Charles Henry Fowler

The New Home and Health and Home Economics

A cyclopedia of facts and hints for all departments of home life, health and

domestic economy

Charles Henry Fowler

The New Home and Health and Home Economics
A cyclopedia of facts and hints for all departments of home life, health and domestic economy

ISBN/EAN: 9783337224073

Printed in Europe, USA, Canada, Australia, Japan

Cover: Foto ©Lupo / pixelio.de

More available books at **www.hansebooks.com**

THE NEW

HOME AND HEALTH

AND

HOME ECONOMICS

A CYCLOPEDIA OF FACTS AND HINTS FOR ALL
DEPARTMENTS OF HOME LIFE, HEALTH
AND DOMESTIC ECONOMY

ILLUSTRATED EDITION, WITH REVISIONS AND ADDITIONS

BY

W. H. DE PUY, A.M., D.D., LL.D.
Editor of *The People's Cyclopedia*, *University of Literature*, etc.

Printed for the Author
HUNT & EATON PRESS
New York
1896

DEDICATION.

This book is dedicated :

1. To our MOTHERS, who made the homes into which we were received.
2. To our WIVES, who make the homes in which we live.
3. To our DAUGHTERS, who are to make the homes for other toilers.
4. To all our READERS who have good homes, and to those who need them.

The first sure symptoms of a mind in health,
Is rest of heart, and pleasure felt at home.
—YOUNGS' NIGHT THOUGHTS.

Home is the resort
Of love, of joy, of peace, and plenty, where,
Supporting, and supported, polished friends
And dear relations mingle into bliss.
—THOMPSON'S SEASONS.

Look to your health, and if you have it, praise God, and value it next to a good conscience. For health is the second blessing that we mortals are capable of—a blessing that money cannot buy. *Value it.*

Surround the sick man with the pomp of kings; let his chair be a throne, and his crutch a scepter; he will look with contemptuous eye on marble, on gold, and on purple, and would deem himself happy could he enjoy, even under thatched roof, the health of the meanest of his subjects.—ZSCHOKKE.

The fireside is a seminary of infinite importance. Few can receive the honors of a college, but all are graduates of the home. The learning of the university may fade from the recollection, its classic lore may molder in the halls of memory; but the simple lessons of home, enameled upon the heart of childhood, defy the rust of years, and outlive the more mature, but less vivid, pictures of after years.—GOODRICH.

I will not, therefore, believe that what is so natural in the house of another is impossible at home; but maintain, without fear, that all the courtesies of social life may be upheld in domestic societies. A husband as willing to be pleased at home, and as anxious to please as in his neighbor's house; and a wife as intent on making things comfortable every day to her family as on set days to her guests, could not fail to make their own home happy.—PHILLIP.

PREFACE.

THIS volume has been prepared for a given purpose. The supreme end sought in it is *usefulness*. It is a book of practical knowledge. No space has been given to rhetoric. *The greatest amount of information in the smallest space* has been the ever-present ideal.

The preparation of these pages has been a constant delight. The privilege of putting so many hundred important suggestions into a hundred thousand homes, to enter into the convictions and manners and lives and destinies of so many young people, and bear the fruit of peace and comfort and gentleness and culture in a million homes of the future, is gratefully accepted as *the opportunity of a life-time.*

In the first edition of *Home and Health* the department of Home was contributed by the Rev. C. H. Fowler, D.D., LL.D., then senior editor of *The Christian Advocate* in New York, (and since then elected a Bishop of his Church;) and this department has been retained without change.

W. H. D.

AUTHORITIES CONSULTED.*

Hand-Book for Home Improvement
The Housekeeper's Manual. By Catherine E. Beecher and Harriet Beecher Stowe.
Life at Home. By Rev. Wm. Aikman, D.D.
Half-Hour Studies of Life. By Rev. E. A. Johnson, D.D
The Art of Conversation.
Hill's Manual of Social and Business Forms.
The American Journal of the Medical Societies. Philadelphia.
Medical and Surgical Reporter. Philadelphia.
The Sanitarian, and Organ of the Medico-Legal Society. New York.
Popular Science Monthly. New York: D. Appleton & Company.
Appleton's Journal. New York: D. Appleton & Company.
New Jersey Eclectic, Medical, and Surgical Journal. Newark, N. J.
American Agriculturist. New York: Orange Judd Company.
Phrenological Journal, and *Journal of Health.* New York: S. R. Wells & Company.
Herald of Health. New York: Wood & Holbrook, Publishers
The Lancet. London, England.
New York Eclectic Medical and Surgical Journal. Edward N. Fishblatt, M.D.
American Journal of Microscopy. New York.
Hall's Journal of Health. New York
Report of Special Committee on Croup of the Illinois State Medical Society, 1878. H. L. Gill, M.D.
Till the Doctor Comes. By Geo. M. Hope, D.D. New York: G. P. Putnam & Sons.
Steele's Fourteen Weeks in Physiology. New York: A. S. Barnes & Company.
We also add, as helpful to us, the names of Rev. L. D. Barrows, D.D., and Rev. John Wesley, A.M.

---

* Partial List

HOME AND HEALTH.

HOME.

Only Man has a Home.—The tired lark sinks in the evening shades down to its quiet nest, and offers its grateful anthems for the boon of a house; but man, wearied with the strifes of the mart and of the field, seeks shelter in his *home*, the sacred retreat of the heart. Foxes have holes, birds have nests, lions have dens, tigers have lairs, dogs have kennels, but men have *homes*. The supreme putting of divine love is found in Jesus, when he forsakes his home, and wanders a stranger, not having where to lay his head; while the extreme display of human sinfulness is found with those human creatures who are "without natural affections."

Virtues of the Hearth are the Securities of the Peoples.—The home is the cradle of the great virtues. The Church was organized in the family. The power to command his household and his children after him was the spring of Abraham's call to be the Father of the faithful and founder of the Church. There is one bond that encircles earth and heaven. It is woven from the most tender longings and hunger of the heart. It binds the humblest home on earth to the Home of our Father on High. It domesticates the angels in cabins. The love of mother is often the last cable that holds a youth to his moorings. Beaten upon by the storm of his passions, every other stay gives way. Every other anchor drags. But the love of mother, that was dropped deep into his soul's substance before he got out of the nursery, holds. While that holds he is almost certain to outride the wildest gales. So the Home, which is the sanctuary where this spirit presides, is a perpetual protection. It is an ark floating with us down the tide of the years. It carries the virtues that make the citizen, and the inspirations that develops the saint. It is not merely a shelter from the storm, it is also a workshop, where the grandest characters are built. It is a preeminent opportunity for the achievement of good. To miss this chief purpose of the home is to lower its grade.

The Home builds the House.—The divine idea of home-life types the building. There is something in every germ of life which determines its form. Time and opportunity bring out only this ideal. The germ of a kernel of barley can be matured, not into a stalk and head of wheat, but into a stalk and head of barley. The germs of the fish and of the bird and of man are, at certain stages of development, indistinguishable. But there is always present a superintending spiritual power, too subtle for our microscopes and chemistries, that determines what form each shall wear. The fish grows into a fish. The bird becomes a bird. The man matures into a man. Each obeys its inner bias. Thus the inner instinct, or thought of the home, fashions the house. Its apartments grow upon this stalk. From the kitchen where the animal is fed, the nursery where the training is ordered, the chamber where the recuperative forces are stored, the sitting room where the social life is nourished, to the reception room or parlor, where the life of society is met and mastered—all these grow about the deeper idea of home. It is this subtle and powerful spirit, born out of the innermost heart, that invariably locates the home where the heart is. The settler's cabin and the peasant's hut, clothed with this inspiration from the heart, become centers of comfort and contentment that time is unable to drive from the mind. Life rises out of this inspiration to its highest values. Thus the home becomes the measure of a nation's stability. A tramp may become a hired soldier, but he can hardly rise to the promptings of patriotism. His life has too little in it to be worth much defending. His life is cheap. He waits for whatever may happen. When a man has a home he becomes immediately interested in the peace of the community. He has given hostages against mobs. It is important for him that the pavement stones should keep their places, and not go flying through the air. Both heads and windows acquire a sacredness from those in which he is interested. A man without a home has little motive for standing against public perils. If a land does not furnish a man so much as a home, he can drift away when it becomes dangerous to remain anchored. Fill any land with good homes, and it must be a good place in which to live. It is one peculiarity of the Anglo-Saxon peoples that they abound in homes. The walls about the hearth shut out all the world, and shut in a kingdom. This is the fort; keep it clean and free, and religion will thrive and liberty will dwell in the land forever.

The Origin of the Family.—The most ancient organization in the race is the Family. It was God's first appointment for man. Other means might easily have been devised for the perpetuation of the race, but God saw that it was "not good that the man should be alone," so he put "the solitary in families."

How the Family Develops Character.—The family is the oldest school known among men. Its molding and educating work begins in that university where the mother's lap is the recitation room, the mother is the professor, and the mother's eye is the text-book. Schools come as public examinations, to determine or show how much the pupil has learned elsewhere. The Church is an after-thought. The family furnishes the elements out of which later character and knowledge are constructed. Other means of influence and instruction touch the soul in spots, but the family furnishes an enveloping atmosphere, that presses upon the absorbing faculties at every point and through every moment. It is too easy to trace family marks through successive generations. Blood runs in channels prepared by nature, but these channels may be reversed or broken over. A given amount of capacity, that is, so much blood and so much brain, may be brought by opposite environments to results as widely separated as the opposite poles of the moral universe. The man with a brogue in his speech, and a club in his hand, and a low passion in his heart, may differ from the statesman with a richness in his accents, and the reins of government in his hands, and a universal philanthropy in his heart, only by so much as the influences of the family in which his capacities were surrounded.

The Family often Ripens Rapidly Those who Carry its Burdens.— Two young people fall into the conviction of approaching oneness. They seem but children. He is trifling, and she is foolish. He divides his time between his old boyish sports and his new boyish love. She turns from her dolls to her lover. They are children, and too young to be thought of as marriageable. But in the courage or folly of their love they take the outer vow. Now watch them. Often they have blundered, but nearly always, when the union was a marriage performed under the sanctions of their hearts, we see them straighten up and sober down. They cease suddenly to be children. We wonder at their dignity and stability. We trembled when they passed into the cloud. But they are clothed upon with higher character. It seems as if nature, fearing lest she should disparage her divinest ordinance, hastens to forgive the folly of premature obedience, and corrects, as far as possible, the mistakes of youth.

The Family Multiplies Happiness.—The road into happiness is always the road out of self. When one has no one for whom he cares more than for himself, the cup of his happiness is very small. The babe, only able to use a rattle, can have but little joy compared with its delight when it can pour itself out for some loved one. Other friendships than those of the family last with the sunshine. But into every life some rain must fall. Then, worn with the rude shocks against the rough world, one returns to his quiet family to be soothed and re-established in the eternal verities of fidelity and integrity. The comforts may be few, but so long as these are not placed above their true rank, and the deeper and abiding realities of the heart are emphasized, there is sure to come a flood of comfort that makes one ready for another strife with the world.

Washington Irving says that "a married man, falling into misfortunes, is more apt to retrieve his situation in the world than a single one, chiefly because his spirits are softened and relieved by domestic endearment and self-respect." The happiness he imparts and receives adds wings to his speed and spurs to his purpose, and difficulties that otherwise would have been too great for a half-formed resolution yield before the supreme impulse from the family.

The Family Blesses in Necessitating Housekeeping.—It is one of the glories of a family that it must come to housekeeping. Boarding is a necessary evil in exceptional cases, but it is not a part of the plan. It may sometimes be an expedient, like a tent, while a house is being built, or on hard campaigns where houses cannot be built. The order of life is *home-keeping*. A family is a unit in society, not a fraction. The home is a man's castle, and he must be the lord of it. To live in a trunk with the feeling that some one else owns the key, and may lock you out by day or in by night, dwarfs the best part of a man's faculties. Boarding houses have their mission, just as any other remedial agency for the sick or deformed or unfortunate in society has its work. People should go to a boarding house just as they do to a hospital, *when they must*, and then be thankful that they can get a good one.

Housekeeping separates the family unit from the fragments of families, and gives it a chance for religious and individual life. The little girl who said to her Sunday-school teacher, "We have not got any Bible, we board," told a secret much deeper than she knew.

Have some house, little if it must be, but have it, and live by yourselves. There you can suit your living to your income. There you can train your children in influences which you can command. There you can create and preserve a Christian atmosphere which shall determine their destiny, and possibly your own. There you will find a fort which you command, a door which you only can open; a place where you are constantly built up into kingship.

According to Jeremy Taylor: "Home is the proper scene of piety and patience, of the duty of parents, and the charity of relatives; here kindness is spread abroad, and love is united and made firm as a center. Marriage hath in it less of beauty, but more of safety than single life; it hath more care, but less danger; it is more merry and more sad; it is fuller of sorrows and fuller of joys; it lies under more burdens, but is supported by all the strength of love and charity, and those burdens are delightful." The family gathered in a Christian home is the type of the eternal home where the whole family of God shall be finally gathered.

So important is a *home* that it is worth much to give any hint that may improve its order, hallow its precincts, sweeten its atmosphere, purify its communions, increase its efficiency, unfold its relations, elevate its affections, exalt its intelligence, protect its virtues, perpetuate its faith, or impress its importance. If we can aid in giving to America men and women who shall abide in the comforts and securities of home, if we ca aidn in rendering more honorable this altar of religion and cradle of patriotism, this model of the Church and unit of the State; if we can aid in checking the worldly rush out of the home into the chase for pleasure, the struggle for gain, and the brawl for fame which sweeps away so many men and infects so many women in our time, we shall be content. If by hints, practical suggestions, rules wrought out of the experience of the good and wise, and instructions gathered from the world's teachers every-where, we can aid the father in being a providence and a parent, the mother in being a queen and a companion, the boy in becoming a vigorous and manly man, and the girl in ripening into the graces of an intelligent, refined woman; if by the words of this book we can help to perfect and actualize the Christian home, so that here and there throughout the land a barefooted boy, or a poor girl, or a weary mother, or a tired father, finding some new hope, or better culture, or higher life, shall rise up and bless these pages, then we shall not be sorry on account of the work, nor on account of the criticism of those who may most need these suggestions.

MARRIAGE.

What God Thinks of Marriage.—In the beginning God created man, and then created for him one woman, because it was not good for him to be alone. He created for him only one woman because it would not be good for him to want to be alone. It is not without a providential purpose that the number of the males is kept so nearly equal to the number of the females for so many ages. "They twain shall be one flesh," said the great Teacher. Not they twenty shall be one flesh, but *twain*. He shall cleave unto his wife, not unto a score of wives. The Lord avoids the perils of both extremes. He wants a man to be the husband of only one wife. It is almost as unnatural for him not to have one as it is wicked to have more than one. For "the Spirit speaketh expressly, that in the latter times some shall *depart from the faith*, giving heed to *seducing spirits, and doctrines of devils; speaking lies in hypocrisy*, having their conscience seared with a hot iron; FORBIDDING TO MARRY." 1 Tim. iv, 1–3.

Principles Governing Marriage.—The following principles are formulated with the full knowledge that it is not possible to give infallible directions for every case. But it is also believed that the chances that these rules will apply are immeasurably greater than that your case is really an exception to the laws that generally obtain over people. Let it not be forgotten that these rules are to find their application and do their helpful work before the interested party is committed either in word or in feeling. Love always blindfolds that he may lead captive. These rules are given not chiefly for those who most need them, but for those who may need them hereafter.

1. *Seek each other's happiness.* A selfish marriage that seeks only its own happiness defeats itself. Happiness is a fire that will not burn long on one stick.

2. *Give your best judgment full authority.* Wedlock is not an impulse, but a life. Like Christianity, it may be miraculously started, but it must depend upon arguments and works of righteousness for its prosperous continuance.

3. *Do not marry suddenly.* It can always be done till it is done, if it is a proper thing to do.

4. *Marry in your own grade in society.* It is painful to be always apologizing for any one. It is more painful to be apologized for.

5. *Do not marry downward.* It is hard enough to advance in the quality of life, without being loaded by clay heavier than your own. It will be sufficiently difficult to keep your children up to your best level without having to correct a bias in their blood.

6. *Do not sell yourself.* It matters not whether the price be money or position.

7. *Do not throw yourself away.* You will not receive too much even if you are paid full price.

8. "*Be ye not unequally yoked together with unbelievers.*" Argument cannot add to the authority of this rule.

9. *Seek the advice of your parents.* Your parents are your best friends. They will make more sacrifice for you than any other mortals. They are elevated above selfishness concerning you. If they differ from you concerning your choice it is because they must.

10. *Do not marry to please any third party.* You must do the living and enduring.

11. *Do not marry to spite any body.* It would add wickedness to folly.

12. *Do not marry because some one else may seek the same hand.* One glove may not fit all hands equally well.

13. *Do not marry to get rid of any body.* The coward who shot himself to escape from being drafted was insane.

14. *Do not marry merely for the impulse love.* Love is a principle as well as an emotion. So far as it is a sentiment it is a blind guide. It does not wait to test the presence of exalted character in its object before breaking out into a flame. Shavings make a hot fire, but hard coal is better for the winter.

15. *Do not marry without love.* A body without a soul soon becomes offensive.

Marriage.

16. *Do not regard marrying as absolutely necessary.* While it is the general order of Providence that people should marry, yet Providence may have some other plan for you.

17. *Beware of spiritual impressions concerning this subject.* Four young preachers consulted their Presiding Elder concerning marrying. Each said he felt called of God to marry one certain lady.

18. *Remember that love does not long survive respect.*

19. *Beware of mere magnetism.*

20. *Test carefully the effect of protracted association.* If familiarity breeds contempt before marriage, it will afterward.

21. *Test carefully the effect of protracted separation.* True love will defy both time and space.

22. *Consider carefully the right of your children under the laws of heredity.* It is doubtful whether you have a right to increase the number of invalids and cripples.

23. *Do not marry simply because you have promised to do so.* If a seam opens between you now it will widen into a gulf. It is less offensive to retract a mistaken promise than to perjure your soul before the altar. Your intended has a right to absolute integrity.

24. *Avoid long engagements.* Touching off a shell with a fuse two or three years long is an uncertain experiment.

25. *Marry character.* It is not so much what one has as what one is.

26. *Do not marry the wrong object.* Themistocles said he would rather marry his daughter to a man without money, than to money without a man. It is well to have both. It is fatal to have neither.

27. *Demand a just return.* You give virtue and purity, and gentleness and integrity. You have a right to demand the same in return. Duty requires it.

28. *Accept nothing in the place of integrity.* Any person who can deliberately lie will do any thing else under favorable circumstances. There is no foundation to character when integrity is wanting.

29. *Require brains.* Culture is good, but will not be transmitted. Brain-power may be.

30. *Remember that health precedes success.*

31. *See where the candidate is going.* The mother of Dr. Henry, the commentator, was told by her father when her hand was sought, "We do not know whence this man came." She replied, "I know whither he is going, and I want to go with him."

32. *Study past relationships.* The good daughter and sister makes a good wife. The good son and brother makes a good husband.

33. *Never marry as a missionary deed.* If one needs saving from bad habits he is not suitable for you.

34. *Beware of one who has been intemperate.* The risk is too great.

35. *Beware of a skeptic.* If he doubts God he will doubt virtue.

36. *Look for thrift in the blood.* If it does not appear, it must leak out through some defect in the character or habits.

37. *Observe the Bible rule concerning consanguinity.* In the transactions of the American Medical Association, published March, 1859, Dr. Bemis of Kentucky gives details of the history of nearly 1,000 married couples who were more or less related before marriage. His facts abundantly prove such marriages to be unfavorable to the health, life, character, and talents of the offspring. About 900 of the children of these parents died young, of consumption or scrofula.

From the reports of Hospitals, Asylums, Penitentiaries, etc., it is found that about 10 per cent. of all the blind, deaf and dumb, idiotic and insane, have parents who were blood relatives before marriage. Similar facts are well known respecting some of the royal families of Europe.

HOW TO PERPETUATE THE HONEY-MOON.

Continue your courtship. Like causes produce like effects.

Do not assume a right to neglect your companion more after marriage than you did before.

Have no secrets that you keep from your companion. A third party is always disturbing.

Do not conceal your marriage for an hour. Busy bodies may perplex you with advice. Madame Le Brun kept her marriage a secret for a short time, when people advised her to drown herself rather than marry Le Brun. Even the Duchess d'Arembourg said, "For Heaven's sake, don't marry him!" The very concealment begets perils. Integrity is the law of safety.

Avoid the appearance of evil. In matrimonial matters it is often that the mere appearance contains all the evil. Love, as soon as it rises above calculation and becomes love, is exacting. It gives all, and demands all.

Once married, never open your mind to any change. If you keep the door of your purpose closed, evil or even desirable changes cannot make headway without help.

Make the best of the inevitable. Persist in looking at and presenting the best side. Such is the subtle constitution of the human mind, that we believe what we will; also, what we frequently tell.

Keep step in mental development. A tree that grows for forty years may take all the sunlight from a tree that stops growing at twenty.

Keep a lively interest in the business of the firm. Two that do not pull together, are weaker than either alone.

Gauge your expenses by your revenues. Love must eat. The sheriff often levies on Cupid long before he takes away the old furniture.

Start from where your parents started rather than from where they now are. Hollow and showy boarding often furnishes the too strong temptation, while the quietness of a humble home would cement the hearts beyond risk.

Avoid debt. Spend your own money, then it will not be necessary to blame any one for spending other people's.

Do not both get angry at the same time. It takes two to quarrel.

Do not allow yourself ever to come to an open rupture. Things unsaid need less repentance.

Study to understand your companion's disposition, in order to please and avoid friction.

Study to conform your tastes and habits to the tastes and habits of your companion. If two walk together, they must agree.

Chang and Eng were the Siamese Twins. Chang made Eng lie down when sick. It killed Eng, and Chang could not survive him. Take care of Eng. Few people survive divorce.

HOW TO BE A GOOD HUSBAND.

Honor your wife. She must be exalted and never dethroned.

Love your wife. The measure is, as Christ loved the Church and gave himself for her.

Show your love. All life manifests itself. As certainly as a live tree will put forth leaves in the spring, so certainly will a living love show itself. Many a noble man toils early and late to earn bread and position for his wife. He hesitates at no weariness for her sake. He justly thinks that such industry and providence give a better expression of his love than he could give by caressing her and letting the grocery bills go unpaid. He fills the cellar and pantry. He drives and pushes his business. He never dreams that he is actually starving his *wife* to death. He may soon have a *woman* left to superintend his home, but his *wife* is dying. She must be kept alive by the same process that called her into being. Recall and repeat the little attentions and delicate compliments that once made you so agreeable, and that fanned her love into a consuming flame. It is not beneath the dignity of the skillful physician to study all the little symptoms, and order all the little round of attentions, that check the waste of strength and brace the staggering constitution. It is good work for a husband to cherish his wife.

Suffer for your wife, if need be. Christ suffered for the Church.

Consult with her. She is as apt to be right as you are, and frequently able to add much to your stock of wisdom. In any event, she appreciates your attentions.

Study to keep her young. It can be done. It is not work, but worry, that wears. Keep a brave, true heart between her and all harm. If you will carefully walk in the way of righteousness you can shield her from cankering care. Providence will not be likely to bring upon her any thing that is not for her good.

Help to bear her burdens. Bear one another's burdens, and so fulfill the law of love. Love seeks opportunities to do for the loved object. She has the constant care of your children. She is ordained by the Lord to stand guard over them. Not a disease can appear in the community without her taking the alarm. Not a disease can come over the threshold without her instantly springing into the mortal combat. If there is a deficiency anywhere, it comes out of her pleasure. Her burdens are every-where. Look for them, that you may lighten them.

Make yourself helpful by thoughtfulness. Remember to bring into the house your best smile and sunshine. It is good for you, and it cheers up the home. There is hardly a nook in the house that has not been carefully hunted through to drive out every thing that might annoy you. The dinner which suits, or ought to suit you, has not come on the table of itself. It represents much thoughtfulness and work. You can do no more manly thing than find some way of expressing, in word or look, your appreciation of it.

Express your will, not by commands, but by suggestions. It is God's order that you should be the head of the family. You are clothed with authority. But this does not authorize you to be stern and harsh, as an officer in the army. Your authority is the dignity of love. When it is not clothed in love it ceases to have the substance of authority. A simple suggestion that may embody a wish, an opinion or an argument, becomes one who reigns over such a kingdom as yours.

Study your own character as husband. Transfer your deeds, with the impressions they might naturally make, to some other couple, and see what feelings they would awaken in your heart concerning that other man. Are you seeking to multiply the joys of your wife, as well as to support her? Are you an agreeable associate among your companions? If not, why should you expect your wife to be pleased with you? Have you acquired the ability to entertain and cheer your friends? If not, it is time you were studying to improve yourself as a husband. If you can, make yourself a model husband.

and that will help your wife to be a model wife, and that will insure your home against shipwreck and your happiness against decay.

Seek to refine your nature. It is no slander to say that many men have wives much more refined than themselves. This is natural in the inequalities of life. Other qualities may compensate for any defect here. But you need have no defect in refinement. Preserve the gentleness and refinement of your wife as a rich legacy for your children, and in so doing you will lift yourself to higher levels.

Be a gentleman, as well as a husband. The signs and bronze and callouses of toil are no indications that you are not a gentleman. The soul of gentlemanliness is a kindly feeling toward others, that prompts one to secure their comfort. That is why the thoughtful peasant lover is always so gentlemanly, and in his love much above himself.

Remember the past experience of your wife. In all probability she has left a better home than the one to which she comes. All the changes for the worse are painful. Only her love for you extracts the pain. She cannot but contrast your pinched accommodations with the abundance she left. It is right that these changes should come. Young people cannot commence where the aged leave off. Yet it becomes you to remember that she has taken you instead of all these comforts, and you must see to it that she has no reason to regret her exchange. Make the most of her better nature. This refinement enters into her value as a mother and a maker of a home.

Level up. If your wife has the advantage in culture and refinement, and this is quite a common condition, as girls usually have a better chance for education and more leisure for books than boys have, do not sink her to your level, but by study and thoughtfulness rise to her plane. The very ascent will improve your home, and add to your value as a husband and to your influence as a citizen.

Stay at home. Habitual absence during the evenings is sure to bring sorrow. If your duty or business calls you, you have the promise that you will be *kept in all* your ways. But if you go out to mingle with other society, and leave your wife at home alone, or with the children and servants, know that there is no good in store for you. She has claims upon you that you cannot afford to allow to go to protest. Reverse the case. You sit down alone after having waited all day for your wife's return, and think of her as reveling in gay society, and see if you can keep out all doubts as to what takes her away. If your home is not as attractive as you want it, you are a principal partner. Set yourself about the work of making it attractive. Find some book to read or to have your wife read to you, or some work that both can be interested in. Find something that shall give interest to the even-ngs. Home is your only retreat. Satan fights a family as Napoleon fought his enemies—divides it, then whips the parts in detail. When you lounge away from home you go into temptation, and send temptation to take your place at home.

Take your wife with you into society. Seclusion begets morbidness. One needs some of the life that comes from contact with society. She must see how other people appear and act. It often requires an exertion for her to go out of her home, but it is good for her, and for you. She will bring back more sunshine. It is wise to rest sometimes. When the Arab stops for his dinner he unpacks his camel. Treat your wife with as much consideration.

HOW TO BE A GOOD WIFE.

Reverence your husband. He sustains by God's order a position of dignity as head of the family, head of the woman. Any breaking down of this order indicates a mistake in the union or a digression from duty.

Love him. A *wife* loves as naturally as the sun shines. Love is your best weapon. You conquered him with that in the first place. You can reconquer by the same means.

Do not conceal your love from him. If he is crowded with care, and too busy to seem to heed your love, you need to give all the greater attention to securing his knowledge of your love. If you intermit he will settle down into a hard, cold life with increased rapidity. Your example will keep the light on his conviction. The more he neglects the fire on the hearth, the more carefully must you feed and guard it. It must not be allowed to go out. Once out you must sit forever in the darkness and in the cold.

Forsake all for him. Looking back may be as fatal to you as it was to Lot's wife. You have voluntarily taken him "for better or for worse." Henceforth your destinies are intertwined.

Confide in him. Distrust is a bottomless abyss

Keep his love. It may require much care and thought, but the boon is vital to your happiness.

Cultivate the modesty and delicacy of your youth. The relations and familiarity of wedded life may seem to tone down the sensitive and retiring instincts of girlhood, but nothing can compensate for the loss of these. However much men may admire the public performance of gifted women, they do not desire that boldness and dash in a wife. The holy blush of a maiden's modesty is more powerful in hallowing and governing a home than the heaviest armament that ever warrior bore.

How to be a Good Wife.

Cultivate personal attractiveness. This means the storing of your mind with a knowledge of passing events, and with a good idea of the world's general advance. If you read nothing, and make no effort to make yourself attractive, you will soon sink down into a dull hack of stupidity. If your husband never hears from you any words of wisdom, or of common information, he will soon hear nothing from you. Dress and gossip soon wear out. If your memory is weak, so that it hardly seems worth while to read, that is additional reason for reading. The disease is advancing to a threatening stage. Keep by you some well selected book. Read little by little, as you can. Think of what you read. Talk to your husband of it when he comes. If your memory fails you in the critical moment, try it again. Persist, and victory is inevitable. Ask him questions about it. Enlist his interest. Any new thing placed before him will awaken his admiration. A careful reading of the daily and religious papers will enable you to keep him posted by incidental references and statements while at table, or while walking or riding, or in the sitting-room. Soon he will come to rely upon you for his information on many matters. Then your throne cannot be shaken. This need not occupy many moments each day. But your time will not be worth having without it.

Cultivate physical attractiveness. When you were encouraging the attentions of him whom you now call husband, you did not neglect any item of dress or appearance that could help you. Your hair was always in perfect training. You never greeted him with a ragged or untidy dress or soiled hands. It is true that your "market is made," but you cannot afford to have it " broken." Cleanliness and good taste will attract now as they did formerly. Keep yourself at your best. Make the most of your physical endowments. Neatness and order break the power of poverty.

Do not forget the power of incidental attentions. The arrow that pierces between the joints of the mail is the one that does the execution. A little time spent by your husband's side, without actually being busied with either work or plans or complaints, is not wasted. A hand on the shoulder, a look, the creeping of your hand into his, any of the thousand little things which your instinct will teach you how to do, may drive away a cloud, and perpetuate the sunshine.

Make your home attractive. This means more than furniture. It means the thousand little touches of taste that drive the darkness out of the corners, and the stiffness out of the parlor, and the gloom out of the house. Make your home so easy that you will feel easy in it yourself. Feel at home in it yourself, then the others will also feel easy there. Keep your house clean, and in good order. It takes less time to so keep things than to neglect them and hunt for them. Even poverty is no excuse for dirt. Many a man is driven by home dirt to the bar-room, and through that to death. Have your table clean. Your food may be coarse and cheap, but if it is clean, and put on in an inviting shape, the meal will be relished. We have relished meals in a cabin where there was but one dish on the table, and that the kettle in which it was cooked. The appetizer was on the floor, which shone from the scrubbing-brush till one could safely eat from it. Your home is your kingdom. Its order and attractiveness will have much to do with your position as a wife.

Preserve sunshine. People shun clouds. Light is life. It does not matter that some things have gone wrong. Things have ways of going crooked. It is not best for you to keep pouring your petty trials into your husband's ears. There are times when he must hear them, but study these times. Do not keep up such a din of complaint that he identifies the idea of home with the idea of distress. In a sense he is your supreme guest. Make the best of what you have. Keep the order at the front, and organize order backward as rapidly as possible. You do not wish to always appear in the role of a beggar who sits by the highway showing his wounds and deformities as reasons for receiving pennies. Some people always retail their distresses and ailments, till one shuns them like a pest hospital. When your husband comes in, let him receive a flood of sunlight. It will do no harm if he comes to think of you as sunlight. True, he is under equal obligation to bring sunlight with him, but you can help him by example. One certain result you will secure, namely, you will avoid all the imaginary storms, be better prepared to meet the real ones, and have a vast deal of sunshine in your own life as a constant compensation.

Study your husband's character. He has his peculiarities. He has no right to many of them, but he has them, and you need to know them; thus you can avoid many hours of friction. The good pilot steers around the sunken rocks that lie in the channel. The engineer may remove them, not the pilot. You are more pilot than engineer. Consult his tastes. It is more important to your home that you should please him than anybody else Patience, time, and tact will enable you to clear out the channel, or make new channels through the very substance of his character. A given amount of study expended on him will yield a larger amount of happiness for your family than it can invested anywhere else.

Cultivate his better nature. Avoid appearing to be shocked at his rude or crude notions, but set him to thinking about things that will elevate the plane of his convictions, tastes, and feelings. Books, extracts, incidents that contain truths which you wish him to imbibe, can be put in his way or read to him in his leisure. As his standard is more elevated his actions will improve. The winter's blast causes us to hug our wraps, but an hour's spring sunshine causes us to throw them open and off.

Study to meet your duties as a wife. Criticise your own defects without mercy. No one else will treat them mercifully. Correct the points that are wrong. If you are indifferent, cultivate interest. If you are negligent concerning your domestic duties, take on care. Whatever a good wife does or ought to do, do that. You can master the science of being a wife as well as you can master any other science.

Seek to secure your husband's happiness. Blessing, you shall be blessed. You cannot anchor your end of the ship in a haven of peace while the other end is carried down the cataract.

Study his interest. Many women wreck their fortune, and darken their future by indifference to the business interests of their husbands. They fix their hearts upon some display which they cannot afford. The husband must choose between bankruptcy and a family quarrel. Hoping against hope, he purchases peace at too high a price, and ruin comes in at the door which the wife opened to admit her pride or comfort. If need be, live in one room. Eat from the end of a trunk, but do not go beyond your means. Nothing is more respectable than independence.

Practice economy. Many families are cast out of peace into grumbling and discord by being compelled to fight against poverty. When there are no great distresses to be endured or accounted for, complaint and fault-finding are not so often evoked. Keep your husband free from the annoyances of disappointed creditors, and he will be more apt to keep free from annoying you. To toil hard for bread, to fight the wolf from the door, to resist impatient creditors, to struggle against complaining pride at home, is too much to ask of one man. A crust that is your own is a feast, while a feast that is purloined from unwilling creditors is a famine.

FACTS FOR PARENTS.

Paternity is earth's highest dignity. The parent is the best human type of God. Paternal authority is the germ out of which are unfolded all governments and all religions. It combines law, authority, power, wisdom, providence, punishments, pardons, remedial agencies, mercy, love, sacrifice, instruction, leadership and companionship. It epitomizes nature, Providence and grace.

Children are boons. They impart dignity to life and furnish a motive for work. They gather up the withering and fading plans for self, and cast them out into the future, renewed in vigor and hope. They cement the family in unity.

Children give new life to a home. They warm the house. They dispel the gloom. They constrain age to renewed youth. They transform a hall into a home.

Children are great teachers of theology. They give new meaning to the important terms in which God seeks to reveal himself. Father, and pity, and pardon, and love, and faith, and authority, and probation, and punishment, and recovery, derive more meaning from a single child than from all dictionaries and grammars combined. They show us the supreme order in confusion and the instrumental character of law. In God's Kingdom it is true of men, "A little child shall lead them."

Parents put their image and superscription upon their children. They beget them in their own image, and train them into their own faith and destiny. Selecting for them their toys, their playmates, their books and their churches, they are responsible for their moral character and social life.

Prepare for the duties of the parental relation. It requires apprenticeship for the common mechanic arts. Long training prepares the surgeon to tamper with physical limbs. What thoughtfulness should precede the assumption of parental relations!

Construct your home for your children. Home may be made the most attractive place on earth. Many lose their children as soon as they can escape. There is a mistake somewhere. If the house is glum and stiff, the children required to keep still while the parents read or doze—if the house is only a feeding and clothing place, or a workshop, it has none of the charms of home, and will be early empty. But the home should be more than a house. Fill it with good cheer, youthful hope, with instruction and entertainment and affection; then it will be a perpetual benediction. Your highest duty is to your children. Make home so winsome to them that they will not go away from your eye for their pleasures. Be yourself a necessary and welcome part of their work and of their study and of their sports. It is not a service of bondage, but a reign of love in the midst of the growing sons and daughters, that you are to maintain.

Remember that children do grow old. We can hardly believe that they can be trusted as we were when we were of their age. We remember them as our little ones.

Recall, as distinctly as possible, your own youth. Profit by your own experience, and let your children also profit by it.

FAMILY GOVERNMENT. FORTY-TWO HINTS.

1. **Family government is to be family government.** It uses authority, authority *in love*, yet authority. It ordains law. It commands the child's moral nature.

2. **It is not merely a provision for temporal relief.** It does more than dress, feed and nurse. It is for higher purposes than exhorting, or advising, or caressing.

3. **It rules in the place of God.** We are created in a system by a plan of reproduction. God creates us second-hand, and governs us in the same way.

4. **It prepares a religion of the hearth.** This seizes upon the infinite Father on the first opportunity. The capacities and faculties for apprehending God are prepared in the home, and are experimented in private, till a distinct idea of God is presented; then this government rises into the spiritual government, and religion is launched upon the soul.

5. **Parental rule must seek the ends sought by the Lord.** Short of this, it is not a system of statesmanship, but a trick of politicians. It must seek purely *Christian* ends. To serve worldly purposes in our children by wanting for them chiefly wealth, or honor, or power, or position, is to fall below any thing worthy of the name of Family Government.

6. **Parents governing on a lower plane lose all inspiration.** The only dignity that can draw the soul up to its own infinite heights is the word of supreme authority. Expediency and advice are conveniences which can never be galvanized into power. Governing in God's place, one cannot miss of inspiration.

7. **Family government may reach real piety.** It is not expected that a mere human order will secure conversion, or that a free use of the rod will reach that result. It is chiefly urged that the child, obeying the representative authority from the motives which God enthrones, may be brought into that spirit of trustful obedience which underlies all piety, and which makes salvation solely a question of God's willingness to save.

8. **The parents must be in the Spirit to attain the highest results.** Their lives must be so steadied, their passions so quieted, as to give them the highest personal authority. All the human agency turns on personal authority. This means genuineness. This means authority rather than sanctimoniousness. Children feel only realities. When the atmosphere of the home is Christian, then they are sure to be encircled.

9. **Instill principles, rather than enact rules or issue commands.** Religious life is removed the farthest possible from a ritual or ceremony. It is a spirit. Enlightened conviction that makes its own applications partakes of the divine plan, while enactments are man's device to leave an offender without an excuse against penalty.

10. **Gentleness must characterize every act of authority.** The storm of excitement that may make the child start, bears no relation to act-

ual obedience. The inner firmness, that sees and feels a moral conviction and expects obedience, is only disguised and defeated by bluster. The more calm and direct it is, the greater certainty it has of dominion.

11. For the government of small children speak only in the authority of love, yet authority, loving and to be obeyed. The most important lesson to impart is obedience to authority as authority. The question of salvation with most children will be settled as soon as they learn to obey parental authority. It establishes a habit and order of mind that is ready to accept divine authority. This precludes skepticism and disobedience, and induces that childlike trust and spirit set forth as a necessary state of salvation. Children that are never made to obey are left to drift into the sea of passion where the pressure for surrender only tends to drive them at greater speed from the haven of safety.

12. After obedience is secured to authority, explanations may follow to strengthen authority for future storm.

13. For a child not wrecked in deceit, appeal to religious motives. These are the love of God, love of virtue, love of purity, approval of their own conscience.

14. For a child dashed under falsehood, threatening the very integrity of the character, operate on lower motive to drive him up into obedience. This distinguishes between fear and terror. God appeals to one for virtue, and may use the other in final retributions.

15. Form in the child habits of self-denial. Pampering never matures good character.

16. Form in the child habits of benevolence. It partakes of the divine mind. It should become a state, and not be an impulse.

17. Emphasize integrity. Keep the moral tissues tough in integrity; then it will hold a hook of obligations when once set in a sure place. There is nothing more vital. Shape all your experiments to preserve the integrity. Do not so reward it that it becomes mercenary. Turning State's evidence is a dangerous experiment in morals. Prevent deceit from succeeding.

18. Guard modesty. To be brazen is to imperil some of the best elements of character. Modesty may be strengthened into a becoming confidence, but brazen-facedness can seldom be toned down into decency. It requires the miracle of grace.

19. Protect purity. Teach your children to loathe impurity. Study the character of their playmates. Watch their books. Keep them from corruption at all cost. The groups of youth in the schools, and in society, and in business places, seethe with improprieties of word and thought. Never relax your vigilance along this exposed border.

Family Government.

20. **In family government threaten the least possible.** Some parents rattle off their commands with penalties so profusely that there is a steady roar of hostilities about the child's head. These threats are forgotten by the parent and unheeded by the child. All government is at an end.

21. **Do not enforce too many commands.** Leave a few things within the range of the child's knowledge that are not forbidden. Keep your word good, but do not have too much of it out to be redeemed.

22. **Punish as little as possible.** Sometimes punishment is necessary, but the less it is resorted to the better.

23. **Reward rather than punish.** Heaven is better than hell.

24. **Never punish in a passion.** Wrath becomes only cruelty. There is no moral power in it. When you seem to be angry you can do no good.

25. **Disorder means ruin.** This is true of the governed and of the government. Order must be enforced.

26. **Brutish violence only multiplies offenders.** Striking and beating the body seldom reaches the soul. Fear and hatred beget rebellion.

27. **Avoid punishments that break down self-respect.** Striking the body produces shame and indignation.

28. **Punish privately.** It is enough for the other children to know that discipline is being administered.

29. **Hold a child sometimes by main force.** This may give the idea of a resistless force without any of the cruelty of blows or fierceness of passion.

30. **Avoid extremes.** Make your punishment severe enough to succeed, but never too severe to show love.

31. **Never stop short of success.** When the child is not conquered the punishment has been worse than wasted. Reach the point where neither wrath nor sullenness remain. By firm persistency and persuasion require an open look of recognition and peace. It is only evil to stir up the devil unless he is cast out. Ordinarily one complete victory will last a child for a life-time. But if the child relapses repeat the dose with proper accompaniments.

32. **Leave no ambiguity about the reason and purpose for which you are punishing.** A whipping is not so many lashes. It is so much moral persuasion. It means results in peace.

33. **You must discover existing offenses.** Disobedience undiscovered breaks down the moral nature. It substitutes cunning in the place of principle.

34. **Avoid apparent espionage.** To be shadowed stirs all the evil within, and awakens all the disgust and wrath against the spy.

35. **Do not show distrust.** Like begets like.

36. **Make no random charges.** There are wiser ways of cross-questioning. False accusations are never forgotten, and are made the excuse for offenses.

37. **Do not require children to complain of themselves for pardon.** It begets either sycophants or liars. It is the part of the government to detect offenses. It reverses the order of matters to shirk this duty.

38. **How to watch.** Notice his directions, question his companions, question him for details. Be on the look-out for omissions. Fill the silent spaces with questions. A child is sure to fall through such an examination. A few discoveries wisely handled discourage the art of sin.

39. **Grade authority up to liberty.** The growing child must have experiments of freedom. Lead him gently into the family. Counsel with him. Let him plan as he can. By and by he has the confidence of courage without the danger of exposures.

40. **Parents must respect each other.** Undermining either undermines both.

41. **Always keep in the spirit of love.**

42. **Form an alliance with the children against the spirit of evil, and get them to help you conquer that evil.** This inspires them by making them feel that they are taking the part of victors rather than of the vanquished.

SUGGESTIONS TO CHILDREN.

Reverence your parents. Always address them in respectful language. Slang terms that would bring them into disrepect with others are offensive. "The governor," "the old man," "the boss," are terms of disrespect. Your heart may not be so coarse toward them, and think such expressions only add spirit to your conversation, but you are working evil to yourself. Honoring your parents secures God's favor.

Appreciate your parents. You will never understand how much they have done for you till it is too late for you duly to show your appreciation. You will never find any other friends who will care for you and cling to you in evil fortune as your parents. They may not have worldly renown, but they deserve your homage. Your best blood you received from them.

Do not shorten childhood by haste. Maturity will come only too soon. Childhood is your probation for life. Extend it, and make the most of it.

Suggestions to Children.

Confide in your parents. Your most sacred and your most dangerous secrets are safer with your parents than anywhere else. Never conceal any habit or course of action from them. If you cannot trust it with your mother it has no right in your bosom. If you would blush to tell her you should blush to know it.

Never read a book you would not show your parents. Vulgar and obscene books or pictures will curse you all your years. The pictures haunt you. They blast you when you least expect it. As you value your peace read no book which you would blush to have your mother see you reading.

In mature years visit and write home frequently. Soon it will be impossible.

MEMBERS OF THE FAMILY.

Brothers in the family. Whatever makes you agreeable to your young lady friends can be added to the charms you have for your sister. Nothing is more attractive in a young man than marked attention to his sister.

Your sister naturally expects certain protection from you. She has a right to receive those delicate attentions that shall protect her from coarseness and vulgarity. Next to your mother or wife she must receive the affection that is glad to comfort.

Never leave her in want of an escort. She has a royal right to be kept from embarrassment so long as you are within reach.

Sisters in the family. The office of a sister is most delicate and important. As a sister, you are preparing your brother to move freely in the society of ladies. You are refining some woman's home. As the string follows and governs the bow so you may seem to follow, yet you do govern your brother.

How to treat the aged. The Chinese set a good example in this matter. Never banish an aged relative to some garret. The aged deserve care and attention in proportion to their years and feebleness. An old person should have the easiest chair, should never be allowed to stand either at home or in a street car, or in any public conveyance, or in public assemblies.

Greet them with a hearty good morning. Inquire after their rest. Pay special attention in seating them at the table and in waiting upon them. Teach the children to wait upon them, and go occasionally to their rooms to see if they need any thing.

As they grow feeble they will entertain doubts about their being welcome. Seek to dispel these doubts by repeated assurances and acts of kindness.

Talk to them. Listen to them. By questions start them on the themes of their early lives. Furnish them with books in proper type. Read to them as you have time, or can take it.

Do not strain them up to your judgment. Humor their whims, if you so call their tastes. The old shoe is the easiest, and they now need ease, not discipline.

God has special care of the aged. When the grasshopper is a burden and the windows are darkened he opens their way to other worlds. If they have grown old in religion he sends his angels to await their translation. It is good to join with the angels in ministries of kindness.

A mother-in-law in the family. Your wife is inexperienced, and the presence of her mother may be her greatest comfort. No one could be more unselfish in her counsels and care. But for your mother-in-law you would have never been blessed with your wife. She has bestowed more care and attention upon your wife than any other mortal.

In many of the trying hours of life she relieves with her experience and love from anxiety and exposure.

If her home is dismembered by death or time so she becomes an inmate and member of your family, you can ordinarily make her presence a blessing to yourself and family by making it a blessing to herself. The secret is in usefulness. The most fearful of all conditions is to feel useless. Some of the cares shifted from the shoulders of your wife will keep both her and her mother from ageing.

The criticism and joking about mothers-in-law is coarse, and indicates a low nature. It is often prejudicial and always wicked. Honor the grand-mother of your children. Children, whose unperverted instincts are good tests of character, seldom go amiss concerning a grand-parent. Care of a husband's mother often becomes a question requiring special consideration. Reverence, affection, employment, and average tact will bless the home forever.

A step-mother in the family. Remember, she makes greater sacrifices in attempting to care for children than they can to make her comfortable. If she is willing the children certainly ought not to object. Few things are more senseless than the constant criticism of step-mothers. No one can tell how soon his own children may need and be glad to secure just such help and love. She is brave; honor her.

SERVANTS IN THE FAMILY.

A good master makes a good servant. But there are certain duties and rights which pertain to the servant. The servant must give the whole time for which he is paid. May aspire to higher positions

May expect promotion from showing capacity in his present place, and from meeting perfectly its duties.

Should identify himself with the interests of his employer. If he is not faithful over things intrusted to his care, who will give him things of his own?

Should preserve the strictest fidelity.

Should serve when out of sight as scrupulously as when under the employer's eye. God sees every-where.

May secure his wishes by requests, not by commands. Should conform his ways of doing given things to the wish of the employer.

Should seek to meet the wish of the employer in spirit, reliability, ability, and activity.

Should secure permanence of engagement by making himself necessary to his employer.

Should carefully study the duties assigned, so as to perform them most perfectly.

Should avoid habits and manners distasteful to his employer.

Should avoid talking much. Speak when spoken to, and when drawn into conversation by your employer.

Should seek to gain and retain respect. Respect is the foundation of all dignity. It is better to be a respected *employé* than a disrespected employer

HINTS TO EMPLOYERS.

The employer should remember that all rights do not center in himself His advantage is an incident of fortune. Kindness to his *employés* is in keeping with his highest dignity. Some things he ought to do in the interest of common manhood:

Identify himself with the interests of his *employés*. Interest begets interest.

Pay honestly what he would expect in a reversed case, and what God requires.

Pay promptly. A man with little credit needs regular payment.

Watch over the morals of his *employés*. Open the future to young men A word or two from his superior judgment may be worth a fortune to the young man, and secure a useful member of society.

Inspire respect by the constant bearing of manhood and royalty of soul.

Encourage the worker in his work.

Instruct with kindliness.

Correct in authority and in gentleness.

MISTRESS IN THE FAMILY.

The mistress should remember that her position gives her certain dignity. She can safely expect her wish to be carried out without descending to a controversy. Her face is the sun or the night in the house.

She must preserve good temper. That will sweeten all the hours. A smile on her face and good-nature in her voice will calm any storm.

Avoid fault-finding. Instruction can be given in a better way. Lead your help into higher capabilities by hints and suggestions. Know what ought to be done, then in a quiet, kindly way see that it is done.

Improve your servants by showing them how they can do better, and what an advantage it will be to them.

Secure their confidence in your kindness, then you can direct them to better ways with ease.

Keep them in self-respect by occasional encouragements about their own neatness and personal appearance. Do not discourage a girl from brushing and ornamenting her hair. Let them keep their own rooms in order, as being parts of the hours. Make them comfortable. Servant-girls need mirrors.

Put your servants into the way of self-care by suggestions, and occasionally helping them to mend and improve their clothes.

Inspire them with the sense of life's worth. The motives from the future are urged upon servants in the New Testament. The heathen master is merged in the idea of God, so they are inspired to render service as unto God.

SUPERIORS AND INFERIORS.

Proper respect for superiors is a due part of liberty. In America we are so determined to be equal, as well as free, that we often reduce our actual grade by disregarding the natural proprieties of our situation. In law and in rights before the courts and at the polls we are equal, but in our employments and social relations we are as diverse as we are numerous.

Children should be subordinate to parents, pupils to teachers, employed to employers, citizens to magistrates, the comfort of the strong and healthy to that of the delicate and feeble.

Superiors in age, office or station have precedence of subordinates, feebleness of strength, women of men.

A parent, teacher or employer may admonish for neglect of duty, may take precedence without remark or apology, while an inferior must first ask leave.

Superiors may use language and manners of freedom which would be improper in inferiors.

Respect is due from all to all. Children should show respect to the feelings of servants.

It is the most exalted philosophy to accept facts. Assertions against the facts do not exalt the lowly or debase the truly exalted.

TRAINING CHILDREN FOR GIVEN ENDS.

What is your purpose in training—not what you would say in class or confession meeting, but in fact? Several distinct purposes animate parents. Look them over and decide what your case is, and what it ought to be.

Training for usefulness. Instill into their minds the conviction that it is greatest to serve most. Train them—

To wait upon themselves, instead of calling for some one to help them.

To do helpful things. Some people think it is a sign of liberal condition to disregard all helpfulness.

To appreciate an economy that saves for the sake of increasing the aggregate of supplies.

To suspect any line of action that seeks mere personal happiness or gratification.

To acquire useful accomplishments. Pastimes may be helpful by adding to the general comfort of the household.

To understand that it is more blessed to give than to receive, to minister than to be ministered unto.

To do good always as they have opportunity.

Training for wealth. Wealth is power, and may be a blessing. We instinctively want our children to have its comforts and advantages. But to train for that, so that every thought shall turn on the dollar mark, is to transform the man into a money bag. Wealth must end in usefulness or in selfishness. To give your children safe views and uses of wealth you must show them greater objects, for the attainment of which wealth is only a means— use your money for great moral or religious purposes. Show them things for which you part with money. When they are inspired with a proper estimate of the value of money in itself, and for the great ends it may accomplish, then you can set them on ways of securing it.

Teach them to earn it. It is dangerous to learn that a dollar can be had in any easier way than to earn it.

Teach them to save it. The boy and the penny pulling one way secure the fortunes.

Teach them to utilize capital. Let them furnish the tools and head-work for men of lower capabilities.

Teac.. them to study and analyze the life and modes of successful men. What has been done may be done again.

Surround them, as far as possible, with thrifty men.

Let them join business with men who are in the habit of succeeding. Shiftless or irresponsible men will always abound, who are willing to join with them.

Warn them against enterprises where they must bear all the risks, and others share the profits.

Warn them against the peril of being in haste for wealth. Never run ahead of the hounds.

Training for greatness. The Spartans brought their children to public tables, and reared them in the presence of their great men, that they might be familiar with the greatness of Sparta. Noble ends may be kept before their minds till they will never think of themselves as capable of little meannesses. Hold them to noble ambitions and great purposes.

Training for refined society. The highest refinement of soul cannot be lost on them. It cannot harm your boy to school him into gentlemanly manners and habits. To reach this advantage he must—

Think. Be at home in his mind. Reflection and thoughtfulness soon show themselves in the face.

Notice the manners of persons familiar with refined society. Object lessons are valuable.

Compare his own conduct with the best models.

Seek information by reading on these subjects.

Practice whatever he learns that will help to refine.

Training for heaven. FOLLOW THE NEW TESTAMENT.

CHOOSING A CALLING.

But few are elected, by either endowment or taste, to any one particular calling or trade. Several doors open about you. It may be true that you can do some one thing better than any of the others, but it is usually true that there are a number of things which you can do with tolerable success.

Study your natural proclivities. Sometimes the sports indicate the gifts. Napoleon played with cannon, Nelson with ships.

Study Providence. There is much in having things open before a boy for his development.

Do not break over your natural qualifications. A successful laborer is happier and more useful than an unsuccessful professional man or tradesman. Poor farmers are sometimes made out of good lawyers. Henry Clay, working with an ox team, would carry the ox goad on his shoulder across the field, and by and by come to himself, to find that he had been waiting for the team to come up, which, understanding his abstraction, had gone aside to graze.

Our wishes are often presentiments of our capabilities.

Having settled the calling, let it remain settled. You have left the ship on that plank, now you must reach the shore. Study on the line of your work You must know all about that. Doubtless you have ability that, well applied, would succeed in several lines. But you have no ability that will succeed in any, if shifting from one to another is the rule.

Pith : **study** self, study Providence, choose, persist.

HOW TO CONDUCT FAMILY PRAYER.

Conduct it according to your strength. Gifts differ, but the spirit is one. Some Christians have great fluency and boldness in prayer, others have the spirit of testimony, but are unable to lead others in prayer. Some, owing to natural timidity, or untoward training in religious exercises, or from the lateness of their conversion, are not able to pray in the hearing of others. This diversity of gifts necessitates diversity in practice. Some few suggestions may not be out of place.

Have family prayer. If you cannot have it in one form have it in another, but *have it*. You are intrusted with the fashioning of the religious life and character of a family; you can hardly do your best without the great help of family worship. The family is the type of the Church. The Church in the family is God's favorite idea. He established his Church first in the family of Abraham, because he knew Abraham that he would order his house and his children after him.

Collect your household as far as possible at a stated hour each morning and evening, in a given room, and then read a portion of God's word, and, all kneeling, render thanks for the mercies received and invoke his blessing for the future.

It is a good custom to have each member of the family take part in the service, reading in turn two or more verses, till a suitable amount has been read. Then sing a hymn, or two or three stanzas. If any in the family can play, and you have a piano or organ, it gives additional impressiveness to the service. After this let the father (patriarch) who is the head and minister of the family church, lead in prayer, closing with the Lord's Prayer, in which all join.

If the father is not a professing Christian, and does not forbid family worship, the duty of leadership devolves upon the mother, the same as in the case of the temporal death of the father. Many a family has been trained into righteousness by the fidelity of the mother. While it is often a great cross for a wife and mother to bear these burdens, yet God honors this fidelity by saving the children, restraining the husband, and often leading him to life.

If the father cannot command courage to lead in prayer, it is often found profitable for him to read the Lord's Prayer instead of offering a prayer of his own construction.

If the father cannot even venture so far, many families have been blessed and nurtured in godliness by all kneeling and uniting in *silent* prayer for a few moments. In the absence of other modes the reading of prayer prescribed by the Church is of service in keeping the Spirit of God in the family.

It is a valuable custom on the Sabbath morning when the family rests from the labor of the week, for the worship to be varied by having other members of the family, the wife, or some of the children, follow the father in leading in prayer.

It is helpful to have a room where all meet for prayer, and have its appointment suited to help the devotional thought. Let the pictures in that room be distinctively spiritual, or religious. It may be the chapel of the house.

GRACE AT THE TABLE.

Render unto God thanks for daily bread. This should be done reverently by the head of the family. Some families stand round the table till the blessing is invoked. Some families sing the long-meter doxology. Some families sing the doxology, and then follow it with the vocal blessing. Some families bow their heads in silence, each invoking God's blessing. Some families repeat each a verse of Scripture. Some families repeat the Scriptures, thus and then ask the blessing. Any form that seems best suited to the tastes and convictions of the family is good enough. The supreme point is to acknowledge and thank God, and invoke his continual blessing.

HOW TO PROFIT BY HABIT.

Habit becomes destiny. God gives us the power to form habits that we may crystallize victories. All improvement in the fingers of the knitter in the eye of the painter, in the tongue of the speaker, in the hand of the artisan, is the gift of habit. Habit is a channel worn in the substance of the soul, along which our purpose and our ability run with increased facility. Prayer, faith, regularity in life, all that builds up steadiness of character, is

How to Profit by Habit.

augmented by habit. Habit is the parent's hold upon the child, and the good man's power against Satan. The formation of a habit reduces to this simple direction: Apply yourself to a given plan industriously, punctually, and persistently.

Having this power in your mind, use it in acquiring habits of obedience and of faith.

HINTS AND HELPS IN CONVERSATION.

The ability to converse instructively and elegantly is one of the greatest endowments and accomplishments. By it other minds, even of the highest order, are led with the greatest ease. It is a delightful way in which to receive and impart information. Varilles said: "Of ten things which I know, I have learned nine from conversation." The gift of speech is man's supreme distinction. This is one impassable gulf between him and the lower grades of life. Its use in the common every-day intercourse of life makes up a large part of the intellectual activity of the race. Nothing in culture can exceed the importance of doing it well. The following hints and helps have been carefully gleaned from a wide range of authorities, and are here presented as matter familiar to many of our readers, but as matter which each successive generation needs to learn for itself:

The soul of refined conversation is the same as the soul of refined manners, namely, good-will toward others and a desire to secure their comfort and increase their happiness. This great law underlies all the rules on this subject. The authoritative putting of this law is, Do as you would be done by.

Say nothing unpleasant when it can be avoided.

Avoid satire and sarcasm.

Never repeat a word that was not intended for repetition.

Cultivate the supreme wisdom, which consists less in saying what ought to be said than in not saying what ought not to be said.

Often cultivate "flashes of silence."

It is the larger half of the conversation to listen well.

Listen to others patiently, especially the poor

Sharp sayings are an evidence of low breeding.

Shun faultfinding and faultfinders.

Never utter an uncomplimentary word against any one.

Compliments delicately hinted and sincerely intended are a grace in conversation.

Commendation of gifts and cleverness properly put are in good taste, but praise of beauty is offensive.

Repeating kind expressions is proper.

Compliments given in a joke may be gratefully received in earnest.
The manner and tone are important parts of a compliment.
Avoid egotism.
Don't talk of yourself, or of your friends, or your deeds.
Give no sign that you appreciate your own merits.
Do not become the distributer of the small talk of a community. The smiles of your auditors do not mean respect.
Avoid giving the impression of one filled with "suppressed egotism."
Never mention your own peculiarities; for culture destroys vanity.
Avoid exaggeration.
Do not be too positive.
Do not talk to hear yourself.
Do not talk to display oratory.
Do not try to lead in conversation, looking around to enforce silence.
Lay aside affected silly etiquette for the natural dictates of the heart.

Direct the conversation where others can join with you, and impart to you useful information.

Avoid oddity. Eccentricity is shallow vanity.
Be modest.
Be what you wish to seem.

If you find bashfulness or embarrassment coming upon you, do or say something at once. The commonest matter gently stated is better than an embarrassing silence. Sometimes changing your position, or looking into a book for a moment, may relieve your embarrassment, and dispel any settling stiffness.

Avoid telling many stories, or repeating a story more than once in the same company.

Avoid repeating a brilliant or clever saying.

Never treat any one as if you simply wanted him to tell stories. People laugh and despise such a one.

Never tell a coarse story. No wit or preface can make it excusable.

Tell a story, if at all, only as an illustration, and not for itself. Tell it accurately.

Be careful, in asking questions for the purpose of starting conversation or of drawing out a person, not to be rude or intrusive.

Never take liberties by staring, or by any rudeness.

Never infringe upon established regulations among strangers.

Do not always prove yourself to be the one in the right. The right will appear. You need only give it a chance.

Avoid argument in conversation. It is discourteous to your host.

Cultivate paradoxes in conversation with your peers. They add interest to common-place matters. To strike the harmless faith of ordinary people in

Hints and Helps in Conversation. 39

any public idol is waste, but such a movement with those able to reply is better.

Never discourse upon your ailments.

Encourage yourself against threatening timidity at meeting a company by the thought that you could talk with any one of them. Like Napoleon, take them in detail.

Use correct language.

Never use slang

Never use words of the meaning or pronunciation of which you are uncertain.

Use Saxon words, and avoid foreign words.

Avoid repetitions and hackneyed expressions.

Avoid discussing your own or other peoples' domestic concerns.

Never prompt a slow speaker, as if you had all the ability. In conversing with a foreigner who may be learning our language, it is excusable to help him in some delicate way.

Never give advice unasked.

Suit your address to the ages of the persons with whom you are speaking.

Do not manifest impatience.

Do not interrupt another when speaking.

Do not find fault, though you may gently criticise.

Do not appear to notice inaccuracies of speech in others.

Do not allow yourself to lose temper or speak excitedly.

Do not always commence a conversation by allusion to the weather.

Do not when narrating an incident continually say, "you see," "you know."

Do not intrude professional or other topics that the company generally cannot take an interest in.

Do not talk very loud. A firm, clear, distinct, yet mild, gentle, and musical voice has great power.

Do not be absent-minded, requiring the speaker to repeat what has been said that you may understand.

Do not try to force yourself into the confidence of others.

Do not use profanity, vulgar terms, words of double meaning, or language that will bring the blush to any one.

Do not allow yourself to speak ill of the absent one if it can be avoided; the day may come when some friend will be needed to defend you in your absence.

Do not speak with contempt and ridicule of a locality which you may be visiting. Find something to truthfully praise and commend; thus make yourself agreeable.

Do not make a pretense of gentility, nor parade the fact that you are a descendant of any notable family. You must pass for just what you are, and must stand on your own merit.

Do not contradict. In making a correction say, "I beg your pardon, but I had an impression that it was so and so." Be careful in contradicting, as you may be wrong yourself.

Do not be unduly familiar; you will merit contempt if you are. Neither should you be dogmatic in your assertions, arrogating to yourself much consequence in your opinions.

Do not be too lavish in your praise of various members of your own family when speaking to strangers; the person to whom you are speaking may know some faults that you do not.

Do not feel it incumbent upon yourself to carry your point in conversation. Should the person with whom you are conversing feel the same, your talk may lead into violent argument.

Do not allow yourself to use personal abuse when speaking to another, as in so doing you may make that person a life-long enemy. A few kind, courteous words might have made him a life-long friend.

Do not discuss politics or religion in general company. You probably would not convert your opponent, and he will not convert you. To discuss those topics is to arouse feeling without any good result.

Do not make a parade of being acquainted with distinguished or wealthy people, of having been to college, or of having visited foreign lands. All this is no evidence of any real genuine worth on your part.

Do not use the surname alone when speaking of your husband or wife to others. To say to another that "I told Jones," referring to your husband, sounds badly. Whereas, to say "I told Mr. Jones," shows respect and good breeding.

Do not yield to bashfulness. Do not isolate yourself, sitting back in a corner, waiting for some one to come and talk with you. Step out; have something to say. Though you may not say it very well, keep on. You will gain courage and improve. It is as much your duty to entertain others as theirs to amuse you.

Do not attempt to pry into the private affairs of others by asking what their profits are, what things cost, whether Melissa ever had a beau, and why Amarette never got married? All such questions are extremely impertinent, and are likely to meet with rebuke.

Do not whisper in company; do not engage in private conversation; do not speak a foreign language which the general company present may not understand, unless it is understood that the foreigner is unable to speak your own language.

Do not take it upon yourself to admonish comparative strangers on religious topics; the person to whom you speak may have decided convictions of

Hints and Helps in Conversation.

his own in opposition to yours, and your over-zeal may seem to him an impertinence.

Dr. Todd has condensed a few rules from Cowper, from which we condense the following:

Choose your company, as you do your books, for profit.
Study your company. If they are superiors, imbibe information; if not impart.
Revive drooping conversation by introducing a topic of general interest.
When any helpful thing is said, retain it.
Bear with much impertinence. It will cure itself.
Be free, and try to make others the same.

GOOD MANNERS.

Politeness is loving thy neighbor as thyself, and showing it in actions.

Affectation is the foe of good breeding. Simple souls, with a smattering of rules of etiquette, and no comprehension of the principles of good manners, have caused many to undervalue a just knowledge of the principles and applications that aid in furnishing the true lady or true gentleman. Many will be helped by knowing that formal etiquette, such as the Japanese monarchs extort from their subjects, has passed out of good society, and its place has been filled with a reign of *common sense* and *good will*. Some people glory in their *rudeness*, which they often dignify with the name of *frankness*. They seem not to understand that the claims of good breeding are as radical and eternal as the fundamental principles of morals.

The divine law of politeness is stated by the Great Teacher in these words, "As ye would that men should do to you, do ye also to them likewise." Politeness has been defined as "only an elegant form of justice," but it involves, also, all the moral and social feelings. It is a sincere regard for the rights of others, in the smallest matters as well as in the largest. It is kindness of heart expressing itself. Good will, good taste and self-control are easily matured into politeness. Kindly affectioned one toward another, is the great secret of good manners.

Bishop Ames saw an Indian Chief at an official interview with President Jackson. The Chief was as graceful as Henry Clay. The Bishop said to the Chief, "How is it you are so graceful, never having studied etiquette?" The Chief replied, "I have no mad talk in me now." Every Christian should be a gentleman or a lady, measured by the etiquette of the thirteenth chapter of First Corinthians. With the Spirit and good-will of the Master in the heart, the refinements of the rules of good breeding are easy. For "politeness is benevolence in little things."

The words *gentleman* and *gentlewoman* came originally from the fact that the uncultivated and ignorant classes used coarse and loud tones, and rough words and movements; while only the refined circles habitually used gentle tones and gentle manners. For the same reason, those born in the higher circles were called "of gentle blood." Thus it came that a coarse and loud voice and rough, ungentle manners are regarded as vulgar and plebeian.

Good manners are important helps in the work of life. When we show ourselves friendly we are always met by the same spirit. Politeness in the hourly intercourse of life smooths away most of the rudeness that otherwise might jar upon our nerves. The parent who instills into his child's mind and habits a simple and clear comprehension of the more reasonable principles and rules of good breeding, has bestowed both new endowments and opened doors for the future.

American manners are said to be "a little free and easy," but a great improvement upon the coldness of the Englishman. Our children need restraining, but, taken all in all, we have great reason to congratulate ourselves on the general good-will of Americans, and their desire to please people. This makes us a nation of ladies and of gentlemen. It would be well to awaken both the zeal of the saint and the pride of the patriot in making Americans the most polite people under the stars.

Study, observation and experiment will easily make any one master of this great accomplishment.

Good manners should be taught to children gradually, and with great patience and gentleness, always enforced by example. Parents should begin with a few principles with their application, and be steady and persevering with these till a habit is formed, and then take a few more, thus making the process easy and gradual. Otherwise the children, hopeless of fulfilling so many requisitions, will become reckless and indifferent to all.

If a few brief, well-considered, and sensible rules of good breeding could be suspended in every school-room, and the children be required to memorize and practice them, it would do much to remedy the defects of American manners.

In presenting these rules we give you the result of a careful selection from a variety of sources and books. We have sought to touch only the most common points, which may be helpful in all homes.

TABLE MANNERS.

Cleanliness is the first element of decency anywhere, and especially at the table. The person should be carefully cleansed and made presentable before coming to the table. Some employments necessarily soil the hands and face

Table Manners. 43

and clothes. Such soiling is honorable. A man should be clad suitably for his business. But this makes no excuse for filthiness or slovenliness at the table. Children should be trained, in preparing themselves for the table or for appearance among the family, not only to put their hair, face, and hands in neat order, but also their teeth and nails, and to attend *habitually* to their nails whenever they wash their hands.

Children should be trained in the family, in order to perfect their manners for the presence of strangers. If they are allowed to chatter while others are talking, they are certain to annoy guests.

Table Rules.—Take your seat quietly at the table, sit firmly in your chair, without lolling, leaning back, drumming, or other uncouth action.

Unfold your napkin, and lay it in your lap.

Eat soup delicately with a spoon, using your bread with your left hand.

Cut your food with your knife, but the fork is to be used to convey it to your mouth. A spoon is employed for food that cannot be eaten with a fork. When eating, take your fork or spoon in the right hand. Never use both hands to convey any thing to your mouth.

Break your bread, not cut or bite it, spreading each piece with butter as you eat it.

Your cup was made to drink from, and your saucer to hold the cup.

It is not well to drink any thing hot; if you drink tea or coffee, wait till it cools.

Eggs should be eaten from the shell, (chipping off a little of the *larger* end,) with or without an egg-cup.

Be attentive to the wants of any lady who may be seated next to you, especially where there are no servants, and pass any thing that may be needful to others.

There are some who insist that when a plate is sent to be replenished the knife and fork must be laid together on the plate. But we are happy to say that idea is being generally discarded. The knife and fork should be taken from the plate when it is passed, and either held in the hand, or laid down with the tips resting on the solitaire, butter-plate, or a piece of bread. The last way is less awkward, and much more convenient than holding them in the hand.

When you have finished the course, lay your knife and fork on your plate, parallel to each other, with the handles toward your right hand.

Wipe your nose if needful. If necessary to blow it, or to spit, leave the table. Never say or do any thing at table that is liable to produce disgust.

Little mistakes, and occasionally a troublesome accident, may occur at table. Always meet them with quiet dignity and self-possession. Do not by undue attention increase the embarrassment.

It is well not to seem too much in haste to commence, as if you were famishing, but neither is it necessary to wait till every body is served before you commence.

It is perfectly proper to "take the last piece" if you want it, always presuming that there is more of the same in reserve.

Table Improprieties.—Never reach over another person's plate.

Never stand up to reach distant articles, instead of asking to have them passed.

Never use your own knife and spoon for butter, salt, or sugar, when it is the custom of the family to provide separate utensils for the purpose.

Never set cups with the tea dripping from them on the table-cloth, instead of the mats or small plates furnished.

Never eat fast, smacking the lips, nor make unpleasant sounds with the mouth.

Never put large or long pieces in the mouth.

Never open your mouth when chewing.

Never leave the table with food in the mouth.

Never attempt to talk with the mouth full.

Never look nor eat as if very hungry, or as if anxious to get at certain dishes.

Never sit at too great a distance from the table.

Never lay the knife and fork on the table-cloth, instead of on the edge of the plate.

Never make unnecessary noise with the knife and fork, or dishes.

Never pick the teeth at table.

Never whisper at table.

Never yawn nor stretch nor indicate restlessness at the table.

Never adjust the hair, clean, nor cut the nails.

Never soil the table-cloth if it is possible to avoid it.

Never carry away fruits and confectionery from the table.

Never encourage a dog or cat to play with you at the table.

Never explain at the table why certain foods do not agree with you.

Never come to the table in your shirt-sleeves, with dirty hands or disheveled hair.

Never express a choice for any particular parts of a dish, unless requested to do so.

Never call loudly for the waiter, nor attract attention to yourself by boisterous conduct.

Never hold bones in your fingers while you eat from them. Cut the meat with a knife.

Never pare an apple, peach, or pear for another at the table, without holding it with a fork.

Never put your salt, or any thing except bread, on the table-cloth.

Table Manners. 45

Never wipe your fingers on the table-cloth, nor clean them in your mouth. Use the napkin.

Never allow butter, soup, or other food to remain on your whiskers. Use the napkin frequently.

Never wear gloves at the table, unless the hands from some special reason are unfit to be seen.

Never, when serving others, overload the plate, nor force upon them delicacies which they decline.

Never pour sauce over meat and vegetables when helping others. Place it at one side on the plate.

Never make a display of finding fault with your food. Very quietly have it changed if you want it different.

Never make a display when removing hair, insects, or other disagreeable things from your food. Place them quietly under the edge of your plate.

Never make an effort to clean your plate or the bones you have been eating from, too clean; it looks as if you left off hungry.

Never, at one's own table or at a dinner-party elsewhere, leave before the rest have finished without asking to be excused. At a hotel or boarding house this rule need not be observed.

Never feel obliged to cut off the kernels with a knife when eating green corn; eaten from the cob, the corn is much the sweetest.

Never eat so much of any one article as to attract attention, as some people do who eat large quantities of butter, sweet cake, cheese, or other articles.

Never spit out bones, cherry pits, grape skins, etc., upon your plate. Quietly press them from your mouth upon the fork, and lay them upon the side of your plate.

Never allow the conversation at the table to drift into any thing but chit-chat; the consideration of deep and abstruse principles will impair digestion.

Never permit yourself to engage in a heated argument at the table. Neither should you use gestures, nor illustrations made with a knife or fork on the table-cloth.

Never pass forward to another the dish that has been handed to you, unless requested to do so; it may have been purposely designed for you, and passing it to another may give him or her what is not wanted.

Never put your feet so far under the table as to touch those of the person on the opposite side; neither should you curl them under nor at the side of your chair.

Never praise extravagantly every dish set before you; neither should you appear indifferent. Any article may have praise.

CHURCH MANNERS.

Be on time. No one has a right needlessly to disturb a congregation or a preacher by being tardy.

Never look around to see who is coming in when the door opens. It diverts your own and others' attention from the exercises, and is discourteous to the leader.

Never talk or whisper in church, especially after the exercises are opened.

Never pull out your watch to see what time it is when the text is announced, or during the sermon. Better to feed on a sermon than to time it.

Conform, if possible in conscience, to the usages of the church in which you worship. Kneel, stand, bow, accordingly.

Never manifest your disapprobation of what is being said by unpleasant sounds, or signs, or by hastily leaving.

Do not fidget, as though the service were a weariness.

Be quiet and decorous to the very end.

Do not put on your overcoat or adjust your wrappings till after the Doxology has been sung.

No gentleman ever defiles a place of worship with tobacco.

Never be one of a staring crowd about the door or in the vestibule, before or after service.

Do nothing out of keeping with the time, place, and purpose of a religious assembly.

Let your politeness be positive. Invite the near stranger to a seat. Offer him a hymn-book, or share with him your own. Be cordial to all. But do not be offended if you are not specially noticed.

INTRODUCTIONS, HOW TO GIVE THEM.

It is neither necessary nor desirable to introduce every body to every body. An introduction is a social indorsement, and you become, to a certain extent, responsible for the person you introduce.

As a general rule, no gentleman should be presented to a lady without her permission being previously obtained. Between gentlemen this formality is not always necessary, but you should have good reason to believe that the acquaintance will be agreeable to both before introducing them.

When two men call upon a stranger on business, each should present the other.

The inferior should be introduced to the superior, the gentleman to the lady, as, "Miss A., permit me to introduce Mr. B." A lady may, however, be introduced to a gentleman much her superior. Equals are mutually introduced; as, "Mr. W., allow me to make you acquainted with Mr. P.; Mr. P., Mr. W."

In presenting persons, be very careful to speak their names plainly; and on being introduced to another, if you do not catch the name, say, without hesitation, "I beg your pardon, I did not hear the name."

If you are the inferior, you will have too much self-respect to be the first to extend the hand. In merely formal introductions, a bow is enough.

In introducing members of your own family, you should always mention the name Say, "My father, Mr. A.," "My daughter, Miss A.," or, "Miss Mary A." Your wife is simply, "Mrs. A.;" and if there happens to be another Mrs. A. in the family, she may be, "Mrs. A., my sister-in-law," etc.

If you are a gentleman, do not permit the lack of an introduction to prevent you from promptly offering your services to an unattended lady, who may need them. Take off your hat, and politely beg the honor of protecting, escorting, or assisting her, and when the service has been accomplished, bow and retire.

SALUTATIONS, HOW TO MAKE THEM.

Salutation is the touchstone of good breeding. You will meet an intimate friend with a hearty hand-shake, and an inquiry indicative of real interest in reference to his health and that of his family. To another person you bow respectfully without speaking. But you should never come into the presence of any person without some form of salutation.

It is a great rudeness not to return a salutation. The two best bred men in England, Charles the Second and George the Fourth, never failed to take off their hats to the meanest of their subjects. A greater than either, George Washington, was wont to lift his hat even to the poor negro slave who took off his.

RECEPTIONS. BEST METHODS.

The duty of receiving visitors usually devolves upon the mistress of the house, and should be performed in an easy, quiet, and self-possessed manner, and without any unnecessary ceremony.

When any one enters, whether announced or not, rise immediately and advance toward him. If a young man, *offer* him an arm-chair; if an elderly man, *insist* upon his accepting it; if a lady, beg her to be seated upon the sofa.

If the master of the house receives the visitors, he will take a chair and place himself at a little distance from them; if the mistress, and she is intimate with the lady, she will sit near her

If several persons come at once, we give the most honorable place to the one who is most entitled to respect. In winter the most honorable places are those at the corners of the fireplace.

If the visitor is a stranger, the master or mistress rises, and any persons who may be already in the room should do the same.

If some who are present withdraw, the master or mistress should conduct them as far as the door. But whoever departs, if we have other company, we may dispense with conducting farther than the door of the room.

VISITS AND CALLS.

There are visits of ceremony, congratulation, condolence, and friendship.

Visits of ceremony should be short.

Visits of congratulation are paid to a friend on the occurrence of any particularly auspicious event in his family, or on his appointment to any office or dignity.

Visits of condolence should be made within the week after the event which calls for them.

Visits of friendship are to be regulated by the peculiar laws of friendship and the universal principles of good manners.

Visiting cards should be engraved or handsomely written. A written card is preferable to a printed card. A gentleman's card should be of medium size, unglazed, and plain. A lady's card may be larger and nicer, and may be conveniently carried in a card-case.

A gentleman attending ladies making morning calls or visits of ceremony should ring the bell, *follow* the ladies in, and be the last to greet—unless he has to introduce.

In terminating the call he should be the last to rise, the last to part, and should *follow* the ladies out.

A morning call being brief, a gentleman may hold his hat, and a lady may keep on her things.

Of course, soiled overshoes and wet wraps should be left outside the reception room.

A gentleman attending ladies should seldom if ever be seated while they are standing.

A gentleman attending should be prompt to serve them as to their parcels, parasols, shawls, etc.

Do not stare around the room.

Do not take a dog or small child.

Do not linger at the dinner-hour.

Do not fidget with your cane, hat or parasol.

Visits and Calls.

Do not make a call of ceremony on a wet day.
Do not turn your back to one seated near you.
Do not touch the piano unless invited to do so.
Do not make a display of consulting your watch.
Do not handle ornaments or furniture in the room.
Do not go to the room of an invalid, unless invited.
Do not remove the gloves when making a formal call.
Do not continue the call longer when conversation begins to lag.
Do not remain when you find the lady upon the point of going out.
Do not make the first call, if you are a new-comer in the neighborhood.
Do not open or shut doors or windows, or alter the arrangement of the room.
Do not enter a room without first knocking and receiving an invitation to come in.
Do not resume your seat after having risen to go, unless for important reasons.
Do not walk around the room, examining pictures, while waiting for the hostess.
Do not introduce politics, religion or weighty topics for conversation when making calls.
Do not prolong the call if the room is crowded. It is better to call a day or two afterward.
Do not call upon a person in reduced circumstances with a display of wealth, dress and equipage.
Do not tattle. Do not speak ill of your neighbors. Do not carry gossip from one family to another.
Do not, if a lady, call upon a gentleman, except officially or professionally unless he may be a confirmed invalid.
Do not take a strange gentleman with you, unless positively certain that his introduction will be received with favor.

In calling, if the person you desired to see is "engaged" or "not at home," leave your card. If several persons, leave a card for each, or request that your compliments be presented to them severally.

If you are going abroad to be absent for some time, and want to take leave ceremoniously, write on your cards T. T. L. [to take leave] or P. P. C., [*pour prendre congé,*] inclose in envelopes, and address them to your friends. In taking leave of a family, send as many cards as you would if making an ordinary visit.

In calling on a friend at a hotel, do not visit his room till, having announced yourself by card, he bids you come. If he is out, add your address to your card, and leave it for him.

If in making an evening visit you happen to find a party assembled, present yourself as you would have done had you been invited. **Converse with** ease for a few moments, and then retire.

In general, visits should be returned personally or by card, just as you would speak when spoken to, or answer a respectful letter.

HOSTS AND GUESTS.

Hosts should give their guests the home-feeling. If a host, do not worry your guests, but let them alone. You should not by over-attentions make them realize they are not at home, and perhaps wish they were.

Promote their convenience and comfort, and open to them reasonable sources of entertainment and improvement, but in such an easy, graceful way as will make it seem no trouble to you, but a pleasure.

You should not let their presence causelessly interfere with your domestic arrangements. Inform them as to the hour for meals and family worship, for retiring and rising—whether there will be a rising-bell. You should let them see that they fall as it were naturally into vacant places in the home circle.

Your rooms and table should be furnished hospitably, but not extravagantly. If any thing extraordinary renders an apology necessary, make it at once, and cease. Do not disgust by depreciating your preparations and "regretting" that you have not better.

When they speak of leaving, you will of course express any desire you feel to have them stay longer, but do not urge them against their and your sense of propriety and duty.

Guests should show their hosts the home-feeling. When a guest, learn as quickly, and conform as fully, as possible to your host's family customs. It is better for you by a little thought and attention to adjust yourself to their household arrangements than for some of them to be inconvenienced, it may be, in their avocations.

By keeping your room tidy, and your articles of dress in order, you will add to their appreciation of you. If they lack help, you may readily find ways of rendering them considerate service.

Appointments. Be exact in keeping all appointments.

If you make an appointment with another at your own house, devote your time solely to him.

If you accept an appointment at the house of a public officer or a man of business, be very punctual; transact the affair with dispatch, and retire the moment it is finished.

At a dinner or supper to which you have accepted an invitation, be strictly punctual. Do not arrive much before the time nor any after. If too late on an occasion where ceremony is required, send in your card wi h an apology, and retire.

Dinner parties. On receiving an invitation answer at once, positively accepting, or declining with "regrets."

Be punctual. Do not keep the dinner waiting. Better be too late for the train!

A gentleman may offer his arm to a lady, and conduct her to the dining-room, the hostess leading the way, and the others following—giving precedence to age or other reasons for respect. A lady takes the left arm of the gentleman.

At the table the lady of the house sits at the head and the gentleman of the house opposite. The places of honor for gentlemen are next the mistress of the house, and for ladies next the master of the house, the right hand being the place of special honor. Husbands and wives or other near relatives may be seated apart for more general conversation.

Nothing on the table should be disturbed till "grace" is said. Then the napkins are spread.

In "waiting," the general rule is to serve from right to left. If two or more wait, the sides may be served at once.

The principal meats are often carved on a side-table, and served by attendants.

Serve pies with forks, puddings and tarts with spoons.

If "finger-bowls" are used, dip the fingers and wipe with the colored napkin.

Interchange civilities and thoughts with those near you.

Evening parties. Evening parties are various, and in general, ceremonious as they are fashionable.

Having accepted the invitation, do not fail to be present if you can reasonably avoid it.

A married man should never accept a lady's invitation to a party, unless his wife is included in the invitation.

On entering a drawing-room where there is a party, salute the lady of the house before speaking to any other. Then mingle with the company, salute your acquaintances. Conversations may be held with others without the formality of an introduction.

If a guest desires to withdraw before the company disperses, he should do so as quietly and as unobserved as proper respect for the hosts will permit.

Christmas. It is a commendable custom to celebrate the anniversary of the birth of Christ. The occasion is peculiarly appropriate for family gatherings, and for the exchange of presents. There are no customs connected with the day requiring special discussion here.

The New Year. In New York and other cities, every gentleman is expected to call on his lady acquaintances on New Year's day, and each lady who receives calls must be prepared to do the honors of her house.

Of late years it has become fashionable for ladies in many cities and villages to announce in the newspapers the fact of their intention to receive calls upon New Year's day, which practice is very excellent, as it enables gentlemen to know positively who will be prepared to receive them on that occasion; besides, changes of residence are so frequent in the large cities as to make the publication of names and places of calling of great convenience.

The practice of issuing personal notes of invitation is not to be commended. It looks very much like begging the gentlemen to come and see them.

Upon calling, the gentlemen are invited to remove overcoat and hat, which invitation is accepted unless it is designed to make the call very brief. If refreshments are provided, the ladies will desire to have the gentlemen partake of them, which cannot conveniently be done in overcoat, with hat in hand. Gloves are sometimes retained upon the hand during the call, but this is optional. Cards are sent up, and the gentlemen are ushered into the reception-room. The call should not exceed ten or fifteen minutes, unless the callers are few, and it should be mutually agreeable to prolong the stay.

Best taste will suggest that a lady having the conveniences shall receive her guests at her own home, but it is admissible and common for several ladies to meet at the residence of one, and receive calls together. In fact, it is pleasant for two or more ladies to receive together, as several ladies can the more easily entertain a party of several gentlemen who may be present at one time. Whether ladies make announcement or not, however, it will be usually safe for gentlemen to call on their lady friends on New Year's, as the visit will be generally received with pleasure.

It is customary for the ladies who announce that they will receive, to make their parlors attractive on that day, and present themselves in full dress. They should have a bright, cheerful fire if the weather is cold, and a table, conveniently located in the room, with refreshments, consisting of fruits, cakes, bread, and other food, such as may be deemed desirable, with tea and coffee. No intoxicating drinks should be allowed. Refreshments are in no case absolutely essential. They can be dispensed with if not convenient.

Ladies expecting calls on New Year's should be in readiness to receive from 10 A. M. to 9 P. M. While gentlemen may go alone, they also frequently go in pairs, threes, fours or more. They call upon all the ladies of the party, and where any are not acquainted, introductions take place, care being taken that persons do not intrude themselves where they would not be welcome. Each gentleman should be provided with a large number of cards with his own name upon each, one of which he will present to every lady of the company where he calls.

The ladies keep these cards for future reference, it being often pleasant to revive the incidents of the day by subsequent examination of the cards received upon that occasion.

An usher should be present wherever many calls are expected, to receive guests, and care for hats and coats. The calls are necessarily very brief, and are made delightfully pleasant by continual change of face and conversation. But however genial and free may be the interchange of compliments upon this occasion, no young man who is a stranger to the family should feel at liberty to call again without a subsequent invitation.

The two or three days succeeding New Year's are the ladies' days for calling, upon which occasion they pass the compliments of the season, comment upon the incidents connected with the festivities of the holiday, the number of calls made, and the new faces that made their appearance among the visitors. It is customary upon this occasion of ladies' meeting to offer refreshments, and to enjoy the intimacy of a friendly visit.

WEDDINGS.

It is well to know that custom gives the parties full liberty to follow their tastes in the style and order of their ceremony.

For a stylish wedding, two or more brides-maids and two or more groomsmen are expected to be in attendance.

For a formal wedding in the evening, invitations should be given at least a week before the occasion. The lady fixes the day. Her mother or nearest female relative invites the guests.

It is a common practice in a well-ordered wedding in the home for the guests to assemble in the parlors, leaving a vacant space at the end selected for the ceremony. At the appointed time the bridal party come into the parlor in the following order: The second brides-maid and groomsman, if there are only two, enter the room first; then the first brides-maid and first groomsman, and lastly the bride and bridegroom. The officiating clergyman meets them so as to stand before them as they take their position on the floor.

When the ceremony is performed in the church, (the best place for it,) the officiating clergyman takes his seat in the chancel or inside the altar, and as the party come up the aisle in the order given above, he rises and passes to his position, and the party form in front of the altar; the bride and groom in the center, the bride at the groom's left hand, the brides-maids at her left and the groomsmen at the right of the bridegroom. Sometimes the first brides-maid and groomsman are stationed at the left of the bride, and the second brides-maid and groomsman at the right of the bridegroom.

Sometimes, following the brides-maids and groomsmen, the bride's mother comes to the altar on the arm of the bridegroom, followed by the bride supported by her father. In this case, during the ceremony the parents stand near and a little back of the bride.

Whatever order of approach to the altar is selected, the ceremony at the altar can most appropriately follow the ritual of the Church where the ceremony is performed, or of the clergyman officiating. The wish of the bride is supreme in these matters.

In the ceremony, if the ring is used, at the proper time the bride gives her left hand to her first maid, who removes the glove. Meantime the bridegroom hands the ring (a plain gold ring) to the clergyman, who holds it till the bride's hand is uncovered, then the clergyman hands the ring to the bridegroom, who puts it upon the third finger of the bride's left hand. Then the ceremony proceeds according to the ritual.

It is proper, if the bride prefers, to have only ushers without brides-maids, or to have brides-maids without ushers or groomsmen.

The *exquisite* order changes with the fancy of each elegant couple.

When the ceremony is ended, the friends remain in their places till the bridal party has left the church. The bridal party, in retiring, reverses the order of their entrance; the groom always leads the way with his bride.

If the ceremony is performed in the house, when it is ended, the company present their congratulations—the clergyman first, then the mother and the father of the bride and the relatives, then the company; the groomsmen acting as masters of ceremonies, bringing forward and introducing the ladies, who wish the happy couple joy, happiness, prosperity.

The bridegroom takes an early occasion to thank the clergyman, and to put in his hand, at the same time, nicely enveloped, a piece of gold, according to his ability and generosity.

FUNERALS.

When any member of a family dies, it is customary to send information and invitation to all who have been connected with the deceased in business or friendship. No answer is required.

At an interment or funeral service, the members of the family have the first places. They are nearest to the coffin, whether in the procession or in the church. No mourning dresses are required.

In general, ministers ought not to be expected to go to the grave, unless it is near by. Others who are not relatives or intimate friends of the deceased are excused from accompanying the procession. The first carriage is for the officiating clergyman if he goes to the grave, then follow the pall-bearers next the hearse, after that the mourners and friends.

IMPORTANT RULES OF CONDUCT.

Always be respectful and deferential to your parents and superiors. The fifth commandment has not been revoked.

Always be polite and courteous to your sisters and brothers.

Remember that the delicate attentions and tender expressions of the lover should not cease after marriage.

Mutual kindness and regard between employers and employed, besides being right, would promote the interests of both capital and labor.

IT IS POLITE:

To inquire courteously after the family and friends of those you meet, and to manifest an interest in them;

To devote a little space in every letter to "remembrances" for friends;

To write occasionally to all from whom you have received special kindnesses;

To conform your dress, and (in reason) your customs to the tastes and feelings of those whose guest or associate you may be;

To inquire after any one of whose acquaintance your friend may have reason to be proud;

To express felt interest in or admiration of those dear to him;

To avoid all remarks which tend to embarrass, vex, mortify, or in any way annoy the feelings of another;

To avoid combating another's religious opinions or politics;

To make ready sacrifices of comfort, as to escort a lady, or help a neighbor;

To avoid all practical jokes;

To avoid noticing personal defects;

To attend closely when addressed in conversation;

To avoid contradicting flatly;

To acknowledge by word or manner all acts of kindness and courtesy even from relatives;

To apologize heartily when you have injured another, or hurt his feelings;

To show the *utmost* kindness to those who have been reduced by adversity;

To interpose and shield another from mortification and wounded self-respect;

To do every thing for another which will gratify him and is not unreasonable.

Never—

Never look over the shoulder of another who is reading or writing.

Never arrest the attention of an acquaintance by a touch. Speak to him

Never, when traveling abroad, be over boastful in praise of your own country.

Never exaggerate.

Never answer questions in general company that have been put to others.

Never point at another.

Never call attention to the features or form of any one present.

Never call a new acquaintance by the Christian name unless requested to do so.

Never appear to notice a scar, deformity, or defect of any one present.

Never wantonly frighten others.

Never exhibit anger, impatience, or excitement when an accident happens.

Never leave home with unkind words.

Never neglect to call upon your friends.

Never punish your child for a fault to which you are addicted yourself.

Never laugh at the misfortunes of others.

Never lend an article you have borrowed, unless you have permission to do so.

Never give a promise that you do not fulfill.

Never enter a room noisily; never fail to close the door after you, and never slam it.

Never send a present, hoping for one in return.

Never pick the teeth or clean the nails in company.

Never be guilty of the contemptible meanness of opening a private letter addressed to another.

Never question a servant or child about family matters.

Never associate with bad company. Have good company or none.

Never will a gentleman allude to conquests which he may have made with ladies.

Never present a gift, saying that is of no use to yourself.

Never fail, if a gentleman, of being civil and polite to ladies.

Never refer to a gift you have made or favor you have rendered.

Never fail to give a polite answer to a civil question.

Never read letters which you may find addressed to others.

Never betray a confidence.

Never attempt to draw the attention of the company constantly upon yourself.

Never pass between two persons who are talking together, without an apology.

Never forget that, if you are faithful in a few things, you may be ruler over many.

Never exhibit too great familiarity with the new acquaintance; you may give offense.

It is Polite.

Never fail to offer the easiest and best seat in the room to an invalid, an elderly person, or a lady.

Never neglect to perform the commission which the friend intrusted to you. You must not forget.

Never send your guest, who is accustomed to a warm room, off into a cold, damp, spare bed, to sleep.

Never enter a room filled with people, without a slight bow to the general company when first entering.

Never leave a room with your back to the company.

Never fail to answer an invitation, either personally or by letter, within a week after the invitation is received.

Never accept of favors and hospitalities without rendering an exchange of civilities when opportunity offers.

Never cross the leg and put out one foot in the street-car, or places where it will trouble others when passing by.

Never fail to tell the truth. If truthful, you get your reward. You will get your punishment if you deceive.

Never borrow money and neglect to pay. If you do, you will soon be known as a person of no business integrity.

Never write to another asking for information, or a favor of any kind, without inclosing a postage stamp for the reply.

Never fail to say kind and encouraging words to those whom you meet in distress. Your kindness may lift them out of their despair.

Never refuse to receive an apology. You may not revive friendship, but courtesy will require, when an apology is offered, that you accept it.

Never examine the cards in the card-basket. While they may be exposed in the drawing-room, you are not expected to turn them over unless invited to do so.

Never, when walking arm and arm with a lady, be continually changing and going to the other side, because of change of corners. It shows too much attention to form.

Never should the lady accept of expensive gifts at the hand of a gentleman not engaged to her. Gifts of flowers, books, music or confectionery may be accepted.

Never insult another by harsh words when applied to for a favor. Kind words do not cost much, and yet they may carry untold happiness to the one or whom they are spoken.

Never fail to speak kindly. If a merchant, and you address your clerk; if an overseer, and you address your workmen; if in any position where you exercise authority, you show yourself to be a gentleman by your pleasant mode of address.

Never attempt to convey the impression that you are a genius by imitating the faults of distinguished men. Because certain great men were poor penmen, wore long hair, or had other peculiarities, it does not follow that you will be great by imitating their eccentricities.

Never give all your pleasant words and smiles to strangers. The kindest words and the sweetest smiles should be reserved for home. Home should be our heaven.

AMUSEMENTS. THEIR IMPORTANCE.

The way to keep the enemy out of the fort is to occupy it yourself. If the street and the grocery are not to occupy the time and attention of your boys, the home must. There have been too many children in the world to leave it an open question that they must have some amusement. It is now simply a question as to what amusements are most suitable. Even if authority keeps the children in-doors, something more subtle must keep evil thoughts from rioting in their minds. Cheerfulness in the home makes it attractive, and gives its ideas great advantage in the strife for control.

When amusements become sinful. When they fail to prepare body or mind for the better discharge of duties.

When they interfere with duties or employments.

When they produce excessive fatigue, weary the mind, or deprive of necessary sleep.

When they tend to injure the health or physical constitution.

When they tend to weaken the intellectual powers.

When they give a distaste for moral and religious truth.

When they turn on an element of chance.

When they require public patronage for their maintenance.

When they inflict needless pain.

When they cause fright or vexation to people or animals.

When they endanger life.

When by their exciting nature, or their connection with temptation, they tend to harm the individual or community.

HOME ENTERTAINMENT.

Provide in the home not only instructive, but also entertaining reading. The philosophers in the family are not the difficult questions. They care for themselves. You must arrange to entertain those who will not grapple with hard reading or dry books. A good story may induce them to read, and, reading, they can be led to better books. While it is true that any good author will awaken inquiries which can be satisfied only by research, it is still necessary to select the stories with great care. Stories that present some historical characters, and thus become a center in the memory for locating other events of an age, are good bait for a child without taste for reading. It is true that the parables are inventions, but they partake more of the character of high moral instruction than of amusement.

Provide a good supply of pictures and toys for very young children. It is not extravagant, as it may seem. It fills their time, keeps out bad thoughts, quickens their faculties, and prevents evils that can be corrected only with great labor and pains.

Enter into the sports of your children. Lyman Beecher was a champion racer on all fours with a child on his back.

Lead the children to cultivate fruits and flowers. It develops the love of the beautiful, and gives opportunity and means for blessing other people.

Cultivate music, instrumental and vocal. It cheers the home.

Collect shells, plants, and specimens in geology and mineralogy. Not to weary as a study, but to interest the children in studying the specimens, and learning all about them. Encourage all sorts of harmless games, which tend to quicken the observation, strengthen the memory, or develop the body. Tableaux and charades give much amusement, and call forth a good deal of ingenuity and intelligence, and there are various games invented—literary, historical, geographical, and so forth—which are very cheap, and which convey a good deal of useful information. It is amusing to give out a word, and call upon every one to make two or more rhyming lines containing that word. Spelling matches are very lively and profitable, and when the company is disposed to be grave, a word such as "tree" or "water" might be given out, and every one be asked to mention where it is found in the Bible.

Give the boys boxes of tools. It develops their mechanical skill and ingenuity.

Give little girls dolls, and nice large dolls to larger girls. With this incentive they will speedily be introduced into the intricacies of dressmaking, millinery, and housekeeping more easily than in any other way.

Interest the children in decorating the home. It is a good investment to furnish them materials with which to make little ornaments for the house. Put emphasis on the value these things possess because made by themselves.

Celebrate birthdays and holidays and anniversaries. It adds to home's attractiveness for a child to feel that there is one place where they are glad that he ever came.

As far as possible let each child have a companion near its own

age, with congenial tastes. It gives a chance to draw upon some forces outside of the family.

Use hospitality. Keep your home open to the good and wise. Your children and yourself will gain much information by meeting people at your table. The unwritten history in things is always the most instructive. God urges hospitality more than any other social duty. It combines the benevolence of the Church with the instruction of the university.

Establish a reading circle. Have this meet in your home if you can, or in the Church or some home of the Church. A dozen or more young men and women of congenial tastes, habits, and social belongings, can easily meet once during every week through five or six months of the year. With a small fund they can buy good books, and over these, read aloud by one and another of their number, they can spend an hour and a half most pleasantly and profitably. They will find in these books topics of conversation for the remainder of the time they spend together. These gatherings may be varied with music and the use of the various gifts of the members—original compositions, declamations, and the like.

Keep up family relations after leaving the home. Some have adopted the following practice: On the first day of each month some member of the family, at the extreme point of dispersion, fills a part of a page. This is sealed and mailed to the next member, who reads it, adds another contribution, and then mails it to the next. Thus the family circular once a month goes from each extreme to all the members of a widely dispersed family, and each member becomes a sharer in the joys, sorrows, plans, and pursuits of all the rest.

HOW AND WHAT TO READ.

We live among books to find the good, the beautiful, and the true in them, and by them to be inspired and led into the heart of nature and into the soul of mankind. A few hints in this labyrinth is better than a master. Indiscriminate reading will give much information and lose more. It fixes no centers around which future acquisitions crystallize.

A course of reading should develop all the intellectual faculties.

A few books may give culture. Poverty, preventing you from buying many costly books, need not keep you from undertaking the culture of your mind. Lincoln read chiefly the Bible and Shakspeare. Good books can be frequently re-read w'th profit.

Choosing books is important business. A single book may make or mar a life. Voltaire learned an infidel poem when he was five years old, and it molded his life. Hume, when a boy took the infidel side of a question in a debating society, and cast his die. What books will you let come into the place of your parents and friends?

Youth should be left to themselves in the selecting of books no more than in the selecting of companions.

The desirableness of books depends upon their truth to nature, their euphony, language, ideas, and vigor. The best books are those that elevate the character by moving the heart.

Some books should be read, whether we like them or not, because they are necessary to education and culture.

Some books should be read because they are so often alluded to by other writers and in general conversation.

One should be thoroughly acquainted with the books and names of the authors of his own land. Patriotism should lead a man to know the glory in the midst of which he lives.

Read occasionally good essays, biographies, standard books of travel, and a little standard fiction. Sometimes too protracted reading of heavy histories wearies the purpose of the uncultured, and the mind refuses to hold the results. Change of diet is good for body and mind.

Let each prominent fact become a center of arrangement for other facts. When the piles are thus driven, it is wonderful how soon the sea washes in a new formation and foundation for future building. Every book, and almost every paper, will add something to the stock of knowledge.

Some find a blank book and a pencil good companions in reading. Thus, marked passages can be retained for reference, or impressed on the mind by the work of writing.

If convenient, read with a friend. Discussion clears and fixes in the mind what you read.

Read aloud portions of every book. It enables you to test the style of the author.

Never read second-class stories. They steal the time and weaken the mind.

Never read what you do not wish to remember.

HEALTH.

HEALTH AT HOME.

Health is Wealth.—Health is one of the foundation pillars of happiness in the home. It is a condition of the best instruction and the best education. It is an essential preliminary to the best success in the best work, and to the highest attainment in the widest usefulness. Without it there is sadness at the hearth-stone, silence and sorrow, instead of cheerful words and happy hearts.

> "A clear bright eye,
> That can pierce the sky
> With the strength of an eagle's vision,
> And a steady brain,
> That can bear the strain
> And the shock of the world's collision;—
>
> "A well-knit frame
> With the ruddy flame
> Aglow, and the pulses leaping
> With the measured time
> Of a dulcet rhyme,
> Their beautiful record keeping;—
>
> "A rounded cheek,
> Where the roses speak
> Of a soil that is rich for thriving,
> And a chest so grand
> That the lungs expand
> Exultant, without the striving;—
>
> "A breath like morn,
> When the crimson dawn
> Is fresh in its dewy sweetness;
> A manner bright,
> And a spirit light
> With joy in own completeness;—
>
> "O give me these,
> Nature's harmonies,
> And keep all your golden treasures;
> For what is wealth
> To the boon of health,
> And its sweet attendant pleasures!"

What are fortunes and honors in the absence of the future health and vigor of our loved ones? What is home itself, where disease abides as a permanent visitor, and poisons every perfume with a malarious infection?

Special Home Ministry.—An eloquent French author correctly says that the whole of maternity is comprised in these four words: "Blood, food, care, devotion." Paternity is an equal sharer here, both as to privilege and responsibility. What ministry is more delicate, more difficult, and more sublime? What work is greater than to give to coming parent and citizen a sound body, a strong mind, and a good heart?

This Ministry Must Begin Early.—There is an old Spanish proverb that "What enters with swaddling, comes out only with the shroud." Wordsworth truthfully wrote in rhyme, "The child is *father of the man*." Manhood inherits childhood. Parentage is responsible for the character and value of the inheritance.

This Ministry Illustrated.—"Behold a man!" said Napoleon to his officers when he first met Goethe, who was the embodiment of physical and mental vigor. The great poet lived to a great age, working on beyond his fourscore years, and remaining "robust and energetic to the last," says his biographer, after he had seen three generations swept by him to the grave. When he died—at *eighty-four*—the medical authorities at Weimar, being curious to learn the physiological problem of such great work at such an advanced age, made a *post-mortem* examination, which showed that all the internal as well as the external organs of the body were in "perfect condition." And yet Goethe was feeble and sickly in childhood. Parental care, in the direction of thorough hygienic culture, with his own resolution to indulge in not a single sinful habit superadded, brought strength, and life, and usefulness.

Another Illustration.—Alexander von Humboldt was another example of the good fruits of early and wisely directed health training. Hence it was that his biographers were able to present him to the world as "the Corypheus of physical science, and a man of universal culture; a man also of 'society,' and of courtly life." He crowded into his ninety years of successful life whole centuries of the life and toil of other men with equal natural endowment, but less carefully and less wisely trained. On the 3d of May, 1859, the journals of Berlin announced: "Alexander von Humboldt has been confined to his bed the last twelve days; his strength has been gradually failing, *his mind retaining all its clearness*." In three days more, writes Dr. Abel Stevens, as the sunlight poured into his window, he exclaimed, "How grand those rays! They seem to beckon earth to heaven!" and died. For twenty years or more of the time in which men are usually said to be beyond "the allotted period of life," when they usually decay mentally, he was writing the "Cosmos," the grandest work of his life, and one of the greatest of his generation. Sanitary work is brain work; and the successful brain work of mature age is the inheritance of the most careful sanitary work in the nursery of an intelligent home.

CHOOSING A PHYSICIAN.

Select the Physician Early.—Choose him, if possible, before he is needed. There is time for the greater care in the selection. There come emergencies in every home. If no selection has then been made, the messenger may rush from door to door seeking help from the first one met. There may then be no time for discrimination, and the practitioner may be one of doubtful excellence. The questions involved may be too important for such hurry.

Select a Physician of Integrity.—No amount of medical or surgical skill can compensate for the lack of good morals and a scrupulous conscience. The relation is too intimate and sacred for the admission of any one of doubtful habits or reputation. Shun the physician of bad habits, as you would a person bearing the infection of yellow fever or the plague. Is he "only a drunkard?" Pity him; try to reform him; be a "Good Samaritan" to him; but do not trust to his professional services, which demand a clear head and a firm hand.

Choose a Physician of Clean Lips.—No one of impure speech, of reckless or even careless words, or hints bordering on the obscene or immodest or vulgar, should find a place, even professionally, in any home. Don't excuse such a fault and pass it by with the expression, "O he means well!" In nine cases out of ten such a man does *not* mean well, and if he does, his immodest expressions are so unnecessary, and so directly in conflict with the best teachings and with the best practice of his profession, as to leave him without the least possible excuse for their utterance. Mothers, sisters, fathers, brothers, invite *no* such person, even professionally, to your home, and if, by any lack of information, or by any mistake of judgment, he may have come there, see to it that his visits are not repeated.

He should be Able, and Thorough as a Student, and of Untiring Industry in his Profession.—The trusts placed in his keeping include that of life itself. They demand the most intelligent, capable, and devoted service. That service may not rest with even the best knowledge of the best teachers. The new phases of diseases, and the new information furnished by additional observation and experiment, must be constantly sought for and promptly appropriated for the benefit of his patrons.

Which School of Medicine should be Preferred?—We cannot tell. Our own personal preferences may not be the best for others. We may not intrude them uninvited into the home circles of our friends. Their prejudices, like ours, may be the result in part of early education and in part of personal observation. There are other questions more important than those which determine the physician's school of medicine. In their light does he measure up to the line required?

Having Chosen Him, Give Him your Confidence.—A good physician will repay in thoroughness and zeal what is awarded him in ready and unmistaken confidence. However strong in his own convictions and rigidly earnest in his professional work, he is sensitive almost to a fault. A word or a look of mistrust disheartens him in his work; while a word or a look of unreserved trust becomes an inspiration to an intense zeal for the patient.

Having Chosen Him, Be Considerate of his Time and Rest.—His season for sleep and for recreation should be respected. In case of necessity it may be appropriately disturbed, but "before doing it," says a well known medical writer, "one should think twice." "It is his trade" is a harsh expression, and unworthy of considerate and devoted patients. Consider carefully your physician's hours for repose, for meals, and for church, and then care for him as you would have him care for you. Such appreciative care on your part will be reciprocated by him a hundred-fold.

Don't Abuse his Confidence by Trivial Calls.—If you run for him on every slight indisposition, and with unnecessary alarm excite his solicitude, and lead him to disarrange his regular plans of visitation, he will soon learn to place a lower estimate upon your demands, and to respond to them with less promptness and solicitude. "Physicians dread fussy mothers."

The Physician in the Intervals of Sickness.—We quote from the observations of Prof. Poussagrieves of Paris: "There is another mistake, which I must point out to mothers, (without, however, slighting the fathers, they may well believe)—that, namely, of looking upon the physician, once chosen, as having no part or function in the family except when illness calls him there. It is a very narrow and a very dangerous conception of his *rôle*, and one which simply ignores one half of practical medicine, *that is*, hygiene. It is said that the Chinese pay their physicians with a liberality proportioned to their freedom from sickness during the year. I do not advise that we should imitate the Chinese; but this stimulus to hygienic care certainly smacks of the judicious. We make our first appearance in families to take charge of patients, many grave questions being resolved without *our* participation. Children often receive a guidance the reverse of what is proper, and we are called upon to fulfill the ungrateful office of repairing the damages we might generally have prevented."

It is Better to Care for a Man's Health than for his Disease.—"I would that the relations of physicians with their families were established on such a footing that the former should make visits as often as they should judge necessary for the prevention of disease. This would be a very precious protective measure. To select a good physician, to put the health of the whole household into his keeping, to expect of him ordinarily, besides unforeseen calls, a visit at certain intervals—once a month for instance—how comforting would it be for the parental conscience?"

Why do Successful Medical Men often die Prematurely?—This question is satisfactorily answered by Dr Bennett: "Mortality in the medical profession after fifty years is greater than in any other profession, and greatest of all among its most eminent and successful members. The peculiar feature of the medical profession is, that work increases with age, and the public do not consent to look upon ageing medical men as veterans, but expect from them to the end the labor of youth. . . . The barrister has his junior counsel who prepares his briefs, the solicitor his head clerks, the vicar his curates, etc., but the successful consulting physician or surgeon must stand alone, whatever his age, and do his work entirely himself as long as he practices."

The Physician Should be Reverential.—If that profound naturalist, Agassiz, surrounded by his pupils in his laboratory, where were the fossils representing the past ages of life, would not enter upon his work without first uncovering his head in silent prayer to God, how should a physician feel on entering the mysterious chamber where disease and health, life and death, time and eternity, are brought into juxtaposition. If we speak of responsibility in connection with other professions, how immeasurably greater is the responsibility connected with the medical profession!

Qualities of a Good Doctor by a Doctor.—Here is a very suggestive *summary* of hints covering the question of choosing a physician. It has the authority of an experienced and able member of the profession. Read and ponder:—

Avoid the *mean* man, for you may be sure he will be a mean doctor, just as certainly as he would make a mean husband.

Avoid a dishonest man; he will not be honest with you as your physician.

Shun the doctor that you can *buy* to help you out of a scrape; a good doctor cannot be bought.

Avoid the untidy, coarse, blundering fellow, though he may bear the parchments of a medical college.

Avoid the doctor who flatters you, and humors your lusts and appetites.

Avoid the man who puts on an extra amount of *airs;* be assured that it is done to cover his ignorance

Avoid the empty blow-horn, who boasts of his numerous cases, and tells you of his seeing forty or fifty patients a day, while he spends two hours to convince you of the fact. Put him down for a fool.

To be a doctor one must first be a *man* in the true sense of the word.

He should be a moral man, honest in his dealings.

He must have good sense, or he cannot be a good doctor.

He should be strictly temperate. No one should trust his life in the hands of an intemperate doctor.

He must have some mechanical genius, or it is impossible for him to be a good surgeon.

It is a good sign if he tells you how to keep well.

It is a good sign if the members of his own family respect him.

It is a good sign if the children like him.

It is a good sign if he is neat and handy at making pills and folding powders.

It is a good sign if he is still a student, and keeps posted in all the latest improvements known to the profession for alleviating human suffering.

PREVENTION OF DISEASE.

Early and Strange Notions of Disease.—It was supposed formerly that diseases were caused by the evil spirits or demons which were supposed to have entered the body and deranged its action. Hence it was said of the dumb that they had a "dumb devil." Incantations, exorcisms, etc., were constantly resorted to in order to drive them out. It was thought by others that diseases came arbitrarily, or as a special visitation of an overruling power, and hence they were to be removed by fasting and prayer.

What is Disease?—Modern science teaches us that disease is not a thing, but a state or condition. When our food is properly assimilated, the waste matter promptly excreted, and all the organs working in perfect harmony, we are well; but when any derangements of these functions occur, we are sick. Sickness is discord, while health is concord. If we abuse or misuse any instrument, we destroy its ability to produce a perfect harmony. A suffering body is simply the penalty of violated law, and follows as necessarily as an effect follows a cause.

Many Diseases may be Avoided.—A large proportion of the ills which now afflict and rob us of so much time and enjoyment might easily be avoided. A proper knowledge and observance of hygienic laws would greatly lessen the number of such diseases as pneumonia, consumption, catarrh, gout, rheumatism, scrofula, dyspepsia, etc. It is a lamentable fact that in densely populated cities nearly one half of the children die before they are five years old. Every physiologist knows that at least nine tenths of these lives could be saved by an observance of the laws of health. Professor Bennett, of Edinburgh, estimated that 100,000 persons die annually in Scotland from diseases easily preventable, and the same testimony could be obtained from the medical profession in this and other countries.

Methods of Prevention.—With the advance of medical science the causes of many diseases have been determined. Vaccination has been found to prevent or mitigate the ravages of small pox. Scurvy, formerly so fatal among sailors that it was deemed "a mysterious infliction of Divine justice against which man strives in vain," is now entirely prevented by the use of vegetables or lime juice. Cholera, whose approach strikes dread in the community and for which no certain specific has been found, is but the penalty for filthy streets, bad drainage, over-crowded tenements, and general filthiness, and it may be controlled, if not prevented, by suitable sanitary measures. The same may be said of that dreadful scourge, the yellow fever. There is no quarantine like cleanliness, good drainage and ventilation.

Responsibility of Health Commissioners.—Health commissioners in our cities should be men well skilled in the medical science, and the health of the community should not be intrusted to ignorant political partisans. A great deal of responsibility rests upon the municipal authorities in regard to the prevention of disease.

The Divine Plan.—It is no doubt the intention of the all-wise Creator that we should wear out by the general decay of all the organs, rather than by the giving out of any particular part of the system; and that all the organs should work together harmoniously until the vital forces are exhausted. There is no reason why it should be otherwise; why all human organisms should not be preserved like a tree or an animal of the forest, until its allotted period of life is reached, and then decay and die. Unfortunately, as it is, the average life of man is short, and after deducting infancy, sickness and old age, scarcely more than one half is available for the active purposes of life. When we observe the almost constant violation of the laws of health so common in every community, the wonder is that people live at all.

Why Medicine is Taken.—The first step in the cure of any disease is to obey the law of health which has been violated. If medicine is taken, it is not to destroy the disease, since that is not a thing to be destroyed, but it is *to hold the deranged action in check* while nature repairs the injury, and brings the system again into harmonious movement. This tendency or power of nature is the physician's chief reliance. *Vis medicatrix naturæ* is the great sheet-anchor, the power of nature to repair the breach made by violated law. The very best and most skillful physicians have little confidence in medicine itself.

THE HUMAN SKELETON—ILLUSTRATIONS.

Preliminary to furnishing the reader of the numerous practical health notes in this volume for the convenience of the latter reference, attention is called to the descriptive illustrations of the human skeleton:

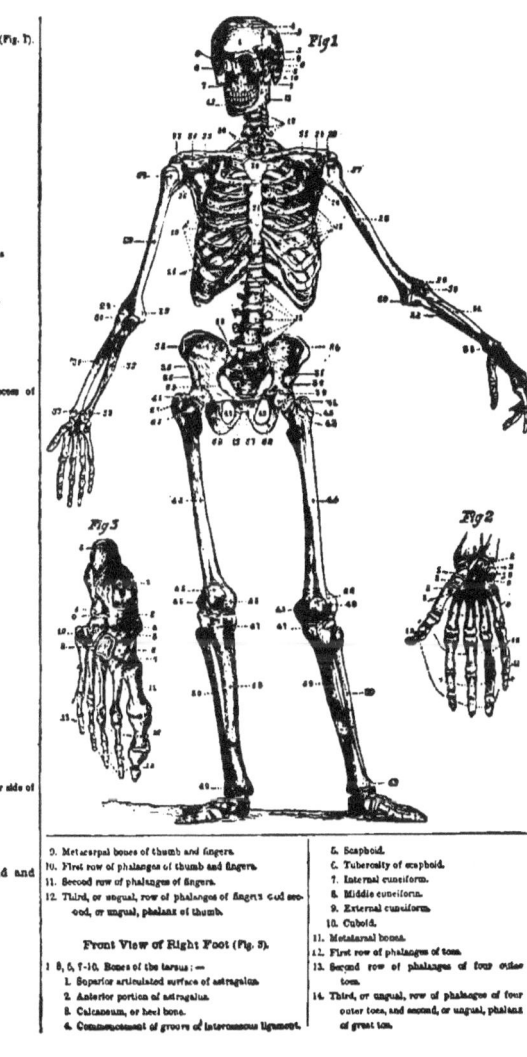

EXPLANATION.

Bones of Head, Trunk, Legs, and Arms (Fig. 1).

1. Frontal bone.
2. Parietal bone.
3. Temporal bone.
4. Coronal suture.
5. Malar or cheek bone.
6. Nasal bone.
7. Superior maxillary, maxilla, or upper jawbone.
8. Orbits.
9. Side of occipital bone.
10. Condyloid process of mandible or lower jaw.
11. Angle of mandible.
12. Symphysis of mandible.
13. Four lower cervical vertebræ (7 in all).
14. Two upper and two lower dorsal vertebræ (12 in a
15. Lumbar vertebræ (5 in number).
16. Sacrum.
17. Coccyx, the lower part hidden } False Vertebræ. by the pubic bones.
18. Cartilages of ribs.
19. Ribs.
20. Manubrium of sternum or breast bone.
21. Mesosternum, or body of sternum.
22. Xiphisternum, metasternum, or ensiform process of sternum.
23. Clavicles, or collar bones.
24. Coracoid process of scapula (shoulder blade).
25. Acromion process of scapula.
26. Subscapular fossa, anterior surface.
27. Head of humerus or arm bone.
28. Body of humerus.
29. Condyles of humerus.
30. Head of radius or outer bone of forearm.
31. Body of radius.
32. Ulna, or inner bone of forearm.
33. Carpal ends of radius and ulna.
34. Internal iliac fossa.
35. Anterior superior process of ilium.
36. Anterior inferior process of ilium.
37. Pubic symphysis.
38. Tuberosity of ischium.
39. Brim of pelvis.
40. Obturator foramen.
41. Head of femur or thigh bone.
42. Neck of femur.
43. Great trochanter of femur.
44. Shaft of femur.
45. Condyles of femur.
46. Patella, or kneepan.
47. Head of tibia or thick bone on anterior and inner side of leg.
48. Shaft of tibia.
49. Lower extremity of tibia.
50. Fibula, or thin bone on external side of leg.

View of Palmar Surface of Right Hand and Wrist (Fig. 2).

1-8. Bones of the carpus, or wrist:—
1. Scaphoid.
2. Semilunar.
3. Cuneiform.
4. Pisiform.
5. Trapezium.
6. Trapezoid.
7. Magnum.
8. Unciform.

9. Metacarpal bones of thumb and fingers.
10. First row of phalanges of thumb and fingers.
11. Second row of phalanges of fingers.
12. Third, or ungual, row of phalanges of fingers and second, or ungual, phalanx of thumb.

Front View of Right Foot (Fig. 3).

1 5, 6, 7-10. Bones of the tarsus:—
1. Superior articulated surface of astragalus.
2. Anterior portion of astragalus.
3. Calcaneum, or heel bone.
4. Commencement of groove of interosseous ligament.
5. Scaphoid.
6. Tuberosity of scaphoid.
7. Internal cuneiform.
8. Middle cuneiform.
9. External cuneiform.
10. Cuboid.
11. Metatarsal bones.
12. First row of phalanges of toes.
13. Second row of phalanges of four outer toes.
14. Third, or ungual, row of phalanges of four outer toes, and second, or ungual, phalanx of great toe.

MUSCLES OF THE HUMAN BODY—ILLUSTRATIONS.

Side View of Full Figure (Fig. 5).

1. Occipito-frontalis — Used to raise the eyebrows, wrinkle the skin of the forehead, and move the scalp backward and forward.
2. Temporalis — Helps to elevate the lower jaw.
3. Orbicularis palpebrarum — Closes the eyelids.
4. Masseter — Helps to elevate the lower jaw, and move it forward.
5. Sterno-cleido-mastoideus — A pair of muscles which together bow the head forward; one acting by itself is able to turn the head, and therefore the chin, to the opposite side.
6. Trapezius — The trapezii muscles, acting together, draw the head directly backward; one of them, acting alone, inclines the head to the corresponding side; the superior part of the trapezius raises the point of the shoulder.
7. Platysma myoides — Assists in depressing the angle of the mouth.
8. Deltoides — Raises the arm, and aids in carrying it backward and forward.
9. Biceps flexor cubiti } Act together in bending the forearm.
10. Brachialis anticus
11. Triceps extensor cubiti — Antagonist of the two former, when the forearm is bent, the triceps, by drawing to the extremity of the ulna, is able to extend it on the humerus, and thus bring both parts of the limb into a right line.
12. Supinator longus — A flexor of the forearm.
13. Extensor muscles of thumb.
14. Extensor muscles of wrist.
15. Pectoralis major } Conjointly with teres major (situate at
16. Latissimus dorsi the inferior and posterior part of the shoulder) these muscles lower the arm when it has been elevated, press the arm closely to the side, and pectoralis major will by itself carry the arm along the side and front of the chest.
17. Serratus magnus — Assists in advancing the scapula and elevating the shoulder.
18. Obliquus externus abdominis } Coöperate with the other
19. Rectus abdominis, in its sheath abdominal muscles in supporting the abdominal viscera.
20. Gluteus medius } The gluteal set alternately on the thigh
21. Gluteus maximus bone and pelvis; 21, by the direction of its fibers, is fitted to draw the thigh bone backward, whilst it turns the whole limb outward if it be kept extended.
22. Tensor vaginæ femoris — Renders the fascia tense, and turns the limb inward.
23. Vastus externus — Contributes to extend the leg upon the thigh.
24. Biceps flexor cruris — Assists in bending the leg on the thigh, and in turning the limb slightly inward and outward.
25. Gastrocnemius — Along with the soleus this muscle forms the calf of the leg; they jointly draw on the heel bone, lifting it from the ground, and cause the foot to represent an inclined plane.
26. Tibialis anticus — Coöperates with 31 in bending the foot on the leg; acting separately, each gives a slight inclination toward the corresponding side.
27. Extensor longus digitorum — Aids in extending the toes, and in bending the foot upon the leg.
28. Soleus — See 25.
29. Peroneus longus } Act together in drawing the foot back.
30. Peroneus brevis
31. Peroneus tertius — A flexor of the foot on the leg, coöperating with 26.
32. Abductor minimi digiti — Bends the little toe, and separates it from the others.
33. Extensor proprius pollicis — Extensor of the great toe.
34. Flexor longus digitorum — Bends the toes toward the sole of the foot.
35. Tendo Achillis — Formed by junction of tendinous expansions of 25 and 26; the strongest tendon in the body.

Front View of Right Arm (Fig. 6).

1. Deltoides — See 8 of previous section.
2. Pectoralis major — See 15 of previous section.
3. Coraco brachialis — Smallest muscle of upper arm; assists in moving the arm forward and upward.
4. Biceps flexor cubiti — See 9 of previous section.
5. Brachialis internus — Part of brachialis anticus; see 10 of previous section.
6. Triceps extensor cubiti — See 11 of previous section.
7. Pronator radii teres — Turns the palm of the hand downward, and aids in bending the forearm on the arm.
8. Supinator radii longus — Acts as antagonist to pronator of the hand (7), turning the palm upward; it is also a flexor of the forearm.
9. Flexor carpi radialis — Bends the wrist, and becomes a flexor of the forearm.
10. Palmaris longus, with fascia — Bends the hand upon the forearm, and aids in its pronation.
11. Flexor profundus digitorum — Bends the fingers toward the palm, acts on the wrist, and assists in the bending of the arm.
12. Flexor carpi ulnaris — Bends the wrist, and becomes a flexor of the forearm.
13. Abductor pollicis manus — Carries the thumb outward and forward from the palm.
14. Flexor brevis pollicis — Flexor of first joint of thumb.
15. Palmaris brevis — A small cutaneous muscle connected with the muscles of the little finger.

Front View of Right Leg (Fig. 4).

1. Gluteus medius — See 20 of first section.
2. Tensor vaginæ femoris — See 22 of first section.
3. Psoas and iliacus — Bend the thigh on the pelvis, and rotate the limb outward.
4. Pectineus — Contributes to bend the thigh bone on the pelvis.
5. Adductor longus — One of the adductors of the thigh.
6. Sartorius — Bends the leg upon the thigh; it is known as the "tailor's muscle."
7. Gracilis — Acts along with adductor muscles of thigh.
8. Rectus femoris } Extend the leg upon the
9. Vastus externus thigh; the rectus and sartorius (C) help to maintain
10. Vastus internus the erect position of body.
11. Biceps flexor cruris — See 24 of first section.
12. Insertion of ligament of patella into tibia.
13. Tibialis anticus — See 26 of first section.
14. Extensor longus digitorum — See 27 of first sect.
15. Peroneus longus — See 29 of first section.
16. Gastrocnemius — See 25 of first section.
17. Soleus — See 28 of first section.
18. Peroneus brevis — See 30 of first section.

NERVOUS AND ARTERIAL SYSTEMS—ILLUSTRATIONS.

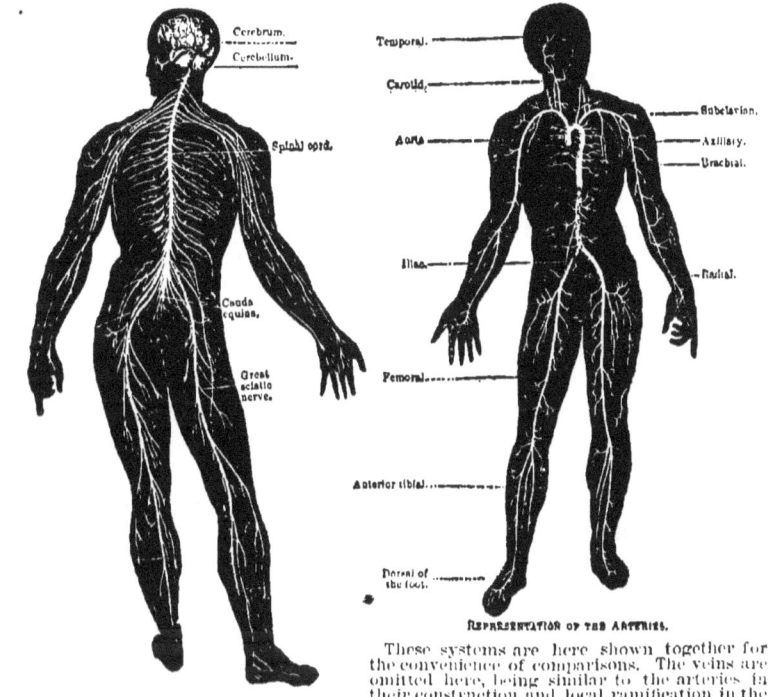

GENERAL REPRESENTATION OF THE NERVOUS SYSTEM.

REPRESENTATION OF THE ARTERIES.

These systems are here shown together for the convenience of comparisons. The veins are omitted here, being similar to the arteries in their construction and local ramification in the body.

The great nerve centers are the brain and the spinal cord. From both of these, in double vertical masses, the branch nerves ramify into all parts of the human system. An inspection of the left-hand cut and that on page 73 will show the sources of all nerves and branches in all parts of the body, and why it is that an injury to the nerves in one part of the system paralyzes the nerves in particular localities, and will explain the results of many such injuries. Thus a violent injury on the head may kill, or only stun for a time some of the cranial nerves. If an injury to the backbone takes place, the lower portion of the extremities on either side may be paralyzed.

The arterial system here represented in the right-hand figure has its source of motion in the heart. The blood of the body is not held as in a sponge, but in pipes called *blood-vessels*, bearing the names respectively of *arteries, capillaries,* and *veins*. The largest of the first class is called *aorta,* and rightly appears in the figure as severed from the heart. The aorta soon branches off into smaller and smaller channels until the smallest pipes, called the capillaries, are reached. The latter form a fine and close network, closer than fine silk, so that a fine needlepoint might be inserted without opening one of the pipes. The blood, after being carried by pulsations into the capillaries where it reaches the remotest extremities, then enters upon its return any channel in the veins, first in smaller and then in the larger ones, until it reaches the heart. "The walls of the capillaries are so very thin that, although there are no openings in them, a portion of the blood soaks through into the surrounding tissues; and, on the other hand, fluids containing waste matter soak into them to be carried away."

If we should examine, with the knowledge and the skill of a surgeon, the "funny bone," we should find it to be a flat shining cord about an eighth of an inch broad, and tracing the cord down the arm and to the tip of the little finger we would find it grown smaller and smaller, and divided into innumerable cords, so fine as to be visible only by the aid of the microscope.

If we should resume our inspection of the nerve cord at the elbow, and follow it up the arm, we would find it joining other cords until it enters through one or more openings between the joints of the backbone, (vertebræ,) and into the spinal cord, and at last up to and into the brain.

"The nervous system," says Professor Smith, M.D., "may be compared to the telegraphic system of a railroad. The nerves are the wires. The gray matter of the spinal cord contains the offices of the district superintendents. In the cerebrum is the office of the superintendent of the road. Suppose a mosquito lights on your face and puts in his bill. He cannot put it in, small as it is, without hitting one or more little nerve fibers. Instantly a message goes along those nerve fibers through the nerve trunks, through the spinal cord, and finally to the general superintendent s office. The message is, 'Something wrong here.' Immediately an order is sent out along other nerve trunks and fibers to the muscles of the shoulder and arm, and they contract so as to strike the mosquito."

The new message is carried toward the brain from any point of the body at the rate of about ninety feet per second. Hence it is that the remote points of the nervous system require greater time for recognition at the cerebrum, the chief headquarters of the mind. The cut will show which classes of nerves go direct to the brain, and which go there by way of the spinal cord.

Considerable variations exist in the size and weight of the human brain, both in different races and in different individuals of the same race, and in the sexes. The white races have the heaviest brains, the average weight of the brain of an adult European male being 49 to 50 ounces, and that of the female 44 to 45 ounces. A man's brain, therefore, is ten per cent heavier than a woman's. The brain begins to lose weight at about sixty years; in males it falls to about 45 ounces, and in females to 41 ounces.

Heavy brains do not always mean great intellectual ability. There is, however, a minimum weight below which intellectual power is not found. Authorities differ somewhat as to this limit, but it is generally placed at about 37 ounces in males, and 32 ounces in females. Cudier's brain weighed 64½ ounces; Dr. Abercrombie's, 63; Professor Goodsir's, 57¼; Spurzheim's, 55; Sir J. Y. Simpson's, 54; Agassiz's, 53⅔; and Dr. Chalmer's, 53. Insane persons have often been found to have heavy brains, and in some cases idiots have had brains weighing more than 50 ounces.

Barnard Davis's researches have shown that the average brain weight is higher in civilized races than among savages; that the range of variation is much greater in the former than in the latter; that there is an almost complete absence of brains weighing more than 54 ounces in the exotic races; that while the male brains are heavier than the female there is not the same amount of difference in the average brain weight between the sexes in the uncultivated as in the cultivated people.

THE BRAIN AND THE CRANIAL NERVES.

The origin of the twelve pairs of cranial nerves is shown in the illustration below, together with the brain. *F, E*, the cerebrum; *D*, the cerebellum, showing the arbor vitæ; *G*, the eye: *H*, the medulla oblongata; *A*, the spinal cord without the backbone, in which it is ordinarily encased; and *C, B*, the first two pairs of spinal nerves. References of numerals;

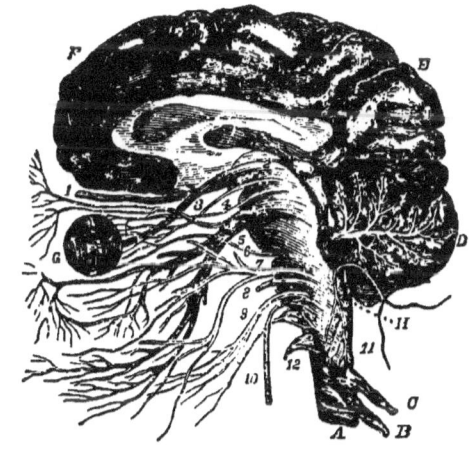

1. The *olfactory*, or first pair of nerves, which ramify through the nostrils, and are the nerves of smell.

2. The *optic*, or second pair of nerves which pass to the eyeballs, and are the nerves of vision.

3, 4, 6. The *motores oculi* (eye movers) are three pairs of nerves used to move the eyes. See illustration of eye, page 140.

5. The *tri-facial*, or fifth pair of nerves, divides each into three branches, whence its name: the first, to the upper part of the face, eyes, and nose; the second, to the upper jaw and teeth; the third, to the lower jaw and the mouth, where it forms the nerve of taste. These nerves are affected in toothache and neuralgia.

7. The *facial*, or seventh pair, are distributed over the face and give to it expression.*

8. The *auditory*, or eighth pair, go to the ears, and are the nerves of hearing.

9. The *glos-so-pha-ryn-ge-al*, or ninth pair, are distributed over the mucous membrane of the pharynx, tonsils, etc.

10. The *pneu-mo-gas-tric*, or tenth pair, preside over the larynx, lungs, liver, stomach, and one branch extends to the heart. This is the only nerve which goes so far from the head.

11. The *accessory*, or eleventh pair, rise from the spinal cord, run up to the medulla oblongata, and thence leave the skull at the opening with the ninth and tenth pairs. They regulate the vocal movements of the larynx.

12. The *hy-po-glos'-sal*, or twelfth pair, give motion to the tongue.

From each half of the brain twelve nerva † cords go out through holes in the skull; from each half (vertical) of the spinal cord thirty-one nerva cords go out through holes in the backbone. This cord is about half an inch thick, and about eighteen inches long in adults.

Each half of the cord is divided longitudinally into three equal parts by the lines of attachment of two parallel series of delicate bundles of nervous filaments, the roots of the spinal nerves. The roots of the nerves which arise along that line which is nearer the posterior surface of the cord are called posterior roots; those which arise along the other line are the anterior roots. A certain number of anterior and posterior roots on the same level on each side of the cord converge and form anterior and posterior bundles, then the two bundles, anterior and posterior, coalesce into the trunk of a spinal nerve, but before doing so the posterior bundle presents an enlargement— the ganglion of the posterior root. ‡

The trunks of the spinal nerves pass out of the spinal canal by the intervertebral foramina, or apertures between the vertebræ, and then divide and

---

* "If it is palsied, on one side there will be a blank, while the other side will laugh or cry, and the whole face wi'l look funny indeed. There were some cruel people in the Middle Ages who used to cut the nerve and deform children's faces in this way for the purpose of making money at shows. When this nerva was wrongly supposed to be the seat of neuralgia or tic doloureux, it was often cut by surgeons. In this way the patient suffered many dangers without relief from pain."—*Maporther.*

† English authors give only nine groups of cranial nerves, but Continental and American anatomists classify as they are here given.   ‡ Dr. Huxley.

subdivide their ultimate ramifications going to the muscles, and to the skin.

If the trunk of a spinal nerve be irritated in any way, as by pinching, cutting, galvanizing, or applying a hot body, two things happen: in the first place, all the muscles to which filaments of this nerve are distributed contract; in the second, acute pain is felt, and the pain is referred to that part of the skin to which fibers of the nerve are distributed. In other words, the effect of irritating the trunk of a nerve is the same as that of irritating its component fibers at their terminations.

THE BLOOD—ITS RELATION TO LIFE AND HEALTH

Change and Waste.—A great change is constantly taking place in every part of the human system. The old particles of the body are incessantly passing off in the respiration, perspiration, and excretion. Careful and intelligent observation leads to the belief that the entire body is changed once in seven years. Many parts change much oftener—those which are constantly active many times in a single year. The same body, in its form, appearance, and functions, may remain, but every particle of flesh, bones, skin, etc., is removed and the place occupied by a new particle. So that in all its material element the body is renewed in seven years.

Supply from the Blood.—The chief supply in repairing this great waste is furnished by the blood. The blood is "liquid flesh." It is a repository of the ingredients of nutrition. Its materials are so varied and so refined that they penetrate the minutest parts of the physical system, and become assimilated to muscle, bone, skin, hair, cartilage, and nerve.

Quantity of the Blood.*—The entire quantity of blood in the vessels is about one eighth part, by weight, of the whole body; so that in a man weighing 140 pounds the quantity of blood is nearly 18 pounds. The quantity of blood, however, as well as its composition, varies somewhat at different times. Soon after digestion it is considerably increased; for it has absorbed all the nutritious materials taken with the food, and these materials must necessarily pass through the blood in order to reach the tissues. After long abstinence it is diminished in quantity to a corresponding degree. For the same reason, its composition varies to a certain extent, since its different ingredients will diminish or increase according as they have been discharged or absorbed in greater or less abundance.

---

* This and most of the subsequent paragraphs on the physiology of the blood are condensed from excellent works of Prof. Dalton on the subject.

Effects Produced by Loss of Blood.—Only a small proportion of the blood in the body can be lost without causing a serious effect upon the system. Generally speaking, the loss of one pound of blood causes faintness, and that of a pound and a half or two pounds is followed by complete unconsciousness. If the bleeding be then stopped, the patient usually recovers, but if a still larger quantity of blood be lost, recovery becomes impossible.

"Transfusion of Blood."—In cases of great exhaustion, caused by excessive bleeding, strength has sometimes been restored by injecting into the blood-vessel healthy blood from some other person. This is called the "Transfusion of Blood." Instance: If blood be drawn from an animal until it is seemingly dead, and then that from another animal be injected into its veins, its vitality will be restored.* This practice became quite common in the seventeenth century. The operation was even tried on human beings, and the most extravagant hopes were entertained. A maniac was restored to reason by the blood of a calf. But many fatal accidents occurring, it soon fell into disuse. It has, however, been successfully practiced in New York in a few cases within the last three years, and is a method still in repute for saving life.

The Composition of Blood.—The *blood* is a thick opaque fluid of a deep red hue, so peculiar that it may usually be distinguished by its color alone. It contains many different ingredients, of which the most important are, first, *water;* second, *mineral substances;* and third, *albuminous matters.*

The Water of the Blood.—This is what gives the blood its fluidity. For if the water be driven off by evaporation the other ingredients remain behind in the form of a dry mass, which would be entirely useless for the purpose of nutrition. But in its natural condition the water of the blood unites all its other ingredients into a uniform liquid, which easily moves through the blood-vessels, and dissolves the new substances, which are absorbed from without. Taken altogether, the water forms rather more than three fourths of the whole mass of the blood.

The Mineral Ingredients.—These are present in much smaller proportion. The most abundant is common *salt,* which we know is taken with the food, and is a necessary ingredient of all the tissues. It forms, however, only about four parts in a thousand of the whole blood. The combinations of *lime,* which the bones and teeth require for their nourishment, are found in still smaller quantity dissolved in the animal fluids of the blood. Other mineral substances of various kinds are also present in their requisite quantity.

---

* Brown-Séquard tells of a curious instance in which the blood of a living dog was transferred into one just dead. The animal rose on its feet and wagged its tail, but died a second time in twelve and one half hours afterward.—*Steele's Fourteen Weeks in Physiology.*

Albumen in the Blood.—But the most remarkable of all the ingredients of the blood are its albuminous matters. It is these substances which give to it its thick and animal consistency, and which also act the most important part in the nutrition of the body. They are of two different kinds, which are naturally mingled together in the blood in a liquid form.

Albumen.—The first of these is the *albumen*. We can obtain a tolerably correct idea of the character of albumen from the fresh white of egg, which has received a similar name. This is not exactly the same thing with the albumen of the blood, but still the two resemble each other very closely. They may both be coagulated by boiling, when they become solid, white, and opaque. The principal difference between them is, that the fresh white of egg is partly gelatinous in consistency, while the albumen of the blood is perfectly fluid, and may readily be made to flow through the veins, or to run from one glass vessel into another.

Quantity of Albumen.—The albumen is about forty parts in a thousand, or one twenty-fifth of the whole blood. It represents, in great part, the concentrated nourishment derived from the food, for it is probably into this substance that most of the albuminose is converted, after being absorbed from the intestine in the digestive process. It is the material out of which the tissues of the body are afterward formed.

Fibrine.—The other animal matter in the blood is the *fibrine*. Although this is in very small quantity, namely, only two parts in a thousand, it is an exceedingly curious and important ingredient. For it possesses a property which does not belong to any other animal substance, namely, the property of "spontaneous coagulation"—that is, it will coagulate by itself without being boiled, or brought into contact with an acid, or treated by any other chemical substance. We shall see hereafter what an important character this property gives to the blood.

Other Substances.—But these substances are only the liquid portions of the blood. They are all dissolved in each other, and form a perfectly transparent and almost colorless fluid. Besides them there are a multitude of little rounded bodies contained in the liquid mixture, which make the blood opaque, and give to it its red color. They are so abundant that they are crowded together by thousands in each drop of blood, and so minute that they are only visible by the aid of the microscope. They are called the *blood-globules*.

Described Globules of the Blood.—If we examine a drop of blood under the microscope, we see the blood-globules floating in profusion in the fluid parts. Each one is a delicate circular plate or disk, somewhat like a piece of money in form, only with the edges rounded, and rather thicker than the central part. In human blood they are about $\frac{1}{3000}$ of an inch in diameter, when measured across their flat surfaces, and about $\frac{1}{8000}$ of an inch in thickness.

Remarkable Characteristics of the Globules.—The blood-globules are exceedingly soft and flexible in consistency. In fact, they are nearly fluid, like drops of very thick oil or honey, only they do not dissolve in the other parts of the blood, but retain their own form and substance. Consequently, when moving about in the fluid, as they often do under the microscope, following accidental currents in the blood, passing through narrow channels, and turning corners among the other globules, they may be seen to twist about, and bend over, and elongate in various ways, and then resume their natural figure as before. This peculiar semi-fluid and flexible consistency is one of their greatest peculiarities.

Color of Blood-Globules.—When seen by transmitted light and in thin layers, they are of a very pale amber color, and nearly transparent. Nevertheless, they contain all the red color of the blood, and when seen heaped together in layers only five or six deep, they show distinctly the ruddy color which belongs to them. Besides, if they are separated by filtration or any other means, or if they are not formed in their natural quantity, the blood becomes paler exactly in proportion as its globules are deficient.

Opacity of the Blood.—They also communicate to the blood its opacity. Although each globule by itself is transparent, yet, when they are crowded together, and mingled with the fluid parts of the blood, the whole becomes opaque, and apparently impenetrable to light. This is because the globules of the blood and its fluid parts are of a different nature and composition. The same thing will happen when oil is emulsioned by a watery alkaline solution. The oil is transparent by itself, and the alkaline liquid is transparent by itself; but if you mix the two together the whole becomes white and opaque like milk. So the globules of the blood and its fluid parts, mingled together, produce a thick red and opaque liquid.

The red globules are the vivifying elements of the blood. They communicate to it its animating and stimulating properties, by which all the organs are maintained in a condition of vital activity.

White Globules.—Besides the red globules, the blood contains other little bodies of a different form and aspect. These are the *white globules*. They are very much less numerous than the red, as there are not more than three or four of them for every thousand of the others. They are of a little larger size, measuring about $\frac{1}{2500}$ of an inch in diameter, of a rounded form and a finely granulated texture. They are usually concealed for the most part, in the greater abundance of the red globules.

When the ingredients of the blood are examined by analysis, they are found

The Blood.

to be mingled together in the following proportions—the proportion being that in one thousand parts:—

Water	795
Globules	150
Albumen	40
Fibrine	2
Other animal matters	5
Mineral substances	8
	1,000

Coagulation of the Blood.—Such are the properties and constitution of the blood while circulating in the interior of the body. But if it be withdrawn from the vessels a very remarkable change takes place, which alters its whole appearance. This change is its *coagulation*.

Time for Coagulation.—When a patient is bled from the arm or is accidentally wounded, the blood runs from the opened vein in a perfect liquid stream; but soon afterward it begins to appear thicker than before, and will not run in drops, nor moisten the fingers so easily when touched. When this alteration has once commenced it goes on rapidly increasing, the blood growing thicker and thicker, until it finally sets into a uniform, firm, elastic, jelly-like mass. It is then said to be "coagulated" or "clotted." This change is usually complete in about twenty minutes after the blood has been withdrawn from the veins.

Cause of Coagulation.—This coagulation of the blood is entirely dependent upon its fibrine. This substance alone has the property of coagulating spontaneously. None of the other ingredients can solidify in this way, and if the fibrine be taken out, the blood loses altogether its power of coagulation. The fibrine, though in a very small quantity as compared with the other substances in the blood, is diffused uniformly throughout the whole; and when it coagulates, therefore, on being withdrawn from the vessels, it entangles all the other ingredients with it, and holds them imprisoned in its own substance. The water of the blood, accordingly, the albumen, the globules, etc., are all mechanically retained by the coagulating fibrine.

Serum of the Blood.—But not long afterward a partial separation takes place between them. The fibrine solidifies still more; and, by contracting upon itself, squeezes out the liquid portions of the blood from between its meshes. Drops of a clear, amber-colored fluid begin to exude from its surface, and these drops, growing larger and larger, run together into little pools, which still increase in size until the entire surface is covered with the transparent liquid. The remainder grows at the same time smaller and firmer, un til at last the whole is permanently separated into two parts, a solid and a liquid. The solid part is called the *clot;* the liquid part is the *serum.*

A "Clot" of Blood.—If we examine a cupful of blood, at the end of twelve hours after it has been drawn from the veins, we will find that it is no longer a uniform mass, but a solid clot floating in the transparent serum. The clot at this time is still firm, red, and opaque, since it contains all the globules of the blood as well as the fibrine. For these globules cannot escape from the clot, owing to their form and size, and are therefore retained by the meshes of the coagulated fibrine. The serum, on the other hand, is transparent, and nearly colorless. It contains all the albumen, the water, and other substances dissolved in them.

Importance of Coagulation.—The coagulation of the blood is a property of the greatest importance; for it is the only thing which prevents our bleeding to death after the slightest incision or injury to the blood-vessels. Whenever these vessels are opened by an accidental cut in the skin or in the muscles, the blood at first flows with great freedom, according to the size of the wound. But if we press firmly upon the injured part with a bandage or with the fingers, and then, after a short time, remove the pressure, we find that the bleeding has stopped altogether. This is because the thin layer of blood between the edges of the wounded vessels has coagulated and blocked up the opening. No matter how thin this layer may be, it still coagulates; for every particle of the blood, however small, contains its due proportion of fibrine, and, consequently, solidifies at the proper time. The clot thus formed adheres to the edges of the wounded parts, and so acts as a continuous bandage or plug, until the tissues have again grown together and become permanently united.

Coagulation Stops Bleeding.—It is in this way that the bleeding from all ordinary wounds is usually arrested by nature. No matter how freely the blood may flow at first, if you keep the parts steadily compressed for twenty minutes or half an hour, the fibrine will then be coagulated and the bleeding will stop. But when the wound is very deep, or when any of the principal arteries have been severed, this means will not succeed; for the blood comes with so much force from those larger vessels that it cannot be kept back by ordinary pressure, and no time is allowed for its permanent coagulation. Then we must call for the assistance of the surgeon, who is often compelled to search for the blood vessels in the deeper parts of the wound, and to tie up their open mouths with a fine cord or ligature. Why this operation is successful requires a further explanation.

Coagulation in the Interior of the Body.—It is a curious fact that the blood will coagulate, not only when it is discharged externally, but also even in the interior of the body, *whenever it is withdrawn from the ordinary*

The Blood.

course of the circulation. Thus, if we receive a bruise, and the little vessels beneath the skin are torn, the blood which flows from them coagulates in the neighborhood of the injury. Any internal bleeding produces, after a time, a clot in the corresponding situation where the blood is effused. After death, also, coagulation takes place in the cavities of the heart, and in the great veins near it; and whenever any part of the body is so injured as to stop its circulation, the blood necessarily coagulates in its vessels.

The Ligature and Coagulation.—When the surgeon places the ligature upon a wounded vessel, he stops the circulation through it. The blood is imprisoned in the neighborhood of the ligature, and soon afterward coagulates and blocks up the cavity of the vessel with its solidified fibrine. After a time the ligature separates and is thrown off, and the wounded parts unite by the healing of the tissues.

Coagulation Spontaneous.—The coagulation of the blood is a property, therefore, that belongs to the fibrine, and it is spontaneous. As soon as the fibrine is formed it possesses this property, by which it is distinguished from all other substances. It is not manifested immediately, for it requires a certain time for its completion; but owing to the very nature of the fibrine, wherever it may be, within a short period after it is shut off from the circulation it exhibits this peculiar character, and coagulates inevitably.

Why Coagulation does not Stop the Circulation.—Why, then, does it not coagulate in the vessels, and thus stop the circulation of the blood? To understand this, we must remember that the history of all the animal substances in the living body is one of incessant change. None of them remain the same, but all undergo successive transformations. The albuminose formed in digestion is no sooner taken up by the blood-vessels then it is converted into albumen. The oily matters absorbed with the chyle, and the sugar produced in the liver, are also rapidly decomposed, as we have seen, and disappear in the circulation. What is destroyed in this way for the purposes of nutrition is constantly replaced by a fresh quantity formed in the same organs.

This is also true of the fibrine. That which is circulating in the blood-vessels to-day is not the same fibrine which was there yesterday, but a new supply, freshly produced in the process of daily nutrition. It is estimated by physiologists that all the fibrine which exists in the blood is destroyed and reproduced *at least three times over in the course of a single day.* What the new substances are which are formed by its decomposition is still unknown, for we cannot yet follow out all the details of these changes which take place so rapidly in the living body. But there is every reason to believe that the renovation of the fibrine in the blood takes place as constantly and rapidly as that of its other ingredients.

The blood, therefore, does not coagulate while the circulation is going on, because its fibrine is being incessantly altered and converted into new substances. It has been found that in certain of the internal organs, especially in the liver and kidneys, the fibrine disappears, and that little or none of it is contained in the blood returning from them. When we come to learn with what rapidity the circulation is carried on, we shall easily understand how coagulation may thus be prevented. But if the blood be withdrawn from the circulation altogether, or confined in any part by a ligature, then its fibrine can no longer go through with the natural changes of its decomposition, and it accordingly coagulates, as we have above described.

Two Different Kinds of Blood in the Body.—Finally, there is a most remarkable difference in the appearance of the blood in different parts of the body. In one half of the circulation, that is, in all those vessels which are called "arteries," it is of a brilliant scarlet hue; while in the "veins" it is of a deep bluish-purple, almost black color. These two kinds of blood follow each other in the circulation, changing alternately from one color to the other; so that, although there is always red blood in the arteries, and always blue blood in the veins, yet the same blood is alternately scarlet and purple, as it passes from one set of vessels to another. The dark, impure blood of the veins is purified in the lungs by the air.

FOOD AND HEALTH.

Food Makes Blood for the Body.—We have already noted the relation of the blood to life and health. The relation of water to health has also been shown. Blood is derived chiefly from the food we eat. The nutritious part of the food after being taken into the stomach is converted by the process of digestion into blood, and then into living, healthful tissues.

Amount of Food Daily Needed.—To replace the daily outgo we need about two pounds of food and three pounds of drink. With the eight hundred pounds of oxygen taken from the air a man uses in a year about a ton and a half of material. Our bodies are but molds in which a certain quantity of matter receives a definite form. They may be likened to an eddy in a river which retains its shape for a while, yet every instant each particle of water is changing. Our strength comes from the food we eat. The food contains within it a latent force, which it gives up when it is decomposed. Putting food into our bodies is like placing a spring within a watch; every motion of the body is only a new direction given to this spring-force, as every movement of the hand on a dial is but the manipulation of the power of the bent spring in the watch. We use the pent-up energies of meat, bread, and vegetables which are placed at our service, and transfer them to a higher sphere of action.

Kinds of Food Needed.—In order, therefore, to produce heat and force, we require something that is combustible, something with which oxygen can combine. Three kinds of food are needed.

1. *Nitrogen.* That which contains a considerable proportion of *nitrogen.* This is a prominent constituent of the tissues of the body, and is necessary to their growth and repair. The most common forms are whites of eggs, which are nearly pure albumen, caseine, the chief constituent of cheese, lean meat, and gluten, the viscid substance that gives tenacity to dough. Bodies that have much nitrogen readily oxidize.

2. *Carbon.* The next is *carbonaceous* food, or that which contains much carbon. This consists of two kinds: first, the sugars. These contain hydrogen and oxygen in proportion to form water, and about the same amount of carbon. They may, therefore, be considered as water with carbon diffused through them. In digestion, starch and gum are changed into sugar. All these are burned to produce heat. The second are the fats, which are like sugars in composition, but contain less oxygen, and not in the proportion to form water. They combine with more oxygen in burning, and thus give off more heat.

3. *Mineral Matters and Water Needed in Food.* Food should contain mineral matter in addition to water—such as iron, sulphur, magnesia, phosphorus, salt, and potash. About three pints of water are needed daily to dissolve the food, and carry it through the circulation, to float off waste matter, to lubricate the tissues, and by evaporation cool the system. A man weighing one hundred and fifty-four pounds contains one hundred pounds of water; enough if collected in a body to drown him. Iron goes to the blood disks; lime combines with phosphorus and carbonic acid to give solidity to the bones and teeth; phosphorus is essential to the activity of the brain; salt is necessary to the secretions of some of the digestive fluids, and also to aid in working off the waste products.

Process of Digestion.—Nature has provided an entire laboratory for the process of digestion. The food is chewed, mixed with the saliva of the mouth, and swallowed. It is then acted upon by the gastric juice in the stomach, passed into the intestines, where it receives the bile, pancreatic juice, and other liquids which completely dissolve it, absorbing the nourishing parts in the stomach and intestines; the remainder goes to the blood-vessels, and enters the general circulation.

Nutritious and Healthy Articles of Food.—There are some articles of food of the greatest nutritive value. We mention the following: Beef, mutton, fish, milk, cheese, eggs, bread, potatoes, corn, oat-meal, rice, ripe fruits, tomatoes, peas, beans, etc., all of which articles of food are more or less nutritive.

Beef and *mutton* possess the greatest nutritive value of any of the meats.

Lamb is less strengthening, but more delicate. Like the young of all animals, it should be thoroughly cooked, and at a high temperature, to properly develop its flavor.

Pork has much carbon, and hence is very heating; the delicate and sedentary have no need of such food. It sometimes contains a parasite called trichina, which may be transferred to the human system, and produce disease and death. If eaten it should be cooked thoroughly.

Fish is rich in phosphorus, and is commended as food for the brain. It loses its mineral constituents and juices when salted.

Oysters are highly nutritious, and are more easily assimilated when eaten raw.

Milk is a model food, containing albumen, starch, fat, and mineral matter.

Cheese is very nourishing, one pound being equal in value to two of meat.

Eggs are most easily digested when cooked "soft."

A Suggestive Conversation.—Many comparatively healthy persons eat pork; but such persons usually toil at out-of-door work, and because of the great strength of their physical constitutions they can endure even the use of pork. The hog is the filthiest of animals; and experiments show that when the flesh is made the only or chief article of food for a few days the physical system begins rapidly to suffer. Scrofulous persons suffer the soonest and the most largely, and there is good reason to believe that much of the scrofula prevalent in this country is caused by pork-eating, either by the patient or by his parents.

"But it is often difficult to get other meat than pork."

" My answer is, Eat pork *if you must*, in other words, from necessity; never from *choice*."

" How should pork be cooked?"

"I will answer in the language of a veteran physician: ' *Cook it done.*' Other meats may be eaten rare if desired; pork must be cooked thoroughly. My advice to you is, Unless you are an out-of-door laborer, eat pork rarely and sparingly, and see to it that the cook puts it over a hot fire, and keeps it there until it is 'twice done.' "

Onions.—Few people dream of the many virtues of onions. Lung and liver complaints are certainly benefited, often cured, by a free consumption of onions, either cooked or raw. Colds yield to them like magic. Don't be afraid of them. Taken at night all offense will be wanting by morning, and the good effects will amply compensate for the trifling annoyance. Taken regularly, they greatly promote the health of the lungs and the digestive organs. An extract made by boiling down the juice of onions to a syrup, and taken as a medicine, answers the purpose very well, but fried, roasted, or boiled onions are better. Onions are a very cheap medicine, within every body's reach, and they are not by any means as "bad to take" as the costly nostrums a neglect of their use may necessitate.

Tomatoes.—The tomato is one of the most healthful as well as the most relished of all vegetables. Its qualities do not depend on the mode of preparation for the table; it may be eaten thrice a day, cold or hot, cooked or raw, alone or with salt or pepper or vinegar, or altogether, to a like advantage, and to the utmost that can be taken with an appetite. Its excellence arises from its slight acidity, and the seeds which it contains. The acidity refreshes and tones up the system in the same manner as fruit, while the seeds act as mechanical, gentle irritants to the inner coating of the bowels, causing them to throw out a large amount of fluid matter, and thus keeping them free. The tomato is also very nutritious.*

Healthful Bread.—The nutritive value of all food depends much upon the amount of gluten which it contains, as this is the substance which goes to form muscle. The proportions of gluten in whole grain, bran, and fine flour are as follows: Whole grain, twelve per cent.; fine flour, ten per cent. By sifting out the bran we therefore render the flour less nutritious as well as less wholesome. As bran constitutes from one eighth to one fourth of the whole weight of wheat, on the average one sixth, there is a great waste of muscle-forming material by bolting.

Graham Bread when made well is especially healthy for dyspeptics.

Unground Wheat.—A very healthful and relishable dish for breakfast, dinner, or supper, can be made from unground wheat, boiled. The freshest and cleanest wheat, with the plumpest kernels, should be selected. The white and the amber-colored wheats cook the most readily, and they are also preferable on account of having a thinner skin. Time is saved in picking it over, to have it first run through a smut machine and then washed, though the looking over is indispensable. Put it to boil with five or six parts water to one of wheat, by measure. Cover close, and after it begins to boil set it where it will barely simmer. Cook it four or five hours, or until the kernels mash readily between the thumb and finger. Hard wheat of any kind will require still more time, and some kinds may be cooked all day without softening. When done it should be even full of water or juice, which thickens

---

* The tomato season ends with the frost. If the vines are pulled up before frost comes, and are hung up in a well-ventilated cellar with the tomatoes hanging to them, the "love-apple" will continue ripening until Christmas. The cellar should not be too dry nor too warm. The knowledge of this may be improved to great practical advantage for the benefit of many who are invalids, and who are fond of the tomato.

and becomes gelatinous on cooking. Salt, and send to the table warm, to eat with meats and vegetables at dinner. It can also be eaten by itself, trimmed with sugar or butter, or both, or syrup, or milk. It molds nicely, and may be served cold at breakfast or supper, or it may be steamed up and served hot at breakfast. The long cooking it requires of course precludes its being served fresh at that meal. After it has once cooled, however, it cannot be made so soft and liquid as at first by any subsequent cooking. Like other starch, when it once sets, it loses its liquidity.

A Very Nutritious Bread.—Valuable economy in the manufacture of nutritious bread is secured by the following process: Gluten to the amount of ten or twelve per cent. is extracted by boiling water from bran, and the flour is kneaded with this infusion, whereby from twenty to thirty per cent. more bread is obtained. The bread, of course, is not so white as that of first quality, but is much more nutritious.

Fresh or Stale Bread, Which?—Fresh bread and warm biscuits are less digestible and less nutritious than old bread. In Germany bakers are prohibited from selling bread until twenty-four hours after it is baked. Nothing is more common in Germany than to hear the buyers at bake-shops ask for "Alt gebackenes Brod." Is German robustness to be attributed to this fact?

Oat Meal.* —Oat meal is a food of great strength and nutrition. It is especially serviceable as a brain-food. It contains phosphorous enough to keep a man doing an ordinary amount of brain-work in good health and vigor. All medical authorities unite in the opinion that, eaten with milk, it is a perfect food; and, having all the requisites for the proper development of the system, it is a pre-eminently useful food for growing children and the young generally. Oat meal requires much cooking to effectually burst its starch-cells, but when it is well cooked it will thicken liquid much more than equal its weight in wheaten flour. The oats of this country are superior to those grown on the Continent and the southern parts of England, but certainly inferior to the Scotch, where considerable pains is taken to cultivate

---

* The two principal ways of cooking oatmeal are as porridge and cake, for which the following are good recipes: To three pints of boiling water add a level teaspoonful of salt and a pint of coarse meal, stirring while it is being slowly poured in; continue stirring until the meal is diffused through the water—about eight or ten minutes. Cover it closely then, and place it where it will simmer for an hour; avoid stirring during the whole of that time. Serve hot, with as little messing as possible, accompanied with milk, maple syrup, or sugar and cream. To make oatmeal-cake, place in a bowl a quart of meal, add to it as much cold water as will form it into a soft, light dough, cover it with a cloth 15 minutes to allow it to swell, then dust the paste-board with meal, turn out the dough and give it a vigorous kneading. Cover it with the cloth a few minutes, and proceed at once to roll it out to the eighth of an inch in thickness; cut in five pieces, and partly cook them on a griddle then finish them by toasting them in front of the fire.

them, and it is needless to point out that the Scotch are an example of a strong and robust nation, which result is justly set down as being derived from the plentiful use of oat meal. Dr. Guthrie has asserted that his countrymen have the largest heads of any nation in the world—not even the English have such large heads—which he attributes to the universal use of oat meal.

Professor Forbes, of Edinburgh, during some twenty years, measured the breadth and height, and also tested the strength of both the arms and loins, of the students in the University—a very numerous class, and of various nationalities, drawn to Edinburgh by the fame of his teaching. He found that in height, breadth of chest and shoulders, and strength of arms and loins, the Belgians were at the bottom of the list; a little above them, the French; very much higher, the English; and highest of all, the Scotch and Scotch Irish, from Ulster, who, like the natives of Scotland, are fed in their early years with at least one meal a day of good oat meal porridge.

Poisonous Properties of Moldy Bread.—A recent case of fatal poisoning has been directly traced to the use of moldy bread for pudding. The pudding was eaten by the cook, the proprietor of the eating-house in which it was prepared, several children of the proprietor, and a number of strangers. All were made alarmingly sick, and two, a child and an adult, died. The doctors attending the case ascribed the effects to poisonous fungi in the mold.

Healthfulness of Fruits.—The liberal use of various fruits as food is conducive to good health. Fruit is not a solid and lasting element like beef and bread, and does not give strength to any great extent. But fruits contain those acids which refresh and give tone to the system during the season when it is most needed. They should never be eaten unless thoroughly ripe or cooked. Stale fruits or those which have been plucked some time are unhealthy in the extreme. The proper time to eat fruit is in the morning and early afternoon. At night it is "leaden," according to the Spanish, who call fruit "golden in the morning and silver at noon."

Fruit Saves Doctors' Bills.—An experienced physician in the West writes as follows: "My bills are cut down in families in proportion as they eat fresh fruit. Strawberries, currants and tomatoes are better medicine than calomel or jalap, and 'rather better to take.' Apples freely eaten do the work of vermifuge or lozenges. Every fruit or berry has its mission to man hidden away within it. Therefore, set out a strawberry bed, if you haven't one. If there is no other place, border your garden walks, and with a sharp hoe and straight line keep the edges cut clearly, leaving a rich mat of vines two feet wide. Plant currants. A fresh cutting will grow if you but stick it in the ground. Border the fence with raspberries. Walk around your place during the early spring days, and make a mental inventory of every spot where you can stick in a fruit tree or a berry bush. Plant something."

Danger of Eating Fruit to Excess.—In the use of fruit excess should be avoided. While advantageous when consumed in moderate quantity, fruits prove injurious if eaten in excess. Of a highly succulent nature, and containing free acids and principles prone to undergo fermentation and change, they are, when eaten out of due proportion to other food, apt to act as a disturbing element, and excite derangement of the stomach and bowels. This is particularly likely to occur if eaten either in the unripe or overripe state: in the former case, from their acidity and unfitness for digestion; in the latter, from their strong tendency to ferment and decompose within the alimentary canal. The prevalence of stomach and bowel disorders, noticeable during the height of the fruit season, affords proof of the inconveniences to which the too free use of fruit, especially if unripe, may give rise.

Special Danger in Summer Vacation.—There is special danger to persons who leave the large towns for a vacation in the country during the early fruit season. The children often indulge in eating unripe fruit, and in this way suffer so much harm as to lessen if not to neutralize the benefits of a summer vacation. Will mothers read this, and enter upon a line of greater watch and care?

Are Nuts Healthful?—Most kinds of nuts are only suited to persons of strong powers of digestion, while some are positively baneful to all. A good rule is to eat them sparingly, and only those found by personal experience to be suitable.

Salt with Nuts.—Here is a suggestive record by a physician: "While enjoying a visit from an Englishman, hickory nuts were served in the evening, when my English friend called for salt, stating that he knew of a case of a woman eating heartily of nuts in the evening who was taken violently ill. The celebrated Dr. Abernethy was sent for, but it was after he had become too fond of his cups, and he was not in a condition to go. He murmured 'Salt! salt!' of which no notice was taken. He went to the place next morning, and found the patient a corpse. He said had they given her salt, it would have relieved her; and that if he was allowed to make an examination he would convince them. When the stomach was opened, the nuts were found in a mass. He sprinkled salt on it, and it immediately dissolved. I have known of a sudden death myself, which appears to have been the effect of the same."

HINTS ABOUT HEALTHFUL EATING.

A Good Appetite Healthful.—Many persons regard a hearty desire for food as something unrefined, indelicate, and to be constantly discouraged. This is a great mistake. The people who strive to check a wholesome and natural appetite regard dinner merely as a "feed," not an agreeable social custom, and as the domestic event of the day. A good appetite is a good thing, and is just as necessary to the health of the man who works only with his brain as it is to the day-laborer who earns his bread by the sweat of his brow, "breaking stones or plowing." The stomach and the brain are brethren, the former being the elder, and having prior right to care. Let that be well provided for, and it will sustain its brother.

Appetite not an Infallible Guide.—The opinion prevailing among many that if people like a thing they may eat it without harm is a great mistake. If sweetened drinks, candies or things containing poison be given to children, they will eat them readily without detecting the danger. Brute animals are guided in the selection of food by their instinct, and their wonderfully developed organs of smell. Human individuals do not show such instinct, but are, or should be, governed by their superior intelligence.

Evil of Rapid Eating.—Eat slowly, thoroughly masticating your food. Rapid eating is one of our national evils, and is the chief cause of dyspepsia. The saliva does not flow too rapidly to mix with the food to promote digestion, and the coarse pieces swallowed resist the action of the digestive fluid. The food washed down with drinks which dilute the gastric juice and hinder its work will not supply the place of the saliva. Failing to get the taste of the food by rapid mastication, we think it insipid, and hence use condiments which over-stimulate the digestive organs. In these ways the system is overworked, and, the tone of the stomach being affected, a foundation is laid for dyspepsia.*

How to Regulate the Quantity of Food.—If the food be swallowed no faster than the gastric fluid is prepared to be mixed with it, hunger or the desire for food will cease when just enough has been taken; but if the food is crowded down rapidly, after the manner of thousands of American eaters, the appetite will continue until more than enough is eaten, and often until two or three times too much is eaten. Remember that the appetite will only cease with the secretion and flow of the gastric fluid; hence we should eat slowly, or we shall eat too much. The slow eater should stop with the cessa-

---

* "In this country rapid eating is a prevailing evil. Every year its slain are counted by thousands. Not long since a friend wrote me inquiring why it is that there are so many more dyspeptics in America than in other populous countries? 'Because,' I responded, 'there are more rapid eaters.'"—HENRY LUSON, M. D

tion of his appetite; the rapid eater before. Rapid eating frequently begets irritability, dyspepsia, or disease of the stomach.

Eating too Much.—Eating too fast generally involves eating too much—more than is needed for the support and nutrition of the body—and the reason for this is, that the organs of taste, which are our guide in this matter, are not allowed sufficient voice; they are not allowed time to take cognizance of the presence of food ere it is pushed past them into the recesses of the stomach. They do not, therefore, have opportunity to represent the real need of the system, and hence allow the crowding of the stomach. "I hold," wrote Dr. Jackson, "that thirty minutes should be spent at each meal, and spent, too, in chewing the food a good portion of the time, and not in continued putting in and swallowing, but in pleasant chat and laugh, instead of the continuance of the intense nervous pressure of the office or library. If you arrange to spend thirty minutes in this way at your meals, you may rest assured you will not eat too much, and what you do eat will be in the best condition for appropriation to the needs of your system."

Food should be Thoroughly Chewed.—There is one simple rule, the observance of which will go a great way toward securing the full benefit of what we eat, and so will be conducive to good health; it is, that all food should be thoroughly chewed before being swallowed. The effects, both mechanical and chemical, of thorough mastication, are the preliminary conditions for healthy digestion and nutrition. Aside from the grinding, the service which the saliva is capable of performing, if we give it time, is similar to, if not identical with, that of the juice of the stomach. And in a general way, it may be said that the more nearly the food is reduced to a fine pulp in the mouth, the less remains for the rest of the digestive apparatus to do, the more completely their task is performed, and the more perfect is the preparation of the food for its purpose—the formation of blood and the nutrition of the whole body.

Hint about "Small Mouthfuls."—Our children will receive a great service from us, if we require them early to form the habit of eating in small mouthfuls and chewing their food well. The same rule holds good for every age, and should be especially regarded in advancing years, when the teeth become imperfect and mastication less effective. Adherence to this simple rule will not only be of great benefit to health, and largely contribute to prevent indigestion and dyspepsia, but will increase the pleasures of the table, and retain the natural strength of the digestive organs, which exert so wide an influence upon both bodily and mental comfort.

How Much Shall We Eat?—Great eaters never live long; spare eaters never accomplish much. The best rule is, Eat moderately. Never eat so much as to feel uncomfortable. If more food is taken than sufficient for the wants of the system, it remains undigested, and becomes a source of irritation and oppression. The quantity of the food required varies with the age and habits of a person. The diet of a child should be largely vegetable and abundant. A sedentary occupation requires less food than an active, out-door life. The greatest workers should be the greatest eaters, as a powerful engine needs a corresponding furnace. Cheerfulness is essential to digestion. A good laugh is the best of sauce. Care and grief are the bitterest foes of digestion. A bright face and a light heart are friends to a long life, and nowhere do they serve better than at the table. God designed that we should enjoy eating, and that, having stopped before satiety was reached, we should have the satisfaction always attendant on a good work well done. To eat until one can eat no longer is gluttony, and should never be indulged. One has said that as many lives have been destroyed by gluttony as by drunkenness.

Loss of Appetite, and How to Recover it.—The appetite is often lost through excessive use of stimulants, food taken too hot, sedentary occupation, liver disorder, and want of change of air. To ascertain and remove the cause is the first duty. Exercise, change of air, and diet will generally prove sufficient to recover the appetite. Children, if they have plenty of out-door exercise, are regular in their habits, and eat only plain, nourishing food, will seldom, if ever, complain of a lack of appetite. See, also, chapter on exercise.

Rest Before and After Eating.—A season of rest after dinner pays well, but it is not more important than the rest before eating, if one is very weary. This rule is of the utmost importance to business men, or persons engaged in brain labor, and its violation is one of the chief causes of dyspepsia. The length of time required to complete digestion varies according to various circumstances, such as the healthy condition of the stomach, the kind and quantity of food taken, exercise, etc. Ordinarily from two to five hours, or longer, are needed.

Eating Between Meals.—This is another of the causes of dyspepsia, for which the foundations are laid in childhood. When the ordinary meals of the day are sufficiently near each other, nothing should be taken into the stomach between meals. Even fruit, which so many consider healthy at all times, robs the stomach of its needed rest.*

Best Times for Meals.—*Breakfast* should be eaten as soon as possible after rising. If not convenient to eat at once, a single cup of warm wheat or

---

* CONVERSATION WITH A DOCTOR.—"Well, doctor, *is it injurious to eat between meals?*"
"That depends on the length of the interval."
"I mean the ordinary or usual meals of the day, as observed in communities generally."
"It is; the stomach, after being taxed with the work of digestion after the ordinary meals, needs rest, and must have it, or it will suffer sooner or later."
"Then you think the eating of *fruits* between meals is not well?"
"I do. The only proper rule is to give the stomach its necessary rest; rob it of that, and soon the penalty must come."

corn, coffee or chocolate, with plenty of milk, will remove the feeling of languor and faintness for an hour or more.

Dinner should be eaten late in the afternoon or early in the eve.ling. It is the principal meal of the day, and, to be enjoyed as well as digested, admits of neither hurry nor interference. The work of the day should be over; and a long rest should follow before bed-time. Eat no late suppers.

Luncheon in the middle of the day is the meal most abused. It is rarely that sufficient time is taken for it. This meal should consist of substantial food, but light in quantity. The pressure of work at midday is so great that the digestive organs should not be heavily taxed at that time. Take all meals at regular hours.*

Comparative Value of Different Modes of Cooking.—All meats, pork excepted, are the most healthful when cooked so as to retain their juices. This is best done by roasting. Broiling ranks next, then comes boiling, and last we have frying. Cook meat, as far as possible, in its own juices. Vegetables follow the same rule.†

Variety of Vegetables at the Same Meal.—"Shall we eat several kinds of vegetables at the same meal?" is a question often asked. A well known physician answered it thus: "I would not burden you with severe restrictions here; but if my good wife should ask me for 'mine good opinion,' I would gently hint to her to cook not more than two." "Should she ask for the reason, what then?" "I would answer, that most vegetables digest more easily alone. Indeed, this is true of most kinds of food. I think, tak-

---

* "Blessed art thou, O land, when thy king is the son of nobles, and thy princes eat in due season, for strength, and not for drunkenness!"—Ecclesiastes x, 17.

"The natural division of the day for necessary repasts, is Breakfast, *eight*, or *half after;* Dinner, *one*, or *half after;* Supper, *eight*, or *half after*. And these, or even *earlier* hours, were formerly observed in these countries. Then we had scarcely any such thing as *gout*, and no *nervous disorders*.

"In ancient nations the custom was to eat but *once;* and then about midday."—Dr. ADAM CLARKE, *in loc.*

† A Conversation: "Doctor, how shall we cook vegetables?"

"I will give you the same general rule as before: The best mode is to cook them so as to retain their own juices. Baking, therefore, is my preference. Beets baked are far preferable to boiled beets. In boiling, much of the most valuable ingredients which are in the juice, is lost."

"You surprise me; I have never eaten baked beets."

"Then try them. Have your cook thoroughly bake them. In eating, slice them, and spread with butter. In some sections of Europe the baked beet is sold to the peasantry as a good substitute for the bread-loaf, and is eaten in the same way. I need not say that it is relished."

"Now, as to other vegetables?"

"I need not tell you that baked potatoes are the best; fried are the worst. Let the rule be to cook them with as little grease as possible. Milk is much more healthful with vegetables than grease."

ing society as it is, the best advice I can give you is to eat a variety of food, but not many kinds at the same time."

"**How Long to Starve.**"—A man will die for want of air in five minutes, for want of sleep in ten days, for want of water in a week, for want of food at varying intervals, dependent on constitution, habits of life, and the circumstances of the occasion. The captain of a Boston whaler was wrecked. For eight days he could not get a drop of water, nor a particle of food. On the day of the wreck he weighed a hundred and ninety pounds; when rescued he weighed one hundred pounds. A teaspoonful of brandy was given to each sailor; but before they could be taken aboard the vessel which saved them they became unconscious, and remained so for two days, but all eventually recovered. Many persons have been killed by eating too much after having fasted for a long time; the safe plan of procedure, and which every reader should bear in mind, is to feel the way along, as persons who are traveling in the dark and fear a precipice ahead; there can be no one rule given, because there are so many modifying circumstances. Give a tea-spoonful of hot drink at a time, and if no ill result, repeat in five minutes, and the same amount of soft food, boiled rice, or softened bread, or gruel; for the stomach is itself as weak as the sufferer in proportion, and can only manage a very small amount of food.

FOOD FOR THE SICK.

Toast and Water.—Toast about three inches of the *crust* of bread till it is of a light brown on both sides; then plunge it into cold water, and let it stand for half an hour in a covered vessel. When the crumb is used it soon sours in a warm room, and when made with boiling water it is insipid and unrefreshing.

Barley Water.—Get some pearl-barley, wash it in four waters—that is, water poured on it four times and thrown away, so that it may be clean; rub two or three pieces of sugar *on* a lemon cut open, and put them in a jug with the washed barley and a few slices of lemon; then pour boiling water on the whole, and cover it over until it is cold.

Barley Gruel.—Boil two ounces of pearl barley in half a pint of water to extract the coloring matter, throw this away and put the barley into three pints and a half of boiling water, and let it boil till it is one half the quantity; then strain it for use.

Oatmeal Gruel.—Take two table-spoonfuls of oatmeal, half a blade of mace, a piece of lemon peel, three quarters of a pint of water or milk, a little sugar. Mix two spoonfuls of oatmeal very smooth in a little water, and put it gradually to three quarters of a pint; add a little lemon peel, and half a blade of mace; set it over the fire for a quarter of an hour, stirring it constantly. Then strain it, and add sugar to taste.

Parched Corn Gruel.—There are frequently sick people whose stomachs reject all kinds of nourishment until conditions follow that in many cases of this kind terminate fatally. In many cases where the popular sick-bed nourishments are prescribed and rejected, a simple saucer of parched corn pudding or bowl of gruel will seldom be refused. The corn is roasted brown, precisely as coffee is roasted, ground as fine as meal in a coffee mill, and made either into mush, gruel, or thin cakes, baked lightly brown, and given either warm or cold, clear, or with whatever dressing the stomach will receive or retain.

Ground Rice Milk.—This is an agreeable way in which to administer rice to the sick: Boil together two tablespoonfuls of ground rice with a pint of milk. Sweeten it according to taste, adding the juice of a lemon. Let the whole boil half an hour over a moderate fire. Eat it warm.

Bread Jelly.—Take one roll, one lemon, one quart of water, and sugar to taste. Or take the crumb of a penny roll; cut it into thin slices, and toast them of a pale brown on both sides. Put them into a quart of spring water. Let it simmer over the fire till it has become a jelly. Strain it through a thin cloth, and flavor it immediately with a little juice and sugar.

Iceland Moss Jelly.—Wash and bruise Iceland or Irish moss, and soak it all night; dry and boil it, putting an ounce to a quart, till it is reduced to one half the quantity of water; strain it through a sieve. Take it with milk, or flavored to taste. It may be boiled in milk and turned into a shape when cold.

Apple Tapioca.—Pare, core, and quarter eight apples; take half a spoonful of tapioca; put it to soak and swell all night in the water; put in half a teacupful of white sugar and a little lemon peel; put this into a stew-pan, and let the tapioca simmer ten minutes, then put in the apples and stew ten minutes more. When the tapioca is clear, it will form a jelly around the apples.

Tapioca Jelly.—Take four tablespoonfuls of tapioca; rinse it thoroughly, then soak it five hours in cold water, enough to cover it. Set a pint of cold water on the fire; when it boils, mash and stir up the tapioca that is in water, and mix it with the boiling water. Let the whole simmer gently, with a stick of cinnamon or mace. When thick and clear, mix a couple of tablespoonfuls of white sugar with half a tablespoonful of lemon-juice; stir it into the jelly; if not sweet enough, add more sugar, and turn into cups.

Meat Jelly.—Take half a pound of mutton, half a pound of beef, and half a pound of veal or pork, with a small piece or bone of bacon; put in water enough to keep it from burning, and cover it close; let it simmer for three or four hours till the juice of the meat is entirely out, then strain it off, and let stand till cold. If there is any fat, it can then be removed. A person recovering from an illness must not be left all night without food. Some of this jelly placed beside him, where he can reach it easily is a very excellent thing.

To Make Arrow-root.—Put one teaspoonful of arrow-root into a basin; rub it very smooth with two spoonfuls of cold water; pour over this half a pint of boiling water or milk in such a proportion as may be allowed, stirring well the whole time. It is generally better to boil it for two or three minutes. Sweeten to taste.

Apple Water.—Slice two large apples, put them into a jar, and pour over them one pint of boiling water. Cover close for an hour; pour off the fluid, and sweeten if necessary.

Apple Tea.—Roast eight fine apples in the oven, or before the fire; put them in a jug with two spoonfuls of sugar, and pour over them a quart of boiling water. Let it stand one hour near the fire.

Currant Drink.—To a pint of fresh-gathered currants (stripped) put a pint of water; let them boil together ten minutes or a quarter of an hour, then strain and sweeten to taste; a few raspberries added give a pleasant flavor. The same may be produced in winter by simmering two tablespoonfuls of currant jelly in half a pint of water.

Beverage of Figs and Apples.—Have two quarts of water boiling; split six figs, and cut two apples into six or eight slices each; boil the whole together twenty minutes; pour the liquid into a basin to cool, and pass through a sieve when it is ready for use. The figs and apples may be drained for eating with a little boiled rice.

Ice Cream and Beef Juice.—Here is the prescription for a relishable dietary article highly commended by an Illinois physician:—

℞. Cream, ... 120 grams
Sugar, ... 30 "
Extract of vanilla, . . . 8 "
Beef juice, ... 8 "

Any confectioner can make it, or it may readily be prepared at home with a freezer. Its uses are obvious.

Broth from Fowls.—Take an old fowl; stew it to pieces with a couple of onions. Season lightly with pepper and salt; skim and strain it.

Chicken Broth.—Cut up a young fowl into several pieces, put in a stew-pan with three pints of spring-water set on the stove fire to boil; skim well, and add a little salt; take two tablespoonfuls of pearl barley, wash it in several waters, and add it to the broth, together with one ounce of marsh-mallow roots cut into shreds, for the purpose of better extracting its healing properties. The broth should then boil one hour, and be passed through a napkin into a basin, to be kept ready for use.

To Cook Birds for Convalescents.—Lay them upon the gridiron; broil until they have a light brown color, then put them in a stew-pan; pour over hot water enough to cover them. Let them stew until tender. Season with a little fresh butter, pepper and salt. Chickens, birds, and squirrels, stewed in a double kettle, are very delicate for invalids. If permitted, stuff the fowls and birds with minced oysters.

Mutton Broth.—Take one pound of scrag of mutton, put it into a saucepan with two pints of water and a little salt; let it simmer gently for two hours; strain it through a sieve, and when cold carefully remove every particle of fat. It may be thickened with a little arrow-root or ground rice, as required.

A Strong Broth.—One pound of veal; one pound of beef; one pound of the scrag end of a neck of mutton; a little salt; three quarts of water. Put the above quantities into three quarts of water, with a little salt, and a few whole peppers. Boil it until reduced to one quart.

Calves' Feet.—Take two calves' feet; two pints of water; one pint of new milk; a little lemon peel or mace. Put the ingredients into a jar, cover it down, and keep it in the oven for four hours. When cold, remove the fat. Flavor it with lemon peel or mace, as preferred. This is very strengthening if taken the first thing in the morning and the last at night.

Nourishing Soup.—Two pounds of lean veal or beef; a quarter of a pound of pearl barley; a little fresh celery; a little salt. Boil two pounds of lean veal or beef, with a quarter of a pound of pearl barley in a quart of water very slowly, until it becomes the consistency of good cream; flavor it with a little fresh celery. Strain it when done through a fine hair sieve, and serve. This soup will only keep until the next day, therefore not more than the quantity required must be made.

Honey should not be eaten by the sick and feeble, as it continues for a long time in the stomach, and frequently causes "sourness" and flatulence.

Isinglass may be put into the invalid's tea, morning and evening, a good pinchful for a teacup. It may also be introduced, as much as possible, into the food of the weak, as it is most strengthening.

Brewis.—This is very good food for children. It is nothing more than a thick top crust of bread put into the pot where salt beef is boiling, and is nearly done; it draws the fat, becomes relishing with the flavor of meat and salt, and is nourishing to the stomach.

Suet and Milk.—One tablespoonful of shredded beef-suet; half a pint of fresh milk. Mix these ingredients, and warm them sufficiently to melt the suet completely. Skim it. Warm the cup into which you pour it, and give it to the invalid to drink before it gets cold.

Mucilage of Gum-arabic.—One ounce of gum-arabic in powder; mix well with two tablespoonfuls of honey; shave a little rind of lemon; clean off the white pith, and cut the lemon in slices into a jug; then stir on it, by degrees, a pint and a half of boiling water. This is particularly good in any complaint that affects the chest, as cough, consumption, measles, etc.

Strong Tonic Drink.—A quarter of an ounce of camomile flowers; a quarter of an ounce of sliced gentian root; a quarter of an ounce of bruised calumba; a quarter of an ounce of dried orange peel; fifty cloves, bruised; a pint and a quarter of cold spring water. Put these ingredients into a jug, and pour over them rather more than a pint of cold water; let it stand twenty-four hours, then pour off the clear liquor. Take three tablespoonfuls for a dose, fasting every morning.

Bran Tea.—This is sometimes invaluable for softening the throat, and most nourishing for the sick and aged. Take two or three tablespoonfuls of middle-sized bran, (not coarsest, as that is greasy,) put it into a jug, and pour on it one quart of boiling water; let it stand for about a quarter of an hour, and then pour off the water from the bran. The tea may be sweetened with white sugar or fine honey. When wine has been ordered for the patient, it may be added, or a little lemon juice. It is, however, not unpleasant without either of these additions. A wine-glass full of this tea may be taken many times in the day. Several persons in France have been kept alive with no other nourishment for weeks.

Savory Custard.—A savory custard, much relished by sick people, is made in the following manner: Take the yolks of two eggs, and the white of one, and put in a small basin; add one gill of beef-tea, and a quarter of a salt-spoonful of salt; whip up the eggs and the beef-tea; take a small cup, which will hold the mixture, and butter it; take a piece of white letter paper, and butter that, and tie it on the cup; have a sauce-pan with hot water, and put it on the fire to boil; when the water is boiling put in the cup so that the water stands below the top of the cup; let it simmer for a quarter of an hour; serve hot.

Raw Beef.—Physicians often administer to consumptives and persons of frail constitutions a diet of finely chopped raw beef, properly seasoned with salt, and heated by placing the dish containing it in boiling water. This food is given, also, in cases where the stomach rejects almost every other form of food. It assimilates rapidly and affords nourishment, while patients learn to long for and like it.

Some of the severest forms of that distressing ailment called dysentery are sometimes entirely cured by the patient eating a heaped tablespoonful of raw beef at a time, cut up very fine, and repeated at intervals of four hours until cured, eating and drinking nothing else in the meanwhile.

Recipe for Beef Tea.—Mince finely one pound of lean beef, placed in a preserve jar or other suitable vessel, and pour upon it one pint of cold water. Stir, and allow them to stand for about an hour, so that the goodness of the meat may be dissolved out. Next place the jar or vessel in a sauce-pan of water over a fire, and let the water boil gently for an hour. Remove the jar and strain. The beef tea which runs through contains a quantity of fine sediment, which is to be drunk with the liquid, after being flavored with salt to suit. The jar may also be placed in an oven for an hour, instead of in the water, as above. Beef tea, thus prepared, represents a highly nutritive and restorative liquid, with an agreeable, rich, meaty flavor. The old method of boiling the beef over a fire in a saucepan makes a soup or broth, not a tea.*

---

*BEEF TEA.—Some of the medical profession differ regarding the action of beef tea. Some declare it very inferior as a food; others believe it a most useful substance to sustain the body under great exhaustion. It is an established fact, that the greater portion of the albuminous tissue in the body is furnished by animal or nitrogenous food, and there seems no reason to doubt that the same elements can be supplied to the body in the more concentrated form of beef tea, or meat-juice, such tea thus making one of the most valuable tissue builders we possess. It has certainly had a great reputation from the earliest times, and there are many instances in which it has saved lives.

Among many cases we may cite a striking example of the useful and nutritive efficacy of beef tea in a case of inanition in an infant now six months old. The mother of the patient had three children, the first of which was still-born, the second died nine days after birth from inanition, and the third began to decline when she was three weeks old. Knowing the tendency to death in her second child, and suspecting it was due, probably, to the inefficiency of the mother's milk, a thoroughly supporting treatment was adopted, and fifteen drops of "Valentine's preparation of meat-juice," three times a day, together with diluted cow's milk and lime-water were given. The mother's supply of milk was also kept up. The cow's milk had a tendency to curdle, in spite of the lime-water, and so was discontinued. The child began to improve in a few days, and, in the words of the mother, "got fat and solid." In the course of a few months the stock of meat-juice became exhausted, and the mother concluded to do without it, "since the child had improved so remarkably." She was, however obliged to resume it again, as she relates "that on the second day after the meat-juice was left off, the little girl went quite thin and soft over the whole body, and became very fretful;" but on its renewal, in three or four days the child became healthy and well again. The meat-juice furnished more than the salts which it contains, as the child became fat, and her flesh hardened, showing an improvement in the muscular structure. Milk is the natural and suitable food for infants, but in this case, and doubtless in many others, the child would have been reduced to starvation if compelled to depend alone upon the mother's breast for nourishment.

WATER—ITS RELATION TO HEALTH.

The water we drink has been correctly described as a "life-giving and life-destroying element." Pure water, like pure air, is essential to good health. Polluted water, like impure air, is one of the most common sources of disease. Its natural history reveals the secret of its true quality.

Its Source.—Traced to its origin, water, in its continuous circulation through the atmosphere and oceans of our globe, is first pure distilled water, evaporated at comparatively low temperature by the heat of the sun, and raised far up in mid-air, and drifted slowly toward the poles of the earth by the return trade-winds. When warm air-currents, saturated with watery vapor, meet with colder ones, their capacity for holding water in solution is diminished; a portion of the latter is condensed and is precipitated in the form of rain, snow, hail or dew, in a state of almost absolute purity, upon the mountains and lowlands. Thus it comes down pure upon the ground, filters through a wholesome soil, issues in abundant springs, gravitates toward the water basins of the earth, and gradually drains into the ocean, from which, in process of time, it will again be converted into vapor, and re-enter into its ceaseless circulation. All supplies of fresh water are, therefore, derived from condensation of the watery vapor contained in the atmosphere.

Spring and Well-water in the Country.—In rural districts the water of springs and wells is comparatively pure. The pure rain (always pure when it first falls unless the air through which it passes is filled with noxious gasses) percolates through the soil, and filtrates into the subterranean water strata or fountains, and thence issues in a comparatively pure condition at the open spring or well. Of course, the "purer the soil filter, the purer the spring."

How Water Becomes Polluted.—The pure water after falling from the clouds filters through the soil, and carries from the rocks and soil certain soluble parts, the nature and amount of which depend upon the nature of the rock and soil. It is always contaminated by passing through a drainage area of polluted ground. In this respect, the increasing density of population and the encroachment of civilization upon the primeval state of the earth's surface have largely altered these conditions for a supply of pure water. Not only in crowded centers of population and industry, but also in some agricultural districts, the soil is more or less contaminated with sewage and all kinds of effete or decaying matters.

Well-water Often Dangerous.—Few wells, as ordinarily constructed, are free from surface pollution. Their walls are open from bottom to top for the inflow of the water from the contaminated soil and surface-water around. A densely crowded population soon impregnate the surface soil with filth, which drains into the water-course below, especially if such water is near the surface; the walls of the wells are so constructed as not to prevent its inflow. "Artesian wells" and "deep driven wells" from which the surface water is excluded furnish the best water, (except pure rain water,) which can be obtained with the expense of lengthy and tightly-closed conduits, in which the water is brought from a distance and from unpolluted reservoirs.

Caution in Locating Wells.—Every well should be widely separated from barn-yards, cess-pools, pens, sinks, and similar places, and should not be simply stoned up with loose stones or bricks, so that any surface liquid that filters through the soil has free access; but its walls should be made water-tight with cement, so that nothing can reach them except that which has been filtered through dense beds of unpolluted ground below. If this precaution is neglected, the best and deepest well may become continually contaminated by infiltration from the surrounding surface. If, at any time, no good drinking water can be had, or its purity appears doubtful, the only way to remove its dangerous qualities is to filter the water through thick layers of fine sand, or, better, through ground charcoal or animal charcoal.

Care in Constructing Cisterns.—*Cisterns* should be constructed of suitable material, carefully built and covered, and so placed that no foul air can pass through or over the water they contain. The overflow pipes from cisterns should be free from connection with any other pipes. Roofs and gutters supplying cisterns must be frequently inspected, and some simple contrivance should be adopted to insure their careful cleansing before the water is allowed to run into the cistern. Cistern water ought to be frequently examined, and be kept free from color, odor, or other indications of impurity.

How to Examine Suspected Water.—A simple method of examination is by dissolving a lump of loaf-sugar in a quantity of the suspected water in a clean bottle, which should have a close-fitting glass stopper. Set the bottle in the window of a room where the sunlight will fall on it. If the water remains bright and limpid after a week's exposure, it may be pronounced fit for use. But if it becomes turbid during the week it contains enough impurity to be unhealthy. Such water should not be used for drinking purposes until it has been boiled and filtered; after which it should be aerated by any simple process, such as pouring several times from one vessel into another in the open air. This is Heinsch's water test.

Purifying Water With Alum.—It is not generally known that pounded alum possesses the property of purifying water. A tablespoonful of pulverized alum sprinkled into a hogshead of water (the water stirred at the time) will, after the lapse of a few hours, by precipitating to the bottom the impure particles, so purify it that it will be found to possess all the freshness and clearness of the finest spring water. A pailful containing four gallons may be purified by a single teaspoonful.

Is Soft Water Better than Hard Water for Drinking Purposes?—Waters which contain only small quantities of these lime and magnesia compounds are said to be "soft," while those which contain them in greater proportion are described as being "hard." It is not advisable to use habitually a very hard water either for culinary or dietetic purposes; the presence, however, of a fair amount of these saline impurities—the occurrence of which constitutes "hardness"—rather increases than impairs the value of water as a beverage. There are, though, it should never be forgotten, certain other impurities sometimes found in water which render it quite unfit for use, and which have, indeed, been the cause of much disease and suffering, when water containing them has been used for dietetic purposes. Spring water is best adapted for drink when it is soft, although it is often oppressive to weak stomachs. It often proves injurious to domestic animals when they are confined to it, and is particularly disliked by horses.

Water-Cure or Hydropathy.—Water has been used in the treatment of disease from very early times. By the Priessnitz system water alone is used as a cure for nearly all diseases. Among the processes of hydropathy are the Sitz bath, the douche, the shower bath, and cold water compresses. For the beneficial application of water treatment in various diseases, the reader is referred to the ensuing pages.

Water a Powerful Absorbent.—Few persons know how certainly and rapidly water imbibes the impurities of the air. Many of us think if the water be clear and cold it must be perfectly pure, though it has stood in a close bedroom twenty-four hours; but this is far from true. If a pitcher of water be set in a room for only a few hours it will absorb nearly all the respired and perspired gases in the room, the air of which will have become purer, but the water utterly filthy. The colder the water is, the greater the capacity to contain these gases. At ordinary temperatures, a pail of water can contain a great amount of ammonia and carbonic-acid gas; and its capacity to absorb these gases is nearly doubled by reducing the water to a temperature of ice.

Caution Concerning Standing Water.—The inference is, therefore, plain and irresistible that water kept in a room over night is totally unfit for drinking purposes, and should not be used to gargle in the throat; also, that a large pail of water standing in a room would help to purify the atmosphere, but should be thrown away the next morning; it also teaches us the reason that the water from a pump should always be pumped out in the morning before any is used.

Distilled Water.—Absolutely pure water is only to be obtained by distil lation. It is then so insipid that we are unable to drink it, because it does not contain the solid matter we are accustomed to drink.

Do Lead Pipes Poison the Water?—So general is the impression that water becomes impregnated with the poison by standing in lead pipes and metallic lined water pitchers that many writers on hygiene recommend that lead pipes should be avoided when possible; and then when used the water should "run awhile before using." This precaution can do no harm, and yet the question whether water is poisoned by flowing through lead pipes was lately discussed in the French Academy of Sciences, with results that are calculated to quiet the apprehensions of those who get their water supply through such pipes. M. Dumas stated that in his chemical lectures he had long been accustomed to employ a very simple experiment for the purpose of showing that water corrodes lead only under special conditions. He takes distilled water, rain water, spring water, river water, etc., and drops into each a piece of lead. It is found that only the distilled water acts on the lead, the salts of lime in the rest of the specimens preventing the reaction. M. Belgrand read to the Academy a memoir giving the results of his investigations into this subject. The ancient Romans employed lead water pipes on a large scale, but yet no Latin medical writer says any thing of lead poisoning produced by the water. According to M. Belgrand, one sixth of a grain of calcareous salts to the quart prevents the dissolution of the lead. He exhibited to the Academy pieces of lead pipes which had been in service from the time of Louis XIV., without showing any sign of corrosion; and analysis of water that had passed through a long line of lead pipes showed the complete absence of lead.

ICE WATER AND HEALTH.

Ice Water Hinders Digestion.—Cold water is a less rapid solvent than warm water, as cold air is a better preservative than warm air. So ice water taken into the stomach chills the coats and contents of that organ, and thus suddenly checks and hinders the digestion of the food.

Iced Drinks Affecting the Head.—An intelligent and influential medical journal says very sensibly, "Drinks should be sipped, not gulped," and adds: "The intimate connection between stomach and brain is known to every body, and it must be obvious that to pour an iced draught into the stomach must at once send the blood to the head. Very few who have indulged in the rapid drinking of these beverages have failed to notice that a sudden pain in the head was the result. It may have been a sharp shoot, or a mere feeling of dullness, and it may have passed off in a moment, but it was at least incipient congestion of the brain."

Other Evils of Iced Drinks.—Another eminent hygienic authority urges that "no well man has any business to eat ices or drink iced liquids in any shape or form, if he wants to preserve his teeth, protect the tone of his stomach, and guard against sudden inflammations and prolonged dyspepsia. It is enough to make one shudder to see a beautiful young girl sipping scalding coffee or tea at the beginning of a meal, and then close it with a glass of ice-water; for at thirty she must either be snaggle-toothed, or wear those of the dead or artificial."

A Suggestive Caution about Ice.—Dr. W. W. Hall, in one of his Health Tracts, has these suggestive words: "If the reader is down town or away from home on a hot day, and feels as if it would be perfectly delicious to have a glass of lemonade, soda-water, or brandy toddy, by all means let him resist the temptation until he gets home, and then take a glass of cool water, a swallow at a time, with a second or two interval between each swallow. Several noteworthy results will most assuredly follow.

"After it is all over, you will feel quite as well from a drink of water as if you had enjoyed a free swig of either of the others.

"In ten minutes after you will feel a great deal better.

"You will not have been poisoned by the lead or copper which is most often found in soda-water.

"You will be richer by six cents, which will be the interest on a dollar for a whole year!

"You will not have fallen down dead from the sudden chills which sometimes result from drinking soda, iced water, or toddy in a hurry."

How to Cool Drinking Water without Ice.—Fresh spring or well water is abundantly cool for any drinking purpose whatever. In cities where water is artificially supplied, the case is somewhat different; but even then there is no good excuse for drinking ice-water, because, even if the excuse were good in itself, the effects on the stomach and teeth are the same.

Make a bag of thick woolen doubled, lined with muslin; fill it with ice; have in a pitcher an inch or two of water above the faucet, and let this bag of ice be suspended from the cover within two inches of the surface of the water. The ice will melt slowly and keep the water delightfully cool, but not ice cold. A still better effect will be produced if the pitcher is also well enveloped in woolen. Again, water almost as cool as it can be, unless it has ice actually in it, may be had without any ice at all by enveloping a closed pitcher partly filled with water with several folds of cotton, linen, or bagging, and so arranging it that these folds are kept wet all the time by water dripping from another vessel, on the principle of evaporation.

Water which is not iced may be drank freely throughout the meal, as the natural thirst demands.

SUMMER BEVERAGES.

Avoid all Alcoholic Drink.—Any drink which contains alcohol, (even cider, beer, and domestic cordials,) is not only not harmless, but positively injurious, because a single atom of alcohol, by using the strength of the present, leaves the system just that much weaker than it would have been had not that atom of alcohol been taken. The atom of alcohol has not one particle of nutriment, and hence cannot supply the system with one atom of strength. See chapter on "Alcoholic Drinks."

Good Cool Water.—The first and the best, because the safest, drink for laborers, invalids, the sedentary, for all times of the day and night, is half a glass at a time, repeated in ten minutes, if desired, of common water. As already indicated in the chapter on "Water," it should not be used too cold, nor in large quantities at a time. All the water taken into the stomach must pass away. If it be in excessive quantities, the strain upon the system will be too great. The skin, the kidneys, bowels, lungs, all are drawn upon. The result is, as may be naturally expected, exhaustion. For this reason, the man who drinks much water, particularly during the summer, and in the hottest weather, is less able to endure fatigue. The excess of water is of no benefit to him. A safe rule is to drink only a little at a time.

To Allay Thirst Without Drinking.—Cold water applied to the head is very refreshing to harvesters. Wading in water abates thirst. Persons cast away at sea will suffer less from thirst if the clothing is kept wringing wet with salt water. A piece of silk fitted in the hat at an equal distance from the hair and top of the hat is a great protection to the head against sun heat; it is an absolute protection if one side is well covered with gold leaf. As there is always a space between the top of the head and the crown of the hat, hatters should utilize this idea.

The Best Kind of Water.—According to Dr. Gautier, the best drinking water should be destitute of any particular taste, and must be positively rejected should it contain any odor whatever. Its temperature should be comprised between forty-two degrees and sixty degrees Fahrenheit. As the water introduces not only oxygen and hydrogen into the system in the proportions necessary to form water, but also such mineral substances, in solution, as are indispensable to life, it will be readily understood that absolutely pure water is not suited for the sustenance of life. There must, however, be a limit to the quantity of such foreign ingredients, under the penalty of injury to health.

Lemonade and Lemons.—Lemonade is a simple and grateful beverage. To make it "best," roll the lemons on something hard till they become soft; cut or grate off the rinds, cut the lemons in slices, and squeeze them in a pitcher, (a new clothes-pin will answer for a squeezer in lieu of something better;) pour on the required quantity of water, and sweeten according to taste. After mixing thoroughly, set the pitcher aside for half an hour, then strain the liquor through a jelly strainer, and put in the ice. Do not drink lemonade if your physician tells you there is an excess of acid in your system.

Lemon Sugar for Travelers.—Travelers who find it inconvenient to use lemons can carry a box of lemon sugar, prepared from citric acid and sugar, a little of which in a glass of water will furnish quite a refreshing drink, and one that will help oftentimes to avert sick-headache and biliousness. Citric acid is obtained from the juice of lemons and limes.*

Lemons for Excessive Thirst.—When persons are feverish and thirsty beyond what is natural, indicated in some cases by a metallic taste in the mouth, especially after drinking water, or by a whitish appearance of the greater part of the surface of the tongue, one of the best "coolers," internal or external, is to take a lemon, cut off the top, sprinkle over it some loaf sugar, working it downward into the lemon with the spoon, and then suck it slowly, squeezing the lemon, and adding more sugar as the acidity increases from being brought up from a lower point.

Lemons for Invalids.—Invalids with feverishness may take two or three lemons a day in this manner, with the most marked benefit, manifested by a sense of coolness, comfort, and invigoration.

Lemons at "Tea-time."—A lemon or two thus taken at "tea-time," as an entire substitute for the ordinary "supper" of summer, would give many a man a comfortable night's sleep and an awakening of rest and invigoration, with an appetite for breakfast, to which they are strangers who will have their cup of tea or supper of "relish" or "cake" and berries or peaches and cream. †

Organic Matter in Drinking Water.—The presence of organic matter in waters has been considered one of the principal causes of any injurious

---

* While traveling recently, says Dr. A. N. Bell in the *Sanitarian*, our attention was inconveniently called one morning to empty water tanks. But there were others, children especially, who, on crawling out of the sleeping bunks, were in want of water more than we were—to drink. It was long, however, before the cars halted, and the tanks were filled from a road-side stream. Of this the thirsty drank. We ventured to suggest to the porter that possibly this water was not wholesome. But the suggestion that "water as clear as that" was not clean, to him was absurd. The same suggestion to the conductor was equally incomprehensible. It is just such water that collects and holds in solution the poison of typhoid fever, which summer travelers so often take home with them.

† The lemon thus eaten was the great physical solace of General Jackson in his last illness, which was consumption combined with dropsy. It loosened the cough, and relieved him of much of that annoying hacking and hemming which attends diseases of the throat and lungs, being many times more efficient, speedy, and safe than any lozenge or "troche" ever swallowed.

qualities they may possess; to their presence being attributed the development of such diseases as diarrhœa, dysentery, intermittent fever, typhoid fever, etc. Of these ingredients, carbonate of lime is the most common, and of this there may be, without inconvenience, 10-100 to 20-100 of a gramme to the litre. An appreciable percentage of phosphate of lime renders the water unfit for domestic and industrial uses; and for general purposes there should not be a greater percentage than 2-100 to 5-100 of a gramme to the litre. Small percentages of the chlorides generally affect water disadvantageously for drinking purposes. The maximum, however, should be 8-100 to 10-100 of a gramme to the litre.

Various Drinks.—If any thing is added to the summer drink it should contain some nutriment, so as to strengthen the body as well as to dilute the blood for the purpose of a more easy flow through the system; as any one knows that the thinner a fluid is the more easily does it flow. Some of the nutritious and safe drinks are given below, especially for those who work in the sun of summer, all to be taken at the natural temperature of the shadiest spot in the locality. To any of them ice may be added, but it is a luxurious, not a beneficial, ingredient nor a safe one.

1. Buttermilk.
2. A pint of molasses to a gallon of water.
3. A lemon to half a gallon of water and a teacupful of molasses, or as much sugar.
4. Vinegar, sugar, and water are substitutes, but the vinegar is not a natural acid, contains free alcohol, hence is not as safe or healthful.
5. A thin gruel made of corn or oats, drank warm, is strengthening.
6. A pint of grapes, currants, or garden-berries to half a gallon of water is agreeable.

Orangeade Medically Prescribed.—Dr. Walter Lewis, in describing the precautions against cholera adopted at the General Post-office, in London, Eng., says: "The men employed in sorting letters and newspapers suffer much from thirst, especially in the hot weather, and consequently drink much water while engaged in their duties. Although the post-office is supplied with excellent water, much diarrhœa was, nevertheless, the result of this practice. To remedy this, the officers, clerks, and men of all classes, have of late been supplied from the medical department with a most agreeable drink, which not only assuages the thirst, but has, moreover, strong antiseptic and anti-diarrhœa properties. It is called orangeade, and is thus composed: Take of dilute sulphuric acid, concentrated infusion of orange peel, each twelve drams; syrup of orange peel, five fluid ounces. This quantity is added to two imperial gallons of water. A large wine-glassful is taken for a draught, mixed with more or less water, according to taste. The officers drink this with pleasure. It is being consumed in large quantities daily, and I am convinced it will be the means of warding off a great deal of sickness."

Ices and Ice-cream.—The growing use of ices, and the custom of taking ice-water or other very cold drinks or food, as ice-cream, etc., cannot but prove unfavorable to health, especially when one has low vital power, with insufficient power of the stomach to react and restore the degree of heat actually demanded that digestion may proceed naturally. Digestion is arrested as soon as the temperature of the stomach falls below about 90 degrees Fah., and when cold drinks are taken by the weak, at least some considerable time must elapse before it is restored; in some instances hours, attended by great waste of power, and a derangement of the stomach. Cold drinks also excite and inflame the throat, causing an artificial thirst, never satisfied by such drinks, to say nothing of the danger of contracting colds by this unnatural chilling of the stomach, often followed by bowel derangements, inflammation of the stomach, and by still worse ailments.

TEA AND COFFEE AND HEALTH.

How Tea is Grown.—The tea-plant is a native of China, and resembles the low whortleberry bush in many respects. The Chinese raise it very much as we raise corn—three to five plants in a hill, raised from the seed. The plants are not allowed to grow more than one and a half feet high. Only the medium-sized leaves are picked, the largest being left to favor the growth of the plant. The picking occurs (1) in April, of the young and tender leaves; (2) about the first of May, of the full-sized leaves; and (3) about the middle of July, the last making an inferior quality of tea.

Preparation of Tea for Market.—Tea leaves are first wilted in the sun, then trodden in baskets by barefooted men to break the stems, next rolled by the hands into a spiral shape, then left in a heap to heat again, and finally dried for the market. This constitutes black tea, the frequent exposure to the air and to heat giving it its dark color.

For green tea the leaves, instead of being first exposed to the air, are fired for a short time as soon as gathered, then rolled and quickly dried over a fire.

The green tea of commerce is artificially colored with tumeric powder and a mixture of gypsum and Prussian blue, the latter in very minute proportions.

Canton teas are usually scented by the infusion of the blossoms of certain aromatic plants.

In this country damaged teas and the "grounds" left at hotels are re-rolled, highly colored, packed in old tea-chests, and sent out as new teas.

Certain varieties of black tea, even, receive a coating of black lead to make them shiny.*

The Chinese always drink black tea, using no milk or sugar, and prepare it, not by steeping, but by pouring hot water on the tea, and allowing it to stand for a few moments.

The Tea Plant in Respect of Quality.—The tea plant will bear a wide range of climatic variation without serious deterioration. The richness of the soil and the mode of cultivation exercise a paramount influence on the quality of the tea. In this respect the tea-plant is like the tobacco-plant or the mulberry-tree.

The youngest leaves give the best tea; hence the high price of choice teas, for to produce any considerable weight of young leaves a great number of plants are required, while the same weight of old or full-grown leaves is produced by a comparatively small number of plants. The age of tea leaves may be ascertained by a chemical examination of the ash left on burning them. As the leaves grow they lose in potash and phosphoric acid, both absolutely and relatively, and gain in lime and silica. Examinations made at periods of fourteen days asunder exhibit these phenomena with sufficient distinctness. In the practical examination of teas there is a very valuable and simple rule: *Much potash and phosphoric acid, together with little lime and silica, means good tea, and the reverse poor tea.*†

Tea and Digestion.—Tea possesses an active principle called *theine*. It contains tannin, which, if the tea is strong, coagulates the albumen of the food—actually *tans* it—and thus delays digestion.

Tea-Drinking and Sick-Headache; An Illustration.—The importance of the question involved in this caption leads us to insert here—though in a re-arranged form—the history of a case, reported originally by R. B. Gregg, for the *Homeopathic Quarterly Review*, and later printed by permis-

---

* A splendid specimen of tea, grown in the Himalayas, was chemically examined by Zöller, and the following results obtained. In 100 parts of the tea there were 4.95 parts of moisture, and 5.63 parts of ash. The ash contained in 100 parts, showed the following ingredients:

Potash	39.22	Sulphuric acid	trace.
Soda	0.65	Chlorine	3.81
Magnesia	6.47	Silica	4.85
Lime	4.24	Carbonic acid	24.30
Oxide of iron	4.38		
Protoxide of manganese	1.03	Total	100.00
Phosphoric acid	14.55		

† "*Oolong* "—A variety of black tea, possessing the flavor of green tea.

"*Hyson* "—A fragrant species of green tea.

" *Gunpowder* "—A species of green tea, each leaf of which is rolled into a small ball or pellet.

" *Souchong*"—A kind of black tea.

sion in a health magazine edited by one of the compilers of the present volume. The entire case is presented in the language of the writer—a competent witness.

The Doctrine Stated.—The writer says: "From considerable observation I have come to view tea as a more prolific cause of that terrible suffering, so aptly described by the phrase sick-headache, than any other one thing, if it is not the cause of more cases of this disease than all else besides; and I will give examples which seem to confirm this view most positively.

A Home Case.—"The first of these, and one of the clearest and most positive in its evidence, occurred in my own family, and although it may be regarded by some as a violation of propriety in such matters to so definitely designate the patient, still the case seems of too much importance, too clear in its proof, to allow any alternative, or tolerate, in short, any doubt to arise as to its genuineness by withholding the name. Besides, it will readily be seen that a physician could hardly become so familiar with all the details of a case, and remain so for so long a time, outside of his own household.

Was the Case Hereditary?—"My wife was several years a victim to frequent and most terrible paroxysms of sick-headache. She commenced suffering from it in the twenty-fourth year of her age, soon after the birth of our first child. Her father, mother, and grandmother upon the mother's side, were also all great sufferers from the same—the grandmother till she died, the father and mother are so still. From this fact I attributed its appearance in my wife's case to a strong hereditary predisposition, developed into activity by the change her system had recently passed through, and so regarded it for four or five years. And believing, as I do, that inherited diseases ought to be cured so long as they remain functional, or before any real organic changes have taken place in them, I gave my attention to the means of cure, without regarding the cause beyond what has just been mentioned.

Failure of Remedies.—"In regard to curing, however, I was doomed to disappointment, for not the slightest curative action was established in her case. During the first three or four years medicines frequently mitigated the severity of the paroxysm, but these would recur just as often; in fact they increased in frequency from year to year, until they occurred commonly every week, and became so violent that nothing afforded any relief; and then she used to say that, in addition to the frequent paroxysmal attacks, she did not pass a minute at any time, when awake, without more or less pain in the head. Under this state of things other and more serious symptoms began also to manifest themselves, which appeared as though they must sooner or later lead to paralysis, if they were not arrested.

More Careful Investigation.—"Medical aid having now, for so long a time, completely failed to do what it certainly seemed that it ought, and what results in the treatment of other maladies would lead us to expect, I began more seriously to consider the cause of her trouble, to see if this was not in part, at least, to be found in some daily habits of living, instead of its all being hereditary; or if not this, then to see if there was not something in those habits which was continuously acting in a manner to prevent medicines from developing their curative effects.

The True Cause Suspected.—"I then recalled the facts, that she had never drank tea until after she was married; that she had drank it, invariably, three times a day from that time—she was not in the habit of drinking coffee; that she never had a sick headache until some three years after commencing the use of tea; and that she never went without it one meal after the headaches began to trouble her but she was *sure to have one of her most severe paroxysms*. From this last fact, and the more I reflected upon it, the more confident I became that the tea had something, at least, to do either in causing or aggravating her disease.

The Usual Answer.—"Upon this conviction becoming more fully impressed upon my mind, I urged her to leave off drinking tea entirely, and substitute cold water for it. This, however, she thought both very unpleasant and difficult to do. So time passed on for a year or two longer, and with it an increase of suffering, until it became still more clear that something must be done, or very serious consequences in the way of paralysis, or some kindred disease, would certainly ensue.

First Efforts for Relief.—"She then abstained from her tea entirely. I told her she would no doubt suffer severely for a few days, as this appeared unavoidable, from the fact that she always experienced such increased severity of pain from going without it one meal; and we were not disappointed. For nine or ten days her sufferings were continuous, and about half of this time they were terrible. On the fourth day the pain in the head was so extreme it seemed that congestion and inflammation of the brain must result, if it continued. She was writhing in agony the most of that day, entirely unable to sit up, yet found it almost impossible to lie down, therefore was constantly changing her position in bed, to find a little relief After this worst day, however, the intensity of the pain subsided in a measure, though she still suffered, much of the time greatly, until the tenth day, when all the acute pain ceased, but the whole head, both internally and externally, was left very sore.

Relief at Last.—"The soreness continued a week or more, when that, too, passed off, giving place to a very weak feeling through the head, of some days' duration; and then she went along some three weeks before another attack of headache, longer than she had gone before in two or three years, and this was much lighter, and of shorter duration, than former paroxysms. After this she went six or seven weeks before another attack, and this was still lighter, and soon passed over entirely, leaving the head more free from all symptoms than it had been for years. Following this she had no more trouble until the succeeding December, about six months from the last paroxysm, above mentioned.

Relapse and Recovery.—"At that time our little daughter had scarlet fever, and my wife seemed to contract diphtheria from it. At least, she had a severe attack of this disease, as did very many other adults in this city, that winter, in families where children had the scarlatina. This left her throat so sensitive for a short time that she could not drink cold water, but drank tea three or four days, when she was seized with another severe paroxysm of sick-headache. Then she abstained from it the second time, and from that day to the present, nearly three years, she had had but little distress of any kind from the head, until during a short illness last February, when she drank tea again, for a week or ten days, and in that time it commenced developing all the old symptoms. Upon this she wholly abandoned the idea of ever again using it, convinced that it is one of those agents that her system will not tolerate.

Was the Case "Peculiar?"—"Now, all this might, with some plausibility, be said to be the result of a very unusual peculiarity of constitution, a highly-marked idiosyncrasy, and, therefore, not important in its bearing upon other cases. But let us consider this point. Fortified with the facts that this case furnished me, I have advised all patients consulting me the last two years, for sick-headache, to abandon at once and wholly the use of tea, of any and all kinds. It has been difficult, though, to induce any to do so, the hold which habit had upon them being so strong, and utterly impossible to persuade others to make the sacrifice.

A Remarkable Test.—"Of the few who have complied with my request there were three men past middle age, and otherwise tolerably healthy, but who were among those the worst afflicted with this malady of any that I have ever met. One of these was upward of sixty years of age, and had suffered his entire lifetime, or from his earliest recollection, with sick-headache, frequently as often as every week, and sometimes for two days at a time. I prescribed for him several times, but with no other result than to partially relieve the severity of the attacks—did not break in at all upon the frequency of their recurrence—so finally prevailed upon him, two years ago last spring, to abstain from the use of tea.

As he lived out of the city I never learned the result until three or four months since, when I one day met him upon the street, and he remarked,

'Well, doctor, I got rid of my sick-headaches by stopping tea.' He further said that his pain was much greater than common for a few days after leaving it off, but he then went much longer than usual before another attack, which was also less severe, and after two or three such recurrences, each at longer intervals and in less violence, they disappeared entirely. And that of late he had tried to use tea again, but even when taken very weak it brought on many of the former symptoms.

A Second Remarkable Test.—"Another of the three cases was that of a man aged about fifty years. He had been afflicted some thirty years or over, or from his early manhood, with sick-headache. For some two years or more I was called to him repeatedly for attacks of this disease, and in several instances had to attend him two and three days before the symptoms would yield. His distress at such times was really terrible. No other expression would at all adequately describe it. He would sometimes go two and even three days without sleep, and all the time under apparently as extreme pain as a man could endure and retain his consciousness. Indeed, during two or three of these attacks he did become very delirious. And finally, also, he began to show marked symptoms of paralysis, his extremities becoming numb, and in several instances losing the use of his legs in a great measure, during the severity of the paroxysm. I had urged him repeatedly to leave off the use of tea, and finally about a year since, during one of the worst attacks he had ever had, I told him there was no need of all this, and no sense in his refusing longer to abandon what I believed to be the cause of it all; and that there was not a doubt in my mind that his legs would be paralyzed in another year if he continued it. He stopped the tea then in the midst of that attack, had but one or two light returns of it afterward, passed the winter free from them, and left here for the West this last spring, saying he had not been so well in years.

A Third Remarkable Test.—"The third and last of these three cases was that of a man aged from forty-five to fifty years. He, too, was a great and frequent sufferer from the disease under consideration, and had been for many years, though the duration of the paroxysms was seldom, if ever, so long as in either of the other cases; and he found relief just the same in abandoning tea.

Relief for Most Headache Sufferers.—"Now, then, in view of these cases, is it not important that all who suffer from sick-headache should be warned against drinking tea? It should be understood, however, that the claim is *not made that all such cases are caused by this agent*, for I well know the contrary to be true, having met with a few persons who suffered from it that never drank tea. But from the two or three years observation, since my mind was more especially called to the subject, I have no hesitation in declaring my belief that a large proportion, if not, indeed, a large majority, of those afflicted with this disease who do drink tea, will find great, and many entire, relief from abandoning at once and wholly the use of this beverage.

The Kinds of Tea Used.—" With regard to the kinds of tea, there seems to be no particular difference in their effects upon the nervous system: in the cases given, so that the drinkers of *black* teas can claim no advantages in this, as is done in other respects, over those who use the green teas, nor *vice versa* The relief was just as prompt in abandoning the one as the other My wife never drank any other than black tea, and always used it weak. The first one of the three other cases reported drank black tea also, but strong; the next one used both black and green strong; while the third, or last, generally drank green tea very strong. Neither did it appear to make any difference in regard to temperaments with these cases, one of the four having black hair and black eyes, another dark brown hair and hazel eyes, another sandy hair and blue eyes, and the fourth more of a flaxen hair, and very light blue eyes.

Other Suspected Bad Effects of Tea.—" The possible effects of tea in producing other and more serious diseased conditions than we have been considering should not be overlooked. . . . It will have been seen that in two of the cases reported there were marked indications of paralysis, and there were certainly reasons to fear that it might become permanent in both. Then, when we reflect that this disease is so alarmingly on the increase—that, contrary to what used to be the case, so many young or youngish persons are becoming paralyzed—it is of the utmost importance to investigate its causes, and see if tea may not be one of them in some of these cases. Delirium, too, is not an uncommon attendant upon the severer paroxysms of sick-headache, and may not this possibly afford a clue to the cause of a few, at least, of the rapidly-increasing numbers of cases of insanity throughout the civilized world?"

Tea a Powerful Excitant.—It is not asserted that tea does operate as a cause of such troubles, for there is no positive proof of it as yet. We all know that this article is a powerful excitant of the nervous system, and from this fact alone is as liable to produce insanity as many other agents which affect the brain.

Tea a Powerful Astringent.—Again, the known astringent properties of tea would seem as though they must make it a cause of chronic constipation with many who drink it.

How to Test Each Case Properly.—As for hoping to *cure* sick-headache by medical treatment, when tea-drinking is the cause of it, and this is continued, it is utterly useless to waste time in the endeavor, and the height of absurdity to expect to produce such a result. No disease was ever yet really cured, where, through the ignorance or perverseness of the patient, the cause of it was constantly or frequently renewed. It is not possible that it should be done; therefore let the physician do his duty in all such cases, and raise the warning voice; then place the responsibility where it properly belongs, if his advice is not heeded.

How to "Stop" Drinking Tea.—If patients are advised to break off "gradually," the gradual is seldom reached, and when it is, they see no improvement for so long a time—from the fact that the weaker article is sufficient to keep the symptoms active after the resisting power of the nervous system has once been broken down—that they will almost always abandon the effort, and stoutly maintain that tea has nothing to do with it. Besides, all the benefits of the powerful reaction accruing from the sudden stoppage are lost, and the patient will drag along for months, if not years, to reach that exemption from the effects that those stopping suddenly will get in a few days, or at most in a few weeks. When any thing is actually causing suffering, how absurd to continue it in less strength, hoping that thereby we can compromise with Nature and stop her protests!

The Old Cry Stated.—But the old mistaken logic often comes to the physician, thus: "Why, doctor, when I have the headache nothing gives me so much relief as a good *strong* cup of tea." This is the best evidence that it injures them. It is only the temporary relief afforded by a more powerful re-stimulation, while the next paroxysm must come so much the sooner, or in greater severity, as a result of the renewed attack upon the nervous forces. In fact, though not so disreputable, it is only the old cry of the inebriate in his cravings: "Give me my drinks, they are all that relieve me."

How Tea was Banished from a Minister's Table.—Rev. Dr. X., a well-known minister, furnished us the following record of his experience on the tea question: Over twenty-five years ago I was in feeble health. One day I visited an able physician, stated my case, and requested his counsel as to the most suitable treatment. He responded, "Let us first determine, if possible, the cause of your imperfect health: do you use tea!"

"I do."

"I thought so," said the doctor.

"How so?"

"Your countenance and your general physical symptoms told me the **story**."

"Then you really think the drinking of tea is hurtful?" I inquired with some emphasis.

"Often," carefully and considerately responded the doctor, adding, "It certainly harms you."

I shall never forget the unpleasant surprise I felt at his opinion. I had no confidence in its correctness, and left him with a feeling akin to contempt for his judgment—not doubting, however, his sincerity. Soon after, I met an other physician, of much larger experience, and of wider renown, especially as to his knowledge of the pathology of disease. I asked his opinion.

"I would advise you to abstain from the use of tea," was his very first word of counsel.

"But, doctor, how do you know I use it?"

"The symptoms betray you; I suppose they give correct witness!"

I was nonplused again. After leaving the doctor, I considered the whole question, and by the time I had reached the parsonage I had nearly determined to test, by the most careful personal experience, the correctness of the unexpected and doubtful professional opinion which had now been repeated. My wife suggested that in a matter of so much importance as health, it would be "better to err on the safe side;" the omission could "do no harm." The thing was settled—tea was banished from the table, except when guests were present, and then it was only used by them. My general health began to improve, and in less than three months the whole tone of my nervous system became so transformed for the better as to be a matter of special notice and congratulation on the part of my friends. From that day to this neither my wife nor myself have used tea of any kind as a beverage. We occasionally sip it in "homeopathic doses" when abroad, so as not to excite remark, but its use is only the record of twenty-five years ago.

Is Tea Good for Well People?—Tea derives its beneficial qualities not from its supply of nutrition, for it supplies none, but from its affording theine, the effect of which in the system is to diminish the waste, thus making less food necessary at the time tea is taken. Whether such effect is needed depends largely upon the previous habits of the drinker. Its stimulus is peculiarly grateful to the aged who have been accustomed to drink it. Our advice to all, however, is *never to drink strong tea, except* as a medicine, and under the advice of a competent and reliable physician. Unless a stimulus is required, some other warm drink, as "wheat-tea," "corn-tea," or "rice-tea," etc., with the milk and sugar added, is always to be preferred. The latter are much relished by those who are accustomed to use them. *

Coffee as a Beverage.—Coffee, though of a taste little allied to tea, de-

---

* It is an incontrovertible physiological fact, says Dr. Hall, that any artificial stimulus continued for a few days makes the system feel the want of it, instinctively lean upon it, and look for it; but this is not all; the same amount of stimulation is demanded every day; but to create that amount, a larger and an increasing quantity of the stimulus becomes necessary, or it must be more frequently supplied. No habitual user of spirits, or of tea and coffee, can possibly deny this after ten years' practice. As proof, see how much oftener they drink, or smoke, or chew than when they first entered on the miserable, useless, and degrading career of self-indulgence. The truth is, there is no safety except in absolute refusal even to taste a drop or chew an atom. He who takes one drop may die in the gutter; he who has the high moral courage to refuse that first drop, that first atom, never can!

rives its efficiency in precisely the same manner and from nearly the same substances. Its value and effects in the system are therefore the same as those above stated. Yet it must be generally conceded that a free coffee drinker will almost invariably complain of biliousness and present a cadaverous appearance. For working people, as a rule, coffee will seldom produce this effect; but for all persons of sedentary habits, who take but little exercise, coffee is not to be recommended. In the case of coffee, as in that of tea, *it should not be drunk strong, except as a medicine.* As a rule, coffee is less harmful than tea.

Substitutes for Coffee.—Chocolate is generally much more healthful than coffee; but care should be used to get it pure. Corn coffee, wheat coffee, and the other kinds of coffee made from the use of the roasted cereals, are to be preferred, as in the case of tea.*

THE AIR WE BREATHE.

The Wonder of Breathing.—The perfection of the organs of respiration excites our wonder. "The hand that formed them must have been divine." So delicate are these organs, that the slightest pressure would cause exquisite pain, yet tons of air surge back and forth through their intricate passages, and bathe their innermost cells. Every year we perform seven million acts of breathing, inhaling one hundred thousand cubic feet of air, and purifying over three thousand five hundred tons of blood. This gigantic process goes on constantly, and never wearies or worries us, and we only wonder at it when science reveals to us its magnitude. In addition, by a wise economy, the process of respiration is made to subserve a second use no less important, and the air we exhale, passing through the organs of voice, is transformed into prayers of faith, songs of thanksgiving and praise, and words of love and social enjoyment.

Fresh Air Constantly Needed.†—None of the wants of the human body are so constant and pressing as that of air. Other demands may be met by occasional supplies, but the air must be furnished every moment or we sicken and die.

---

* "Children who drink tea and coffee," says Dr. Ferguson, of England, "as a rule, only grow four pounds per annum between the ages of thirteen and sixteen, while those who drink milk night and morning grow fifteen pounds each year. When diseases are prevalent in the neighborhood children who use these drinks have less power to resist sickness than others.

† Mr. Louis Winters, a sculptor and mason at Stoke-Newington, England, describes an interesting natural curiosity in his house. Some years ago he observed on the banks of the Thames, at Kew, a small wasp's nest. This he carefully secured, after stupefying the insects by the fumes of wetted gunpowder. Removing the nest, then about the size of an ordinary apple, to his house, he placed it in a glass case inside the outer wall of the build-

What is Pure Air?—The air we breathe is composed of nitrogen, oxygen, carbonic acid, and watery vapor. The first forms four fifths, the second one fifth, the third about $\frac{4}{10000}$, and the last a variable amount. The nitrogen and oxygen form so large a part, that they are considered in ordinary calculations to compose the whole atmosphere. In the animal world the oxygen is the life-giving element, and carbonic acid the destroyer, while in the vegetable world this order is exactly reversed. Thus, deprived of plants we should soon exhaust the oxygen from the air, supply its place with carbonic acid, and die; while they, removed from us, would soon exhaust the carbonic acid, and die as certainly. The nitrogen is of a negative character, and neither supports life nor destroys it. Yet we cannot live without it, for the oxygen would be too active, and our life would be excited to a pitch of which we can scarcely dream, and would sweep through its feverish course in a few days. The watery vapor supplies the animal and vegetable worlds with water. Were the air perfectly dry, our flesh would become shriveled like a mummy's, and leaves would wither as in an African simoom. Any thing that changes the proportion of these elements render air impure.

How Fresh Air Purifies the Blood.—In the delicate cells of the lungs the air gives up its oxygen to the blood, and receives in turn carbonic acid gas and water, foul with waste matter which the blood has picked up in its circulation through the body. The blood thus purified and laden with the inspiring oxygen, goes bounding through the system, while the air we exhale carries off the impurities. In this process the blood changes from purple to red, while if we examine our breath we can readily see what it has removed from the blood.*

---

ing, through which he bored a small hole for ingress and egress, and carved the figure of a beehive on the outside. The wasps took kindly to their new abode, especially as several gardens and nurseries adjoin the house. They have subsequently increased wonderfully in numbers, and have enlarged the nest until it is nearly a foot in diameter. It is calculated that the present number of wasps must be at least several thousands. The glass case, which is usually covered and darkened, permits the unflagging diligence of the little architects to be closely watched. But the most interesting feature of the community within is their persistent and systematic attention to *ventilation*. In this respect they are a model to human householders. During the recent hot weather from four to six wasps were continually stationed at the hole of egress, and, while leaving space for entrance or exit, *created a steady current of fresh air by the exceedingly rapid motion of their wings. After a long course of this vigorous exercise, the ventilators were relieved by other wasps.* During the cooler weather only two wasps at a time were usually thus engaged. The utmost harmony and industry appeared to pervade this strange and crowded establishment of interesting but much maligned little creatures.

* Let those who wish to test this, breathe into a jar, then lower into it a lighted candle. The flame will be extinguished immediately, thus showing the presence of carbonic acid gas. Or breathe upon a mirror, and a film of moisture will show the vapor. If the breath is confined in a bottle for a time, the animal matter will decompose, and give off an offensive smell. —STEELE.

Our exhaled breath, therefore, is the air robbed of its vitality, and containing in its place a gas which is as fatal to life as it is to a flame, and effete matter which at the best is disagreeable to the smell, injurious to the health, and may contain the germs of disease. Air containing only three or four per cent. of carbonic acid gas acts as a narcotic poison, and a much smaller proportion will have an injurious effect. Careful investigations show that air containing more than *six tenths of one per cent. of carbonic acid in one thousand parts of air,* is really adverse to comfort, and obnoxious to health, the vitiated condition increasing in proportion to the increase of the carbonic acid.

Capacity of the Lungs for Air.—There are in an average sized and well-developed human body about *six hundred millions of air cells,* into which the air passes in order to purify the blood. According to Hutchinson, a man of medium height will expel at a single full breath about two hundred and thirty cubic inches, or a gallon, and for each inch in height between five and six feet, there will be an increase of eight cubic inches. In addition, it is found that the lungs contain about one hundred cubic inches which cannot be expelled, thus making their entire contents about three hundred and thirty cubic inches, or eleven pints. The extra amount always on hand in the lungs is of great value, since thereby the action of the air goes on continuously, even during a violent expiration.

Amount of Air we Breathe.—A full sized man takes into his lungs at each breath about a pint of air; while in there all the life-nutriment is extracted from it; and on its being sent out of the body, it is so entirely destitute of life-giving power, that if re-breathed into the lungs again without the admixture of pure air, the individual would suffocate, would die in sixty seconds. As a man breathes about eighteen times in a minute, and a pint at each breath, he consumes over two hogsheads of air every hour, or about sixteen hogsheads during the eight hours of sleep; that is, if a man were put in a room which would hold sixteen hogsheads of air, he would, during eight hours' sleep, extract from it every atom of life-nutriment, and would die at the end of eight hours, even if each breath could be kept to itself, provided no air came into the room from without.

Healthful Respiration.*—Respiration consists of two acts, *inspiration,*

---

* *Sighing* is merely a prolonged inspiration, followed by an audible expiration.
Coughing is a violent expiration in which the air is driven through the mouth.
Sneezing differs from coughing, the air being forced through the nose.
Snoring is a sleeping accompaniment, in which the air passes through the nose and mouth. The peculiar sound is produced by the palate flapping in this divided current of air, and so throwing it into vibration.
Laughing and *Crying* are very much alike, the expression of the face being necessary to distinguish between them. The sounds are produced by short, rapid contraction of the diaphragm.

taking in the air, and *expiration*, expelling it from the lungs. When we draw in a full breath we straighten the spine, and throw back the head and shoulders so as to give the greatest advantage to the muscles. At the same time the diaphragm descends and presses the walls of the abdomen outward, both of which processes increase the size of the chest. Then the elastic lungs expand to occupy the extra space, while the air rushing in through the windpipe pours along the bronchial tubes, and crowds into every cell.

When we forcibly expel the air from our lungs the operation is reversed. This is called *expiration*. We bend forward, draw in the walls of the abdomen, and press the diaphragm upward, while the ribs are pulled downward—all together diminishing the size of the chest, and forcing the air outward. Ordinary, quiet breathing is performed mainly by the diaphragm, one breath to every four beats of the heart; or eighteen per minute.

Relief from Hiccough.—The following simple directions have proved successful in numerous cases, and bear the indorsements severally of responsible names:—

1. "Holding the breath" as long as possible.
2. Drinking as many successive swallows as possible without breathing.
3. Startling the patient by a sudden motion or communication.
4. Eating sugar, or drinking "sugared water." The latter is often given to infants by their nurses as a "sure cure."
5. Concentrating the mind intensely upon some subject.
6. Hold up the right arm, extending the hand as far as possible, and look at it.

How to Check Sneezing, Coughing, etc.—Dr. Brown-Sequard, in one of his Boston lectures, says: "There are many facts which show that morbid phenomena of respiration can be also stopped by the influence of arrest. Coughing, for instance, can be stopped by pressing on the nerves on the lip in the neighborhood of the nose. A pressure there may prevent a cough when it is beginning. Sneezing may be stopped by the same mechanism. Pressing in the neighborhood of the ear, right in front of the ear, may stop coughing. It is so also of hiccough, but much less so than for sneezing or coughing.

"Pressing very hard on the top of the mouth, inside, is also a means of stopping coughing. And I may say that the will has immense power there.

Hiccough is confined to inspiration, and is caused by a contraction of the diaphragm, and a constriction of the glottis.

Yawning or *gaping* is like sighing. It is distinguished by a wide opening of the mouth, and a deep, profound inspiration. Both processes furnish additional air, and, therefore, probably meet a demand of the system for more oxygen. Frequently they are like laughing, sobbing, etc., a sort of contagion which runs through an audience, and seems almost irresistible.

There was a French surgeon who used to say, whenever he entered the wards of the hospital, The first patient who coughs here will be deprived of his _ood to-day. It was exceedingly rare that a patient coughed then.

"There are many other affections associated with breathing, which can be stopped by the same mechanism that stops the heart's action. In spasm of the glottis, which is a terrible thing in children, as you well know, as it sometimes causes death, and also in whooping-cough, it is possible to afford relief by throwing cold water on the feet, or by tickling the soles of the feet, which produces laughter, and at the same time goes to the matter that is producing the spasm, and arrests it almost at once. I would not say that we can always prevent cough by our will; but in many instances those things are possible, and if you remember that in bronchitis and pneumonia, or any other acute affection of the lungs, hacking or coughing greatly increases the trouble at times, you can easily see how important it is for the patient to try to avoid coughing as best he can."

Evil Effect of Breathing Respired Air.—If we take back into our lungs that which has been expelled, we soon feel the effect. The muscles after a time become inactive, the blood stagnates, the heart acts slowly, the food is undigested, the brain is clogged. The constant breathing of even the slightly impure air of our houses cannot but tend to undermine the health. The blood is not purified, and is in a condition to receive the seeds of disease at any time. The system uninspired by the energizing oxygen is sensitive to cold. The pale cheek, the lusterless eye, the languid step, speak too plainly of oxygen starvation.

In such a soil catarrh, scrofula, pneumonia and consumption run riot. Black, in his "Ten Laws of Health," says, "The lack of what is so abundant, and so cheap—good, pure air—is unquestionably the one great cause of pulmonary consumption."

The foul air which passes off from the lungs and the pores of the skin does not fall to the floor, but diffuses itself through the surrounding atmosphere. A single breath will to a trifling extent taint the air of a whole room.

The Air in Rooms Vitiated by Lighted Fires.—It is estimated that a light or a fire will vitiate as much air as a dozen persons. Carbonic oxide gas, a product of combustion more deadly than carbonic acid gas, leaks out from a stove through the pores of the hot iron, and, besides the air which it draws from the room, it actually poisons that which we breathe. Many breaths and lights rapidly unfit the air of a room for use.

Impure Air in Small Rooms and Tenement Houses.—Small, ill ventilated sleeping rooms, in which re-heated air is ever present, are nurseries of consumption, and an eminent physician says that this disease could as effectually be guarded against by proper attention to ventilation, as small pox by vaccination. To a lack of pure air may be attributed the existence of nearly all the prevalent diseases classed under the head of scrofulous diseases. Some physicians attribute the prevalence of intemperance among the lower classes to the effect of bad ventilation in the crowded tenements, which produces a degree of lethargy sufficient to drive them to the rum shop for stimulants.

How to Ventilate Houses.—Every sleeping apartment should have a fire-place with an open chimney, and in cold weather it is well if the grate contains a small fire, enough to create a current and carry the vitiated air out of the room. In such cases, however, it is necessary to see that the air drawn into the room comes in from the outside of the house. Summer or winter, it is well to have a free ingress for pure air. The aim must be to purify the air without causing a great fall of temperature. To accomplish this, the windows may be drawn down an inch or two from the top, and a fold of muslin placed over the aperture to prevent draught.*

Where the body is kept warm and pure air only inhaled, there is no more danger of taking cold in sleeping directly between two windows all the year round than there is of taking cold in riding in an open sleigh when thoroughly warmed by wrappings of furs and robes; and such a thing as taking cold under such conditions never occurs, providing, always, the thorough warming of the feet and back, which are often neglected.

Air in Sick Rooms.—Fresh air is one of the most important and difficult things to obtain and retain in a sick room. The following simple arrangement will remedy the evil of foul gas, generated by burning a kerosene lamp all night in a nursery or sick room:—

Take a raisin-box or any other suitably sized box that will contain the lamp when set up on end. Place the lamp in the box, outside the window, with the open side facing the room. When there are blinds, the box can be attached to each by leaving them a little open, and fastening with a cord; or the lamp box can be nailed to the window casing in a permanent manner. The lamp burns quite as well outside, and a decided improvement of the air in the room is experienced.

Bad Air in School and Lecture Rooms.—Our school rooms, heated by furnaces or red hot stoves, often have no means of ventilation, or, if provided, these are seldom used. Pupils starved by scanty lung food (and we might add brain food) are stupefied by foul air, and are listless and dull. This proc-

---

* Dr. August Smith gives a good rule for ascertaining the amount of carbonic acid in the air of a house:—

"Let us keep our rooms so that the air does not give a precipitate when a ten and half ounce bottleful is shaken with half an ounce of clean lime-water"—a sanitary regulation which can easily be carried out.

ess goes on from year to year, and the weakened and poisoned body at last succumbs to disease, and a "mysterious Providence" is charged with sickness and death. The voice of nature, as well as nature's God, cries aloud, "Do thyself no harm!" Those who violate the God-given laws of life and health may expect the penalty. Whatsoever we sow we shall inevitably reap. If we sow the seeds of disease, we must reap sickness and death. To breathe the atmosphere of many school houses, lecture rooms, and theaters, is to breathe the atmosphere of death.

Teachers and Bad Air.—With the vile atmosphere of the school room constantly pouring over the lining membranes of the nasal cavities, surging about the linings of the throat and vocal organs, driving down the bronchial tubes, and deluging the lungs, what wonder the teacher first suffers from vitiated blood, then from clogged membranes, and lastly from catarrh, bronchitis, dyspepsia, and perhaps pulmonary consumption! It is next to impossible that the more nervous constitutions should not succumb.

Foul Air in Churches.—We sit in our churches, from which the air and light of heaven have been excluded six days out of seven, and, though ventilated as well as heated for the seventh, we bewail our listlessness and want of interest in the life-giving Gospel, and we charge it either to the preacher or to our own depravity, when the fact is, no temporary ventilation can take from the carbonic-impregnated crypts and walls the depravity which has there fixed its abode. The foul air left by the congregation on Sunday is often shut up during the week and heated for the next Lord's day, when the people assemble, to be re-breathed as polluted atmosphere.

How to Remove the "Foul Air" Evil from Churches.—The best time to change the air in the churches is immediately after the congregation has departed. When the services for the day are concluded, and while the audience room is still warm, if the windows and doors are left open for a short time the cooler air of out-doors will rapidly displace that which has been breathed over and over again by the throng of worshipers. A better arrangement would be to so provide for ventilation in the structure of the church that the foul air shall be constantly passing out and fresh air shall be constantly supplied; but in the absence of such an arrangement the sexton or janitor should, in the way here suggested, thoroughly ventilate the church edifice after each service. If the intervals between the services are long, it may be well, also, to rechange the air a short time before the succeeding service.

Bad Air vs. Religion.—An old number of the *Educational Monthly* makes some suggestive hints under this caption, which we quote: "Many a farmer and housekeeper wonders why it is that they must needs take a nap every Sunday in sermon-time. When the parson gets comfortably into the second or third head of his discourse, and his congregation have settled into the easiest position to listen, gentle sleep begins to steal over their faculties, and the good man is surprised at finding his argument less cogent than it seemed when prepared in the solitude of his study. At home the busy matron never thinks of napping at eleven o'clock in the morning, and the man of business would consider his sanity or common sense sadly called in question should a friend propose a half-hour's nap at that hour of the day. Nevertheless, they both sleep like kittens in their pews, and logic, rhetoric, eloquence, are alike wasted in the vain attempt to rouse their sluggish souls. The question of the poet, so often sung in our assemblies,

"'My drowsy powers, why sleep ye so?'"

is exactly in point, and we propose as an answer, 'Because we are all breathing carbonic acid gas—deadly poison; because the sexton did not let the foul air of last Sunday's congregation out of the doors and windows, and the fresh, pure air of heaven in.'

"Look round at the audience; that feverish flush on the face isn't heat, it is poison. The lady nodding over there, her nose and cheeks like a scarlet rose, is not too warm, for the thermometer doesn't stand over 70 degrees; she is partially suffocated; what she wants is fresh air. That hard-working mechanic or farmer doesn't sleep because he watched with a sick child last night, but simply for want of oxygen to keep the flame of intellectual and physical activity brightly burning.

"Nobody can rise on wings of faith in a poisonous atmosphere. Oxygen and religion cannot be separated in this unrighteous manner. We cannot live in conformity to spiritual laws while in open violation of the physical.

"Is your sexton a man of intelligence sufficient to understand the necessity and reason of ample ventilation? Does he know that every human being vitiates, at the least estimate, four cubic feet of air every minute? Linger when the congregation leaves, and see if he shuts every door and window tight to keep in all the heat till evening service. Then see how thin the lamps burn in the vitiated air; how hard the minister tries to raise himself and his listeners to the height of some great argument, and how stupid they are—nothing but bad air.

"Now for the remedy, which costs labor and money both, for ventilation is a question of dollars and cents. Saturday the sexton should be instructed to open all the doors and windows; to let out all the dead and foul air, and let in such as is fresh. It takes no more coal on Sunday morning to heat the church to 70 degrees because of this purification. Sunday noon let the openings of the church be again thrown wide—warmth and bad air will alike disappear, and though extra coal may be required to raise the temperature, the minister will preach so much better in consequence, and the hearers will listen with such increased relish to the sacred word, that the loss of the pocket will be infinitely compensated by the gain of the soul."

Night Air Healthy.—Many are afraid of night air. Florence Nightingale replies to this objection by asking, "What can we breathe at night except night air?" Her rule is to keep the air within as pure as that without the house. Don't be afraid to sleep by an open window. It is a common fallacy that cold air is necessarily pure, and that apartments need less ventilation in winter than in summer. Coolness does not always indicate freshness, and disagreeable warmth does not indicate chemical impurity. Draughts are pernicious in their effects, and must be avoided. In sleeping in an unavoidable draught, turn the face to meet it.

Water as a Purifier.—A pan of water standing in an inhabited room becomes utterly filthy and unfit for drink in a few hours. This depends on the fact that the water has the faculty of condensing, and thereby absorbing, all the gases, which it does without increasing its own bulk. The colder the water is, the greater its capacity to contain these gases. The "breathed" atmosphere of the room is, therefore, improved by the water, if often changed, and proves a good purifier.

Sea Air.—Sea air, as a rule, is beneficial to health. This is shown by the fact that the average life among seamen is larger than among those of most vocations on land. The occupations of the former are such that, were it not for the healthfulness of the sea air, their lives would probably be shorter than those of the latter. The sea air is appetizing, and bracing to the general system.

Air at the Seaside.—Physicians who have traveled widely and investigated the subject thoroughly arrive at the conclusion that the healthfulness of seaside resorts is owing more to the fact that those who go to such places are in the habit of spending much time in the open air, than to any special property the localities may possess. In short, if in all sections the people were in the habit of being in the open air, their general health would be greatly improved.

Are Winds Healthful?—Stagnation in the air or water is always harmful. The wind expels the stagnant air, and introduces fresh. Railway trains or street cars passing rapidly and frequently by a dwelling stir up the atmosphere, and in this respect render important service. It often occurs that in localities where fevers prevail those persons who reside close to a railway escape the disease. The writer knew a case in an eastern town where nearly every household suffered except those by the track of frequently passing cars.

The prevailing direction of the wind each month of the year is as follows: In January, north-westerly; in February, north-westerly; in March, north-westerly; in April, northerly; in May, southerly; in June, south-westerly; in July, westerly; in August, south-westerly, (easterly as often;) in September, easterly; in October, south-westerly; in November, northerly; in December, north-westerly.

Dampness of the Air and Health.—Dry air as a rule is healthier than damp or humid air. Hence if rains continue long, or if fogs prevail for several days, the system suffers by the increased saturation. While oxygen and nitrogen and pure air itself are almost entirely diathermous, the absorptive power of moisture is very great. It seems that a molecule of aqueous vapor has sixteen thousand times the absorptive power of an atom of oxygen or of nitrogen; and carbonic acid, marsh gas, ammonia, etc., are also extremely absorptive. Now, when the sun shines on an atmosphere that is dry, his rays pass through it in all their power, but when the air is damp the rays are much weakened before they reach the earth. On the other hand, when the air is dry, the heat from the earth radiates into space much faste than when it is moist. The importance of these facts from a medical stand-point is very great. All the agents just mentioned as powerful absorbents of heat are found in greatest abundance near the earth; consequently they absorb a large amount of the heat radiated from the earth, which, it must be borne in mind, is the chief source of the heat diffused in the atmosphere. Usually over ten per cent. of the heat from this source is absorbed within ten feet of the ground.

On the northern Atlantic coast the south and east winds are, as a rule, moist winds; next come the northerly; next the south-west; next the west; next the north; and last the north-west. The sudden veering of a wind from a southerly to a northerly wind is usually attended with a precipitation of moisture; and the same is true of a sudden change of a northerly to an easterly.

Sea and Mountain Air Compared.—An able Italian physician, Dr. C. Alberto, in a recent work says: "The marine air produces the same benefit as that of the mountain, but each has a different *modus efficiendi ;* the former acts more forcibly and energetically on the constitution which retains some robustness and internal resources to profit by it, while the second acts more gently, with slower efficacy, being thereby more suitable to the weaker, and less excitable organizations. From this important distinction, the conscientious physician who takes the safety of his patient much to heart, ought to be able to discriminate whether the alpine or the marine atmosphere is the better suited to the case he has before him."

Mutual Diffusion of Air.—The physical law known as that of "mutual diffusion" plays an important part in all questions relating to the mixture of different gases, such as of oxygen, nitrogen, and carbonic acid, which make up our atmosphere. By virtue of this law it occurs that two gases when brought together, no matter what their relative weights, become thoroughly mixed together, in proportions which are stated as being inversely as the square roots of their densities.

Carbonic acid is a gas so heavy that it may be decanted from one vessel into another; and hydrogen is so light that a balloon filled with it ascends, as we all know, into the air. Yet if a vessel filled with the latter be inverted over one containing the former, and a piece of membrane be placed between the mouths of the two, it will be found that, after a while, some of the carbonic acid has ascended into the upper vessel, and the hydrogen has descended in the lower one, and mingled with the carbonic acid. A mixture will be thus formed in both vessels.

It is the same in nature. Animals are perpetually exhaling carbonic acid into the atmosphere, and were it not for this wonderful property of "diffusion" a stratum of foul air would lie over the earth, and would possibly extinguish animal existence. The great value of connecting the air of our rooms with the free and purer air outside is, therefore, apparent.

Our Great Enemies, the Marshes.—M. Lombard, of Geneva, shows, from a great collection of statistical documents, that winter and spring are the seasons of greatest mortality in the north and center of Europe. In the south, on the contrary, summer and autumn are the most destructive seasons; but marsh miasm where it exists, transforms the period and character of the mortality. The same influence, as M. Simmoneau has shown, is the great obstruction to the acclimatization of Europeans in hot climates. It is to the perfect drainage of the soil that our efforts must be directed in both cases.

DISINFECTANTS—HOW TO PREPARE AND USE THEM.

Fresh Air and Sunlight.—First and always let in fresh air and sunlight, that they may purify every place they can reach. Open and dry all cellars and vaults, and keep the grounds and surfaces about dwellings as dry and clean as possible. Sedulously cultivate habits of the strictest cleanliness in person, clothing and habitation, indoor and out; as well in the cellar as in the parlor; as well in the darkest closet as in the hall; not neglecting a corner or a crevice in the whole building, keeping an eye to one point always, that wherever there is dampness there is disease, and that moral purity and filth in any form are absolutely incompatible.

Water.—We have already seen the value of water as an absorbent and disinfectant. Dishes of water may be placed in any place required. Care should be used to remove the water frequently. Cold water is better than warm for this purpose. A pailful of water in a freshly-painted room will often remove the sickening odor of the paint. Try it.

Charcoal.—Powdered charcoal is one of the best of disinfectants. It is very prompt in absorbing affluvia and gaseous bodies, as well as rendering harmless and even useful those bodies which are easily changed. Charcoal powder has long been used as a filter for putrid water. When the impurities are absorbed they come in contact with condensed oxygen gas, which exists in the pores of all charcoal which has been exposed to the air, and in this way become oxidized and destroyed. A layer of pulverized charcoal will prevent the escape of all offensive odor from any decomposing substance.

Charcoal and Lime.—These may be mixed with notable advantage in many cases. This compound is known in the shops as "Calx powder." It is useful in absorbing putrid gases. Use it dry and fresh.

Clay.—For many purposes dry clay is not only the cheapest but the best deodorant. It *destroys* or *absorbs* the foul odors, instead of partially overcoming them by substituting chlorine or coal tar in their place. The presence of clay has a great influence upon the health of communities. There are oftener cases of typhoid fever and dysentery on a sandy or alluvial soil than on a clay soil. This is probably owing to the fact that the water used is made pure by filtering through the clay soil, while in passing through sandy soil it retains to some extent its impurities, or adds to them.*

Quicklime and Gypsum.—*Quicklime* and *gypsum* or *land-plaster* are good absorbents, and may be used advantageously in damp places, cellars, gutters, etc. They should not, however, be used in drains, catch-basins, sewers, soil-pipes, etc.; nor where they are liable to be washed into such places, lest they, by decomposing soap-water, form lime-soap, and obstruct the passages.

Sifted Ashes are very useful in country water-closets, where they may be scattered as often as any odor is perceptible.

Surface Soil.—Any surface soil or mold pulverized forms a convenient and effective absorbent and deodorizer for use in out-houses. The fresh dug earth is the best. It should be used in the same manner as above noted in the case of clay.

Fresh Stone-lime.—To absorb moisture and putrid fluids use fresh stone-lime finely broken; sprinkle it on the place to be dried, and in damp rooms place a number of plates or pans filled with the lime powder.

Copperas.—Common copperas, called sulphate of iron, in its crude state

---

* There is another advantage in the country in using clay for privies. The removal of the contents is no longer a disgusting operation, while the farmer or gardener has a valuable supply of fertilizing material for his grounds.

can be purchased for five cents a pound; this, dissolved in two gallons of water, and thrown over ill-smelling places, is one of the cheapest, simplest, and most convenient deodorizers, and is applicable to privies, sinks, gutters, and heaps of offal.

Chloride of Lime.—To give off chlorine, to absorb putrid effluvia, and to stop putrefaction, use chloride of lime; and if in cellars or close rooms the chlorine gas is wanted, pour strong vinegar or diluted sulphuric acid upon plates of chloride of lime occasionally, and add more of the chloride. We have known a large manufactory filled with deadly sewage air cleansed in a single half hour by throwing a half bushel of chloride of lime into the vaults from which the poisonous gas emanated. Chloride of lime is often deleterious in close dwellings because of the chlorine evolved. It may be used safely in the open atmosphere.

Salt and Lime Paste.—A cheap and available disinfectant and deodorizer is made by dissolving a bushel of salt in a barrel of water; then adding enough unslacked, that is, fresh lime, which has never been exposed to dampness, to make the whole into a thin paste, to be applied as often as necessary to all places yielding offensive smells, such as gutters, sinks, cesspools, etc. This is home-made chloride of lime.

Carbolic Acid.—A weak solution of carbolic acid may be used in saucers, or shallow earthen dishes; or a cloth saturated with it may be hung in the room where the offensive odor is suspected. In large cities the streets in the most densely populated wards have been watered on alternate days with a weak solution of carbolic acid with excellent results. There is no doubt that this excellent antiseptic and disinfectant has been very beneficial. The inhabitants of those streets have often expressed satisfaction at the freshness and removal of disagreeable smells which this acid produces, and they regard it as an addition to their comfort.

Salt and Nitrate of Lead.—Dissolve half a dram of nitrate of lead in a pint of boiling water, and two drams of common salt in a pail of water; then mix the two solutions and allow the sediment to settle. A cloth dipped in the liquid and hung up in the apartment is all that is required to purify the most fetid atmosphere. It is recommended for its cheapness, a pound of the materials costing about twenty-five cents. One pound of nitrate of lead, dissolved in a pailful of water, is excellent for sinks, sink-drains and vaults.

"Disinfecting Mixture."—Common salt, three ounces; black manganese, oil of vitriol, of each one ounce; water, two ounces. Carry this mixture in a cup through the apartments of the sick.

General Disinfecting Compound.—For general disinfection the following compound is available and valuable, and far better than most of the patented

Disinfectants.

articles offered: Sulphate of iron, (copperas,) forty pounds; sulphate of lime, (gypsum or plaster,) fifty pounds; sulphate of zinc, (white vitriol,) seven pounds; powdered charcoal, two pounds. Mix well and scatter dry, or wet it in small quantities and make into balls ready for use. Where a liquid is needed, stir in water in the proportion of a pound of the powder or ball to a gallon of water, and sprinkle where needed.

Coffee as a Disinfectant.—Experiments with roasted coffee prove it to be a powerful means of rendering harmless and destroying animal and vegetable effluvia. A room in which meat in an advanced state of decomposition has been kept can be instantly deprived of all smell by simply carrying through it a coffee roaster containing a pound of newly-roasted coffee. The best mode of using the coffee is to dry the raw bean, pound it in a mortar; and then roast the powder on a moderately heated iron plate, until it becomes a dark brown color. Then sprinkle it in sinks and cesspools, or expose it on a plate in the room to be purified.

Sunflowers as Disinfectants.—Experiments in France and Holland have shown that sunflowers, when planted on an extensive scale, will neutralize the pernicious effects of exhalations from marshes. This plan has been tried with great success in the fenny districts near Rochefort, France; and the authorities of Holland assert that intermittent fever has wholly disappeared from districts where the sunflowers have been planted. It is not yet determined what effect the flower produces on the atmosphere—whether it generates oxygen, like other plants of rapid growth, or whether, like the *coniferæ*, it emits ozone, and thus destroys the organic germs of miasms that produce fever.

Boiling for Infected Clothing.—When foul clothing or infected things can be boiled, or have a boiling heat steadily applied and kept up for an hour, this is one of the simplest and best modes of disinfection. But until such high heat is actually applied to the infected things, some one of the disinfecting solutions must be used. A common steam tub, in a laundry or elsewhere, with a tight cover, is a good disinfecting vat. The clothing must be thrown into the water at boiling heat, and that temperature should be kept up for an hour.

Soaking for Foul Clothing.—Soiled, impure garments may be put to soak in a half pound of sulphate of zinc (white vitriol) to three gallons of water. It will not stain or discolor most fabrics. One ounce of chloride of lead dissolved in a pint of hot water, and then a pailful of water added, into which a handful of common salt has been thrown, serves a similar purpose; also a half ounce of permanganate of potash to a gallon of water.

Boiling after Disinfection.—Permanganate of potassa may be used in disinfecting clothing and towels from cholera and fever patients during the night, or when such articles cannot be instantly boiled. Throw the soiled articles immediately into a tub of water, in which there has been dissolved an ounce of the permanganate salt to every three gallons of water. Boil the clothing as soon as it is removed from this colored solution.

Carbolic Acid for Clothing.—Carbolic acid, when used to disinfect clothing, should be of good quality, thoroughly mixed with its own quantity of strong vinegar, and next be dissolved in two hundred times its own quantity of water before the clothing is immersed in it. This mixture with vinegar insures such complete solution of the carbolic acid that the clothing will not be "burned" by undissolved drops of acid when disinfected in the carbolic water. This weak solution—1 part to 200—will not injure common clothing. But to destroy clothing as well as infection, instantly, use the acid diluted only 10 to 30 times its quantity of water. The disinfecting and antiseptic power of good carbolic acid is so great that 1 part to 50 or 100 parts of water is sufficient for ordinary purposes. For drains, sewers, foul heaps, stables, and privies, the cheap "dead oil" of coal tar, or the crude carbolic acid, answers every purpose when freely applied. Coal tar itself is available as a disinfectant to paint upon the walls of stables, privy vaults, and drains. By mixing with sawdust or dry lime, coal or crude acid may be used on foul grounds or heaps of refuse.

How to Fumigate Rooms.—To fumigate and cleanse the air of an apartment, there is no more simple way than to heat a common iron shovel quite hot, and pour vinegar slowly upon it. The steam arising from this process is pungent, and of a disinfectant character. Open windows and doors at the same time.

Another way is to fumigate with sulphurous acid, thus: Arrange to vacate the room for twelve hours. Close every window and aperture, and, upon an iron pipkin or kettle with legs, burn a few ounces of sulphur. Instantly after kindling it, every person must withdraw from the place, and the room must remain closed for the succeeding eight hours.

If any other kind of fumigation is resorted to, as that by chlorine, bromine, or nitrous acid, a sanitary officer or chemist should superintend the process. Fumigation should be resorted to in dwelling-houses only by official orders or permission, as the disinfecting gases are very poisonous.

To Disinfect Water-closets.—To disinfect a water-closet or a quantity of earth that is contaminated by cholera excrement, or liable to be infected, use solution of carbolic acid and copperas, mixed, as follows: To every cubic foot of soil or filth give from one to three pints of the strong solution. To every privy and water-closet allow at the rate of one pint, to be poured in daily at evening, for every person on the premises. This practice should be kept up while cholera is in the country. This method of systematic dis infection would be useful in every household; but when cholera is present in any city or country, such thorough application of this means of protection cannot be safely neglected in any city or place to which persons may come from towns where cholera is epidemic. The best sanitary chemists advise that the estimated quantity of these privy and sewer disinfectants required for each person daily, in the presence of cholera, should be half an ounce sulphate of iron, and half a dram or half a teaspoonful of carbolic acid.

To Disinfect Dead Bodies.—All chances of infection will be prevented and all effluvia destroyed from dead bodies by wrapping them in sheets saturated with a solution of carbolate of camphor.

Comparative Permanent Value of Different Disinfectants.—Owing to its cheapness, the impure sulphate of iron, ordinarily known as copperas, (*green vitriol*,) is the most available chemical disinfectant for sewage, outhouses, etc. The common mistake is in not using it in sufficient quantity. Its value does no rest, it must be remembered, upon theory only, but also upon experiment. In February, 1873, Albert Eckstein published an account of his attempts to disinfect an outhouse which was used daily by one hundred persons, and the results are so interesting that they are here transcribed:—

1. Two pounds of sulphate of iron in solution. After from two to three hours all bad smell had disappeared, but in twelve hours all the influence of the disinfectant was lost.

2. Sulphate of copper, (*blue vitriol*,) in solution, the same.

3. Two pounds of sulphate of iron in crystals; its effect lasted two days.

4. Sulphate of copper, the same.

5. Sulphurous acid in solution rapidly lost its effect, and was exceedingly irritating to the respiratory organs.

6. Two pounds of impure carbolic acid filled the house for two days with such a disagreeable smell, that it was impossible to tell whether the original odor was destroyed or covered up.

7. Two pounds of sulphate of iron in a parchment sack exerted a disinfecting influence for full three days, and when the parchment sack was drawn up it contained only some dirty, odorless fluid.

8. Two pounds of the best chloride of calcium in the parchment sack disinfected the outhouse for at least nine days.

In conclusion, to sum up the points·

1. It is useless to attempt to permanently disinfect the atmosphere, and, therefore, care should be exercised to destroy, as far as possible, the poison-germs so soon as they leave the body.

2. Copperas is the most available disinfectant for ordinary purposes; in certain cases, (chiefly for water-closets,) chloride of calcium is very good.

3. Carbolic acid, on account of its odor, is very disagreeable; further, it is not so efficient as some other substances. For the purpose of killing disease-germs, and for the purifying of cholera discharges, copperas in solution or powder is to be preferred.

Caution in Removing Foul Air from Wells.—It is well known that many accidents occur to persons going down into wells to clean them, owing to the noxious gas in such places. To remove the gas before descent is made in any well, a quantity of burned but unslaked lime should be thrown down. This, when it comes in contact with whatever water is below, sets free a great quantity of heat in the water and lime, which rushes upward, carrying all the deleterious gas with it, after which the descent may be made with perfect safety. The lime also absorbs carbonic acid in the well. Always lower a light before descending; if it is extinguished there is still danger of suffocation.

Precautions in Visiting Infected Rooms.—When the great philanthropist Howard was asked what precautions he used to preserve himself from infection in the prisons, hospitals, and dungeons which he visited, he responded with his pen as follows:—

"I here answer once for all that, next to the free goodness and mercy of the Author of my being, *temperance and cleanliness* are my preservatives.

"Trusting in Divine Providence, and believing myself in the way of duty, I visit the most noxious cells, and while thus employed *I fear no evil.*

"I never enter a hospital or prison before breakfast; and

"In an offensive room I seldom draw my breath deeply."

No better precautions than these need be given. The answer of Howard should be indelibly impressed on every memory.

Heat and Steam.—Heat has long been known as among the most efficient of disinfectants. And the use of steam, as a facile means of communicating it, against yellow fever especially, was effectually demonstrated as long ago as 1848. Since that time, in addition to the common use of steam for the disinfection of vessels, it has been extensively used for the disinfection of personal clothing and bedding, and to this end steam disinfecting chambers, abroad, at least, have long since ceased to be a novelty. The first one constructed in this country was in connection with the New York Quarantine hospitals, where it continues to be a prominent feature.

A New Disinfectant.—Dr. John Day, of Geelong, Australia, recommends for use in civil and military hospitals, and also for the purpose of destroying the poison germs of small-pox, scarlet fever, and other infectious diseases, a disinfectant, ingeniously composed of one part of rectified oil of turpentine and seven parts of benzine, with the addition of five drops of oil of verbena to each ounce. Its purifying and disinfecting properties are due to the power which is possessed by each of its ingredients of absorbing atmospheric oxygen, and converting it into peroxide of hydrogen—a highly-active oxidizing agent, and very similar in its nature to ozone. Articles of clothing, furniture, wall paper, carpeting, books, newspapers, letters, etc., may be perfectly saturated with it without receiving the slightest injury; and when it has been once freely applied to any rough or porous surface, its action will be persistent for an almost indefinite period. This may, at any time, be readily shown by pouring a few drops of a solution of iodide of potassium over the material which has been disinfected, when the peroxide of hydrogen which is being continually generated within it, will quickly liberate the iodine from its combination with the potassium, and give rise to dark brown stains.*

SUNLIGHT AND HEALTH.

Power of Sunlight.—Sunlight is one of the most powerful forces in nature, kindling the whole vegetable world into being, and making animal life possible by its extraordinary chemical agency.

Seclusion from Sunshine.—Seclusion from sunshine is one of the great misfortunes of our civilized life. The same cause which makes the potato vines white and sickly when grown in dark cellars, operates to produce the pale, sickly girls that are reared in our parlors. Expose either to the rays of the sun, and they begin to show color, health, and strength.

Philosophy of the Influence of Sunlight.—Recent discoveries seem to prove that there is conveyed to animals, by the direct action of the sun's rays, a subtle current of iron. It does not exist in light, or but very slightly, if at all, but it is a part of the sun's rays. Therefore, we must enjoy these rays if we would feel their full effect. This iron it is which is supposed to give color to plants and animals, and to impart strength and beauty. With strength and beauty come health and good spirits, and despondency and fear are banished.

Sunlight and Plants.—It is well known that no valuable plant can grow well without being visited by the direct rays of the sun; no plant can bear seed, no fruit can ripen without it. Any vine grown in the dark is white and strengthless. Grass, grain, and flowers do not thrive under the shadow of a tree.

Sunlight and Domestic Animals.—It is well known that no valuable domestic animals can thrive without being visited often by the sunshine. The fish of the Mammoth Cave are white; their eyes are not opened, because they

---

* British Medical Journal.

have never felt the glorious light; they are weak and imperfect, a kind of idiots, if fish are liable to that wretchedness.

Swine which are shut under the farmers' barns, and where every thing is favorable except the lack of sunshine, do not thrive as well as those which have the ordinary run in the open air.

Cows and horses stalled continuously in dark stables become feeble and unhealthy, and become useless in less than half the time of those which run in the open air, or whose stalls permit them to enjoy the influence of the sun light. The same is true of all other domestic animals.

Dr. Ellsworth, of Hartford, says: "Take a rabbit and shut him from the sunlight, and he will die of consumption in a few weeks. The tubercles will be just as perfectly formed in his lungs as in the human species, and the symptoms in every respect will be the same."

Sunlight and Human Life.—Sir James Wylie says that, "The cases of disease on the dark side of an extensive barrack at St. Petersburgh, have been uniformly, for many years, in the proportion of three to one to those on the side exposed to strong light."

Dr. Forbes Winslow in his volume entitled "Light, its Influence on Life and Health," uses the following language: "It may be enunciated as an indisputable fact, that all who live and pursue their calling in situations where the minimum of light is permitted to penetrate, suffer seriously in bodily and mental health. The total exclusion of the sunbeam induces the severer forms of chlorosis, green sickness, and other anæmic conditions depending upon an impoverished and disordered state of the blood. Under these circumstances the face assumes a death-like paleness, the membranes of the eyes become bloodless, and the skin shrunken and turned into a white, greasy, waxy color; also emaciation, muscular debility and degeneration, dropsical effusion, softening of the bones, general nervous excitability, morbid irritability of the heart, loss of appetite, tendency to syncope and hemorrhages, consumption, physical deformity, stunted growth, mental impairment, and premature old age. The offspring of those so unhappily trained are often deformed, weak, and puny, and are disposed to scrofulous affections."

Another Testimony.—"It is a well-established fact that, as the effect of isolation from the stimulus of light, the fibrine, albumen, and red blood-cells become diminished in quantity, and the serum or watery portion of the vital fluid augmented in volume, thus inducing a disease known to physicians and pathologists by the name of *lukæmia*, an affection in which white instead of red blood-cells are developed. This exclusion from the sun produces the sickly, flabby, pale, anæmaic condition of the face or exsanguined, ghost-like forms so often seen among those not exposed to air and light. The absence of these elements of health deteriorates by materially altering the physical composition of the blood, thus seriously prostrating the vital strength, enfeebling the nervous energy, and ultimately inducing organic changes in the structure of the heart, brain, and muscular tissue."—Dr. FORBES WINSLOW.

Sunlight and Miners.—The lack of pure light and pure air in mines tells seriously upon the health of miners. "Fourcault affirms that where life is prolonged to the average term, the evil effects of the want of light are seen in the stunted forms and general deterioration of the human race. It appears that the inhabitants of the arrondissement of Chimay, in Belgium, three thousand in number, are engaged partly as coal miners, and partly as field laborers. The latter are robust, and readily supply their proper number of recruits to the army; while among the miners it is in most years impossible to find a man who is not ineligible from bodily deformity or arrest of physical development."—FORBES WINSLOW'S *Influence of Light*.

Paralysis Cured by Sunshine.—One of the ablest lawyers in our country, writes a physician, a victim of long and hard brain labor, came to me a year ago suffering from partial paralysis. The right leg and hip were reduced in size, with constant pain in the loins. He was obliged, in coming upstairs, to lift up the left foot first, dragging the right foot after it. Pale, feeble, miserable, he told me he had been failing for several years, and closed with "My work is done. At sixty I find myself worn out." I directed him to lie down under a large window, and allow the sun to shine on every part of his body; at first ten minutes a day, increasing the time until he could expose himself to the direct rays of the sun for a full hour. His habits were not essentially altered in any other particular. In six months he came running upstairs like a vigorous man of forty, and declared, with sparkling eyes, "I have twenty years more of work in me."

Neuralgic, Rheumatic, and Hypochondriac Cures by Sunshine.—Writes the same physician quoted above: "I have assisted many dyspeptic, neuralgic, rheumatic, and hypochondriacal people into health by the sun cure. I have so many facts illustrating the wonderful power of the sun's direct rays in curing certain classes of invalids, that I have seriously thought of publishing a work to be denominated the 'Sun Cure.'"

Florence Nightingale on Sunlight.—"Who has not observed the purifying effect of light," says Florence Nightingale, "and especially of direct sunlight upon the air of a room? Go into a sick room where the shutters are always shut, (in a sick room or bed-chamber there should never be shutters shut,) and, though the room has never been polluted by the breathing of human beings, you will observe a close, musty smell of corrupt air, *i. e.*, unpurified by the effect of the sun's rays. The mustiness of dark rooms and corners, indeed, is proverbial. The cheerfulness of a room, the usefulness of light in treating disease, is all-important. 'Where there is sun there is thought.' All physiology goes to confirm this. Where is the shady side of deep valleys, there is cretinism. Where are cellars and the unsunned sides of narrow streets, there is the degeneracy and weakliness of the human race, mind and body equally degenerating. Put the pale, withering plant and human being into the sun, and if not too far gone, each will recover health and spirit."—NOTES ON NURSING.

Sunlight Shut Out by Parasols.—Many persons keep themselves pale and sickly by means of parasols, umbrellas, shaded rooms, and indoor life generally. Parasols should be dispensed with excepting in the hottest seasons. Sailors who are ever in the pure air and sunlight, and children who play much out of doors, generally present a ruddy, healthy appearance. The following severe cut on our American house-keepers, from an editorial of a Chicago daily, is well merited: "In this country there seems to be an implacable feud between people and the sun—the one striving vigorously and even fiercely to get into the houses, and the other striving just as fiercely and vigorously to keep him out. The average American house-keeper does not think she has fulfilled her whole duty until she has made the rounds of the whole household, shut all the doors, closed all the shutters, and drawn all the curtains on the east and south sides of the house. This is the morning's job. In the afternoon she makes the same grand round on the west side of the house. She is not quite happy and contented until the sun has gone down and darkness sets in. She is substantially aided in her raid against the sunlight by the heaviest of shades, curtains, and lambrequins. Thus the fight goes on day by day, and season by season. In summer she shuts out the sun because it is too hot. In winter she shuts it out because it will spoil her carpets. In spring and fall she has other reasons. She has reasons for all seasons. Thus she keeps the house in perpetual shade, in which the children grow up sickly, dwarfed, full of aches and pains, and finally have to be sent off into the country post-haste so that they may get into that very sunlight which they have been denied at home, and in which the country children run and are glorified."

The Sunlight and Blinds.—"I wish God had never permitted man to invent 'green blinds,'" said a thoughtful and brilliant woman. Why did she say it? Because she saw, wherever she went over our fair and sunshiny land, that green blinds were closely shut upon our comfortable houses, excluding the sun's light, which we may be sure God sends down for some blessed purpose. That blessed purpose is to promote growth, to give strength, to impart color, to gild with beauty, to inspire good thoughts, and to insure light hearts and cheerful faces."

Sunlight and Carpets.—"Do not be afraid of a little sunshine, either," wrote another excellent authority on healthful housekeeping. "It may ir crease your color, but a nut-like brownness is more becoming to a woman's face than the deathly whiteness of the lily. Sunshine is quite as good in its way as fresh air, and it should come into every room in the house. Does it fade the carpet? Then spread down a rug or a piece of drugget. A better way is to select colors that will not run away from the sunshine. For bedrooms Canton matting is good. It will not fade; it is easily swept; it will not hold dust readily, nor contract bad smells; it can be taken up and cleaned, and the floor washed every month if desired. I like painted floors, too, and, better still, I like the hard wood inlaid floors. Rugs may be placed where wanted to stand upon. It is said that the French very seldom carpet a whole house, and laugh at the idea as a New World notion. True, "French" is out of fashion now, but I take a good thing wherever I find it, put my own common sense to it, which I am obliged to do in order to make it serve me harmoniously, and then make the most of it."

Give the Children Sunshine.—Children need sunshine quite as much as flowers do. Half an hour is not enough. Several hours are required. The most beautiful flowers that ever studded a meadow could not be made half so beautiful without days and days of the glad light that streams through space. Light for children. Sunshine for the little elves that gladden this otherwise gloomy earth. Deal it out in generous fullness to them. Let the nursery be in the sunshine. Better plant roses on the dark side of an iceberg than rear babies and children in rooms and alleys stinted of the light that makes life.

"Yes, mothers," writes an intelligent friend from the country, "give your children the sunshine. You could not give them a gift which would cost you ess, nor yet one qualified to profit them more. It will make them what we in the country call tough and hardy. They require sunshine just as much as plants do. All scientific persons are now united in this decision. The world is full of delicate and weakly women, and, my word for it, more of the cause lies in an effort on our part to make 'fair' ladies of our daughters than in any thing else."

Sunlight in the School-Room.—Dr. Andrew Winter, in the *Pall Mall Gazette*, London, says: "When the St. Martin National School, leading out of Endell-street was built some years ago, we noticed with pleasure that a playground was built at the top of the school, where light and air was plentiful. The necessity of light for young children is not half appreciated. Many of the affections of children, and nearly all the cadaverous looks of those brought up in great cities, are ascribable to this deficiency of light and air. When we see the glass-rooms of the photographers in every street, high up on the top-most story, we grudge them in their application to a mere personal vanity. Why should not our nurseries be constructed in the same manner? If mothers knew the value of light to the skin in childhood, especially to the children of a scrofulous tendency, we should have plenty of these glass-house nurseries, where children may run about in a proper temperature, free of much of that clothing which at present seals up the skin—that great supplementary lung—to sunlight and oxygen."

The "Solaries" of the Ancients.—The ancients often had terraces, called *solaries*, built on the tops of their houses, where they were in the habit of taking their solar air baths. Pliny says that, for six hundred years Rome had no physicians. Using such natural methods of retaining or gaining physical power as vapor baths, manipulation, sunlight, exercise, etc., they became the mightiest of nations. By this remark I throw out no slur against true and wise physicians, who are a blessing to the community, but would call their attention more to nature's finer methods rather than to the use of so many drugs blisters, moxas, bleedings, leechings, and other violent processes which so weaken and destroy the beautiful temple of the human body.

Sunlight and Digestion—An Illustration.*—Very intimate relations exist between the sun and digestion. Digestion and assimilation becomes weak and imperfect if the man or animal is not daily exposed to the direct rays of the sun. Mr. P., one of our merchants, came to see me about his stomach. Dyspepsia was written all over his face, was shown in his movements, and heard in his voice. The conversation between us was essentially as follows:—

Mr. P. "Doctor, if you will excuse a street vulgarity, I am 'played out.' I can't digest, I can't work, I have lost my courage, I feel I must stop."

"Tell me about your diet."

"If you will excuse me, I know that is all right. I have studied the subject, and I know my food is all right."

"How about your exercise?"

"I have a little gymnasium in my store, and exercise an hour or two every day. I sometimes tire myself out with these exercises."

"How about your sleep?"

"Why, Doctor, I go to bed with the chickens. At any rate I am always in bed by nine o'clock, and I rise by six o'clock in the morning, take a bath, a plain breakfast, and go to my counting-room. Once in the forenoon, and once in the afternoon, I exercise in my gymnasium half an hour or so, but I am getting worse all the time. Isn't it curious?" My wife thinks I must have a cancer in the stomach. Nothing seems to help me. I live the most physiological life, but my digestion grows worse and worse."

"About your counting-room; is that light? is it sunny?"

"No, that is one nuisance we have in our store. The store is every way

---

* Narrated by Dr. Dio Lewis, in *Talks about People's Stomachs.*

pleasant, only that the counting-room is so dark, we have to use gas nearly all the time."

"That's it, Mr. P., that explains your cancer."

"Of course, you don't mean that; but I suppose it would be better if the counting-room was sunny."

"Why, Mr. P., no plant or animal can digest in the dark. Try it. Plant a potato in your cellar. Now watch it carefully. If there is a little light, that potato will sprout and try to grow. But surround it with the best manure, water it, do the best you can for it, only keep it in the dark, it cannot digest and grow. See how slender and pale it is. Now open a window in another part of the cellar, and notice how the poor hungry thing will stretch that way. Or give the stalk a little twist, and see how it will lie down. It has no strength to raise itself again. No matter how much of the best food and drink you give it, it can't digest. The process of digestion, the great function of assimilation, can't go on without the sunshine. Why, Sir, with your excellent habits, if your counting-room were in a flood of sunlight, you would be better in a week, and well in a month. Mr. P., did you ever go into the country late in the summer? Of course you have been. Well, did you never notice, where grain is growing in orchards, that the part under the trees is smaller than that outside and away from the trees? The land is actually richer there. For years the leaves have fallen and decayed, but notwithstanding this, the wheat is only half size, and never fills well. Now, what is the difficulty? The sun shines upon it more or less. Yes, that is true, but that under the trees does not receive as much sunshine as that away from them. That which is thus partly in the shade, can't digest so well. Why, Sir, if you will move your counting-room upstairs, in front, and stand where the sun can have a chance at you, even though it is only three or four hours a day, you will begin to digest your beef better within three days. Have you ever noticed that the only grapes that become perfectly ripe and sweet; that the only peaches that take on those beautiful red cheeks, and offer that luscious sweetness, are those that are on the outside, entirely uncovered by the leaves, and perfectly exposed to the sun? God's laws are the same in the animal world. It is just as true, the only girls with red cheeks and sweet breaths, the only girls who become fully ripe and sweet, are those who baptize themselves freely in God's glorious sunshine. Don't you see a good many pale girls in your store, girls with a bloodless, half-baked sort of face, whose walking, whose voice, whose whole expression, is devoid of spirit and force? Those girls are in the green state. Look at their lips and cheeks; they are not half ripe. Send them out in the country, let them throw away their parasols, put on their little jockey hats, and live out in the sunshine three months, and I would give more for one of them in any work requiring soul and spirit, than for a dozen of those pale things that live in the shade. A pale woman! She makes a very good ghost, but not much of a woman."

ILLUSTRATIONS OF THE HUMAN EYE.

The essential parts of the eye are inclosed in a tough outer coat, the sclerotic, to which the muscles moving it are attached, and which in front changes into the transparent cornea. A little way off the cornea the crystalline lens is suspended, dividing the eye into two unequal cavities; a smaller one in front, filled with a watery fluid, the aqueous humor. The sclerotic is lined with a highly pigmented membrane, the choroid, and this in turn is lined in the back half of the eyeball with the nearly transparent retina, in which the fibers of the optic nerve ramify. The choroid in front is continuous with the iris, which has a contractile opening in the center, the

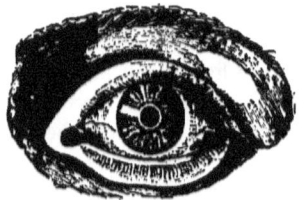

THE EYE.

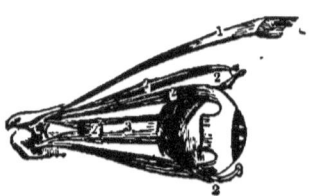

MUSCLES OF THE EYE-BALL.—1. Muscle of the upper lid. 2. Muscles of the ball. 3. Optic nerve.

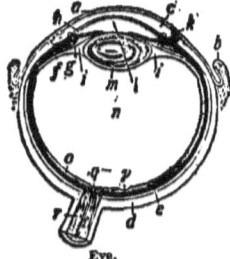

Eye.

HORIZONTAL SECTION OF RIGHT HUMAN EYE-BALL, SEEN FROM ABOVE.—a, b, Conjunctiva; c, Cornea; d, Sclerotic; e, Choroid; f, Ciliary Muscle; g, Ciliary Process; h, Iris; i, Suspensory Ligament; k, Posterior Aqueous Chamber between h and i; l, Anterior Aqueous Chamber; m, Crystalline Lens; n, Vitreous Humor; o, Retina; p, Yellow Spot; q, Center of Blind Spot; r, Artery of Retina in the center of the Optic Nerve.

pupil, admitting light to the lens which brings the rays to the focus and forms an image upon the retina, which light, falling upon delicate structures called rods and cones, causes them to stimulate the fibers of the optic nerve to transmit visual impressions to the brain.

How We See.—The eye is like the camera with which a photographer takes pictures. The lens is like the glass lens in the end of the tube. The lining of the cavity of the eyeball is colored dark, like the inside of the box of the camera. The retina is like the sensitive plate which the photographer puts in just before he takes the picture. The brain behind the eye is represented by the photographer himself looking through from behind his instrument.

When we look at an object a picture of it is made on the retina. This picture can be seen by a skillful observer looking into the eye with an instrument called an ophthalmoscope. It may be seen by looking from behind through an eye taken from an animal just killed, as the photographer looks through his camera.

The retina, which is the ending of the optic nerve, carries in to the brain the impression which makes the picture. It is not the eye that sees. If the optic nerve is cut off we do not see, although a picture will still be formed on the retina as before. It is the brain that sees. The eye is its instrument.

Causes of Trouble in the Eye.—The eye is sometimes weak, and gets very tired and sore by use, simply because the whole body is weak. But generally when there is redness, swelling, or pain in the eye, there is something wrong in itself. It may be that the delicate lining of the lids, the conjunction, is inflamed, just as the lining of the throat is inflamed at times. The lids then feel rough, as if there were sand under them.

Too Long Sight.—One of the commonest causes of aching eyes and head, after reading, is too long sight. When we look at a near object the shape of the lens is changed a little by an effort of the eye. Too long-sighted eyes have to make more effort to do this than eyes with natural sight. The strain tires and irritates them, and may make them very weak. This trouble can be entirely relieved by glasses.

Too Short Sight.—Short-sighted persons do not commonly have aching and inflamed eyes. Their eyes do not have to make the effort that those of long-sighted people do to see near objects. Reading does not tire them. But short-sightedness is liable to increase. It makes the vision of every thing more than a few feet away indistinct. It may be remedied by glasses, but they are an inconvenient necessity.

Too short sight is very common among students. It is found that when children begin to go to school few of them are short-sighted. In each higher class there are more short-sighted pupils, and the number increases so fast that we infer that there is something in the habits of school-children that makes them short-sighted.

Causes of Too Short Sight.—If we inquire what this cause of short sight is, we find that it is not any one thing, but many things. Every thing that tires and strains the eyes of school children tends to make them short-sighted. Causes of short sight are: 1. Too much use of the eyes. 2. Bad light. 3. Wrong position when reading.

Functions of the Iris.—The iris constitutes a diaphragm which regulates the amount of light entering the eyeball. The aperture in the center, the pupil, may be dilated by contraction of a system of radiating fibers of involuntary muscle, or contracted by the action of another system of fibers forming a sphincter at the margin of the pupil. The radiating fibers are controlled by the sympathetic, while those of the circular set are excited by the third cranial nerve. The variations in diameter of the pupil are determined by the greater or less intensity of the light acting on the retina. A strong light causes contraction of the pupil; with light of less intensity the pupil dilates. In the human being, a strong light acting on one eye will often cause contraction of the pupils of both eyes.

The pupil contracts under the influence: (1) Of an increased intensity of light; (2) of the effort of accommodation for near objects; (3) of a strong convergence of the two eyes and (4) of such active substances as nicotine, morphia, and physostigmine. It dilates under the influence: (1) Of a diminished intensity of light; (2) of vision of distant objects; (3) of a strong excitation of any sensory nerve; (4) of dyspnœa; and (5) of such substances as atropine and hyoscyamine. The chief function of the iris is to so moderate the amount of light entering the eye as to secure sharpness of definition of the retinal image. This it accomplishes by diminishing the amount of light reflected from near objects; by cutting off the more divergent rays and admitting only those approaching a parallel direction, which, in a normal eye, are focused on the retina.

CARE OF THE EYES.

The eye is one of the most delicate and sensitive organs of the human body. It is most closely connected with the brain, and with the general system of civilization. It shares with the brain in all the various conditions of nervous excitement or depression, labor or repose. It is affected by all the obstructions and irregularities of the general circulation, and suffers, therefore, from any injury or lack in the general health.

Strange Neglect of the Eyes. It is a remarkable fact that this organ is more neglected than any other. "I have known," says a recent writer," [*] "fond and doting mothers take their children of four and five years of age to have their first teeth filled, instead of having them extracted, so that the jaw might not suffer in its due development, and become in later years contracted, while the eye, the most intellectual, the most apprehensive, and the most discriminating of all our organs, receives not even a passing thought, much less an

---

[*] Harper's Magazine, 1879.

examination. It never seems to occur to the parents that the principal agent in a child's education is the eye; that through it it gains not only its sense of the methods and ways of existence of others, but even the means for the maintainance of its own; nor does it occur to the parents for an instant that many of the mental as well as bodily attributes of a growing child are fashioned, even if they are not created, by the condition of the eye alone A child is put to school without the slightest inquiry on the part of the parent, and much less on the part of the teacher, whether it has the normal amount of sight; whether it sees objects sharply and well defined or indistinctly and distorted; whether it be near-sighted or far-sighted; whether it sees with one or two eyes; or, finally, if it does see clearly and distinctly, whether it is not using a quantity of nervous force sufficient after a time not only to exhaust the energy of the visual organ, but of the nervous system at large."

How the Eye is Kept Clean.—For us to be able to see objects clearly and distinctly, it is necessary that the eye should be kept clean. For this purpose it is furnished with a little gland, from which flows a watery fluid, (tears,) which is spread over the eye by the lid, and it is afterward swept off by it, and runs through a hole in the bone to the under surface of the nose, while the warm air, passing over it while breathing, evaporates it. It is remarkable that no such gland can be found in the eyes of fish, as the element in which they live answers the same purpose. If the eye had not been furnished with a liquid to wash it, and a lid to sweep it off, things would appear as they do when you look through a dusty glass.

How the Eye is Protected from Irritation.—All along the edges of the eyelids there is a great number of little tubes or glands, from which flow an oily substance which spreads over the surface of the skin, and thus prevents the edges from being sore or irritated, and it also helps to keep tears within the lid. There are also six little muscles attached to the eye, which enable us to move it in every direction; and when we consider the different motions they are capable of giving to the eye, we cannot but admire the goodness of Him who formed them, and thus saved us the trouble of turning our heads every time we wish to view an object.

How to Improve the Eyelashes.—If the eyelashes be irregular or short, they can be lengthened by simply clipping the split ends once a month. Ladies in Oriental lands often resort to this method with invariable success.

Over-straining the Eyes.—This is done by trying to read or work with partial or imperfect light. How common is our habit of using the eyes in the evening twilight and just before "lighting up." We desire to complete some work, as writing, reading, or sewing, by daylight, and so exert ourselves with insufficient light. Every family should carefully guard against this. So also care should be used that there shall be sufficient light after nightfall

When needed for the comfort or convenience of the eyes, another candle, lamp, or gas-burner must be lighted. The extra cost to the person will be more than saved in the preservation of the sight.

Eye-strain Sometimes the Cause of Headache.—Recent experiments show what the earlier physicians suspected, but could not demonstrate, that very troublesome headaches are sometimes the immediate result of straining the eyes. In order to test such cases, Dr. Wm. Thomson (*Am. Journal of Medical Science*, 1870) recommends the use of "test disks." The simplest and most convenient one, that described by Dr. Mitchell as a piece of closely-perforated Bristol-board or card, may be made to answer as a qualitative test. If we pierce in a card, close together, half a dozen pin holes, and view with one eye through these a tip of gas-jet or a small candle flame at least fifteen feet distant, if there be myopia or hypermatropia, the patient will see a number of points of light, while the perfect, normal eye will see but one. If the disordered eye be astigmatic, the multiplied images will be spread out laterally, if the defect be in the horizontal meridian, or will be at right angles to this if it be in the perpendicular meridian. Physicians out of reach of the resources of the great cities will find Dr. Thomson's test disks well worth learning to use. Without it or more complex means no one can feel sure that in any case of headache the cause may not be in the organs of vision. If found there, its treatment will be at once suggested.

Danger of Too-Continuous Use.—Even when the light is abundant, the eye often wearies after continuous use for a few hours. Especially is this true after some physical debility. When such weariness arises work should be stopped for a time. A brief rest of the eyes *will* generally bring relief, and permit a renewal of the work without danger. It may be well to close the eyes for a little while, or to walk out and use the eyes on distant objects, or else so change the work in-doors for a little time as to lessen the fatigue.

Proper Distance of the Object.—Great care should be used in holding the object at a proper distance from the eye. Generally, persons have the bad habit of lowering the head to the object. In most cases 12 inches should be the *least* and about 20 inches the maximum distance for the book or work from the eye, in ordinary cases. Seats ought always to be so adjusted to the height of tables or desks, that it shall not be necessary for persons to stoop over into a "round-shouldered" position in order to work or to read or write.

Proper Quantity of Light.—It is well known that we cannot look at the sun with impunity. Even luminous objects, far less brilliant than the sun, cause a painful sensation when their rays strike directly upon the eye. The more uniformly the light is dispersed and the less directly its rays penetrate the eye, the more beneficial is its action. The uniformly-dispersed daylight serves as the best example. Every violent and sudden contrast between light and darkness is disagreeable, and becomes injurious if frequently repeated. Flickering light is likewise unpleasant and fatiguing. The simultaneous action of luminous contrasts is also harmful. Such contrasts are produced when a bright light is covered by a dark shade. The small space lighted is intensified by the broad dark zone of shadow around it; and under the influence of such contrary states of illumination, the eyes are strained and so tire easily. A shade of ground glass or porcelain, covering the flame and causing a somewhat subdued but uniform illumination, is far preferable to a dark shade. In these materials we possess a powerful means of softening the dazzling light by dispersion of its rays.

Best Direction of the Light.—The best authorities assure us that "skylight," or light from above, is the best light for all work not requiring a bent position of the head, and, therefore, deserves a far more general application in the construction of factories, work-shops, schools, and other buildings, or in the methods of artificial illumination. In writing or similar handwork the work should strike from the left side, in order to avoid the shadow cast by the right hand; and in all cases it is far better that the light should come from above than from below. For this reason, those window-shades that raise and lower from the bottom, are preferable to the ordinary ones that are rolled at the top, or to the window-awnings that shut out the light of the sky, and admit it only from below. It is, therefore, important that parents and teachers in schools should also see to it that pupils do not study with the direct rays of the sunshine falling on the book, or desk, or floor, and that they do not, on the other hand, sit directly facing low windows, as the eyes become dazzled by either of these errors and injury may result.

The Use of Colored Glasses.—When there is perceived any great sensitiveness of the eyes toward very bright or excessive light, toward white and reflecting objects of work, or toward the reflection of the sun-light from snow and other white surfaces, the use of spectacles with plain light-blue or gray (so-called London smoke) glasses is generally safe and a great relief and protection; as it softens the painful brilliancy, without interfering with ready sight. Blue veils, to some extent, answer the same purpose as blue glasses.

Relieving Near and Far-sightedness.—Near-sightedness is remedied by wearing concave glasses, and far-sightedness by convex glasses. Some think that by manipulation of the eyes, such as pressing them if too convex, and rubbing them up from the corners if too concave, will remedy the effect, but all this action is not only useless, but also injurious. For the kind of glasses consult an optician, and for any defect or disease of the eyes, consult an oculist. The eye is too delicate an organ to be treated except by a skillful physician.

Changing Sight not a Cause for Alarm.—As a rule the sight begins to fail about the fortieth year. The first sign is a disposition to hold things at a distance to see them well, as in reading. The circumstance may alarm a man, who may hastily infer that disease is surely upon him. Eyes are sometimes put out by false notions with regard to this condition of the sight. Resort is had to artificial helps, as globes, manipulations, eye-washes, and perhaps salves. In the first place, the reader should ascertain whether his age is not the natural cause. He should then procure an eye-glass adapted to his sight in such a way that he can see easily and readily what he could not before.

Use Glasses as Soon as Needed.—The opinion prevailing with some that the early use of glasses is harmful "in the end," is erroneous. When eye-glasses will improve the sight, they should be worn; any delay will be liable to injure the eyes by straining their already impaired power. Nearly all persons should use glasses to read with as soon as they begin to hold a book more than eight inches from the eyes.

Double Glasses sometimes Useful.—A New York optician has succeeded in helping eyesight which requires a very short focus. This he does by putting together two plane-convex lenses with their convex sights toward each other.

Squinting and its Remedy.—This painful affection of the eyes generally appears about the fifth year, though sometimes as late as the eighteenth. The former of these ages points to the methodical employment of the eyes upon near work, as in learning to read, etc. There are times in all cases of strabismus (squinting) when it is only observable during near vision; and the squint alternates, as sometimes one eye is used, sometimes the other; or one may be used for near, the other for distant sight. And soon the patient gets into the habit of using one eye only, and the one disused becomes less and less sensitive to the rays of light, until it is nearly or quite blind. Thus no further calls are made for exertion upon the ciliary muscle, the internal muscle relaxes, the external asserts itself; and the strabismus commences to disappear; but if the vision were now tested, the eye will be found blind.

The obvious treatment for extreme strabismus is to prevent its confirmation by putting correcting glasses on the child while the sight is still good for distant vision. The objections often urged against the use of glasses by children—"risk of breakage" and "appearance"—are unworthy of answer. What is the temporary loss of a few cents, or of temporary change of the child's appearance, compared to a permanent loss of sight!

A skillful surgeon will generally cure strabismus by cutting the ligament which, by contraction, draws the eye out of place. The operation is neither dangerous nor very painful.

Near-sightedness in Children.—Children troubled by near-sightedness should not lean forward at their work, as thus the vessels of the eye become overcharged with blood. They should avoid fine print, and spare their eyes in every possible way. If a person reach middle age without especial difficulty of sight, he is comparatively safe.

How to Remove Foreign Bodies from the Eye.—If any foreign substance, (as cinders, grains of sand, and broken eye-lashes,) gets into the eye, it should be removed before inflammation takes place. If cinder or dust get into the eye, and no surgeon is at hand, the eyes should be closed that tears may accumulate in sufficient quantity, then take the point of a cambric handkerchief, and opening the eye so as to turn back the lid, the substance can be removed. Some use a small loop made from fine smooth wire, which may be moved around under the lid.

"**Eye-stones**" **or Grain of Flaxseed for the Eye.**—The popular idea of the charm of "eye-stones" is a delusion. While they seem to remove cinders, they really raise the eyelid and allow the tears to *do their proper work*. *A grain of flaxseed answers quite as well.*

"**Wild Hairs,**" or hairs which have grown on the inner side of the lid, must be extracted with forceps, and all matter which may have collected around the root washed away.

"**Cataract**" **in the Eye.**—Cataract is a disease in which the crystalline lens or its capsules become opaque, and thus obscure the vision. A skillful surgeon can remove the lens or cause it to be absorbed, and the wearing of convex glasses will remedy the defect. The treatment of such cases must always be referred to competent medical authority.

Color-blindness.—The most frequent of this peculiar blindness (or Daltonism) is, that the patient cannot distinguish red; next green; while such blindness for blue is rare. Persons have been known to be blind in respect of two of the base colors, and occasionally for all colors.

In an examination of 1,154 persons in Edinburgh, 5·6 per cent. were found color-blind; and among 611 students of Harvard University and the Boston Institute of Technology, 5 per cent. of the number were found to be affected by it. Among the 3,000,000 of persons thus affected in France, the number of females as compared with men is about one to ten. Experience has proven that a great number are thus defective in this respect without themselves or others suspecting it.

Color-blindness Explained.—This strange fact is explained by our senses of the exterior world being in a manner entirely practical. Objects are permanently invested by us with qualities which are first noted. Thus if we say this *carpet is red*, it will afterward seem to us to be a *red carpet*. So not only by the color do we recognize it, but by a complex combination of qualities among which the real sensation of color plays a small part. Thus we learn the sky is blue, grass green, bricks red.

The Question of Color-blindness Important.—The traveling public, both on sea and land, know the use of red and green signals is universal. The only security against collisions and other accidents—especially at night—is a proper interpretation of such colors. Hence the importance of securing for important posts *employés* of whose correct sight there can be no doubt. Among the examining tests which have been tried, the simplest and best seems to be the one used more than twenty years ago by Wilson, of Edinburgh, more recently revived by Holingren; and which is now generally adopted in Europe. The person examined is directed to match different-colored worsteds.

Cure of Color-blindness.—In nine out of ten cases it may be easily cured in young subjects. The best method of treatment consists in methodical exercise of the eyes on colored objects. The women of a family ought to undertake the development of the chromatic sense in children, and especially those who may commit errors in the denomination of colors. They should be careful not to ridicule these "Daltonians." In future no one ought to be admitted into the service of the railways, the marine, or schools of painting without an examination as to colors. "Daltonians" should never be intrusted with any service connected with colored signals. Regular exercises in colors should be instituted, both in the marine and army. Examinations and exercises in colors should be established in all schools.

Medical Treatment of Color-blindness.—By a recent discovery Daltonism, or "color-blindness," can be cured by looking through a layer of *fuscine* (a dark-colored substance obtained from animal oil) in solution. A practical application of this discovery has been made by M. Joval, in France, by interposing between two glasses a thin layer of gelatine.

False Sight Explained.—Dr. Clarke's attention being drawn to this subject by striking cases of hallucination of sight, explains these phenomena as according with the accepted facts of anatomy and physiology. "The apparatus of human vision," he says, "may be described as a mechanism consisting of fine organs, closely connected and in intimate communication with each other. Each member of this apparatus has its special function, and each one is supposed to do its own part or duty honestly; that is, never to send a report to a station above which it has not received from below. Nevertheless, modified by disease, disturbed by drugs, or influenced by the brain itself, it sometimes plays false." Dr. Clarke claims that false sight is analogoes to that well known false sensation of pain in a limb days or weeks after amputation, and describes several forms of false sight (pseudopia) arising from different cerebral conditions; sometimes provoked by an abnormal habit like somnambulism and somnolentia, and sometimes by active cerebral disorder like delirium tremens; sometimes by febrile excitement, sometimes by anxiety and mental strain, by stimulants; and by an act of volition aided by habit, association and emotion.

How to Treat a Sty.—The sty is a small boil protruding from the eyelid. It will usually pass away of itself, but its cure may be hastened by applying a warm poultice of bread and water in a small linen bag. Apply three or four times a day, and each time foment the eye with warm milk and water.

Important hints Concerning Eyesight.—Unless circumstances demand it, it is better that no one should read, sew, or use the eyes for any close work on objects near by before breakfast or immediately after a full meal.

Bad air and bad food often cause diseased eyes.

Cold water is about the safest application for inflamed eyes. Poultices should never be used.

Avoid all sudden changes between light and darkness.

Avoid looking suddenly from a near object to one in the distance.

Never sleep so that on awaking the eyes shall open on the light of the window.

Do not use eyesight by light so scant that it requires an effort to discriminate.

Never read or sew directly in front of the light of a window

It is best to have the light from above, or obliquely, or over the left shoulder.

Too much light creates a glare, and pains and confuses the sight. The moment you are sensible of an effort to distinguish, that moment stop and talk, walk or ride.

As the sky is blue and the earth green, it would seem that the ceiling should be a bluish tinge, the carpet green, and the walls of some mellow tint.

The moment you are instinctively inclined to rub the eyes, that moment cease to use them.

ILLUSTRATIONS OF THE HUMAN EAR—HOW WE HEAR.

In man and the higher vertebrates the organ of hearing is very complicated, and is divisible into three parts: the external ear, which includes the pinna, or auricle and meatus, or external opening; the middle ear, drum, or tympanum; and the internal ear, or labyrinth.

The waves of air enter the external auditory canal and strike the drum-head. They make the drum-head vibrate. Across the cavity of the drum, from the drum-head to the opposite wall, the three little bones of the ear—the "hammer," the "anvil," and the "stirrup"—are stretched in a chain. The hammer is joined to the drum-head and to the anvil, and the anvil to the stirrup.

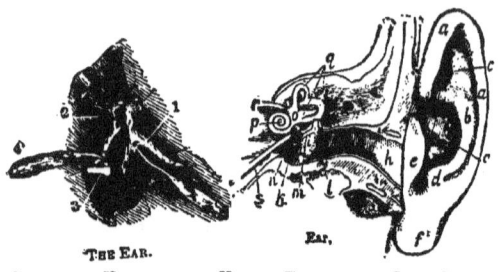

THE EAR.

SECTIONAL VIEW OF THE HUMAN EAR OF THE LEFT SIDE.— *aa*, Helix; *b*, Antihelix; *c*, Fossa of the Antihelix; *d*, Antitragus; *e*, Tragus; *f*, Lobule, or Lobe; *g*, Concha; *h*, External Auditory Meatus, or Auditory Canal; *i*, Tympanic Membrane; *k*, Tympanum; *l*, Mallens; *m*, Incus; *n*, Stapes; *o*, Vestibule; *p*, Cochlea; *q*, Three semicircular Canals; *r*, Auditory Nerve; *s*, Eustachian Tube.

BONES OF THE LEFT EAR, SEEN FROM THE INSIDE.—1, Hammer; 2, Anvil; 3. Stirrup; 4, Stapedius.

When the drum-membrane vibrates, these little bones are made to vibrate. The last one in the chain, the stirrup, is joined to a small membrane in the inner wall of the drum, which is like a little drum-head. On the other side of this little drum-head is the inner ear, which is filled with water. As the stirrup vibrates it sets the little inner ear vibrating, and the little waves strike the ends of the nerve of hearing, and by it the impression is carried in to the brain.

The middle ear is a cavity connected by the Eustachian tube with the pharynx, separated from the opening of the external ear by the tympanic membrane, and containing a chain of three small bones or ossicles, named malleus, incus, and stapes, which connect this membrane with the internal ear. The essential part of the internal ear where the fibers of the auditory nerve terminate is the membranous labyrinth, a complicated system of sacs and tubes filled with a fluid (the endolymph), and lodged in a cavity, called the bony labyrinth, but is partially suspended in it in a fluid (the perilymph). The bony labyrinth consists of a central cavity, the vestibule, into which three semicircular canals and the canal of the cochlea (spirally coiled in mammals) open. The vestibular portion of the membranous labyrinth consists of two sacs, the utriculus and sacculus, connected by a narrow tube, into the former of which three membranous semicircular canals open, while the latter is connected with a membranous tube in the cochlea containing the organ of corti. By the help of the external ear the sonorous vibrations of the air are concentrated upon the tympanic membrane and set it vibrating; the chain of bones in the middle ear transmits these vibrations to the internal ear.

An ear-ache is commonly caused by inflammation of the lining of the drum. It swells, and discharges a fluid that fills the cavity, and makes pain by pressure. Sometimes, as the inflammation subsides, the fluid is absorbed. Sometimes the drum-membrane bursts and lets out the fluid, and then the pain stops. A discharge from the ear commonly comes from an inflamed middle ear through a hole in the drum-head. If the hole is small it may heal up when the discharge stops. If a large part of the drum-membrane is gone it will not heal up.

The loss of the drum-head does not destroy the hearing, but it impairs it.

Ear-wax is made by glands in the skin lining the auditory canal. It is not a safe practice to dig it out with hair-pins or other instruments. Ear-wax is necessary to keep the canal and drum-head soft and moist, and it will take care of itself. If it forms hard lumps, and stops the ear, as it sometimes does, it may be removed by carefully syringing with warm water.

A tuning fork may be set vibrating if its own particular note, or one harmonic with it, be sounded in its neighborhood. In other words, it will vibrate under the influence of a particular set of vibrations, and no others. If the vibrating ends of the tuning fork were so arranged as to impinge upon a nerve, their repeated minute blows would at once excite this nerve.

Suppose that of a set of tuning forks, tuned to every note and distinguishable fraction of a note in the scale, one were thus connected with the end of every fiber of the cochlear nerve, then any vibration communicated to the perilymph would affect the tuning fork which could vibrate with it, while the rest would be absolutely or relatively indifferent to that vibration. In other words, the vibration would give rise to the sensation of one particular tone and no other, and every musical interval would be represented by a distinct impression on the sensorium. It is believed that the fibers of Corti are competent to perform the function of such tuning forks; that each of them is set vibrating to its full strength by a particular kind of wave sent through the perilymph, and by no other; and that each affects a particular fiber of the cochlear nerve only.

The fibers of the cochlear nerve may be excited by internal causes, such as the varying pressure of the blood and the like. And in some persons such internal influences do give rise to veritable musical spectra, sometimes of a very intense character. But for the appreciation of music produced external to us we depend upon the intermediation of the scala media and its Cortian fibers.

It has already been explained that the stapedius and tensor tympani muscles are competent to tighten the membrane of the fenestra ovalis and that of the tympanum, and it is probable that they come into action when the sonorous impulses are too violent, and would produce too extensive vibrations of these membranes. They therefore tend to moderate the effect of intense sound in much the same way that, as we shall find, the contraction of the circular fibers of the iris tends to moderate the effect of intense light in the eye.

The cochlea discriminates the quality rather than the quantity or intensity of sound. There is great reason to believe that the excitement of any single filament of the cochlear nerve gives rise, in the mind, to a distinct musical impression, and that every fraction of a tone which a well-trained ear is capable of distinguishing is represented by its separate nerve fiber. Thus the scala media resembles a key-board in function as well as in appearance, the fibers of Corti being the keys, and the ends of the nerves representing the strings which the keys strike. If it were possible to irritate each of these nerve fibers experimentally, we should be able to produce any musical tone at will.

The function of the Eustachian tube is probably to keep the air in the tympanum, or on the inner side of the tympanic membrane, of about the same tension as that on the outer side, which could not always be the case if the tympanum were a closed cavity.*

CARE OF THE EAR.

How Sound is Produced.—Whenever one body strikes another in the air, waves are produced, just as when we throw a stone into the water a series of concentric circles surround the spot where it sinks. These waves of air strike upon the membrane. This vibrates and sends the motion along the chain of bones in the middle ear to the fluids of the labyrinth. Here, bristles, sand, and stones pound away, and the wondrous harp of the cochlea, catching up the pulsations, carries them to the fibres of the auditory nerve, which conveys them to the brain, and gives the mind the idea of sound.

Careful Attention and Treatment.—The ear needs the greatest care. Cold water should not be allowed to enter the external ear. If the wax accumulates, never remove 't with a hard instrument, but with a little warm water, turning the head to let it run out. The hair around the ears should never be left wet, as it may chill this sensitive organ.

Temporary Deafness.—This may be caused by the gathering and hardening of ear-wax, in which case the cause may be removed as shown above. Temporary deafness, sometimes from imperfect action of the Eustacian tube,*

---

* The Eustacian tube extends from the mouth to the middle ear, or cavity inside the ear-drum. for the purpose of admitting the air freely inside of the tympanum or ear-drum.

caused by inflammation of the ear. In such cases the muscles that open the tube should be kept in action by a gargle of alum, or chlorate of potash, or cold water.

Insect in the Ear.—If an insect gets into the ear, pour a little sweet oil into it and kill it, and then remove it with warm water. If this treatment fails, plug the external meatus with a piece of "cotton-wool," thoroughly saturated with a strong solution of common salt or vinegar, and large enough to close the orifice completely. After its introduction, turn the patient on the side affected, and press the hand firmly on the ear. In a few minutes the noise and irritation caused by the insect, will cease, and, if the plug be withdrawn, the insect will probably be found partially imbedded in its substance.

Other Small Bodies in the Ear—To remove small bodies, a stream of water may be thrown gently into the canal, or a scoop or bent probe may be used.

Fungus in the Ear.—Exposure of the external ear to an impure, damp atmosphere, coupled with neglect to cleanse the ear, often results in the growth of fungus, which can be detected by the microscope. One physician reports that he can "count such cases by the hundred." The fungus affects the walls of the external ear. One physician reports the case of a cobbler who was accustomed to sit on a bench with his left side close to a window opening into a damp, low atmosphere. He became nearly deaf in that ear from the growth of the fungus "on the old wax."

Remedy for Fungus.—Wash away the large masses with a syringe, and apply a weak solution of sulphate of zinc—eight grains to the ounce; after the fungus is removed, to prevent its return, keep the meatus of the ear free and dry.

"Singing in the Ear."—Michael, who was well acquainted with the sedative influence of nitrite of amyl on the sympathetic system, and especially on the vaso-motor nerves, resolved (*Archives Med. Belges*) to try whether it would not prove equally successful in singing in the ear, and eventually obtained good results in nineteen cases out of twenty-seven.

From two to five drops of nitrite of amyl were inhaled in one dose. The inhalation was continued as long as the following symptoms lasted, viz., a flushed face and injection of the vessels of the eye, and was discontinued the moment the patient began to feel giddy. It was noticed that all the patients who subsequently improved, complained that the noise in the ears increased during inhalation, but as soon as the flush began to disappear on the face, the singing noise decreased, and was less than before inhalation. In some patients the improvement lasted only one hour, in others for some weeks, but as a rule it lasted from two to ten days. A second inhalation, if not made too soon after the first, had much more marked effects. The author thinks that at least two days must be allowed to elapse between two inhalations; and that the second must not be taken in cases of acute catarrh, or where the singing noise is due to some mechanical cause.—*London Medical Record*, May 15, 1879.

Remedies for Earache.—1. Dr. Browning, of Mississippi, earnestly commends the following prescription as a remedy for acute earache: Tobacco, (cut fine,) one drachm; glycerine, one ounce; mix, and put five drops into the ear once a day.

2. A case is related of a person suffering with intense pain from earache, who, after trying all other remedies without relief, was finally cured by pouring vinegar upon a hot brick, and with a funnel conducting the steam into the ear. Relief was quick and permanent.

3. Take a small piece of cotton-wool, making a depression in the center with a finger, and fill it with as much ground pepper as will rest on a five-cent piece, gather it into a ball and tie it up, dip the ball into sweet oil and insert it into the ear, covering the latter with cotton-wool, and use a bandage or cap to retain it in its place. Almost instant relief will be experienced, and the application is so gentle that an infant will not be injured by it, but experience relief, as well as adults.

4. Generally heat is an efficient remedy. Apply a warm poultice or warm oil to the ear. Rub the back of the ear with warm laudanum. In case of a fetid discharge, carefully syringe the ear with warm milk and water. In all cases keep the ear thoroughly cleansed. Relief is often given by rubbing the back of the ear with a little hartshorn and water.

Earache Relieved by Arnica.—A physician endorses the following: There is, however, one remedy which the experience of twenty years has taught us is unfailing. We have seen it repeatedly tried in our own family, and have frequently recommended it to others, always with the same satisfactory result. No house should be without its bottle of arnica. It is indispensable in cases of cuts, burns, and bruises, and in earache it is a sovereign cure. As soon as any soreness is felt in the ear, which feeling mostly precedes the regular "ache," let three or four drops of tincture of arnica be poured in, and then the orifice filled with a little cotton to exclude the air, and in a short time the uneasiness is forgotten. If the arnica is not resorted to until there is actual pain, the cure may not be so speedy, but it is just as certain. If one application of the arnica does not effect a cure, it will be necessary to repeat it, it may be several times. It is a sure preventive of gathering in the ear, which is the usual cause of earache. We have never yet known any harm or serious inconvenience to attend the use of arnica; though if the spirits with which it is made are strong, it may be diluted with a little water, as the spirits, not the arnica, will sometimes cause a temporary dizziness of the head, which is unpleasant.

Don't Treat the Ear for Toothache.—It is a bad practice to put cotton-wool soaked in laudanum or chloroform into the ear for the relief of toothache. It is true that it may sometimes prove effectual and procure a night's rest, for the connection between the teeth and the ear is very close. But let it be borne in mind that the ear is far too delicate and valuable an organ to be used as a medium for the application of strong remedies for disorders of the teeth, and that both laudanum and chloroform, more especially the latter, are powerful irritants, and that such applications are always accompanied with risk. The teeth should be looked after for themselves by some competent dentist; and if toothache spreads to the ear, this is another reason why they should be attended to at once, for prolonged pain in the head, arising from the teeth, may itself injure the hearing. In earache everything should be done to soothe it, and all strong, irritating applications should be avoided. Pieces of hot fig or onion should on no account be put in; but warm flannels should be applied, with poppy fomentations, externally, if the pain does not soon subside.

Don't "Box the Ears."—The practice of boxing children's ears is exceedingly reprehensible. It is known that the passage of the ear is closed by a thin membrane, especially adapted to be influenced by every impulse of the air, and with nothing but the air to support it internally. What, then, can be more likely to injure this membrane than a sudden and forcible compression of the air in front of it? If any one designed to break or over-stretch the membrane, a more efficient means could scarcely be devised than to bring the hand suddenly and forcibly down upon the passage of the ear, thus driving the air violently before it, with no possibility of its escape but by the membrane giving way. Medical authorities assert that children are in this way made more or less deaf by boxing on the ear.

CARE OF THE NOSE.—SMELLING.

The Sense of Smell.—The nostrils open at the back into the pharynx, and are lined by a continuation of the mucous membrane of the throat. The olfactory nerves enter through a sieve-like bony plate at the roof of the nose, and are distributed over the inner surface of the two olfactory chambers. The purpose of the sense of smell is to warn us of the presence of foul air, and to aid us in the selection of food.

The Object May be Distant.—The object to be smelled need not touch the nose, but tiny particles borne on the air enter the nasal passages. Three quarters of a grain of musk placed in a room causes a very powerful odor for a considerable length of time, without any sensible diminution in weight. Odors are transported by the air a long distance. Navigators state that the winds bring the odors of the spice islands to them when far away at sea.

Foreign Substances in the Nose.—Beans, cherry-pits, peas, etc., often cause considerable, but not serious, inconvenience among children. The simplest way of getting rid of the intruder is to close the opposite nostril, and blow forcibly into the patient's mouth. Sometimes sneezing, caused by snuff introduced into the nostril, will dislodge the object. In place of this, a stream of water carried into the nostril by means of a nasal douche, may wash out the material. When simple measures fail, a physician must be called, and the forceps resorted to.

Bleeding from the Nose.—The causes which commonly produce bleeding from the nose, are those which send the blood too strongly to the head, such as strong coffee, too full living, exposure to heat, excess in drinking; any violent mental excitement, constipation, etc. It is also caused by tight lacing, tight neck-cloths, blows on the nose, etc. In the majority of cases it is beneficial, but may be so persistent as to endanger life.

Treatment of Excessive Nose-Bleed.—The patient should be exposed to cool air. The head should not hang over a basin, but be kept raised. Find which nostril the blood escapes from, and on that side raise the arm perpendicularly, and hold the nose firmly with the finger and thumb. At the same time a towel wet with ice-water may be laid on the forehead. A piece of ice, a snowball, or cold water compress applied to the back of the neck will often stop the bleeding. The popular remedy of placing a cold key between the clothes and the back should not be forgotten. A more powerful remedy, one which seldom fails, is that of blowing, by means of a quill, powdered gum-arabic into the nostrils. When clotted blood forms in the nostrils it should be disturbed as little as possible.

Simple Remedy for Nose-Bleed.—A friend who has tried it, says: "Put a piece of paper in your mouth, chew it rapidly, and it will stop your nose from bleeding. This remedy has been tried frequently with success."

A physician says that placing a small roll of paper or muslin above the front teeth, under the upper lip, and pressing hard on the same, will arrest bleeding from the nose, checking the passage of the blood through the arteries leading to the nose.

Catarrh of the Nose.—This disease is not usually absolutely painful, but it is yet in many cases intensely harassing. It is universal, for neither sex and no age is free from liability to acute attacks of it. The one great cause of it is exposure to cold, sitting in draughts, wetting the feet, and all circumstances that conspire to close the pores of the skin, may bring on a severe attack in a few hours. The chief predisposing causes are confinement in over-heated rooms, and the eating and drinking of hot substances.

Treatment of Nasal Catarrh.—No two cases can be treated exactly alike. The special remedy to be used, and the strength of the solution must be determined by the progress of the case. In almost all cases weak solution of chlorate of potash, applied by means of a syringe, will prove beneficial. Carbolic acid, nitric acid, Lugol's solution, iodine and glycerine, tannin and glycerine, are also beneficial, and are to be applied in the same manner, or in the absence of a syringe, be snuffed into the nostrils.

CARE OF THE TEETH.

Number of the Teeth.—The teeth are classed with the mucous membrane, as are the hair, nails, horn, and scales, which though always found in connection with the skeleton, are neither bone nor are they formed in the same manner as bone. They are thirty-two in number, sixteen in each jaw, similarly shaped and arranged.

How the Teeth are Classified.—There are eight teeth in each half jaw, making thirty-two in all. In each half jaw the two nearest the middle of each jaw have wide, sharp, chisel-like edges fit for cutting, and hence are called *incisors*. The next one in each half corresponds to the great tearing or holding tooth of the dog, and is called *canine* (from *canis*, a dog) or eye tooth. The next two have broader crowns with two points or cusps, and hence are called the *bicuspids*. The remaining three on each side in each jaw are much broader, and as they are used to crush the food they are called *grinders* or *molars*. The incisors and eye teeth have one fang or root, the others have two or three each.

Order and Period of their Growth.—We are provided with two sets of teeth. The first or "milk teeth," are small and are only twenty in number. The middle incisors are usually cut about the age of seven months, and the others at the age of nine months; the first molars at the age of twelve months; and the canine at the age of eighteen months; the remaining molars at two and three years of age. The lower teeth precede the corresponding upper ones. At six years of age, when the first set are usually still perfect, the jaws contain the crowns of all the second except the wisdom teeth. About this age, to meet the wants of the growing body, the crowns of the second set begin to press against the roots of the milk teeth which, becoming absorbed, leave the loosened teeth to drop out, while the new ones rise and occupy their places. The central incisors appear at about seven years of age, the others at eight; the first bicuspids at nine, the second at ten; the canines at eleven or twelve; the second molars at thirteen, and the *dens sapientiae* or "wisdom teeth" (further back) in the twenty-second year. Sometimes these are cut at a later period.

The Composition of Teeth.—The interior of the tooth consists of *dentine*, a substance resembling bone. In the tusk of the elephant it is known as ivory. The crown is protected by a sheath of *enamel*, a hard, glistening white substance, containing only two and a half per cent. of animal matter. The fang is covered by a thin layer of true bone. At the center of the tooth is a cavity filled with a soft, reddish-white pulpy substance full of blood vessels and nerves. This pulp is very sensitive and toothache is caused by its irritation. The tooth is not set in the jaw like a nail in wood, having the fang in contact with bone, but the socket is lined with a membrane which forms a soft cushion. While this is in a healthy state it deadens the force of any shock, but when inflamed becomes the seat of excruciating pain.

Causes of Decay.—The decay of the teeth is commonly caused by portions of food which become entangled between them, and on account of the heat and moisture quickly decompose. As the saliva evaporates it leaves on the teeth a sediment which is called *tartar*. This collects the organic matter which rapidly changes and also affords a soil in which a sort of fungus speedily springs up. From these causes the teeth are injured and the breath becomes offensive. The teeth can only be preserved by keeping them clean.

Want of Cleanliness.—This is, perhaps, the most direct of the preventable causes of the most common dental disease, namely, decay; for this is always the result of chemical action, progressing from without inward. Food allowed to remain in the crevices and interstices of the teeth soon decomposes, aided as it is by the heat and moisture of the mouth; an acid being generated attacks the tooth structure, gradually but surely decomposing it—and this decay so formed is capable of again reproducing itself by its attack upon the sound bone beneath it. Time only is needed for the complete destruction of the structure, the rapidity of which is retarded or not by the circumstances of constitution, vital force, etc.

Deposit of Tartar Injurious.—An earthy substance, commonly known as tartar, is in greater or less quantities deposited on all teeth, which, if allowed to accumulate and harden, works great mischief by pressing the gums from their normal position, causing inflammation in them, and instead of being firm are spongy, bleeding from the slightest pressure. The roots of the teeth being thus partially exposed, they gradually become loose and sore, and often teeth which are so perfect in formation as to resist the action of decaying agents, perfectly sound in themselves, lose so much of their vital connection with their sockets as to drop out. So insidiously do both of these diseased conditions progress, especially the latter, that many are just startled from complacent reflection on the fact of never having had toothache, to lament over irrecoverable loss.

How to Care for Permanent Teeth.—The value of the permanent teeth depends largely upon healthfulness of the first or temporary set. The milk teeth should be cared for and preserved till nature is ready to supply their places with the permanent organs; so that the arch of the mouth may be preserved, and that the roots may be absorbed and the material therein may not be lost to the system in the development of the new tooth. Irregularity of the second set would be almost unknown if by frequent visits to a competent dentist the first teeth were retained until nature should have no further use for them, and *then* removed.

How to Care for the Teeth Early.—The child should be taught at five to dampen the brush in water every morning, rub it over a cake of castile soap, and then brush the teeth well, inside and out, front and rear; until, with the aid only of the saliva, the mouth is full of soap-suds: then rinse with tepid water, twirling the brush sideways over the back part of the tongue, so as to cleanse it fully of the soap and leave a good taste; after each meal the mouth should be well rinsed with tepid water, as also the last thing on retiring. The mouth maintains a temperature of ninety-eight degrees; hence, if any food lodges about or between the teeth, it begins to rot very soon, giving out an acid which immediately begins to eat into the tooth, preparatory to an early decay; if solid particles are observed to lodge between the teeth, the child should be taught to use a very thin quill to dislodge it, but not without; for the more a quill is used the greater space between the teeth, which is a misfortune, as it necessitates the use of a toothpick for all after life, consuming a great deal of valuable time. A clean tooth does not decay.

How Often Should the Teeth be Washed?—Grown people should clean their teeth at least five times in the course of the twenty-four hours— on rising in the morning and on going to bed at night, and after each meal. A brush as hard as can be borne without pain should be used, and the best of all applications is pure soap and water, always luke-warm.

Use of Aromatic Water.—It is the custom in some parts of England and France to rinse the mouth with warm aromatic water after eating. It is well to remember that this precaution not only tends to keep the teeth clean, but to clear the voice of those about to sing or converse.

A Mixture for the Teeth.—Dissolve two ounces of borax in three pints of boiling water, and before it is cold add one teaspoonful of spirits of camphor, and bottle for use. A tablespoonful of this mixture, mixed with an equal quantity of tepid water, and applied daily with a soft brush, preserves and beautifies the teeth, extirpates all tartarous adhesions, arrests decay, induces a healthy action of the gums, and makes them look pearly white.

Tooth-Powders often Injurious.—Most kinds of tooth powders are injurious both to the enamel and the gums; and if employed, every particle of them should be removed from the mouth by careful rinsing. The habit which some women have of using a bit of lemon, though it may whiten the teeth, and give temporary firmness and color to the gums, is fatal to the enamel, as are all acids.

"**Cracking Nuts with the Teeth.**"—No one, young or old, should turn their jaws into nut-crackers; and it is dangerous even for women to bite off, as they often do, the ends of thread in sewing.

Importance of Healthful Gums.—Wholesome gums are more essential even than the teeth to the beauty of the mouth. They should be of a firm texture and a lively red color, and well spread over the base of each tooth, but they are often pale or livid, shrunken, fleshless, and sometimes even ulcerated. The excessive use of sugar and candies does great mischief. It is not chiefly the bad effect of the acids produced by their composition, but the grittiness of these substances which wears away the gum, bares the roots of the tooth, and spoils the mouth. This is the chief danger of the use of tooth-powders.

Teething.—Young children, while cutting their first set of teeth, often suffer constitutional disturbance. At first they are restless and peevish, but not unfrequently these symptoms are followed by convulsive fits, and sometimes under this condition the child is either cut off suddenly, or the foundation of serious mischief to the brain is laid. The remedy, or rather safeguard, against these circumstances consists merely in lancing the gum covering the tooth which is making its way through.

Keep close watch over the gums, and when they are swollen and red have them lanced immediately. The teeth will probably come through the day after lancing, but if they do not, and the cut heals, and a scar forms, there is nothing to be feared, as, when the teeth finally appear, the scar will give way much more easily than the uncut gum. If the teeth do not come through after two or three days, the lancing may be repeated; and this is especially needed if the child seems in much pain. The relief children experience in the course of two or three hours from the operation is often very remarkable.

"**Toothache Cures.**"—1. Relief from toothache or neuralgic affections arising from teeth in any stage of decay, may often be obtained by saturating a small bit of clean cotton or wool with a strong solution of ammonia, and applying it immediately to the affected tooth. The pleasant contrast instantaneously produced sometimes causes a fit of laughter, although a moment before extreme suffering and anguish prevailed.

2. One dram of collodium flexile added to two drams of Calvert's carbolic acid is a most excellent application. A small portion should be inserted into the cavity of the tooth by means of a bit of lint.

3. Powdered alum and salt mixed in equal quantities, and placed on a small piece of damp cotton, and put into the cavity, sometimes gives permanent relief.

At a meeting of the London Medical Society, Dr. Blake, a distinguished practitioner, said that he was able to cure the most desperate case of the toothache, unless the disease was connected with rheumatism, by the application of the following remedy: Alum, reduced to an impalpable powder, two drams; nitrous spirits of ether, seven drams; mix, and apply to the tooth.

4. Two or three drops of essential oil of cloves put upon a small piece of lint or cotton-wool, and placed in the hollow of the tooth, will be found to have the active power of curing the toothache without destroying the tooth or injuring the gums.

5. Toothache may be temporarily alleviated by scrupulously cleaning out the cavity of the tooth—as decay has generally hollowed it at some part—and dropping into this cavity a piece of cotton-wool soaked in creosote, or a strong solution of alum. After using the creosote, etc., the hollow of the tooth should be filled up with a pellet of cotton-wool saturated with a solution of gum-mastic in ether, or with a piece of gutta-percha softened in boiling water. The condition of the stomach and bowels should in all cases of toothache be attended to.

6. A Paris journal states that Dr. Bouchard, of that city, finds the use of electricity very efficient in cases of severe toothache, a perfect cure, even where the teeth are greatly decayed, being not unfrequently obtained, and temporary relief almost invariably ensuing. In numerous instances where alleviation was at first of short duration, the effect became more and more marked, and longer, as the treatment was repeated. The method pursued by Dr. Bouchard, in applying the electricity, is to place the positive pole of the current on the cheek opposite the diseased tooth, and the negative upon the anterolateral portion of the neck; and, to avoid ulcerations, the electrodes are made very large, and their places frequently changed. The application is continued for about half an hour, although relief is frequently experienced in ten to fifteen minutes. A battery of about ten elements is used.

What to Do with Decayed Teeth.—Decayed teeth should have attention at once. If only partially destroyed, the decayed part may be cut away, and a filling inserted; but a tooth much decayed should never be allowed to remain in the mouth, as it will destroy its neighbors.

Artificial Teeth.—When teeth become so troublesome as to habitually disturb the nervous system, they should be removed. *Many diseases are caused, and most others greatly aggravated, by toothache.* "Stop the ache, or remove the tooth," should be universally obeyed. Thousands of persons suffer for years in great discomfort to themselves and to all around them, until their constitutions are permanently impaired, when the removal of a single tooth would bring permanent relief.

CARE OF THE HAIR.

Growth of the Hair.—At the root of each hair is a tiny bulb, in which the nutriment is supplied. As long as these bulbs (*papillæ*) remain in a healthy condition, the hair will continue to grow. It is of the first importance, therefore, that the scalp be kept clean, the pores open, and the processes of the nutritive supply free and active.

How to Preserve the Hair.—Wash the scalp often and thoroughly with soft water, and wipe it dry with a towel. Keep the head well ventilated. If the hat is close, lift it often and let in the fresh air. A hat with a crown in which there is room for a reservoir of air, is much better than a close-fitting cap. Hats should not be worn in-doors.

Why Ladies are not Bald.—Ladies, notwithstanding they wear long hair, (which is more likely to fall out,) seldom are bald-headed. Their heads are not kept covered in-doors, and when out-doors they are not closely covered. In sleeping none should confine the hair in a close night-cap.

Why the Hair Falls Out.—Hair falls out for want of nourishment. It dies just as a blade of grass dies in a soil where there is no moisture. This want of nourishment is only "functional," the papillæ sacs and other apparatus remain, but are inactive. The mechanism which supplies it, the apparatus, is there to make it; but it is out of order, and makes it imperfectly; so the hair being imperfectly nourished, is dry, scant, or a mere furze, according to the degree of the defective nourishment.

How to Prevent the Hair from Falling Out.—As to men, when the hair begins to fall out, the best plan is to have it cut short, give it a good brushing with a moderately-stiff brush while the hair is dry, then wash it well with warm soap-suds, then rub into the scalp, about the roots of the hair, a little bay rum or camphor water. Do these things at least once a week. The brushing of the scalp may be profitably done twice a week. Dampen the hair with water every time the toilet is made. Nothing ever made is better for the hair than pure soft water, if the scalp is kept clean in the way we have named.

Care of the Hair.

"**Organic Baldness**" **Incurable.**—"Organic" baldness is when the defect of nutriment arises from the destruction of the papillæ, the apparatus which made it. When the scalp is in any part entirely bare of hair, and *shiny* or *glistening*, that is organic baldness, and there is no remedy.

"**Functional**" **Baldness Curable.**—When the bulbs are uninjured, that is, the nutritive organs remain, but have become partially or wholly inactive, this is "functional baldness," and can be remedied radically and permanently in only one way and that is by taking means to improve the general health.

How to Cure Functional Baldness.—If there is not that shining, glistening appearance, but a multitude of very small hairs, causing a "furziness" over the scalp, that is "functional" baldness; and two things are to be done. Keep the scalp clean with soap-suds—that is a "balm of a thousand flowers." More especially and principally seek to improve your general health by eating plain, substantial food three regular times a day, and by spending three or four hours between meals in moderate exercise in the open air or in some engrossing employment.

A little turpentine applied to the bald patches by means of sponges, will hasten the first appearance of the hair, and the growth of hair, when it recommences, may be stimulated by constant shaving.

Avoid Hair-Dyes.—Hair dyes, or so-called "hair-restorers," should be strenuously avoided, as they tend to fill the pores of the skin, and almost invariably contain poisonous matters, which the system absorbs.

Caution in Using "Hair-Oils."—The frequent use of "oils," "bear's grease," "arcturine," "pomades," "lustrals," "rosemary washes," and such like upon the hair, is a practice not to be commended. These oils and greasy pomades are manufactured from lard-oil and simple lard. No "bear's grease" is ever used. If it could be procured readily it should not be applied to the hair, as it is the most rank and filthy of all the animal fats.

A Good Hair Dressing.—There are many persons whose hair is naturally very dry and crisp; and in most families there is a want of some innocent and agreeable wash or dressing, which may be used moderately and judiciously. The mixture which may be regarded as the most agreeable, cleanly, and safe, is composed of cologne spirit and pure castor-oil. The following is a good formula: Pure, fresh castor-oil, two ounces; cologne spirit, (ninety-five per cent.,) sixteen ounces. The oil is freely dissolved in the spirit, and the solution is clear and beautiful. It may be perfumed in any way to suit the fancy of the purchaser.

Value of Castor-Oil for the Hair.—A competent writer in the Boston *Journal of Chemistry* urges that the oil of the castor-bean has for many years been employed to dress the hair, both among the savage and civilized nations, and it possesses properties which admirably adapt it to this use. It does not dry rapidly; and no gummy, offensive residuum remains, after taking on all the chemical changes which occur in all oils upon exposure to light and air. It is best diffused by the agency of strong spirits, in which it dissolves, the alcohol or spirit rapidly evaporates, and does not, in the slightest degree, injure the texture of the hair. This preparation for dressing the hair of children or ladies will meet nearly or quite all requirements.

A Preparation of Glycerine and Rose-water Recommended.--A cheap and very good dressing is made by dissolving four ounces of perfectly pure, dense glycerine in twelve ounces of rose-water. Glycerine evaporates only at high temperatures; and therefore, under its influence the hair is retained in a moist condition for a long time.

Relative Value of Other Oil Preparations.—As a class, the vegetable oils are better for the hair than animal oils. They do not become rancid and offensive so rapidly, and they are subject to different and less objectionable chemical changes.

Olive-oil, and that derived from the cocoa-nut, have been largely employed, but they are far inferior, in every respect, to that from the castor-bean.

How to Prevent the Hair from Turning Gray.—The hair may be prevented, generally for a considerable time, from turning gray, by keeping the head cool, and by using occasionally sage tea with a little borax added. With a small sponge apply to every part of the head just before or at the time of dressing the hair.

Washing the Hair with Soda-water, Relieves Headache.—Many persons find speedy relief for nervous headache by washing the hair thoroughly in weak soda-water. I have known severe cases almost wholly cured in ten minutes by this simple remedy. A friend finds it the greatest relief in cases of "rare cold," the cold symptoms entirely leaving the eyes and nose after one thorough washing of the hair. The head should be thoroughly dried afterward, and drafts of air avoided for a little while.

Sudden Changes in the Color of the Hair.—Sudden and severe frights have sometimes so affected the nerves connected with the papillae at the roots of the hair, as to produce instantaneous changes in the color of the hair. A German medical magazine, now before us, reports two recent cases.

A Remarkable Case in Berlin.—A physician of Berlin, a strong, healthy, and less than middle-aged man, sent his wife and one daughter to spend last summer at a watering-place. The day that he expected a letter informing him of their arrival, there came one saying that his daughter had been taken sick very suddenly, and was already dead. The shock was terrible, and instantly his hair became entirely gray. He had to visit some patients that same afternoon, and they scarcely recognized him. Their peculiar actions revealed the change to him.

A Remarkable Case in Rotterdam.—Another case was that of a man thirty-five years old, living in the Netherlands. He was one day passing the canal in Rotterdam, when he saw a child struggling in the water. He plunged in and brought it to land, but it was already dead by the time he had rescued its body. Bending over to try to restore life, he discovered that the dead child was his own son. The blow, so sudden and unexpected, and coming upon him when he himself was so much exhausted, turned his hair entirely gray, and left him scarcely recognizable.

Sudden Changes of Color without Fright.—That eminent savan, Dr. Brown-Séquard, in his Archives de Physiologie, discovered a rapid transition in color, on certain portions of his face, while he was in perfect health. After detailing the particulars in the case, he says that, without any appreciable cause, other than that which at a certain age makes the beard turn white, there took place in his case a very rapid change of color, from black to white, in a considerable number of the hairs upon his face. As far as he could ascertain, this change occurred always in the night. He did not examine the whitened hairs with the microscope. He concludes that this experience of his puts beyond a doubt the possibility of a very rapid transformation (probably in less than a night) of black hairs into white.

Utility of Beards.—A recent writer in one of our standard magazines strongly puts the case as follows: There are more solid inducements for wearing the beard than the mere improvement of a man's personal appearance, and the cultivation of such an aid to the every-day diplomacy of life. Nature combining, as she never fails to do, the useful with the ornamental, provides us with a far better respirator than science could ever make, and one that is never so hideous to wear as that black seal upon the face that looks like a passport to the realms of suffering and death. The hair of the moustache not only absorbs the moisture and miasma of the fogs, but it strains the air from the dust and soot of our great cities. It acts, also, in the most scientific manner, by taking heat from the warm breath as it leaves the chest, and supplying it to the cold air taken in. It is not only a respirator, but, with the beard entire, we are provided with a comforter as well; and these are never left at home, like umbrellas, and all such appliances, whenever they are wanted. Moffat and Livingstone, the African explorers, and many other travelers, say that in the night no wrapper can equal the beard. A remarkable thing is, too, that the beard, like the hair of the head, protects against the heat of the sun; but, more than this, it becomes moist with the perspiration, and then, by evaporation, cools the skin.

To Remove Dandruff.—1. Wash the head thoroughly and often with pure soft water, and brush it thoroughly until the hair is dry. 2. The white of an egg rubbed thoroughly into the hair with the fingers, and then washed out with plenty of tepid water, is very good. 3. Borax removes the dandruff quickly and perfectly, but is apt to make the hair dry and stiff. 4. Ammonia, and all other alkalies, should be avoided.

CARE OF THE FEET.

Warm Feet Essential to Health.—Unless the feet be kept warm the circulation of the blood to the extremities is prevented, the whole system becomes deranged, and fever of any kind becomes aggravated as a result. A distinguished medical man declares that, as a result of many years' careful observation in a large practice in his profession, he believes a large part of the sickness prevalent in any community is "nearly or remotely the result of cold feet."

How to Cure the Habit of Cold Feet.—The feet should be placed in a basin of cold water every morning for a few seconds, just deep enough to cover the toes; wipe dry, dress, and walk off. Once or twice a week the feet should be held in water, made comfortably warm, for some ten minutes, adding hot water from time to time, using a little soap; if at the end of this bathing at night the feet were placed in a pan of cold water, toe-deep, for less than a quarter of a minute, it would greatly aid in giving tone to the skin, vigor to the circulation, and softness to the skin, and thus do much toward keeping them comfortably warm.

A tablespoonful of chloride of lime in a basin of warm water is an excellent wash for removing foot odor.

How to Sleep with Warm Feet.—Before retiring to bed, especially in fire time of year, hold both feet before a blazing fire, stockings removed, for ten minutes at least, rubbing them with the hands all the time until they feel perfectly dry and warm; such a process will warm the feet more effectually in five minutes than can be done in an hour by holding them to the fire with stockings and shoes on.

Waking up with Cold Feet.—Sometimes, without apparent cause, a person will suddenly wake up to the knowledge that his feet are cold, and a disagreeable sensation is caused which pervades the whole body, and the mind and temper become fretful and morose. This is often the case in the very midst of summer. When this is observed you are taking cold, and you should instantly treat the feet to a blazing fire as named above. If this is not practicable, give them a hot foot bath as just directed. In either case you will not only avert the cold, but you will also experience a feeling of comfortableness which is delightful. This same kind of bath is the speediest and most comfortable means of warming the feet when they are found to be uncomfortably cold after coming in from a walk, or a long day's work.

To Keep the Feet Dry.—Many ways have been devised for rendering the upper leather of shoes impervious to water; a much better plan is to keep out of the water, for whatever will keep water out will also keep the perspiration and ill odor always in. To make leather impervious is to make it board-like, hard, unyielding, and hot as fire of a summer's day; but if it be absolutely necessary at any time to wear a shoe which shall exclude water, the application of castor oil or petroleum with a brush, and then allow it to dry, is perhaps the most familiar, accessible, and facile mode known.

Short and High-heeled Shoes.—Thousands of people lose their natural ease and grace of motion, and become stiff and awkward walkers, simply from wearing short-heeled shoes, and thereby losing their natural elasticity of step. Another effect of flattening the arch of the foot is to increase its length, and the foot is often lengthened in this way to the extent of half or three-quarters of an inch. The matter is made still worse by wearing the heels very high, and many a foot has been ruined by this pernicious practice. Short and high-heeled shoes also readily permit the easy turning over of the ankle, and many a strained and weakened ankle is the result of them.

Cause of Chilblains.—These are slight inflammations which occur on the toes and fingers, and sometimes the nose and ears—generally in winter, and where a part has been rapidly heated when it was very cold. They consist of red and swollen patches, sometimes accompanied with blisters, and these, upon breaking, are apt to become ulcerated, and to occasion much annoyance.

To Cure Chilblains.—In the simpler forms, some stimulating liniment, such as equal parts of spirit of wine and vinegar, or spirit of camphor, will prove sufficient to cure chilblains, but when ulcerations occur, some stronger remedy will be found necessary.

One very good remedy is to place red-hot coals on a pan, throw a handful of corn meal over them, and hold the suffering feet in the dense smoke.

Severe weather may produce a recurrence of the trouble at intervals, but persistent use of this remedy will prevent it as well as cure it. It has been known to effect very marked cures, where the persons were unusually exposed, and when all other remedies were useless.

A foreign medical journal thinks the cause of chilblains is often due to impoverishment of blood and a languid, weakly condition of the whole system not to be met by any local remedy. Yet there are local applications which sometimes afford relief, if a person can strike on the right one. Turpentine is to many a great blessing. Glycerine is a good thing to rub into the hands before washing with castile soap and tepid water. Warm vinegar sometimes avails. Kid gloves, lined with wool, are recommended, and, in general, care must be taken to keep the hands and feet from wet and cold. The *London Chemist* recommends a lotion, which should be used with some caution ; liniment of belladonna two drams, liniment of aconite one dram, carbolic acid ten drops, collodion one ounce, to be painted over the surface with a brush. If the skin is broken, the aconite should be left out. This will form a film or varnish which will keep the air out.

How to Prevent and How to Remove Corns.—For *prevention* of corns use daily friction of cold water between the toes. For their removal, the following suggestions are given :—

1. *Hard* corns may be carefully picked out by the use of a small, sharp-pointed scalpel or teuolomy knife, and if well done the cure is often radical, always perfect for the time.

2. They may be equally successfully removed by wearing over them for a few days a small plaster made by melting a piece of stick diachylon and dropping on a piece of white silk. The corn gradually loosens from the adjacent healthy skin, and can be readily pulled or picked out.

3. *Soft* corns require the use of astringents, such as alum dissolved in white of egg, or the careful application of tincture of iodine.

4. A simple cure for both hard and soft corns, which rarely fails, is a poultice of bread dipped in *cider* vinegar and applied every night until cured.

5. Lemon juice effects only a temporary cure, unless applied before the corn has gained ground firmly.

6. A large cranberry or raisin split open and bound to the toe is very good.

7. The strongest acetic acid (vinegar) applied night and morning with a camel-hair brush to either soft or hard corns, will remove them in one week's time.

8. The heart of a potato boiled in its skin, placed on a corn and left there for twelve hours will give temporary relief.

9. Apply a good coat of gum-arabic mucilage over them every evening on going to bed.

10. Apply castor-oil, after paring closely, every night before going to bed. This softens the corn, and it becomes as the other flesh.

11. Take a little sweet oil, on getting up in the morning and before retiring at night, and rub it on the corn with the tip of the finger, keeping the corn well pared down. This relieves the friction, which causes corns, and will cure them in a short time.

12. Apply with a brush morning and evening a drop of a solution of the per-chloride of iron. After a fortnight's continued application, without pain, a patient who had suffered martyrdom for nearly forty years, from a most

painful corn on the inner side of each little toe was entirely relieved. Pressure was no longer painful, and Dr. B. believed the cure radical. Two other similar cases were equally successful.

13. After removing the stocking at night, with the nails of the thumb and forefinger loosen the corn at the edges, and gradually peel it across until it comes off. This is done with entire ease when the toe is not inflamed and sore, and if the corn hardens again in a few weeks, as it will be apt to, the process is easily repeated. The main point is, don't pinch the feet with tight shoes.

14. Soak the feet well in warm water, then with a sharp instrument pare off as much of the corn as can be done without pain, and bind up the part with a piece of linen or muslin, thoroughly saturated with sperm oil, or, what is better, the oil which floats upon the surface of the pickle of herring or mackerel. After three or four days the dressing may be removed, and the remaining cuticle removed by scraping, when the new skin will be found of a soft and healthy texture, and less liable to the formation of a new corn than before.

Cause of "Ingrowing Toe-nail."—This affection is of more consequence than is usually supposed. It is sometimes a serious matter to the patient and causes much pain. One principal cause comes from the fashion of wearing very small-toed boots, and another from wearing much-darned stockings. It is not usually the nail that is in fault, but the skin surrounding it. This becomes thickened and ulcerated and gradually the nail becomes overlapped. The nail then becomes bent and grows irregularly, but it is the highly sensitive skin that gives the pain.

Remedies for Ingrowing Nail.—1. Mr. Wood, surgeon of King's College Hospital, recommends broad-toed boots, also scraping the center of the nail thin with a piece of glass. A plug of cotton under the edge of the nail will aid in restoring it to proper shape and position.

2. A Liverpool physician has, for the past twenty years, employed compressed sponge very successfully in the treatment of ingrowing nails. His method is to render the sponge compact by wetting, and then tying it tightly until it is thoroughly dry. A bit of the sponge, in size less than a grain of rice, is placed under the nail, and secured by strips of adhesive plaster. In this way the point of the nail is kept up from the toe until the surrounding soft parts are restored to their normal condition by appropriate means. Of course there is no pain in this remedy, and its application requires only ordinary skill.

3. It is stated that cauterization by hot tallow is an immediate cure for ingrowing nails. Put a small piece of tallow in a spoon, and heat it over a lamp until it becomes very hot, and drop two or three drops between nail and

granulations. The effect is almost magical. Pain and tenderness are at once relieved, and in a few days the granulations all go, leaving the diseased parts dry and destitute of all feeling, and the edge of the nail exposed, so as to admit of being pared away without any inconvenience. The operation causes little if any pain if the tallow is properly heated.

Remedy for Blistered Feet.—On going to bed rub the feet with tallow, dropped from a lighted tallow candle into the palm of the hand.

Bunions.—These may be checked when they first appear by binding the joint with adhesive plaster and keeping it on until all indications of an enlargement disappear. An inflamed bunion demands large shoes and a poultice. An ointment, to be rubbed on gently twice or three times a day, may be made of iodine, twelve grains, lard or spermaceti ointment, half an ounce

To Cure "Frosted Feet."—Warm some pine tar, and apply with a feather to the affected part; heat it by the fire before going to bed. In very bad cases it may need the second or third application. It is a sure cure, and the tar can easily be removed with lard and soap.

Treatment of Scalded Feet.—When the legs and feet are scalded, they should be plunged as soon as possible into cold water, and kept immersed in it a considerable length of time before the stockings are removed. By this means blisters are often prevented.

CARE OF THE SKIN.

Use of the Skin.—The skin is not only a covering and a protection for the body, but also the medium of perspiration. This perspiration consists of ninety-nine parts of water and one part of solid matter. It is called insensible because the vapor is not recognized by the senses, except where its flow is excessive and interrupted, forming drops on the surface which are called in common language, sweat. The daily exhalations through the skin aggregate about an average weight of *two pounds!* The skin also possesses a remarkable absorbing power, and to such a degree that substances may be imbibed through its pores as a medicine, or as a partial relief from thirst and hunger. As an exhalant and absorbent the skin in its functions has been compared to the lungs. Some writers on physiology describe it as "the third lung of the body." By carefully-conducted experiments it has been found that the skin acts in the same way as the lungs in absorbing oxygen from the air, and giving off carbonic acid to an appreciable amount.*

---

* In some of the lower animals the skin plays a still more important part. Frogs, for instance, deprived of their lungs, breathe with almost undiminished activity, and often survive for days, and snakes get their main supply of air through the skin.

Care of the Skin.

Color of the Skin.—Underneath the outer skin are minute cells containing the particles of coloring matter. The particles are about $\frac{1}{3000}$ of an inch in diameter. "In the varying tint of this coloring matter lies the difference of hue between the blonde and the brunette, the European and the African. In the purest complexion there is some of this pigment, which, however, disappears as the fresh, round, soft cells of the cutis change into the old, flat, horny scales of the cuticle. Scars are white, because this part of the cuticle is not restored. The sun has a powerful effect upon the coloring matter, and so we readily 'tan' on exposure to its rays. If the color gathers in spots, it forms freckles.*"

The Pores of the Skin.—These are fine tubes about $\frac{1}{300}$ of an inch in diameter, and a quarter of an inch in length, which run through the cutis, and then coil up in little balls. They are very numerous. In the palm of the hand there are about 2,800 in a single square inch. On the back of the neck and trunk, where they are the fewest, there are yet 400 to the square inch. The entire number on the body of an adult is estimated at about 2,500,000. The mouths of these pores may be seen with a pocket lens along the fine ridges which cover the palm of the hand. Through these pores the body throws off its excess of water and various impurities from the blood, and imbibes oxygen and other substances with which the skin comes into contact.†

---

* This action of the sun on the pigment of the skin is very marked. Even among the Africans, the skin is observed to lose its intense black color in those who live for many months in the shades of the forests. It is said that Asiatic and African women confined within the walls of the harem, and thus secluded from the sun, are as fair as Europeans. Among the Jews who have settled in Northern Europe are many of light complexion, while those who live in India are as dark as the Hindoos. The black pigment has been known to disappear during severe illness, and a lighter color to be developed in its place. Among the negroes are sometimes found people who have no complexion, *i. e.*, there is no coloring matter in their skin, hair, or the iris of their eyes. These persons are called Albinos.—STEELE.

† Persons frequently poison their hands with the common wood-ivy. Contagious diseases are caught by touching a patient, or even his clothing. Painters absorb so much lead through the pores of their hands that they are attacked with colic. Snuff and lard are frequently rubbed on the chest of a child suffering with the croup to produce vomiting. Seamen in want of water drench their clothing in salt spray, and the skin will absorb enough to quench thirst.

On an occasion of great solemnity, Pope Leo X. caused a young child to be completely covered with gold leaf, closely applied to the skin, so as to represent, according to the idea of the age, the golden glory of an angel or seraph. In a few hours after contributing to this pageant of pride the child died; the cause being suffocation, from stopping the exhalations of the skin; although, in the ignorance of the common people of those days, the death was of course attributed to the anger of the Deity, and looked upon as a circumstance of evil omen.

If one is called upon to handle a dead body, it is well, especially if the person has died of a contagious disease, to rub the hand with lard or olive-oil. Poisonous matter has been

Keeping the Skin Clean.—In view of the nature and functions of the skin, the great importance of keeping it clean and healthy is apparent. It should be one of the chief themes in the list of our duties in caring for the health of the body to keep its pores open. To this end the bath, clean bed-linen, and clean, fresh clothing become not only a luxury but a necessity. The skin, so commonly neglected claims, and should receive, the careful attention of parents and instructors.

Diseases of the Skin—Warts.—Warts are over-grown papillæ.

1. They may be removed by the application of glacial acetic acid, or a drop of nitric acid, repeated until the entire structure is softened. Care must be taken not to let the acid touch the skin.

2. The easiest way to get rid of warts is to pare off the thickened skin which covers it, cut it off by successive layers; shave it until the surface of the skin is reached, and until blood is drawn in several places. Rub the part thoroughly over with lunar caustic and the wart will generally disappear. If it does not, cut off the black spot caused by the caustic, and apply it again. Acetic acid may be used instead of caustic.

"Grafting the Skin."—A celebrated French physician (M. Reverdin) reported to the Academy, as early as 1872, that he had for ten years been accustomed to perform veritable transplantations of the skin. He did not sew over the small granulations small pieces of skin, but he covered the whole with large flaps of skin. The cure then takes place. The pieces of skin may be taken either from the patient himself, or from other individuals. He took most of his grafts from limbs amputated on account of accidents occurring to men otherwise healthy. In some cases he had been obliged to take the pieces of skin from the patient himself in order to do away with the pain of the operation. The experiment proved the possibility of transplanting tissues which had been subjected to a low temperature. At that period he demonstrated that pieces of periosteum first frozen and then transplanted under the skin of another animal, could not only retain life, but also produce osseous tissues. Before practicing cutaneous transplantation he applied to the skin a freezing mixture composed of ice and salt. When the skin was frozen, that is to say, when it was white, bloodless, and insensible,

---

fatally absorbed through the breaking of the cuticle by a long nail or a simple scratch. There is a story that Napoleon I., when a lieutenant of artillery, in the heat of battle, seized the rammer and worked the gun of an artillery-man who had fallen. From the wood which the soldier handled, Napoleon absorbed a poison which gave him a skin-disease, by which he was annoyed the remainder of his life.

Cosmetics, powders, hair-dyes, etc., are exceedingly injurious, not only because they tend to fill the pores of the skin, but because they often contain poisonous matters which are absorbed into the system.—STEELE'S PHYSIOLOGY.

be cut out pieces comprising the whole of the dermis, which, when transplanted on the surface of a wound, became perfectly ingrafted.

Dr. Griflin, of Pavia, claims to have had great success by this operation in several cases of extensive burns. The grafting pieces, six in number, were solidly united after the third day, and on the twelfth the excoriations were reduced to half their original surfaces.

Greased bandages, in place of adhesive strips, are preferable, as they can be readily removed for cleansing without danger of dragging out the grafts.

The union of the grafts is aided by the condition of the wound, and the thickness and extent of the graft. Pieces from two to four millimetres in diameter unite most readily. It is very necessary to include part of the derma.

The edges of the wound should be slightly pared whenever union is effected; suppuration diminishes, the granulations become larger, the condition of the wound improves, and cicatrization is favored and accelerated.

Cutaneous grafting as shown by high authority:

1. In all wounds in full and uniform granulation when we wish to accelerate healing.

2. In chronic wounds of old or cachetic persons; in varicose ulcers with callous margins.

3. In those cases of extensive wounds where spontaneous cicatrization would be attended with considerable retraction of the parts—burns.

4. In wounds of hard surfaces covered with skin only, as the front of the tibia.

To Remove Warts.—Warts are not only very troublesome, but disfigure the hands. They may be cured so as to leave no scar. 1. Take a small piece of raw beef, steep it all night in vinegar, cut as much from it as will cover the wart, and tie it on; or, if the excresence is on the forehead, fasten it on with strips of plaster. It may be removed during the day, and put on every night. In one fortnight the wart will die and peel off. The same prescription will cure corns.

2. Apply the juice from the milk-weed (*Asclepias cornuti*) to the wart once, and it will assume a chalky state, disappear, and not return.

3. Pass a pin through the wart; apply one end of the pin to the flame of a lamp; hold it there until the wart fries under the action of the heat. A wart so treated will leave.

4. If the wart is hard, a good method is to cut it off with a knife or scissors, and apply a little caustic to the roots.

5. If the wart has a narrow neck, tie a silk thread or horse-hair around it, and it will soon drop off. A little caustic applied to the roots will prevent it from growing again.

Chapped Lips and Hands.—1. A good salve may be made in this way: Take two ounces of white wax, one ounce of spermaceti, four ounces of oil of almonds, two ounces of English honey, quarter of an ounce of essence of bergamot, or any other perfume. Melt the wax and spermaceti; then add the honey, and melt all together, and when hot add the almond oil by degrees, stirring it till cold. This is superior to glycerine for chapped hands, sunburns, or any roughness on the skin.

2. The following is a well-tested, excellent remedy for chapped hands and sores of this nature: Put together equal weights of fresh, unsalted butter, tallow, beeswax, and stoned raisins; simmer until the raisins are done to a crisp, but not burned. Strain, and pour into cups to cool. Rub the hands thoroughly with it, and though they will smart at first, they will soon feel comfortable and heal quickly.

Freckles.—1. For the benefit of young persons afflicted with freckles, we would inform them that powdered nitre, moistened with water, applied to the face night and morning, will soon remove all traces of them.

2. A French journal recommends the following: Take naphthaline, ten parts; biphenate of soda, one part; tincture of benzoin, cologne, each two thousand parts. Mix. A tablespoonful of this is to be added to a glass of cold water, four to eight fluid ounces, and the face then bathed with it every night and morning.

3. Apply a lotion of Vichy water for two or three minutes, night and morning. The skin should be allowed to dry without wiping it.

Tan and Sunburn.—Ladies who have spent the summer in the country and at the seaside, may be glad to know of some simple remedies for tan and sunburn. When the face is burnt by exposure, it is best to bathe it with a little cold cream; this simple and pleasant wash will remove the discoloration and swelling as if by magic, and leave the skin cool and smooth. To prevent tan and sunburn, take the juice of a fresh lemon and rub it in thoroughly before going into the open air, allowing it to dry on the face; at night dust a little oatmeal upon the skin, and next morning, after washing it off, apply a little cold cream or buttermilk. Such a simple and harmless treatment will be found much more effectual than the use of cosmetics, which close up the pores, and dry and roughen the finest complexion in a frightful way and in a short space of time.

Cause and Cure of Moles.—A low tone of the blood, with a torpid liver, often cause the appearance of moles. The best remedy is to be found in an invigorated circulation. This will cleanse and renew the skin.

Pimples and Sores.—Sores and pimples show that the skin does not act its normal part in throwing off the effete matter or waste of the system; its pores having become clogged, different forms of illness result.

THE HUMAN SKIN—ILLUSTRATION.

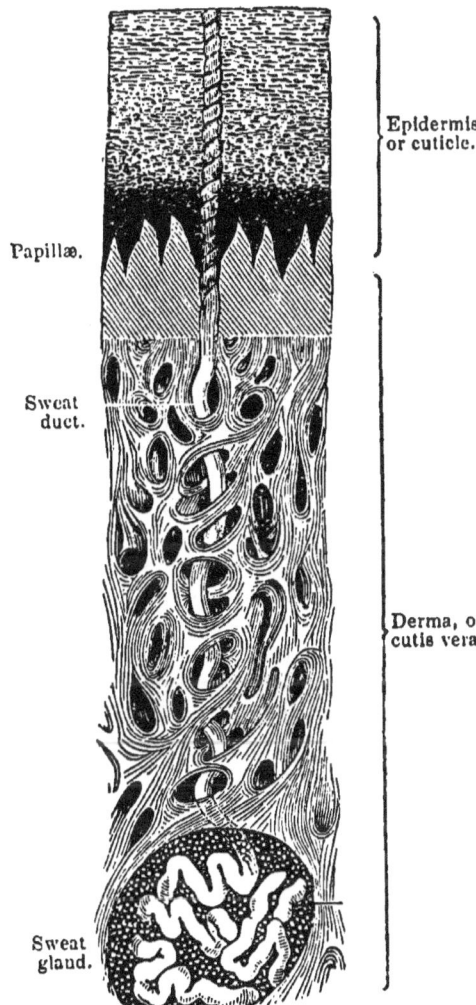

This section of the skin is represented as greatly enlarged under the microscope. The top layer, or *epidermis*, has neither nerves nor blood-vessels, and is not itself painful to the touch. From that part of it covering the scalp dry scales or dandruff are constantly passing off, a large part of which are visible to the unaided eye. These scales are composed of the waste matter which pass out through the pores, and form on the surface of the skin. Smaller scales, chiefly invisible to the naked eye, also pass out through the pores which abound in parts of the skin. These small scales when examined under the microscope appear exactly similar to the particles of dandruff, the only difference being in the size. The constant issue of this dead and useless waste will suggest to the reader the great importance of frequent and thorough washing of the surface of the body.

Under the microscope we can clearly see the round cells of the cutis, and how they become flattened and hardened as they are forced to the surface. Says Hartley: "In one square inch of the cuticle, counting only those in a single layer, there are more than a billion of horny scales."

BATHING AND HEALTH.

Fresh and Salt Water Bathing.—Salt water is a stimulant to the skin, and in many cases is to be preferred for the bath. It is, however, more exhaustive to the system, and special care should be taken in its use by invalids that it should not be prolonged or severe. The sea water is found by experiment to be milder than salt water artificially prepared, and to possess tonic properties superior to the latter.

Bathing at the Sea-side.—The sea-side resort for bathing has its special advantages. The shore and beach are more likely to be free from all products of decay. This does not exist in towns where the populations are massed, nor can we have it in the streams in the country where marshes and forced or neglected vegetation, and various other circumstances, often upset the equilibrium which Nature has so beautifully established between production and decay. "Ah!" said one, "I love the sea, for there is no dust there." That seems really an adequate reason. "When we find," says another, "dust to mean millions of invisible particles, some of which represent life unfavorable to human life, or decay in too concentrated a form, we readily rejoice that on the sea and close by the sea we may be rid of many a dust-mote of disease."

Tonic Value of Sea-side Air.—In connection with sea-side bathing there is value in another sense. In the air by the sea-shore carbonic acid and gaseous impurities are almost entirely absent, while the chlorides of the sea seem to impart to the air especial tonic properties. It is bracing, not merely in sensation, but in an actual sense. It seems as if the lungs were enabled to take in more oxygen, and with it more of those slight stimulants which sea-air contains. Under this influence the system is aroused to greater activity, and the effete products of the blood are more fully consumed. Then there is more active assimilation and construction to make up for this lawful destruction. It has been well said that this "is the kind of blood-purifier that does not need a patent, and has a real significance."

A Caution in Sea-side Bathing.—"We love this air of the sea," writes a correspondent, "and taken aright, which one soon learns, it is a tonic to drink in with exquisite delight. That does not mean that an invalid should face an ocean storm, or that he should ever allow himself to get chilly; for, though cold is often healthful, real chilliness never is. To be borne at all, it must be very temporary. If you do not know how to breathe, and forget that the nose is the chimney, and rush to the sea with the mouth wide open and a yell, you may get as hoarse as the waves, and be the shorn lamb to which the wind will not be tempered. But, if only very briefly, you will adjust yourself to the changed air, avoid at first the dampness of morning or evening, and have changes of clothing ready to adjust to changes of temperature, it is not difficult to avoid contingencies, and to get the full vigor of the ocean life."

Peril at Crowded Sea-side Resorts.—A great danger has arisen at some of the attractive localities opened for the convenience of bathers. This danger has come from the large crowds of people which gather there, and the close contact of residences and other buildings, the lack of good drainage, and of waste removal, and of the consequent befoulment of the air. Where this danger exists, the visits of the bathers should be of brief duration. No one can afford to breathe, even for a night, an atmosphere polluted by the excreta of a crowded population where there is a deficiency of good drainage.

Season for Sea-Bathing.—In the middle Atlantic States the bathing season extends from the middle of June to the middle of September. Farther north the season is shorter, and farther south longer. In the middle States, if there are no indications of unhealthfulness of the place, the season may be safely extended from four to six weeks later.

Duration of the Sea Bath.—On this head much ignorance prevails, and much damage to health and needless delays in the cure of disease are caused by such ignorance. Very many persons, especially of the younger class, stay in the water until they are tired, and are often surprised that they should pay the tax for their rashness in subsequent suffering from some one or more of the following disorders, namely: Defective reaction, as shown by paleness of the skin, blueness of the lips, sleeplessness, loss of appetite, rheumatic pains, headache, bronchitis in those with a delicate chest, earache, fullness of the head, giddiness, and various spasmodic affections. From the same cause arises disturbed digestion, manifested by pains of the stomach, nausea, and diarrhœa.

Proper Limitation of Sea-Bathing.—The allowable range is far short of that in common practice. It ought to be from a single immersion, plunge, or dip, to a bath of a quarter of an hour's duration. We refer now in a more particular manner to invalids. Nervous women, long affected with disease, and depressed by other causes, ought not to take more than one or two, or, at the most, three immersions. Children of a tender age, and of a lymphatic constitution, should not remain longer in the water than from one minute to three minutes. Equally restricted should be the period allowed to very young girls and young women who are subject to cough, and shooting pains through the breast and shoulders; and so on, in graduating scale, for other classes of invalids.

Those who have palsy of the lower limbs bear, and even require, a bath of twenty, and even twenty-five minutes, alternating with a douche or spout bath over the spine. Invalids in this class, and strong subjects, who are sufferers from nervous pains of a rheumatic character, bear two baths daily, namely, in the morning and in the evening.

Plunge-Bathing.—The practice of plunging head foremost into the water is not to be commended. Some of the kinds of headache attributed to bathing originate, in reality, from this precipitate kind of immersion. Only the strong should practice it.

Surf-Bathing.—This kind of sea-bathing is a luxury to those who are strong and vigorous. An eminent physician, however, expresses the opinion that the high surf which many seek, is more harmful than helpful to a majority of those who indulge in it. A low or gentle surf is to be preferred. We strongly recommend the erection of strong inclosures in the surf in such manner as to permit the free ebb and flow of the tide, and yet break the force of the surf wave. Such enclosures in time of the heavy surf would be exceedingly serviceable to a large proportion of sea-side bathers.

Best Hour of the Day for Bathing.—A rule of the most general, if not universal, application is, that the bath should be taken before a meal, and never on a full stomach, or during the first stages of digestion. By general consent, a morning hour is preferred for sea-bathing. Comparatively few, however, choose the time before breakfast for the purpose. Invalids with a cold skin and languid circulation will require a slight refreshment—a cup of good chocolate, a plate of plain soup, or a soft-boiled egg with a roll—before bathing. If an early or noon-day dinner be taken, an evening bath may be used with advantage, and in some cases it is found to agree better with invalids than in the morning.

For the most part, bathing at the watering places in the United States is undoubtedly begun too soon after breakfast, certainly before the digestion of the meal in the stomach is half completed. As a general rule, we are safe in directing invalids to bathe before breakfast, if they rise with a warm and even hot skin, and reach the water before they can be said to have lost the warmth of the bed, or after they have been put in a glow by exercise.

Condition of the Body Before Bathing.—To persons who awake in a perspiration, or whose skin at the time is moist with sweat, bathing under such circumstances would be injurious. The rule is, to bathe when the skin is warm, or hot and dry, and *not when it is chilled or perspiring*. Reaction and glow will follow in the first case; chilliness and headache, and pains in the limbs will be no uncommon result in the last. Great exhaustion after fatiguing exercises forbids the use of the sea to the same extent as the fresh water bath; and hence there is danger in rushing immediately into the sea after a long and fatiguing journey.

Helpful Accessories to Bathing.—**Exercise.**—In most cases the benefit of the bath would be considerably increased if followed by light and instant exercise. Walking in the open air at such a time is to be preferred. This keeps up the glow obtained by the thorough towel rubbing of the body in dressing, and extends the benefit of such glow to the internal organs of the body.

Avoid Exposure.—Avoid chilling the body by sitting or standing undressed on the banks or in boats, after having been in the water, or remaining too long in the water, but leave the water immediately there is the slightest feeling of chilliness.

Bathing In-doors.—This should be frequent and thorough. The bathroom should be an essential part of every dwelling. Every person should use it for "health's sake" *once a week, at least*. In many cases twice a week would be still better, and in some cases a daily bath would be useful. When taken frequently, it should be used only for a few minutes.

Benefit of a "Towel Bath."—A thorough rubbing daily, first with a coarse and then with a soft towel, immediately after the morning wash, is always healthful, provided it can be done without chilliness or exhaustion of the strength. Continue the towel exercise until the body is thoroughly dry, and until the glow of the skin becomes assured.

Temperature of Baths.—The cold bath is a tonic, and must be used with caution. The tepid and warm bath is slightly tonic and sedative, and induces sleep. It should generally be taken immediately before retiring. Hot baths are debilitating when used for any length of time. It is very rarely beneficial to take hot baths unless they are followed at once by a cold shower-bath to tone down the system.

It is the custom of many persons to have a cold water bath immediately on leaving their beds as a daily habit. Nevertheless, but few persons know how to use cold water judiciously for bathing purposes. Delicately-organized ladies frequently have established the same course, considering it conducive to health. There is an impression that it invigorates the individual, hardens the muscles, and strengthens the constitution. The sudden abstraction of caloric or vital warmth in that way has not only injured but destroyed more than were ever benefited thereby. The reaction, as it is called, a glow of warmth that subsequently follows, is a direct draft upon the system to meet a sudden loss of vitality, and is by no means so beneficial as theoretically imagined. A tepid bath makes no such injurious demands, and therefore it is not so injurious or perilous for those of a frail structure.

The Best Bath for Children.—We have no hesitation in recommending a warm bath early in the day, followed by a simple douche of cold water, as far preferable to the cold bath; or a warm bath at night for the sake of cleanliness, and none at all in the morning. It may be taken as a rule that, in the case of children, sudden changes of temperature are dangerous, and that 58 degrees to 60 degrees may be taken as the safe average temperature in which they should be constantly kept.

Turkish and Russian Baths.—The only difference between Turkish and Russian baths is, that in the former the bather is first submitted to hot air, and in the latter to hot vapor. The processes of shampooing, showering, plunging, rubbing, and kneading, are the same in both. In both baths the bather reclines for some time, until he is thrown by the hot air or vapor into a profuse perspiration. He is then rubbed by an attendant, and afterward receives a shower or douche of cold water. The duration of the bath depends upon the constitution and habits of the bather, and may be two minutes or two hours. These baths are of excellent service in rheumatism, neuralgia, and various nervous conditions, aside from their general cleansing and invigorating qualities.

Medicated Baths.—The alkaline bath is especially efficient in curing itching and other diseases of the skin, and is made by putting eight ounces of impure carbonate of potash into thirty gallons of tepid water.

The nitro-muriatic bath is for diseases of the liver, and is composed of two ounces of nitric acid, three ounces of muriatic acid, and ten and a half gallons of water.

Convenient Vapor Baths.—Simple and convenient vapor baths may be made by placing a large pan or pail containing boiling water under a cane-bottom chair. The patient seats himself upon it, enveloped from head to foot in a blanket, which covers the bath as well. Sulphur, spirit, herbal, and other baths, may be obtained in the same manner. They should not be taken unless prescribed by a physician.

Electric Baths.—In these baths electricity is diffused through the water of the bath-tub. Special advantages arise from the improved method of applying electricity in the treatment of disease, over the more ordinary methods. The friends of this system argue that water, at blood temperature, is a better conductor of electricity than the human body; hence the diffusion of the electric current through the water, and to the whole periphery of the body, intensifies and insures more certain results. Moreover, they claim its influence thus conditioned, in promoting the absorption of medicines dissolved in the water, and its power "through chemical affinity, to facilitate the elimination from the body of certain metallic substances, and to further the absorption of morbid deposits." A number of cases are related in support of the theories advanced, and a category of diseases given deemed to be especially amenable to this kind of treatment.

Hot Sand Baths.—One of the most attractive therapeutical novelties for some time past in London—recently introduced from the Continent—consists in the erection of establishments for administering hot sand baths as a remedy for rheumatism, recent cases of nervous disorders, affections of the kidneys, and all cases where heat is needed as the chief remedial agent. The advantages claimed in behalf of this method of treatment are, that it does not suppress respiration, like the hot water bath, but rather increases it, and does not interfere with the respiration, after the manner of the steam bath or Turkish bath. It is found that the body can endure the influence of this kind of bath for a much longer time, and a much higher temperature can be applied.

Bathing Dresses.—A bathing dress for the summer is almost as much a *sine qua non* as a morning dress, for few ladies like to subject themselves to the chances of such as can be hired from the proprietors of bathing-houses; while for those who spend the summer near salt water the cost of the material would be absorbed in a very few days. There is no doubt that the less cumbersome the clothing the more beneficial the bath, and ladies who are fortunate in having private bathing places will find a flannel dress, made with a loose blouse waist and short closed drawers, very nearly perfection; but for the ordinary bather, who has to take her chances with many others, there is no better design than the one which serves also as a gymnastic suit, and consists of a sailor blouse, skirt and trousers. The skirt is plain in front, and there is no more fullness in either blouse or skirt than is necessary to its good appearance. The amount of material required for this entire suit is little less than nine yards. Twilled flannel, dark blue or Russian gray, is the most serviceable material for bathing dresses, as it does not chill or hold the water. White, black, or red braids are the usual trimmings, put on broad and in clusters, or simply as bindings, according to taste.

Twenty-two Brief Hints to Bathers.—In the preceding paragraphs we indicated the principles and methods which should govern the habit of bathing. We now subjoin a summary of directions to bathers, which are condensed from an admirable work by Dr. R. M. Trall:

1. Never bathe soon after eating.
2. A full bath should not be taken less than three hours after a full meal.
3. Do not take any cold bath when in a state of chilliness or fatigue.
4. Always have the feet comfortably warmed, by fire, hot water, or exercise, at the time of taking any cold bath.
5. If inclined to headache, wet the head with cool water before bathing.
6. Never drink cold water just before bathing.
7. Do not eat soon after bathing. An hour should elapse after a full bath, and half an hour after a local bath before taking the meal.
8. Local baths, as hip, foot, etc., may be taken an hour after a light, and two hours after a full meal.
9. Patients who are able should exercise before and after bathing.
10. If not able to exercise, and inclined to chilliness, they should cover up in bed for an hour after bathing.

11. No strong shock, by means of the shower or douche, should be made on the head.

12. After bathing do not sit in a draught of cold air, nor allow the feet to become cold.

13. Avoid all very cold or very hot baths in all cases of great debility, local congestions, or determinations of blood to particular parts; also all processes which disturb the circulation, as shower, douche, and plunge baths.

14. Great heat of the body is no objection to any form or kind of bath, providing the respiration is not disturbed, nor the patient in a state of fatigue.

15. When two or more baths are administered daily the principal and coldest one should be taken in the fore part of the day.

16. All full baths, except the warm, are better in the morning or forenoon than in the afternoon or evening.

17. When baths are taken regularly every day, they should be omitted occasionally, as one day in a week, or two or three days in a month.

18. Whenever the patient feels dependent on any particular form of bath, and persists that he cannot do without it, some other should be substituted for a few days.

19. Patients should never take a bath so cold that fatiguing exercise is necessary to "get up reaction." The better way is to use water of a milder temperature.

20. Very feeble persons should have the water for all bathing purposes at nearly the neutral temperature, which is ninety degrees, varying but a few degrees above or below.

21. Pleasurable sensations for the time are no evidence that the bath is useful. Very cold or very hot baths may be succeeded by agreeable feelings, but be very wasteful of vitality.

22. The temperature of the bathing-room should always be comfortably warmed and well ventilated. For invalids the temperature should be seventy to eighty degrees.

SLEEP AND HEALTH.

Sleep a Necessity.—Sleep is a necessity. Without it we would suffer speedy dissolution. Every act that we perform, every movement we make, every thought that passes through our minds, every emotion that stirs our souls, breaks down a certain amount of nervous tissue, and leaves us weaker than before. These broken cells can be repaired during sleep only. The system, exhausted by physical and mental labor during the day, must be built up and strengthened for the next day's work during the dark, still hours of night.

while the senses are locked in slumber, and the mind and muscles are all relaxed; for at no other time is this process of building up carried on.

What Sleep will Cure.—The cry for rest has always been louder than the cry for food. Not that it is more important, but it is often harder to get. The best rest comes from sound sleep. Of two men or women, otherwise equal, the one who sleeps the best will be the most devotional, healthy, and efficient. Sleep will do much to cure irritability of temper, peevishness, uneasiness. It will cure insanity. It will build up and make strong a weary body. It will do much to cure dyspepsia, particularly that variety known as nervous dyspepsia. It will relieve the languor and prostration felt by consumptives. It will cure hypochondria. It will cure the headache. It will cure neuralgia. It will help cure a broken spirit. It will help cure sorrow.

How We Go to Sleep.—The muscles which move the arms and legs usually become relaxed before those which maintain the body in an erect position. In relation to the social senses, that of sight is the first lost, the eyelids forming a barrier between the retina and the external world; but, independently of eyelids, if they had been removed by the surgeon, or could not be closed by disease, this is still the first sense whose function is abolished. Some animals, as the hare, do not shut their eyes when asleep; and in cases of somnambulism, the eyes remain open, although the sense of sight is temporarily abolished, and their acuteness is much lessened.

Taste is the next to disappear, and then smell; hearing follows, and touch is the most persistent of the senses. So, conversely, a person is most easily awakened by the sense of touch; next in order by sounds, and then by smell.

Position During Sleep.—The recumbent position has much to do with sleep. Undoubtedly sleep may occur in the sitting posture, and even while standing; but these cases are exceptional. It is certain, also, that sleep in bed is generally sounder with a low pillow than with a high one. If, therefore, there be a state of wakefulness at night, the head should be kept low; if, on the contrary, there is undue sleepiness, the head should be kept high. The degree of sleep, and its amount, may be regulated by simply taking care that the head is in the right position. If prolonged recumbency is a necessary part of the treatment, the tendency to sleep too much during the day and too little at night may be thus corrected.

Why High Pillows are Injurious.—It is often a question among people who are unacquainted with anatomy and physiology, whether lying with head exalted or on a level with the body is the more unwholesome. Most, consulting their own case on this point, argue in favor of that which they prefer. Now, although many delight in bolstering up their heads at night, and sleep soundly without injury, yet it is a dangerous habit. The vessels in which the blood passes from the heart to the head are always lessened in their cavities when the head is resting in bed higher than the body; therefore, in all diseases attended with fever the head should be pretty nearly on a level with the body; and people ought to accustom themselves to sleep thus and avoid danger.

Sleeping on the Back or Side, Which?—It is not best to sleep mainly on the back, but it is well to alternate, and sleep occasionally on either side, not always on the right, nor always on the left, but on both. The right side is better of the two sides to lie upon for any length of time, as it leaves the action of the heart free, and precludes the probability of undue pressure on any of the large blood-vessels; but generally the body may be allowed to select its own position.

Evil Effects of Sleeping Exclusively on One Side.—The question is often put to physicians, "Why is my head lop-sided or larger on one side?" It *may* be accounted for by always lying on one side. Young mothers are apt to place the child always in one position when putting it to bed, and the skull being soft and thin, the brain grows most on the under side, and finally assumes permanently this irregular and uneven shape. In cholera times, or when the bowels are cold, constipated, and inactive, it is well to lie on the breast, and thus keep the bowels warm.

Amount of Sleep Necessary.—It is impossible to lay down rules regulating the amount of sleep necessary for each individual; some persons need much more than others. The amount necessary depends much upon the age, health, temperament, and climate.

Testimony of an Experienced Farmer.—Said one of the oldest and most successful farmers in this country: "I do not care to have my men get up before five or half-past five in the morning, and if they go to bed early and can sleep soundly, they will do more work than if they got up at four or half-past four. We do not believe in the eight-hour law, but nevertheless are inclined to think that, as a general rule, we work too many hours on the farm. The best man we ever had to dig ditches seldom worked, when digging by the rod, more than niné hours a day. And it is so in chopping wood by the cord; the men who accomplish the most work the fewest hours. They bring all their brain and muscle into exercise and make every blow tell. A slow, plodding Dutchman may turn a grindstone or a fanning-mill better than an energetic Yankee, but this kind of work is now mostly done by horsepower, and the farmer needs above all else a clear head, with all his faculties of mind and muscle light and active, and under complete control. Much, of course, depends on temperament; but as a rule such men need sound sleep and plenty of it.*

---

* When a boy on the farm I was told that Napoleon needed only four hours' sleep, and the old nonsense of "five hours for a man, six hours for a woman, and seven hours for

Sleep and Health.

Waking Children.—We caution parents particularly not to allow their children to be waked up in the mornings; let nature wake them up; she will not do it prematurely; but have a care that they go to bed at an early hour; let it be earlier and earlier, until it is found that they wake up themselves in full time to dress for breakfast. Being waked up early and allowed to engage in difficult or any studies late, and just before retiring, has given many a beautiful and promising child brain fever, or determined ordinary ailments to the production of water on the brain. Infants cannot sleep too long, and it is a favorable symptom when they enjoy a calm and long-continued rest. They should never be awakened, and thus deprived of the greatest support nature has given them.

Best Hours for Sleeping.—Sleep obtained two hours before midnight, when the negative forces are in operation, is the rest which most recuperates the system, giving brightness to the eye and a glow to the cheek. The difference in the appearance of a person who habitually retires at ten o'clock and that of one who sits up until twelve, is quite remarkable. The tone of the system, so evident in the complexion, the clearness and sparkle of the eye, and the softness of the lines of the features, is, in a person of health, kept at "concert pitch" by taking regular rest two hours before twelve o'clock, and thereby obtaining the "beauty sleep" of the night. There is a heaviness of the eye, a sallowness of the skin, and an absence of that glow in the face which renders it fresh in expression and round in appearance, that readily distinguishes the person who keeps late hours.

Kiss the Children a "Happy Good Night."—If we go to sleep in a happy frame of mind it will help much toward a refreshing slumber. A cheerful "good night" and an affectionate kiss (if there is sufficient spontaneity about it to make it worth any thing) are decidedly *healthful* for the little ones. Never scold or give lectures, or in any way wound a child's feelings as it goes to bed. Let all banish business and worldly care at bed-time, and let sleep come to a mind at peace with God and all the world.

The Great Pleasure of Sleep.—Let us all cherish the thought of our approach to sleep, of which some unknown writer has beautifully said: "It is a delicious moment: the feeling that we are safe, that we shall drop gently to sleep. The good is to come, not past. The limbs have been just tired

fool," is often quoted, but the truth is, that Napoleon was enabled, in a great measure, to accomplish what he did from the faculty of sleeping soundly—of *sleeping when he slept* and *working when he worked.* His favorite traveling carriages were so arranged that he could lie down at full length, and when dashing through the country as fast as eight horses, frequently changed, could carry him, he slept soundly, and when he arrived at his destination was as fresh as if he had risen from a bed of down. Let farmers, and especially farmers' boys, have plenty to eat, nothing to "drink," and all the sleep they can take.—*American Agriculturist.*

enough to render the remaining in one position delightful, and the labor of the day is done. A gentle failing of the perceptions comes slowly creeping over us; the consciousness disengages itself more and more with slow and hushing degrees, like a fond mother detaching her hand from that of her sleeping child; the mind seems to have a balmy lid closed, closed altogether, and the mysterious spirit of sleep has gone to take its airy rounds."

"**Sleeping Alone.**"—It is not well to place a very young person in the same bed with a very old one, as the younger in such a case will suffer by a loss of vitality and heat. One in a bed is better than two, especially where there is a great contrast in age.

Are Feather-beds Unhealthy?—Feathers make a very unhealthy bed, because they retain the heat and keep the temperature of the body too high, thus debilitating the skin and rendering the system liable to contract colds; they also retain the moisture and waste matter thrown out by the lymphatic, which is absorbed, producing disease. A dry straw bed, or, what is better, a hair mattress, should be used.

In what Direction Shall the Bed Stand?—Sleeping-rooms should always be so arranged, if possible, as to allow the head of the sleeper to be turned toward the north. Frequently, in cases of sickness, a person will find it impossible to obtain rest if his head is in any other direction, and often a cure is retarded for a long time. This arrangement for the sleeper puts him in harmony with the electrical currents caused by the motion of the earth on its axis. Try this and see.

Sleep for the Invalid.—An eminent English physician says that a large allowance of sleep to the invalid is possessed of eminent sanitary advantages. "Nothing," he remarks, " is equal to eight or nine hours of undisturbed repose. Take it through the night, or partially through the day and night, but secure enough, and the beneficial effects will not fail to show themselves." In one portion of his essay he adds a hint specially for city invalids: "Go to bed by nine o'clock and sleep till six or seven. Do not sit up till ten or eleven and rise at five, for if you do, no dieting or exercise can supply the waste of the system."

Lack of Sleep Causes Leanness.—Dr. Dio Lewis puts the following suggestive incident on record:—

A very thin young lady of about twenty years, with a friend, came to consult me about her "skin and bones." I had frequently met her when she seemed even more emaciated, but now she "would give the world to be plump." Sitting down in front of me, she began with:—

"Don't you think, doctor, that I look very old for twenty?"

I admitted that she looked rather old for twenty.

"Can any thing be done for me? What can I do? I would be willing to take a hundred bottles of the worst stuff in the world if I could only get some fat on these bones. A friend of mine (her beau) was saying yesterday that he would give a fortune to see me round and plump."

"Would you be willing to go to the Cliff Springs in Arkansas?"

"I would start to-morrow."

"But the waters are very bad to drink," I said.

"I don't care how bad they are; I know I can drink them."

"I asked you whether you were willing to go to the Arkansas Springs to test the strength of your purpose. It is not necessary to leave your home. Nine people out of ten can become reasonably plump without such a sacrifice."

"Why, doctor, I am delighted to hear it; but I suppose it is a lot of some bitter stuff."

"Yes, it is a pretty bitter dose, and has to be taken every night."

"I don't care; I would take it if it was twice as bad. What is it? What is the name of it?"

"The technical name of the stuff is *bedibus nineo'clockibus*."

"Why, doctor, what an awful name! I am sure I will never be able to speak it. Is there no common English word for it?"

"O, yes. The English for it is, 'You must be in bed every night at nine o'clock.'"

"O, that is dreadful! I thought it was something I could *take*."

"It is. You must take your bed every night before the clock strikes nine."

"No; but what I thought was that you would give me something in a bottle to take."

"Of course, I know very well what you thought. That's the way with all of you."

One person eats enormously of rich food till his stomach and liver refuse to budge; then he cries out, "O, doctor, what can I take? I must take something."

Another fills his system with tobacco until his nerves are ruined, and then, trembling and full of horrors, he exclaims, "O, doctor, what shall I take?" I write a prescription out for him — *Quitibus Chawibus et Smokibus*.

I will suppose my patient is not a classical scholar, as I am sure my reader is, and so I translate it for him into English. He cries out at once:—

"O, doctor, I thought you would give me something to take."

Another sits up till thirteen or fourteen o'clock. leads a life of theaters and other dissipations. becomes pale, dyspeptic, and wretched, and then flies to the doctor, and cries, "O, doctor, what shall I take? What shall I take?"

"Now, madam, you are distressed because your lover has been looking at your skin and bones."

"But, doctor, you are entirely—"

"O well, we'll say nothing about him, then. But tell me, what time do you go to bed?"

"Generally about twelve o'clock."

"Yes, I thought so. Now, if you will go to bed every night for six months at nine o'clock, without making any change in your habits, you will gain ten pounds in weight and look five years younger. Your skin will become fresh, and your spirits improve wonderfully."

"I'll do it. Though, of course, when I have company and during the opera I can't do it."

It is regularity that does the business. To sit up till 12 o'clock three nights in the week, and then get to bed at 9 o'clock four nights, one might think would do very well, and that at any rate it would be "so far so good." I don't think this every other night early and every other night late is much better than every night late. It is regularity that is vital in the case. Even sitting up one night in the week deranges the nervous system for the whole week. I have sometimes thought that those people who sit up till 11 or 12 o'clock every night get on quite as well as those who turn in early six nights and then sit up once a week till midnight.

Regularity in sleep is every bit as important as regularity in food.

At length my patient exclaimed, "Doctor, I will go to bed every night for six months before nine o'clock if it kills me, or rather if it breaks the hearts of all my friends."

She did it. Twenty-one pounds was the gain in five months. Her spirits were happily enlivened, and she spent half her time in telling her friends of her delight with the new habit. She had no further cause to complain of skin and bones, and she had the special gratification of appearing more attractive in the eyes of her lover.

Sleeplessness—How to Prevent It.—Sleep is a powerful antidote to a long list of nervous ailments. Sleeplessness is an evil which should be removed without delay. The following are among the good rules which, if observed, will usually bring relief to those afflicted with chronic sleeplessness

1. A good clean bed.
2. Sufficient exercise to produce weariness, and pleasant occupation.
3. Good air and not too warm a room.
4. Freedom from too much care.
5. A clear stomach.
6. A clear conscience.
7. Avoidance of stimulants and narcotics.

Sleeplessness—How to Cure It.—Nervous persons, who are troubled with wakefulness and excitability, usually have a strong tendency of blood to the brain, with cold extremities. The pressure of blood on the brain keeps it in a stimulated or wakeful state, and the pulsations in the head are often painful. Let such persons note the following suggestions, which are collected from various sources:

Rise and chafe the body and extremities with a crash towel, or rub smartly with the hands to promote circulation, and withdraw the excessive amount of blood from the brain, and sleep will follow in a few minutes.

A cold bath, or a sponge bath and rubbing, or a good run, or a rapid walk in the open air, or going up and down stairs a few times just before retiring, will aid in equalizing circulation and promoting sleep.

Wet half a towel, apply it to the back of the neck, pressing it up toward the base of the brain, and fasten the dry half of the towel over so as to prevent the too-rapid exhalation. The effect is prompt and charming, cooling the brain and inducing calmer, sweeter sleep than any narcotic. Warm water may be used, though most persons will prefer it cold. To those suffering from over-excitement of the brain, whether the result of brain-work or of pressing anxiety, this simple remedy is an especial boon.

Sometimes any mental exercise which concentrates the mind on one subject will bring relief.

Playing a game of skill, such as checkers or chess, demonstrating a difficult proposition in geometry, or solving an arithmetical or algebraical problem, has often led to this mental condition, and been followed by a good sleep, which otherwise seemed impossible.

One of the very best methods of "courting sleep" is that of counting. Breathe deeply and slowly (without any straining effort) and with every respiration count one, two, three, etc., up to a hundred. Some persons will be asleep before they count fifty in this manner. Others will count ten, twenty, or thirty, and then forget themselves and cease counting. In such cases always commence again at one. Very few persons can count one hundred and find themselves awake; but should this happen repeat the dose until cured. Counting in some other language, as German or Latin, is very good.

If sleepless at night on account of the heat, try the effect of warm water upon the feet. If that does not give relief, try the virtues of a warm bath, but not often, as its frequent use debilitates.

An Eminent Clergyman's Advice.—Dr. Alexander was often heard to say in substance as follows: "Clergymen, authors, teachers, and other men of reflective habits, lose much health by losing sleep, and this because they carry their trains of thought to bed with them. The best thing one can do is take care of the *last half hour before retiring.* Devotions being ended, something may be done to quiet the strings of the harp, which otherwise would go on to vibrate. Let me commend to you this maxim, which I somewhere learned from Dr. Watts, who says that in his boyhood he received it from the lips of Dr. John Owen—a very good pedigree for a maxim: *Break the chain of thoughts at bed-time by something at once serious and agreeable.*

By all means break the continuity, or sleep will be vexed, if not driven away. If you wish to know my method, it is to turn over the pages of my English Bible, alighting on a passage here, a passage there, backward and forward without plan, and without allowing my mind to fasten on any, leaving any place the moment it ceases to interest me. Some tranquilizing word often becomes a divine blessing of peace. 'He giveth his beloved sleep.'"

Slumber at Will.—The following is given in "Blinn's Anatomy of Sleep; or, the Art of Procuring Sound and Refreshing Slumber at Will," published in London in 1842. The principal feature of Blinn's system is for the patient to fix his attention on his own breathing. "He must depict to himself that he sees the breath passing from his nostrils in a continuous stream, and the very instant that he brings his mind to conceive this, apart from all other ideas, consciousness and memory depart; imagination slumbers, fancy becomes dormant, thought subdued; the sentient faculties lose their susceptibility, the vital or ganglionic system assumes sovereignty—and he no longer wakes, but sleeps."

Sleep Procured by Medicine is rarely as beneficial as that secured naturally. The disturbance to the nervous system is often sufficient to counterbalance all the good results. The habit of seeking sleep in this way, without the advice of a physician, is to be deprecated. The dose must be constantly increased to produce the effect, and thus great injury may be caused. Often, too, where laudanum or morphine is used, the person unconsciously comes into a terrible and fatal bondage. Especially should infants never be dosed with cordials, as is the common family practice. The damage done to helpless childhood by the ignorant and reckless use of soothing-syrups is frightful to contemplate.

"A Pillow for the Sleepless."—A friend once told me, says Rev. H. Woodward, that, among other symptoms of high nervous excitement, he had been painfully harassed for the want of sleep. To such a degree had this proceeded, that if in the course of the day any occasion led him to his bedchamber, the sight of his bed made him shudder at the idea of the wretched and restless hours he had to pass upon it.

In this case it was recommended to him to endeavor, when he laid down at night, to fix his mind on something at the same time vast and simple—such as the wide ocean, or the cloudless vault of heaven; that the little hurried and disturbed images that flitted before his mind might be charmed away, or hushed to rest, by the calming influences of one absorbing thought.

Though not at all a religious man at the time, this advice suggested to his mind that if an object, at once vast and simple, was to be selected for meditation, nothing could serve his purpose so well as the thought of God. He resolved to make the trial and think of him. The result exceeded his most sanguine hopes; in thinking of God he fell asleep. Night after night he re sorted to the same expedient. The process became delightful; so much so that he used to long for the usual hour for retiring, that he might fall asleep, as he termed it, in God. What began as a mere physical operation, grew by imperceptible degrees into a gracious influence. The same God who was his repose by night was in all his thoughts by day, and at the time this person spoke to me, God, as revealed in the Gospel of his Son, was "all his salvation and all his desire." So various are the means and inscrutable the ways by which God can "fetch home the banished."

Sleeping Hints.—Sleep is the best known form of rest, and yet it is only partial, for scarcely any part of the body is completely at rest. The heart beats, the blood courses, the lungs and skin are active.

In sleep the volume of blood in the brain is diminished. Remedies which diminish the amount of blood in the brain (as bromide of potassium) are promotive of sleep.

Sleep is a good thermometer of health. Whatever improves the sleep of an invalid betters his condition.

Sleep with the mouth shut. *Will* to do it and persevere, and you will succeed.

Wash the body before sleeping, especially after a day of dust or sweating.

Exhalations through the skin are more abundant while asleep than when awake; therefore the bed should be well aired before it is made up.

In youth more sleep is needed than in old age, when nature makes few permanent repairs, and is content with temporary expedients. In general, one should sleep until he naturally wakes.

"I have nothing to say about feather beds," says a recent writer. "None of our family like them; but I would willingly provide one for an elderly person to whom habit had made it seem a necessity."

Short Sleepers.—Lord Brougham, and many other great statesmen and lawyers, contented themselves with a remarkably small quantity of sleep. Frederick the Great slept only five hours out of every twenty-four; John Hunter, five hours; General Elliot, the hero of Gibraltar, four hours, the Duke of Wellington, in some of his campaigns, less than four hours; Wesley, six hours. The brevity of their sleep did not prevent their enjoyment of good health, nor their living to a good old age.

Living Without Sleep.—Five young men in Berlin lately made an agreement, for a wager, to see who of them could keep awake for a whole week. They all held out for about five days and a half by drinking largely of strong coffee, and keeping up a constant round of active exercises and exciting amusements. At the end of that time two of them yielded to drowsiness;

a third soon fell asleep while riding, tumbled from his saddle, and broke his arm; a fourth was attacked by severe sickness, and compelled to retire from the list; the fifth held out to the end, but lost twenty-five pounds of flesh in winning the wager. Long ago, Frederick the Great and Voltaire m de a similar experiment, making use of the same stimulant of strong coffee, but they did not succeed in driving away sleep for more than four days. "Tired nature" obstinately refuses to accept of any substitute for her "sweet restorer."

Curious Cases of Long Sleeping.—In the middle of the last century a young Frenchwoman, at Toulouse, had, for half a year, fits of lengthened sleep, varying from three to thirteen days each. About the same time a girl, at Newcastle-on-Tyne, slept fourteen weeks without waking, and the waking process occupied three days to complete.

Dr. Blanchet, of Paris, mentions the case of a lady who slept for twenty days together, when she was about eighteen years of age, fifty when she was about twenty, and had nearly a whole year's sleep, from Easter Sunday, 1862, till March, 1863. During this long sleep (which physicians call hysteric coma) she was fed with milk and soup, one of her front teeth being extracted to obtain an opening into her mouth.

Stow, in his "Chronicles," tells us that "The 27th of April, 1546, being Tuesdaie in Easter weeke, W. Foxley, pot maker for the Mint in the Tower of London, fell asleep, and so continued sleeping, and could not be waked with pricking, cramping, or otherwise, till the first day of the next term, which was full fourteen dayes and fifteen nights. The causes of his thus sleeping could not be knowne, tho' the same were diligentlie searched for by the king's physicians and other learned men; yea, the king himself examined ye said W. Foxley, who was in all points found at his waking to be as if he had slept but one night."

Soft or Hard Beds, Which?—On this question there are wide differences of opinion, some persons advocating soft, and others hard beds. The difference between them is, that the weight of a body on a soft bed presses on a larger surface than upon a hard bed, and consequently more comfort is enjoyed. Hard beds should never be given to little children, and parents who suppose that such beds contribute to health by hardening and developing the constitution, are surely in error. Eminent physicians—both here and in England—concur in this opinion, and state that hard beds have often proved injurious to the shape of infants. Birds and animals cover their offspring with the softest materials they can obtain, and also make soft beds for them; and the softness of a bed is not evidence of its being unwholesome. But if it is not kept sweet and clean by daily airings and frequent beatings—whether it is hard or soft—it is surely injurious to health.

Warm or Cold Sleeping-Rooms, Which?—There is an old notion, and a foolish one, that it is better to sleep in a cold room than in a moderately warm one. Given good ventilation, and a fire in a sleeping-room in cold weather is healthy. There is no gain in the chilliness of dressing and undressing in a temperature near the freezing point, but the shock to the system is positively injurious. Cold bed-chambers always imperil health, and invite fatal diseases. Robust persons may safely sleep in a temperature of forty or under, but the old, the infantile, and the frail, should never sleep in a room where the atmosphere is much under fifty degrees Fahrenheit.

Thorough Ventilation of Sleeping-Rooms.—All persons spend more time in their sleeping-rooms than in any other room in the house. As a rule about one-third of human life is thus spent. The sleeping-room, therefore, should be the best aired, the most comfortable, and in all other respects the most healthful room. Ample ventilation is needed at all hours; but especial attention should be paid to ventilation during sleep. There is no danger in having a sleeping apartment well ventilated, provided one sleeps warm, being well protected by an abundance of blankets.

Time Required for Airing the Beds.—The desire of an energetic housekeeper to have her work done at an early hour in the morning, causes her to leave one of the most important items of neatness undone. The most effectual purifying of bed and bed-clothes cannot take place if the proper time is not allowed for the free circulation of pure air to remove all human impurities which have collected during the hours of slumber. At least two or three hours should be allowed for the complete removal of atoms of insensible perspiration which are absorbed by the bed. Every day this airing should be done; and occasionally bedding constantly used should be carried into the open air, and when practicable, left exposed to the sun and wind for half a day.

Dreaming and Somnambulism.—Those cases in which the brain is hard at work during sleep instead of being totally oblivious of every thing, may be called dreaming or somnambulism, according to the mode in which the activity displays itself. Many of them are full of interest. Some men have done really hard mental work while asleep. Condorcet finished a train of calculations in his sleep which had much puzzled him during the day. In 1756 a collegian noticed the peculiarities of a fellow-student who was rather stupid than otherwise during his waking hours, but who got through some excellent work in geometry and algebra during sleep. Coleridge composed *Kubla Kahn* while asleep.

The Cause of Nightmare.—Nightmare is caused by remaining so long in one position that the blood ceases to circulate. How hard we try to run in our sleep, sometimes, to get out of the way of some terrible danger!

does such a person no good to ask what's the matter. Don't waste time in asking a question, but give relief to the sleeper by *an instantaneous shake*, or even a *touch of the body*, which breaks the dreadful spell in an instant, because it sets the blood going toward the heart.

Snoring, and How to Stop It.—Not long since, John A. Wyeth, M.D., described in the *Popular Science Monthly*,* a novel invention for stopping snoring. We give the description in his own words:—

To those unacquainted with the mysterious parlance of the anatomist, the use of strictly scientific terms might prove discouraging and fail to interest. I shall, therefore, discard the *scientific* in favor of the *every-day* phrases, in explanation of the following figure (1) which, it will be observed, represents a human head split from above downward through the central line.

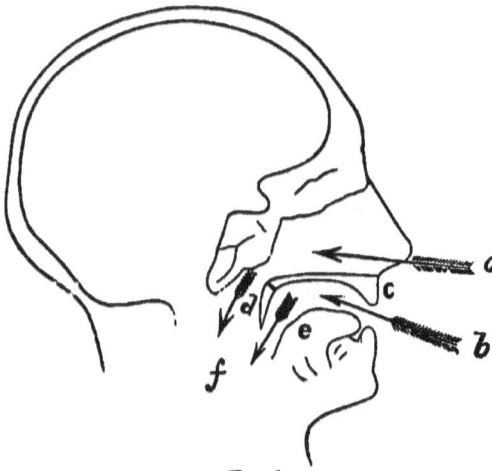

Fig. 1.

Through the only two channels in which the air travels in going to the lungs, namely, through the nose and mouth, are drawn two arrows, *a* and *b*. These two passages unite in a common cavity at *f*, and from that point there is but one tube leading to the lungs.

At *c* is a bone called the *hard palate*, which forms the roof of the mouth and the floor of the nose, separating these two air-channels from each other. At the inner or posterior end of the bone, *c*, is seen a little body, *d*, called the *soft palate*, made of muscle and covered with a delicate skin. This *soft palate* is attached at one end to *c*, the *hard palate*; the other end hangs loose, and moves or flaps in the act of breathing, something like a window-curtain when acted upon by a current of air. This is its condition while we are asleep or awake, though during sleep it lacks in *tonicity*, being much more relaxed, or flabby, than when we are awake. At *e* is represented the tongue.

Now, in order to snore, one must keep the mouth open, as well as the nose, and in this condition the two currents of air, *a* and *b*, passing in and out together during the acts of breathing, catch this little curtain, *d*, between them,

---

* The article was subsequently published also in *The Christian Advocate*, New York.

Sleep and Health.

and throw it into rapid vibration. This vibration, more or less intense and sonorous, is what we call *snoring*.

It is only with the mouth open that snoring can be accomplished during sleep. Awake, if the nose is closed by the thumb and finger, by taking a forcible breath, it is possible to snore, and the same result may be accomplished with the mouth shut and the nose open; but the muscular effort necessary to its accomplishment is more than we can command during sleep, and would wake up the individual who might unconsciously make the effort.

If the mouth be closed, (the natural condition during slumber,) but one current of air will pass to and from the lungs. This current, pressing about equally upon all sides of the canal indicated at *a*, will press the *soft palate*, *d*, forward and downward until it is applied to the tongue, *e*, and will hold it there gently, thus preventing any sonorous vibration.

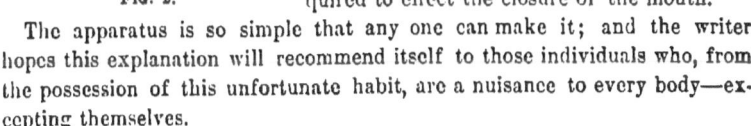

Fig. 2.

It follows that any device which prevents the lower jaw from dropping down during the relaxation of sleep, and opening the mouth, will shut out the one unnatural current of air and prevent snoring.

I have devised the apparatus represented in Fig. 2, which consists of a simple cap, *a*, fitting the head snugly; a cap of soft material, *b*, fitting the chin; and a piece of elastic webbing, *c*, tacked to the chin-piece, and to the head-cap near the ears. The webbing can be made more or less tense as may be required to effect the closure of the mouth.

The apparatus is so simple that any one can make it; and the writer hopes this explanation will recommend itself to those individuals who, from the possession of this unfortunate habit, are a nuisance to every body—excepting themselves.

Are Plants in Sleeping-Rooms Injurious?—Dr. J. C. Draper in a paper in the *Galaxy* furnishes a very clear and able discussion in reference to this question. We condense and quote:—

Plants Give out Carbonic Acid During the Night.—"Though the air is dependent for the renewal of its oxygen on the action of the green leaves of plants, it must not be forgotten that it is only in the presence and under the stimulus of light that these organisms decompose carbonic acid. All plants, irrespective of their kind or nature, absorb oxygen and exhale carbonic acid in the dark. The quantity of noxious gas thus eliminated is however, exceedingly small when compared with the oxygen thrown out dis ing the day. When they are flowering, plants exhale carbonic acid in considerable quantity, and, at the same time, evolve heat. In this condition, therefore, they resemble animals as regards their relation to the air; and a number of plants placed in a room would, under these circumstances, tend to vitiate the air."

Flowering Plants more Injurious than Others.—"While the phanerogamia, or flowering plants, depend on the air almost entirely for their supply of carbon, and are busy during the day in restoring to it the oxygen that has been removed by animals, many of the inferior cryptogamia, as the fungi and parasitic plants, obtain their nourishment from material that has already been organized. They do not absorb carbonic acid, but on the contrary they act like animals, absorbing oxygen and exhaling carbonic acid at all times. It is, therefore, evident that their presence in a room cannot be productive of good results."

Plants Exhale Other Noxious Substances.—"Aside from the highly deleterious action that plants may exert on the atmosphere of a sleeping-room, by increasing the proportion of carbonic acid during the night, there is another and more important objection to be urged against their presence in such apartments. Like animals, they exhale peculiar volatile organic principles which, in many instances, render them unfit for the purposes of respiration. Even in the days of Andronicus this fact was recognized, for he says, in speaking of Arabia Felix, that 'by reason of myrrh, frankincense, and hot spices there growing, the air was so obnoxious to their brains that the very inhabitants at some times cannot avoid its influence.' What the influence on the brains of the inhabitants may have been does not at present interest us; we have only quoted the statement to show that long ago the emanations from plants were regarded as having an influence on the condition of the air; and, in view of our present ignorance, it would be wise to banish them from our sleeping apartments, at least until we are better informed regarding their true properties."

Sleep and Death.—As men grow to be about fifty years old, especially if of sedentary habits, the feeling on rising in the morning is as if they had not gotten sleep enough, not as much as they used to have, and as if they would like to have more, but they cannot get it. They look upon a healthy child sleeping soundly with a feeling of envy. But it is curious to observe that there is a bliss to all in the act of going to sleep, a bliss we become cognizant of only when we happen to be aroused just as we are falling into sound sleep; and there are strong physiological reasons to suppose that this state is a counterpart of that great event that is to come upon all, the act of dying. In fact, those who have in rare cases been brought back to life when on the verge of death, and in several cases those who have been recovered from drowning, and other modes of strangulation or simple smothering, called "asphyxia" by physicians, the expressions have been, on coming to consciousness, "How delicious! Why did you not let me go?" An eminent man thus brought back represented that the last-remembered sensations of which he was conscious were as if he were listening to the most ravishing strains of music.

CLOTHING AND HEALTH.

The Most Healthy Clothing.—The most healthful clothing for our climate, the year round, is that made of wool. If worn next the skin by all classes, in summer as well as winter, an incalculable amount of coughs, colds, diarrhœa, dysenteries, and fevers would be prevented, as also many sudden and premature deaths from croup, diphtheria, and lung diseases. Winter maladies would be prevented by the ability of a woolen garment to keep the natural heat about the body more perfectly, instead of conveying it away as fast as generated, as linen and flaxen garments do, as also cotton and silk, although these are less cooling than Irish linen, as any one can prove by noticing the different degrees of coldness on the application of a surface of six inches square of flannel, cotton, and linen to the skin the moment the clothing is removed. The reason is, that wool is a bad conductor of heat.*

Flannel in Summer as well as Winter.—The incalculable benefit of wearing flannel next the body, in summer as well as winter, cannot be estimated. Flannel is not so uncomfortable in warm weather as many believe. Frequent colds and coughs are almost unknown when flannels are worn. Some women object to them because they are bulky about the waist. This objection can be obviated by shaping them in tight sack fashion, or cutting them out like waists and buttoning them behind. The sudden and frequent changes of our climate are scarcely felt, and certainly do very little injury to those persons who wear flannel constantly. Above all, mothers should clothe the tender bodies of their little ones with under-garments of this material. Warmth is almost as necessary to healthful development as food, and parents should endeavor to clothe their children so as to secure the greatest amount for them.

Best Color for Clothing.—In an article upon "The Clothing We Wear," Dr. Nichols, of the Boston *Journal of Chemistry*, says: "The color of clothing is by no means a matter of indifference. White and light-colored clothes reflect the heat, while black and dark-colored ones absorb it. White is the comfortable and fashionable color for clothing in summer. It reflects heat

---

* Dr. Hall.

well, and prevents the sun's rays from passing through and heating the body. If white is the best color for summer, it does not follow that black is the best for winter. It must be remembered that black radiates heat with great rapidity. Give a coat of white paint to a black steam radiator, which is capable of rendering a room comfortably warm at all times, and the temperature will fall at once, though the heat-producing agency remains the same as before. A black garment robs the body of a larger amount of heat than white, and consequently the latter color is the best for winter garments. It is the best color for both summer and winter. Although this statement may seem like blowing hot and cold, it is nevertheless true. Let those who are troubled with cold feet, and who wear dark stockings, change to white, and see if the difficulty is not in part or wholly removed."

The Texture of Clothing should not be Close.—For all seasons the more porous the clothing is, the better. Porous clothes will give ready escape to the perspiration and a free admission of air to the skin. For this reason woolens, which excel in that quality, should be worn constantly.

Evil of Insufficient Clothing.—One of the great evils induced by fashion is the unequal distribution of clothing upon the person. One part over-clothed, and another not half clad, is a very common condition, especially among women and children. Women are governed by fashion, children are governed by women, and it is the great resource of fashion to produce new effects by piling on the textures, now here and now there, and by leaving other parts exposed. If the declared purpose were to induce disease, no surer or more effectual way could be found to do it than this. The derangement of the circulation is direct and immediate; its healthy equilibrium is destroyed, the thinly-dressed parts lose their blood to the more vascular, and internal derangements give rise to various chronic bodily ailments.

Evil of Low-Necked Dress.—The fashion of wearing low-neck dresses on certain occasions, thus leaving the neck and the upper part of the chest bare, is fraught with evil consequence. It would be less objectionable in countries uniformly warm; but that our daughters, here in the frigid and changeable climate, should expose to the chilling winds a vital part of the body, is one of the evils of fashion which should be discountenanced by every mother, and father, and brother. Of the unseemliness and reckless immodesty often connected with this exposure, it is not necessary to speak in this discussion. *

High-Heeled Boots and Shoes.—Says the *Journal of Chemistry:* "We shall not quarrel with the little jaunty hats of the ladies, for they are indeed

---

* A lady in New York has just died from consumption produced by a cold which she caught by crossing to and from the different hotels at Saratoga, in the evening, in thin satin slippers and low-necked evening dress, and nothing over her shoulders.

pretty, and no harm results from them, as of all parts of the body the head needs the least clothing. But, to pass to the other extremity, we have to say that the detestable high heels to boots and shoes, running, as they do, almost to a point, are spoiling the gait and ruining the ankle-joints of children and young misses. We are careful to order our shoemakers to remove such heels from shoes before permitting them to be brought into our dwelling. Heels of moderate height and good breadth are of great service in elevating the feet, so as to avoid direct contact with moist earth, and they also give support and add firmness to the step. Why should Fashion push good devices to absurd extremes? We must aid in dethroning the tyrant when her decrees lead to the physical or moral injury of the race."

Newspapers as Protectors from Cold.—A newspaper, folded several times and laid across the chest during a cold walk or ride, is a most excellent protector. If the bed-clothing is not sufficiently warm, especially at hotels, two or three large newspapers spread on the bed between the blankets will secure a comfortable night, as far as cold is concerned. A thin shawl may be made warm by folding a paper inside it. The paper is impervious to the wind and cold air from outside, and prevents the rapid escape of the warm air from beneath it. If you suffer from cold feet on a journey, fold a piece of newspaper over your stockings; this is better than rubbers.

Warm Clothing for the Feet.—The lower limbs, especially the feet, should be warmly clothed, both in winter and summer. The fashion that rules otherwise is cruel and deadly. An eminent physician estimates the number who die from ailments induced directly or indirectly from the insufficient clothing of the legs and feet, at nearly *one-third of the cases of mortality on record!*

Frequent Change of Clothing for the Feet.—On no account should this be neglected. Concerning this subject the *Scientific American* very truly says: "Many are careless in the keeping of the feet. If they wash them once a week they think they are doing well. They do not consider that the largest pores of the system are located in the bottom of the foot, and that the most offensive matter is discharged through the pores. They wear stockings from the beginning to the end of the week without change, which become completely saturated with offensive matter. Ill-health is generated by such treatment of the feet. The pores are not repellants, but absorbents, and this fetid matter, to a greater or less extent, is taken back into the system. The feet should be washed every day with pure water only, as well as the arm-pits, from which an offensive odor is also emitted, unless daily ablution is practiced. Stockings should not be worn more than a day or two at a time. They may be worn one day, and then aired and sunned and worn another day, if necessary."

How to Wear Under-Clothing.—All under-clothing should be suspended from the shoulders, in order to relieve the waist, and it is needless to say corsets should be abandoned. To do this, the two principal articles should be joined, forming a garment something like children's night-drawers, but fitting closer to the body. The petticoats and skirts should be hung from the shoulders by straps made of muslin, or other light material.

Bad Effects from Using "Garters."— One of the most frequent and flagrant causes of obstruction in the circulation is the ordinary elastic garter. Children should never wear them at all, as the stockings can be perfectly well kept up by attachment of elastic straps to the waistband. If garters are worn, it is important to know how to apply them with the least risk of harm; at the bend of the knee the superficial veins of the leg unite, and go deeply into the under part of the thigh beneath the ham-string tendons. Thus a ligature below the knee obstructs all the superficial veins, but if the constriction is above, the ham-string tendons keep the pressure off the veins which return the blood from the legs; unfortunately, most people, in ignorance of the above facts, apply the garter below the knee. Elastic bands are the most injurious. They follow the movements of the muscles, and never relax their pressure upon the veins. Non-elastic bands, during muscular exertion, become considerably relaxed at intervals, and allow a freer circulation of the blood.

Muffling the Throat.—There is nothing that makes the throat delicate and sensitive more than muffling it closely in wraps of woolen and fur. The rule is, that the neck should be kept as cool as comfort will allow.

Tight collars frequently cause diseases of the throat and lungs. The neck should be dressed lightly. From the many movements which are made by the larynx in speaking, it is inferred that it is a matter of great importance that the neck in health should be always loosely dressed. Tight cravats are sure to obstruct the proper function of this organ, and bring on irritation, which may lead to bronchitis or consumption. An eminent physician, who devotes his whole attention to the throat and lungs, says *that about three fourths* of all throat diseases would get well by wearing very loose collars, and no neck-tie at all. He also adds: "If you have a disease of the throat, let nature do the curing, and the physician just as little as possible."

Remove Wet Clothing.— Some one inquires, "What shall be done when caught in a shower?" We answer: Put on dry clothing as soon as possible. "Why?" Because damp clothes rapidly chill the surface of the body, the heat being carried off by evaporation. "Suppose your clothes have been wet for some time?" Then give the body a thorough rubbing with a coarse towel at the time of changing the clothes.

Poisonous Clothing—Gloves.—A recent London journal describes the case of a lady whose hands were covered with very irritable blisters. Upon investigation it was found that she had purchased a pair of new silk gloves, and that after wearing them a short time these blisters appeared, and had troubled her ever since. She wore the left glove more than the right, and the left hand was consequently more affected than the right. The gloves were of spun silk, dyed a light brown color—the dye apparently being an aniline dye of coal-tar origin. The use of articles so dyed is dangerous.

Other Cases of Glove Poisoning.—Several English and German papers now before us call special attention to dangerous gloves. In one of them a writer describes the poisonous effect of a pair of the fashionable "bronze-green" silk gloves, when worn by a member of his family. After wearing them a day or two, the patient was attacked with a peculiar blistering and swelling of both hands, which increased to such an extent that for two or three weeks she was compelled to carry her hands in a sling, suffering acute pain, and being, of course, unable either to feed or dress herself. Inquiries among the writer's friends discovered three other ladies similarly afflicted. A German medical journal reports a case of very serious poisoning by a pair of navy-blue kids.

Poisonous Socks.—A clergyman in New York recently purchased a half dozen pair of white cotton socks, having on the top two or three "rounds" of red yarn. After wearing a pair for a couple of days, he found that both legs were poisoned in the parts touched by the red tops of the socks; and, although the red-top socks were discarded, he suffered for three months, a part of the time severely, from the effects of the poison which had been imbibed into the blood. Indeed, the case required very careful treatment by a skillful physician. In the Museum of the College of Surgeons, London, are preserved some brightly-dyed children's socks, which gave rise to a similar affection on the feet of a child.

Other Poisonous Clothing.—Dress goods, of woolen, silk, and cotton, have been found to contain arsenic in dangerous quantities; so, also, gentlemen's underclothing, hat linings, and the linings of boots and shoes. Professor Nichols, of the Massachusetts Institute of Technology, reports the examination of a lady's dress which contained eight grains of arsenic to the square foot. In Troy, New York, lately, the death of a child was attributed to arsenic sucked from a veil which had been thrown over the child's crib to keep off flies.

How to Avoid Such Poisoning.—Use all possible precaution in the purchase of clothing. Buy only of respectable dealers. There are a multitude of shops throughout the country, and especially in the large cities, where goods are exposed for sale by irresponsible and reckless persons, who care nothing for the health of their customers or for the public good. Shun such shops. Shun, also, most of the vagrant, itinerant, and strange pedlars, who carry such goods from house to house, whether in the city or country. Their goods as a rule, have been purchased at cheap and villainous auctions, and are often positively dangerous to the health of those who use them.

How to Cure Such Poisoning.—On the first appearing of such poison, throw off the garment, and either destroy it or submit it to a thorough renovation, by boiling, before wearing again. Use at once the recognized remedies to neutralize the poison in the system. For these, see chapter on "Poisons." If need be, consult your physician without delay.

How to Protect the Public from Such Clothing.—The *Scientific American*, in an article referring to the great extent of the villainous traffic above described, says: "At this rate, it will soon become necessary to test for arsenic all goods purchased before venturing to wear them; or else the label, 'warranted to contain no poisonous dye,' will have to be adopted by all honest and reliable makers. Hitherto, we believe, the retail dealer has not been held legally responsible for damage done in this way. We do not know that he can be, except on the charge of dispensing poisons without a license. Evidently, however, something should be done to put a stop to the rapidly-increasing evil. If the obnoxious tints cannot be secured safely as well as cheaply, then they ought to be prohibited, and another process of dyeing made imperative. Our young chemists will find a fruitful field for the exercise of their inventive powers in the production of the needed dyes."

Injurious Dress of Many School-girls.—A gifted female writer in an article in one of our educational journals, discussing the prospects of the success of girls in our public schools and seminaries, says: "By means of corsets, band, or belt, her liver is divided into an upper and a lower section; the one forced up, to crowd the heart, lungs, and stomach; the other down, to find room as it can, where there is no room for it. Every vital organ is displaced or cramped. Blockades are established by tight shoes, tight gloves, tight garters, tight corsets, or, still more murderous tight skirt-bands; and there the blood must run, by extra force of pumping, every time it passes from the heart to the extremities or back. . . . To study in such a costume is to burn the candle at both ends—but the spirit of the age is upon her; the ages to come press on her; study she must, and die she must."

How Fashionable Dress Interferes with Education.—A student at the Michigan University having remarked that men have more endurance than women, a lady present answered that she would like to see the thirteen hundred young men in the University laced up in steel-ribbed corsets, with hoops, heavy skirts, trails, high heels, paniers, chignons, and dozens of hair-pins sticking in their scalps, cooped up in the house, year after year, with no exhilarating exercise, no hopes, aims, or ambitions in life, and see if they could stand it as well as the girls. Nothing, said she, but the fact that women, like cats, have nine lives, enables them to survive the present *regime* to which custom dooms the sex.

An Increasing Demand for Healthy Clothing.—As a result of better instruction on the general subject above discussed, public opinion seems to be setting in in favor of strong and healthy girls. Pale faces are not thought so interesting nowadays as they used to be. A sneer goes round at the inefficiency of the feeble women who work for a living and ask for good wages. Young men ridicule the idea of tying themselves for life to the sickly girls who exhibit loads of expensive dry-goods upon their persons along the sidewalks, and they begin to praise openly rosy cheeks and stout figures. Indeed, it seems as though the pale and weak young ladies, who, if they were of no practical use in the world, were at least admired and praised as interesting on account of their pallor and languor, were going to have a pretty hard time of it now. But how are women to become healthy? A long stride toward the desired end will be made by wearing proper clothing.

The Tyranny of Fashion.—A lady of extensive and intelligent observation, tells the story of the tyranny of fashion, and of the evil results of fashionable dress: "Fashion kills more women than toil and sorrow. Obedience to fashion is a greater transgression of the laws of woman's nature, a greater injury to her physical and mental constitution, than the hardships of poverty and neglect. The slave-woman at her task will live and grow old, and see two or three generations of her mistresses fade and pass away. The washer-woman, with scarce a ray of hope to cheer her in her toils, will live to see her fashionable sisters die all around her. The kitchen-maid is hearty and strong, when her lady has to be nursed like a sick baby.

"It is a sad truth that fashion-pampered women are almost worthless for all the good ends of human life. They have but little force of character; they have still less power of moral will, and quite as little physical energy. They live for no great purpose in life; they accomplish no worthy ones. They are only doll-forms in the hands of milliners and servants, to be dressed and fed. They dress nobody, they feed nobody, they instruct nobody, they bless nobody. They write no books; they set no example of virtue and womanly life. If they rear children, the latter are left to the care of servants and nurses. And when reared what are the children? What do they ever amount to but weak scions of the old stock? Who ever heard of a fashionable woman's child exhibiting any virtue or power of mind for which it became eminent? Read the biographies of our great and good men. Not one of them had a fashionable mother. They nearly all sprang from strong-minded women, who had as little to do with fashion as the changing clouds."

TIGHT LACING AND HEALTH—IMPORTANT TESTIMONY.

Physical Effects of Tight-pressing Garments.—The free and easy expansion of the chest is obviously indispensable to the full play and dilatation of the lungs; whatever impedes it, either in dress or in position, is prejudicial to health, and on the other hand, whatever favors the free expansion of the chest equally promotes the healthy fulfillment of the respiratory functions. *Stays, corsets, and tight waistbands operate most injuriously, by compressing the thoracic cavity, and impeding the due dilatation of the lungs, and in many instances they give rise to consumption.* I have seen one case in which the liver was actually indented by the excessive pressure, and long-continued bad health and ultimate death was the result.*

Effect on Respiration.—Referring to this subject, a writer states that men can exhale at one effort from six to ten pints of air, whereas in women the average is only from two to four pints. In ten females, free from disease, whom he examined, about the age of eighteen, the quantity of air thrown out averaged three and a half pints, while in young men of the same age he found it to amount to six pints. Some allowance is to be made for natural differences in the two sexes, but enough remains to show a great diminution of capacity in the female, which can be ascribed to no other cause than the use of stays.

Effect on Size.—The organs on which growth depends, namely, the lungs, stomach, and liver, are reduced by the corset to half the natural size and activity. These two causes, with living in the shade, explain the alarming decrease in the size of American women.†

Investigations by Herbst.—Dr. Herbst, of Göttingen, has lately been performing some curious experiments in relation to the quantity of air that is breathed. Now, a person of any understanding will appreciate from them the comfort of full and unrestrained breathing. Dr. Herbst says that a middle-sized man, twenty years old, after a natural expiration or emission of air, inspired or took in eighty cubic inches when dressed, and one hundred and sixty when his tight dress was loosed. After a full dilatation of the chest, he inhaled one hundred and twenty-six inches when dressed, and one hundred and eighty-six when undressed. Another young man, aged twenty-one, after a natural expiration, took in fifty when dressed, and ninety-six when undressed. Had Dr. Herbst made his observations on some of the ladies who carry the use of the corset to extremes, we apprehend he would have obtained results of a nature really alarming.

High Medical Testimony.—A report sent out by the leading medical

---

* Dr. John M. Howe. † Dio Lewis.

association of Great Britain, bears the following testimony: "The chest may be deformed by compression during infancy, and by many of the injurious practices of mothers and nurses; but the chief agents in distorting this part of the skeleton are the various kinds of *corsets*. It is especially from the sixth to the last rib that this pressure is exercised; these, from their greater flexibility, are pressed inward, and all the organs within them—lungs, heart, stomach, liver, etc.—are more or less changed in their position and form; the amount of air introduced into the lungs is lessened, the circulation of the blood through the heart is impeded, the stomach cannot perform properly its functions of digestion, and the liver is displaced downward and presses upon the intestines, laying the foundation for diseases of the chest, consumption, heart-disease, dyspepsia, constipation, and many other ills which shorten and embitter the lives of most of the votaries of fashion.*

Case Reported by the "British Medical Journal."—A female servant died suddenly a short time since in London. The doctor could not account for the death, and made a *post mortem* examination, which showed that the stomach had been reduced to the size of a litttle child's, and the heart pushed out of its proper place through *tight lacing.*

Tight Lacing Pollutes the Blood.†—So does our mode of dressing pollute the blood. One of the worst of blood poisons is the waste matter of the system when not thrown off by its natural channels. And one of the most important of these channels is the lungs. But in order to act properly the lungs must have free play, and this they cannot have with our present style of dress. Originally, the lungs were made to bear an exact proportion to the wants of the body in this respect. Anything, then, which diminishes their capacity destroys the balance, and pollutes the blood by retaining the waste matter in the system. This may develop consumption, scrofula, catarrh, and even some diseases the origin of which is sometimes popularly ascribed to the lower vices. And no woman in ordinary society dresses

---

* A young lady of our acquaintance called on one of our physicians the other day to prescribe for a rush of blood to the head. "I have been doctoring myself," said the languid fair one, with a smile, to the kind M. D., while he was feeling her pulse. "I have taken Brandreth's Pills, Parr's Pills, Strangburg's Pills, Sand's Sarsaparilla, Jayne's Expectorant, used Sherman's Lozenges and Plaster, and—"

"My heavens! madam," interrupted the astonished doctor, "all those do your constitution no good!"

"No! Then what shall I take?" pettishly inquired the patient.

"Take," exclaimed the doctor, eyeing her from head to foot; "take!" exclaimed he, after a moment's reflection, "why—madam—take—*take off your corsets!*"

It is needless for us to state that she is still suffering from the disease.—*Missouri Journal.*

† This paragraph and the one which follows, were written by Miss Julia Colman for *Home and Health.*

as to wholly avoid such results, unless she has made a special study of the matter and planned her dress accordingly.

Weak and Silly Excuses Described.—But how many give the subject this study, or, indeed, any serious thought at all ? We will only reply by referring to the exasperatingly stupid assertion made by almost any woman you meet, learned or unlearned, thoughtful or silly, that her dress is "*not tight!*" Why, the ordinary dress that men wear diminishes their breathing capacity one fourth; and what woman wears her clothing so loose as that? I call a dress too tight that you *hit* when you draw in the fullest possible breath. "But my waist is naturally slender," says one woman. She means that she has inherited small lungs. Her ancestors, more or less of them, compressed their lungs in the same way that we do, and it has become in her case a congenital deformity. This leads us to one of the worst aspects in the whole matter—the transmitted results of indulgence in this deadly vice, and it shows itself in diminished vitality and liability to take on disease of many kinds.

And then the waists. It is pretty well understood now that large waists are the coming style. That is just the way with fashion always—get all to follow it, and then, hey, presto! whirl around to the very thing, whatever it may be, which it will be the most difficult to follow. Here the whole servile crowd that have been literally killing themselves to please fashion find themselves deserted and their "naturally slender" waists held up to pitiless mockery. One would think they would feel outraged by it; but, poor things, like the eels, they take it patiently; "they are used to it."

The only agony is to learn how to obey the dictate. "It is a great deal easier to squeeze the ribs in than to get them out again," says a despairing wasp.

"Well, let's see; take off the corsets."

"O, I can't live without them! I can't hold myself up."

We smile at that, but it comes too near the literal truth. For although there is a backbone in there somewhere, it is possibly very crooked; or, if not, the muscles that ought to steady it have now been so long replaced by corsets that they are not only weak but largely absorbed; they are shriveled down to mere rudiments. That is the inevitable result of the pressure and the lack of use.

If you really cannot sit up, lie down, and have some one use your muscles for you. Once, twice, or thrice a day have them rubbed or worked with the hand of an attendant an hour or more as you can bear it. Then lean over and have the spine crossed with the edges of the hands. The idea is to have muscles which we cannot exercise exercised for us. Then the blood will flow to them and nourish them until they are strong enough to be exercised in the ordinary way.

You want shoulder-braces? Not a bit of it. You have dwarfed your abilities with artificial muscles long enough. You want to use your own muscles, now. Very few, however, will need all this nursing, and you must be brave and strong as you can, for since large waists are the fashion, you must have one, you know.

Are you aware that ladies complained in the same way when corset-boards went out of fashion some years ago? And did it never occur to you to inquire how a great many women live without corsets entirely? How delicate little boys and girls are held together without corsets or other tight clothing? Perhaps some such reflections will convince you that the latter are not wholly indispensable, and that, in spite of your feelings at first, you will soon be able to do without them.

Tight Lacing and General Weakness.—A learned and eloquent, though sarcastic lecture,* was delivered some time ago by a physician of extensive observation, upon this subject. He began by saying that many causes combined to produce the much-lamented delicacy of American women. Chief among these was the system of torture procured by the contrivance called a corset, or corsets. He was always giving hints of this to his lady patients, but never found one who "laced tight," as they called it. They wore "the thing," they acknowledged, but while gasping for breath would declare, "I can put my whole hand between my waist and corset!" And it would not do to contradict them; he could only intimate his unbelief. He did wonder, he said, where some young ladies stowed away their dinner, for it was a curious fact, that as they contracted the space for receiving food, they seemed to enlarge the quantity to be received. It could not, of course, fine room inside the whalebone, and so the stomach must be pushed out of place in order to do its work properly, bringing on dyspepsia and its train of miseries. Then the lungs were compressed, and the heart pushed out of its proper limits, and a little record of rebellion was kept within the system, in place of the beautiful, harmonious account of a grand, healthful action of the whole human machinery. There was the back-bone made for bending, and how could it be bent while splintered and bandaged like a broken limb? Any part of the body made for action, if not allowed to act, grew weak for want of exercise, and a lady should go through, every day, those graceful undulations of form which keep the spine and limbs in healthful action.

Absurdity of Tight Lacing.—There would be no tight lacing if girls could be made to understand this simple fact—that men dread the thought of marrying a woman who is subject to fits of irritable temper, to bad headaches, and other ailments we need not mention; all of which, everybody knows, are the direct and inevitable product of the compression of the waist.

---

* Reported by Miss E. A. Bainbridge.

An unnaturally-compressed waist is far more certain of detection than a mass of false hair or a faint dusting of powder. If the young lady who, to obtain the appearance of a dragon-fly, has been subjecting herself to considerable physical pain, and who has been laying up for herself a pretty store of ailments, which only want time to pronounce themselves, could only see the stare of scarcely-disguised contempt and understand the scornful pity, which greet the result of her labor, we should have a change of the fashion—and it is merely a fashion. Through all changes women remain true only to one fashion. Whether her clothing is as long and lank as that of a Grecian virgin, or whether she builds around the lower half of her figure a rotund and capacious structure of steel, she is ever faithful to the tradition of a small waist; and she will weaken her circulation, she will make her hands red, she will incur headache, she will crack her voice, and she will ruin her digestion, all to produce a malformation which wise men regard with pity and fools with derision. *

The General Question Illustrated. †—" O, indeed, my dress is not tight! My waist is naturally small; I never could wear a tight dress." Such is the universal observation. No lady dresses tightly, none whose dress is not loose. Even the Empress of Austria, who has the enviable reputation of having the smallest waist in the world, would doubtless say her dress was quite loose; and no doubt it is. So the subject of my essay will not apply to any one. I will merely speak of it in the abstract.

First, how we would suppose it would affect the bones. They are apparently hard and unyielding structures, yet will grow in any form or position in which they may be doubled up. In proof whereof, see the thousands of bent spinal columns, from children spending so many hours every day bending over school-desks. "Just as the twig is bent the tree inclines," or, "Mar the young sapling, and the gnarled oak will tell of thee for centuries."

Man is the only animal that is made to look up; but these stooped shoulders and bent spinal columns prevent this, to some extent, and diminish, also the cavity given to the lungs, interfering more or less with their functions. This, of itself, is a serious evil; and, like all other deformities, more apt to come on in young persons, when the bones are somewhat cartilaginous, and yield readily to these forced positions. Yet even in old age the bones are still changing structures, and grow as they are placed. We are told of an old lady who spent the last years of her life in an alms-house, bent over knitting. The bones grew in that cramped position, till across the shoul-

---

* *Athenæum.*

† The remainder of this chapter was written as a separate paper by Mrs. Mary Dixon Jones. M.D., and placed in the hands of one of the present compilers for publication in *Home and Health.*

der measured only five inches, and from top of sternum to pelvis only nine inches.

The heart and lungs are encased in a bony structure, as if to give them a more secure protection. The vertebral, or spinal column, is placed posteriorly. the sternum, or breast-bone, in front, and the ribs around. Only seven of the ribs are joined directly to the sternum; and they by cartilaginous attachments. The rest are more or less floating. so as to allow the fullest expansion to the chest, and the greatest freedom to the lungs. In that form the chest should be naturally expanded, and the ribs free. But the young lady commences with gentle pressure, gradually drawing nearer and nearer together the floating ribs, diminishing more and more the size of the chest, giving less and less room to the lungs, 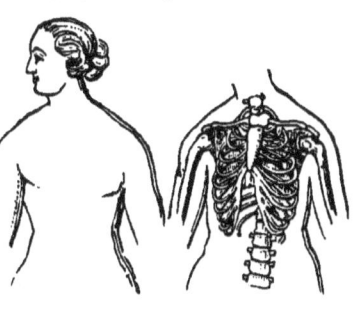 and in that position the ribs grow, and hence will follow *the permanent deformity of a small waist.*

The ribs which curve off so beautifully and gracefully can be brought partly together, or quite, or even be made to lap over. Dr. Merideth Reese dissected a woman in which they were completely lapped, and the flesh seemed bruised. From the lower part of the sternum to the back-bone should measure eight or ten inches, yet so can those bones be compressed and

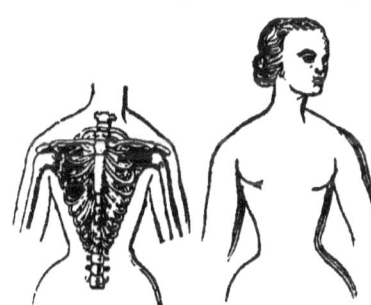 brought together that there are instances of its measuring only one and three fourths inches! Isn't this interfering with the very sources of our existence? We look with horror at the Chinese compressing their feet, and at the flat-headed Indians compressing their skulls. Both customs seem absurd and ridiculous in the extreme, but ours is far more barbarous and injurious. Better compress the feet, head, or any part of the body, than right here, at the very fountain-head, the very citadel of life.

The soft extremity of the sternum, too, is sometimes bent in, and grows and ossifies in that position ; yet we wonder that consumption is so universal, and so generally on the increase. The only wonder is that such persons live at all.

Again. bones become soft from want of exercise, and as our ladies universally dress, the bones of the chest have no freedom of action. Kept in active they become more and more softened, and more and more pliable, and how easy from this condition may follow lateral curvature of the spine. Some physicians have asserted that all fashionably-reared young ladies have this condition to some extent; that it is a universal condition among women, sometimes only a little so—just enough to be graceful! But always it will interfere with the action of the lungs.

The lungs consist only of air-cells, composed of the finest and most delicate mucous membrane. Myendie said there was a great problem to be demonstrated in the construction of the lungs, viz., to establish an immense extent of surface between the atmospheric air and the blood in the small space occupied by the lungs. He might have thought of great vessels or large tubes. No one could have conceived of making six hundred millions of little air-cells, and arranging around their walls millions and millions more of blood-vessels, so that the blood could be brought into immediate contact with the air, over this immense extent of surface, and all wrapped in so small a space. Nothing can exceed the beauty of such a structure. Into these millions of air-cells fresh, pure, invigorating air comes rushing in, filling every one, uniting there with the impure, worn-out particles of the body, and carrying them off in the form of carbonic-acid gas.

But if the chest is compressed the air-cells cannot expand, the air cannot get in, the blood has no way of parting with its impurities, so these impurities are carried back into the circulation, rendering every tissue of the body sickly and every organ unhealthy. The brain suffers with the rest, for to it must come the impure, unhealthy blood to nourish it; its structure becomes diseased, it cannot act healthily, nor is it possible for it to show its full power or activity. The whole nervous system partakes of this same morbid condition, producing a thousand morbid feelings and unpleasant sensations. No doubt this accounts for much of the indisposition and ill-health so general among women. A medical journal lately asserted that "the vitality of American women has been constantly decreasing for many years;" and one of our New York daily papers lately informed its readers that our American women were weak in the back, dyspeptic in the stomach, and nervous to the verge of insanity.

It is impossible that the blood should be thoroughly purified unless every one of these millions of air-cells has the fullest and freest expansion. We cannot afford to dispense with any one of them. And how easy it is to prevent this expansion. Composed of such fine, delicate membranes, they cannot bear up against much force or pressure. Even the weight of a gentleman's clothing is said to interfere with his breathing one fourth, and how much more the cruel compression of corsets, whalebones, and steel, oftentimes requiring all the young girl's strength to pull them together!

If the air-cells are not fully expanded they flab together; in time adhesion must take place, then inflammation, then ulceration—a direct road to consumption. In effect it renders the lungs smaller, which of itself is a predisposing cause of disease. Large and well-developed lungs are the best inheritance we can have; and thus diminishing their size and capacity diminishes our vigor, power, and vitality, and lessens our hold upon life. The larger our lungs are, and the more we breathe, other things being equal, the longer we are going to live, and the more power and vigor we will have. I know they are very unfashionable, yet when we consider how very useful they are, that the larger our waists the better we are off both as to length of life and enjoyment of it, as well as strength and activity of mind, we might have the courage to stem the tide, to dare even to have waists. Not many years ago a rich man died in England, leaving a certain annuity to the bravest man. It was difficult to decide, so for decision it was referred to the brave old Duke of Wellington, and he declared it was the man who shut the gate of a certain city against the surging of battle; so the bravest woman is she who in fashionable life dares shut the gate against the flood-tide of destructive fashion.

Even little girls are brought to this altar of fashion to be sacrificed. Their waists are compressed, their gait rendered unsteady and ungraceful, their vivacity of spirit destroyed. Pale faces, dull eyes, heavy headaches, and a life-time of feebleness and sickness, tell the sequel. Very seldom do we find a young girl dressed so as to give the lungs their proper freedom.

Bringing the ribs together as shown must necessarily press all the internal organs out of place. The liver is pushed and squeezed out of shape, at times pressed quite below the waist; the stomach carried out of position; the colon, which lies just below the waist, was in one instance found in the lower part of the abdomen. A professor once said in the dissecting-room to his class, that to find the position of the internal organs they need never look at a female subject, for in them they are always out of place! The abdominal organs falling down upon the movable uterus topple it over on the floor of the pelvis, bringing on a long train of evils.

The whole process of breathing is by the action of the muscles. The chest is formed largely of muscular structure, great immense muscles branching in every direction—an immense muscular apparatus to expand the chest and help in the process of breathing, to give us the breath of life. It is wonderful how this immense machinery of muscles is arranged to accomplish this end. Besides, the great muscles of the abdomen are brought into play to help—in fact, almost every muscle of the body seems to be brought into action to accomplish more fully and effectually this great act of breathing; and to do this effectively they must have the freest motion and the fullest action, no obstruction in any way. Muscles involuntarily shrink from any impediment.

But this multitude of muscles which God has arranged so beautifully around the body we keep inactive, bind them down with ligatures, press them with heavy clothing, and impede their action by every incumbrance. The breathing apparatus, instead of being free and active, the chest fully and largely expanding about the waist, is bound down and immovably fixed, only a little panting at the upper part of the chest. How fearfully we interfere with the designs of the Creator—how we abuse this beautiful organism!

> "We have wronged it, we do wrong it,
> 'Tis majestically dumb."

The muscles, from being thus inactive, grow weak and powerless, and forget their cunning; even so weak that when the corsets, those unnatural supports, are removed, the muscles have so lost their power, are so feeble, they can no longer sustain the body, and the young girl will say she feels as if she was all falling to pieces, or would break in two. And as the muscles grow yet weaker and more debilitated, she will tell you she can't go without the corsets. I have known some conscientiously try to lay them aside, but would feel so wretched, so miserable without them—so long accustomed to this artificial support that there is no strength in the muscles to hold the body up, or the organs in position, and going without them produces indefinably unpleasant sensations.

The stomach, liver, and intestines which lie immediately under the abdominal muscles are not only misplaced by the weakness of the muscles, but essential to the health of these organs is the constant stimulus of the contraction and relaxation of these same muscles. And when these muscles are kept in a state of inactivity, as is always the case in our mode of dressing, these organs always suffer; the liver becomes torpid, the stomach dyspeptic, bowels constipated, and general inefficiency of every function, either of which conditions will follow legitimately from tight lacing, and either one is sufficient of itself to produce any sickness. And with the complication, how can any one escape general ill-health?

This one cause is doing more to undermine the health of American people than any other thing. It is working more destruction. There is not a function of the human body that is properly performed, not an organ that does its duty. As one writer has said, "It has slain more women in a score of years than the sword does men in a century; stifled more children than the Ganges." It is an historical fact that the same woman invented corsets who instigated St. Bartholomew's massacre; and she has worked more destruction by the former than the latter.

Why is it so universal? Does it add to the beauty of the person? Only our perverted tastes prevent us from regarding it with the utmost horror. When a Swiss once saw a fine-looking Englishman, he exclaimed. "What a pity he has not the goiter." So, we are so accustomed to mutilated waists, that when we see a naturally-formed woman we are apt to say, "What a pity she has not a small waist." If we look at the beautiful specimens of ancient statuary we find no small, contracted chests, nor did Powers take for his model one of our fashion-plates. If they are correct he certainly showed a plentiful lack of taste.

Furthermore, it destroys all gracefulness of carriage. When any muscles of the body are cramped, the movements cannot be easy; there is a certain wiggle—a "divine wiggle." How is the human race to have health with this mode of dressing? Only fashion makes us think it is beautiful, or tolerate it for a moment. We would not otherwise endure the misery it imposes but so accustomed are some to suffering, that they are hardly conscious of it, they don't know when they are dressing tight, don't know when the breathing is oppressed.

When Lady Mary Wortley Montague was traveling in Turkey, while preparing for the bath, laying aside her corsets, one of the women of the Turkish harem took up this little instrument of torture, surveyed it in all directions, and turning to Lady Mary said, "Does your husband make you wear this?" A greater tyrant than our husbands imposes them upon us. If we would only recollect what Carlyle reminds us of, that "rags" are not of as much importance as the person.

EXERCISE AND HEALTH.

Toil and Activity Necessary to Health.—Frederick the Great said: "As for my plan of not sparing myself, I confess it the same as before. The more one nurses one's self, the more feeble and delicate does the body become. My trade requires toil and activity, and both my body and mind must adapt themselves to their duty. It is not necessary that I should live but it is necessary that I should *act*. I have always found myself the better for this method. However, I do not prescribe it for any one else, and am content to practice it myself."

Severe Exercise after Eating Injurious.—Do not take severe exercise immediately after eating. Sir Busick Harwood made a thorough test of this question in this wise. Having fed two hungry pointers with the same kind of food and with the same amount, he allowed one of them to rest in his kennel while he kept the other in constant exercise for a couple of hours. Both dogs were then killed, and their condition carefully examined. It was found that in the dog which had remained in his kennel digestion was nearly completed, while in the other the digestive process had scarcely commenced. The inference was conclusive, namely, the severe exercise should not be taken immediately after a hearty meal.

Light Exercise after Eating is Healthful.—This question has been thoroughly tested in many ways. Light exercise, instead of hindering, promotes digestion, and in this way is helpful to the physical system. It should be light, however, as after a full meal the digestive organs are taxed to their utmost, and repose to the other parts of the system will be helpful.

These Rules Apply also to Mental Exercise.—The brain should not be heavily taxed immediately after a hearty meal. Doing so leads to indigestion and to other disorders consequent thereto. The same law holds good in physical and mental work. Indeed, literary men and those intensely and severely devoted to business are the greatest sufferers from indigestion.

Early Walking and Its Value.—For persons in ordinary health, walking is a very valuable and economic exercise, and every one who can do so should habituate himself to it. A little walk of half an hour upon arising is advisable for strong persons, but cannot be endured so early by persons in delicate health. But to those who can bear it, the early walk, not too brisk, is a most healthful luxury.

How to Make the Walk Most Healthful.—Walking, however, should be walking, and not sauntering. Carry the head erect, expand the chest, and drink in the pure air, and move briskly enough to secure your end. Let the eye turn from one object to another, and not be fixed on the ground in contemplation; note the beauties or deformities of the landscape; take a companion with you if you can, to whom you can refer your opinions on what you see and from whom you can receive suggestive thoughts in return; stop at times and sit upon a rock or fence both for rest and the enjoyment of some striking scene, and let not the pleasure be turned to weariness by any overstraining for the name and fame of a fast walker.

Walking Combined with Useful Investigation.—To those citizens who can spare a week or more in the summer let us recommend the pedestrian journey as a renovator of body and mind. With the physical exercise may be joined geological or botanical, or geographical or historical investigation, and the delighted mind will help the body to its rejuvenescence. Or, if you are an artist, you can use your sketching powers on mountain or stream, and so provide memorials of your tour.

In Walking the Dress Should be Loose.—A tightly-dressed person cannot enjoy walking. One cannot inflate the lungs with the increased quantity of air needed for the increased activity of the system. To promote this there should be a gentle movement of the arms. All untrammeled men and women, and boys and girls, naturally move their arms more or less in walking. It is not needful to swing them like a steam engine, but a natural movement of this kind will be graceful in persons otherwise graceful. This also gives character to the gait and bearing of the individual, and imparts life and animation.

Walk Untrammeled.—Ladies should break up the pernicious fashion of always carrying something in their hands. With a short walking-dress the hands would seldom be needed to manage that. With a broad-brimmed hat the face may be shaded enough to make the carrying of a parasol superfluous, except in the hottest part of the day in hot weather. If a long dress must be worn, let the skirt be hooked or pinned up, *so that the hands and arms may be free.*

Effect of Tight Lacing on Walking.—Tight lacing weakens the action of all the muscles directly. They are so intimately bound together that if one suffers, all the others suffer with it. Bind any animal about the middle so that the muscles there cannot work, and all the other principal muscles must work under restraint. So, set one of these ligatured bodies to walking, and the whole operation is a very constrained and mechanical affair; the lower limbs move mostly by themselves, and the lay figure slides along very much as if on castors. This gives the characterless gait somewhat peculiar to our American women. The upper part of the figure is still. The ligature about the waist has cut off the sympathy which should exist between the two, and so cheats the walker out of nearly all the benefit to be derived from the exercise. She says that walking hurts her, and in that she is right. Then she desists from walking, and in that she is wrong. She should put herself into proper condition for walking, and persist in it, though discreetly, of course; not to utter exhaustion.

Exercise for Delicate Women.—Perhaps it would be better for delicate women to take a large proportion of their exercise in other ways at first. Croquet, riding, and driving might be tried, but nothing will help them much until they dress right. Rambling in the fields and woods, berrying, gathering flowers and botanizing, are among the best forms of exercise for women, next to out-of-door work. Gardening is the best, perhaps, all things considered. It is active, gently exciting, tasteful, and available to most women, for very few of those who read these pages are so shut up that they do not have a chance in a court-yard at least, however small it may be. And it is surprising to see what can be done in some of our city yards.

Wear the Right Kind of Shoes.—Our foot-gear also affects our walking. The shoes at present worn are strong and thick-soled, and that is well, but it stiff enough to make corns, that mars the pleasure of walking. High heels will also do that by driving the foot painfully into the forward part of the shoe. Insist on having *all* the heel removed, and then have only one or two thicknesses of leather or "lifts" put on, quite as wide as the sole and as long as the heel. Then, if your shoes are large enough, you will enjoy your walking as you never could with high and narrow heels. Besides, by wearing these unnatural heels we derange the whole basis of our physical structure, and sow the seeds of our innumerable ills which we are but just beginning to reap. Ladies (and gentlemen, too,) are almost as perverse about tight shoes as they are about tight dresses, and shoemaking is in a very barbarous state.

Exercise a Cure for Many Diseases.—There are many diseases, at least many forms of indisposition, which, with a strong will, may be walked away, provided the exercise be taken systematically and rendered a prominent feature in the daily treatment. Tone is imparted by this means to both mind and body, cheerfulness replaces gloom, and sympathy for others a morbid dwelling on self. The exercise should be active, and not consist of either strolling or sauntering out of doors, or even amateur gardening. A brisk walk may be taken by a strong person at a pace of at least three miles an hour, but always stopping short of fatigue.

Exercise "About the House" Not Enough.—People will be often heard to say that they take plenty of exercise about the house, and that they are on their legs many hours of the day. What is wanted for the health is exercise without fatigue, for fatigue is exhaustion, and the desired object is only to be gained on the terms just stated.

Exercise by Rule Firmly Observed.—The distance walked could be increased daily, and it will be found that increasing strength will give the readiness and wish for increasing exercise. There is an accumulation of incapability in those who are afflicted with what are vaguely called nervous disorders, which render such persons restless, fidgety, irritable, and full of strange fancies, and which is best brought down to a healthy standard by exercise in the open air, and its concomitant change of scene and new trains of thought.

Exercise as a Cure for Low Spirits.—Exercise of body and mind has been well described as the grand constituent of health and happiness, the central point upon which every thing turns. Motion seems to be a great preserving principle of nature, to which even inanimate things are subject; for the winds, waves, the earth itself, are restless, and the waving of trees, shrubs, and flowers, is known to be an essential part of their economy. A fixed rule of taking several hours' exercise every day, if possible, in the open air, if not, under cover, will be almost certain to secure one exemption from disease, as well as from attacks of low spirits, *ennui*—that monster who is ever waylaying the rich indolent. "*Throw but a stone*, the giant dies." Low spirits cannot exist in the atmosphere of bodily and mental activity.

Abuse of Physical Exercise.—One of our magazine writers has well stated that those who have gone through the severest training become, in the end, dull, listless, and stupid, subject to numerous diseases, and in many instances the ultimate victims of gluttony and drunkenness. Their unnatural vigor seldom lasts more than five years. It was especially remarked by the Greeks that no one who in boyhood won the prize at the Olympic games ever distinguished himself afterward. The three years immediately preceding seventeen are years of great mental development, and nature cannot at the same time endure any severe taxing of the physical constitution. Prudence, therefore, especially at this critical period of life, must ever go hand in hand with vigor, for the evils of excess outweigh by far the evils of deficiency.

False Criticism Concerning Exercise Answered.—A modern author, after discussing the general question of sedentary occupations, and referring to the fact that the number thus engaged has become very large, goes on to say that occasionally such persons break away for a day's active exercise. A large number go into the country for a month during the summer. Once at the old homestead, or in the mountains, they plunge into the hay-field or climb the hill. Most of them are led to doubt the value of exercise because of the effects which follow these exertions. Without doubt, the labor is generally excessive for such persons; but if they would manage their table habits rightly, the results would generally be more than satisfactory.

When a man is tired, he is tired all through—the stomach not less than the legs. Now, what is the usual custom? After a walk of twenty miles, or a day at haying, when every fibre of the body is exhausted, the stomach is stuffed with hearty food. The man goes to bed with flushed face and rapid pulse, and awakens in the morning with a bad taste in his mouth, loss of appetite, and a sense of languor. If he had taken a cup of tea and a slice of toast instead, he would find himself the next morning none the worse for the previous day's work and perspiration.

We all understand well when the body is weak from fever that the stomach partakes in the general weakness, and must not be overloaded. But when the body is exhausted from labor, and every part is pleading for rest, then we crowd the stomach full of beef, pudding, pies, and fruit, and spend the next day in declaring to our friends that exercise is not what it is said to be.

When we are tired we should seek restoration in sleep—not in calling upon the legs, the arms, the back, the stomach, or any other part, to undertake five or six hours of continuous hard labor. The laboring man would find himself much better in the morning if the third meal were made more light in quantity and easy of digestion.

Riding and Rowing, and Other Kinds of Exercise.—"Horse-back riding" and boat-rowing are valuable kinds of exercise, and should be often resorted to by those who have the opportunity. Nearly all work about the house, or in the shop or field, (except that which fails to use the lower limbs,) is to be recommended in the department of exercise. In doing such work care should be taken to give freedom and fullness to the breathing and to the circulation of the blood. *Let the neck, waist, and feet be free.*

Swimming as Exercise.*—Swimming, when done at the right hours, and not to excess, is an appropriate and healthful exercise. If we go in several times a day, soon after eating, or when much fatigued, and stay in long, it will injure us. In order that swimming may prove beneficial as well as pleasant, the following rules, referred to more fully in the chapter on bathing, should be observed:—

1. Never go into the water less than two hours after eating; it is better still to make it three.
2. Never go into the water when feeling much exhausted. It will do no harm to go in when you are warm and perspiring, if you are not tired.
3. Never go into the water when you feel cold and chilly.
4. Never stay in long enough to make you feel chilly.
5. Swim and exercise vigorously while in the water.
6. Wipe dry before dressing. If the sun shines, expose the body to its rays a short time before dressing.
7. As a rule, do not go in more than once a day.

---

* PADDLING VERSUS SWIMMING.—The advantages of "paddling" and "treading water," as a means of escaping from drowning when one is suddenly precipitated into deep water, are set forth by a writer in the *Sanitary Record*. The motions performed in the acts of paddling and treading require no previous instruction, and in the great majority of cases would save life. In swimming the mouth is on a level with the water in the intervals of the strokes; in paddling the head is well elevated—the individual is able to look about, he can deliberate as to what is best to be done, and he is much less liable to take water into the larynx or glottis. Without prejudice to the art of swimming, children should be exercised from the tenderest age in the art of paddling and treading water, so as to impart confidence to them. Even without any preliminary practice whatever, there is nothing to hinder man, woman, or child, from beating the water with the hands and feet, just as the lower animals do, and so keeping themselves afloat for a protracted period—a period that in a multitude of instances would be sufficient to invite rescue and preserve life. The action of the feet alone will sustain the body; *a fortiori*, the action of both feet and hands will prove yet more effectual. In this, as in many other things, man is often unaware of his own immense capacities.

CRYING, LAUGHING, AND SINGING.

Crying and Health.—Probably most persons have experienced the effect of tears in relieving great sorrow. It is even curious how the feelings are allayed by free indulgence in groans and sighs. A French physician publishes a long dissertation on the advantages of groaning and crying in general, and especially during surgical operations. He contends that groaning and crying are two grand operations by which nature allays anguish; that those patients who give way to their natural feelings more speedily recover from accidents and operations than those who suppose it unworthy a man to betray such symptoms of cowardice as either to groan or cry. He tells of a man who reduced his pulse from one hundred and twenty-six to sixty in the course of a few hours by giving full vent to his emotions. "If people are at all unhappy about any thing, let them go into their room and comfort themselves with a loud boo-hoo, and they will feel a hundred per cent. better afterward." Then let the eyes and mouth be regarded as the safety-valve through which nature discharges her surplus steam.

Laughing and Health.—It is said by good medical authority that there is not the remotest corner or little inlet of the minute blood vessels of the human body that does not feel some wavelet from the convulsion occasioned by good hearty laughter, and also that the "central man" or life principle, is shaken to its innermost depths, sending new tides of life and strength to the surface, and thus materially tending to insure good health to the persons who indulge therein. The blood moves more rapidly—probably caused by some chemical or electric modification occasioned by the convulsion—and conveys a different impression to all the organs of the body as it visits them on that particular mystic journey, when the man is laughing, from what it does at other times. For this reason every good hearty laugh in which a person indulges tends to lengthen his life, conveying as it does new and distinct stimulus to the vital forces.

The Laughing Cure.—"We doubt not the time will come," says another authority, "when physicians, conceding more importance than they now do to the influence of the mind upon the vital forces of the body, will prescribe to the torpid and melancholy patient a certain number of hearty peals of laughter, to be undergone at stated periods, and believe that they will, in so doing, find the best and most effective method of producing the required effect upon the patient. Our advice to all is, indulge in good, hearty, soulful laughter, when the opportunity offers, and if you do not derive material benefit therefrom, charge us with uttering false principles of *materia medica*."

Physical Influence of Singing.—So many injuries to the health have been attributed by the public—and perhaps also by a portion of the medical profession—to frequent and prolonged use of the voice, as to demand just such a careful and impartial investigation of the alleged ill consequences as has lately been made by a Russian author, and published in a German journal in St. Petersburg. Although the paper presents no very novel views, it is of value as showing the result of his examination of two hundred and twenty-two singers, whose ages varied from nine to fifty-three years. These were examined with reference to size, chest circumference, and breathing capacity. Among the principal deductions to be drawn from these examinations, we observe in particular that vocal training appears to exert a remarkably beneficial influence upon cases having a tendency to consumption. Contrary also, to the popular impression, emphysema is not superinduced by this form of exercise. The following are some of the conclusions of the author of the paper.

The circumference of the chest is greater in vocalists than in non-singers. This difference increases, not only with variations in size or age, but also with the number of years spent in singing. The greatest difference between these classes is observed in the period of life immediately following puberty. Persons of consumptive and intemperate antecedents, have, other things being equal, smaller-sized chests.

The chest circumference is absolutely and relatively greater in singers. Intemperance checks the growth of the chest.

Not only the circumference but the chest capacity is greater in singers. It increases with the size (up to the average) with age, (up to 24 years,) and with the number of years of vocal training; more of course in their earlier than in their later years.

Although the chest movements are restricted in persons of consumptive habit, they are still more so in persons of equal age who are intemperate.

The pulmonary alveoli are not lessened but increased in size by singing. Both inspiratory and expiratory strength is clearly related to the general constitutional condition.

Vital capacity of the lungs is greater in singers, and increases with size and years spent in singing. It is greater even in singers of consumptive families than in other healthy persons, while it is still less in chronic tipplers. While laryngeal catarrh is common, bronchial catarrh is quite rare among singers.

Their mortality is slight. Few die of consumption. A not unfrequent affection, even among temperate singers, is Bright's disease of the kidneys.

Singing is an excellent prophylactic against consumption, and is the best means of developing and strengthening the chest, ranking indeed above ordinary gymnastics. The cause of this lies in the training of the lungs to deeper and stronger respiration.

Age for Vocal Training.—A distinguished vocal-music teacher, after carefully testing the question whether the voices of girls may be safely trained between the ages of thirteen and seventeen, says: "My pupils at such ages responded more successfully to the vocal discipline than did those who were older. The period of greatest difficulty I found to be between seventeen and twenty-two years. During these years the voice was treacherous, husky, dull, or wanting; the throat tender, liable to frequent colds, or even to temporary loss of voice. This was true not only of those who had previously studied, but of those who at that age attempted their first musical note... To me it seems like a libel upon nature to assert that for an important fraction of human existence woman at that period (thirteen to seventeen years of age) is disqualified to critically perform the important function of vocalization. Looking at the question in the light of physiology, I find every thing to oppose the notion; while, in reviewing my experience, I can truthfully say that I have never in one single instance seen the year, the month, the day, nor the hour, when, with functional respiration and laryngeal efforts, youthful voices have shown the faintest suspicion of a greater degree of fatigue, or even huskiness, than at an earlier or later age. On the direct and fortunate contrary, they were at that period more clear, more bright, more enduring, save in instances of precociously bad muscular habits, than at any later period; while to reformatory discipline they responded with an alacrity never to be expected from their senior sisters, whose greatest difficulty, be it observed, was the means of forcing muscular habits engendered during this very period of advised neglect.

OCCUPATIONS AND HEALTH.—VITAL STATISTICS.

Mental Labor and Health. An Illustration.—To the question, "Is severe intellectual work incompatible with good health?" a negative answer must be given. Here is an illustrative case: The renowned Jeremy Bentham, a most able and powerful writer on jurisprudence, the author of more than a *hundred different works*, died in England, in 1832, at the age of eighty-five. In early life he was puny and exceedingly feeble in health, and this continued for sixteen years; the whole remainder of his life exhibited this fact, that the greater his mental application, the better was his physical health.

There are Hundreds of Similar Cases.—Bentham's was not an exceptional case. A multitude of similar instances could be cited. Indeed, a careful observation of the tables of statistics compiled to show the average longevity of persons of different occupations, assures us that, as a rule, those who are engaged largely in intellectual pursuits, live longer than those of less mental occupation. Here are a few instances:—

Benjamin Franklin	84	Halley	86
Sir John Herschel	84	Voltaire	85
Galileo	78	Baron Von Humboldt	90
Sir Isaac Newton	85	Thomas Jefferson	83
Lord Bacon	78	John Quincy Adams	81

All these are eminent examples, and the list might be indefinitely extended. A friend, himself a physician, carefully went through one of the encyclopedias and noted down the ages of one hundred of the greatest men of history He found that the aggregate ages of these men was 7,500, giving an average of *seventy-five years!*

Average Longevity of Diverse Avocations.—The following table was reported by Dr. Jarvis, giving the average longevity in some of the leading occupations in the States of New York, Massachusetts, and Rhode Island. The table was compiled with great care:—

Occupations.	Deaths.	Av'ge Age.	Occupations.	Deaths.	Av'ge Age.
Clergymen	389	55·36	Merchants & Clerks,	2,386	47·46
Lawyers	576	54·26	Tanners	230	47·90
Physicians	540	54·32	Cabinet-makers	253	46·34
Blacksmiths	822	51·51	Shoe-makers	3,233	43·03
Carpenters	2,052	49·72	Painters	500	43·37
Masons	492	48·29	Tailors	486	41·08

A study of such figures gives abundant assurance that mental pursuits are conducive to health, rather than injurious to it. Our Creator has so wisely made us that the employments of the mind and heart—our higher nature—bring with them the fullest possible reward. Diligence in study, provided it be coupled with daily physical exercise, will increase rather than shorten life.

Order of Mortality in Certain Classes of Manual Labor.—Thirty years ago the British returns gave the following as the order of comparative freedom from mortality in several different branches of manual labor:—

1. Farmers,   3. Weavers,   5. Carpenters, 7. Laborers, 9. Bakers,
2. Shoe-makers, 4. Blacksmiths, 6. Sailors,   8. Miners,   10. Butchers.

Comparative Ages of Persons Active in Business.—The registry in the city of Boston gave the following average ages of persons then counted and still actively engaged in the different pursuits compared:—

		Av'ge Age.			Av'ge Age.
305	Laborers	40·30	45	Clerks	32·98
69	Marines	38·59	20	Shoe-makers	24·35
35	Tailors	39·08	15	Teamsters	34·40
32	Merchants	58·81	11	Printers	39·45
32	Traders	49·68	10	Masons	40·20
33	Carpenters	45·76	9	Machinists	33·77
22	Painters	40·36	8	Bakers	38·62
8	Farmers	57·12	7	Blacksmiths	35·00
6	Ship-carpenters	51·16	4	Curriers	28·50
5	Physicians	48·80	4	Engineers	45·75
5	Clergymen	53·80	5	Lawyers	60·20
4	Coopers	40·50			

Vital Statistics—Births.—In countries where the records of births are kept, it is found that the annual number of births to each 1,000 of the population varies from 29 to 40, more in some countries than in others, and more in the rural districts than in cities. Fewer births occur in cold than in warmer climates. More boys are born than girls, the proportion being in Russia 109 boys to 100 girls; the mean proportion for Europe being 106 boys to 100 girls. In Great Britain the average proportion is 104 boys to 100 girls. More children are born during the first three months of the year than during any other quarter. Of 1,000 births, 312 occur between midnight and 6 A.M.; 249 between 6 A.M. and noon 183 between noon and 6 P.M.; and 256 between 6 P.M. and midnight.

Vital Statistics—Marriage.—Under ordinary circumstances, marriage is favorable to longevity. Married men from 25 to 30 years of age die at the rate of 6; unmarried, at the rate of 10; and widowers, at the rate of 22 per 1,000 per annum; and from 30 to 35 years of age, married men at the rate of 7½; unmarried, 13; and widowers, 17½ per 1,000 per annum. From 30 to 35 years of age, maids die at the rate of 11, and married women at the rate of 9 per 1,000 per annum. A man married at 25 will live to the age of 65, while an unmarried man at the same age will live only to the age of 60. A married woman at 25 will attain the age of 65, the unmarried that of 56 only. Less crime is committed by the married; more by the widowed; and most by those who have never married. The chances of females being married before the age of 20, are as 1 to 5 of all their probabilities of ever marrying; at the age of 20 the chances are one fifth less; at 25, two thirds less; and at 30, six sevenths of all their probabilities are lost.

Vital Statistics—Deaths.—The greatest number of deaths occur during the third quarter of the year, and the smallest number during the fourth quarter. The other two quarters have nearly the same proportion. Estimates vary as to the time of day when the most deaths occur, some claiming the hours from midnight to 6 A.M. as the most fatal, and others from 6 A.M to noon. More deaths occur during the first *half* of the day than the last half. Of all the deaths that occur throughout the world, about one half are of children under five years of age.

Expectation of Human Life.—After the first year the chances of living increase up to the fourth year, and then slowly decline. Rural laborers may expect to live, on an average, 45·32 years; carpenters, 45·28; domestic servants, 42·03; bakers, 41·92; shoe-makers, 40·87; weavers, 41·92; tailors, 39·40; hatters, 38·91; stone-masons, 38·19; plumbers, 38·13; mill operatives, 38·09; blacksmiths, 37·96; brick-layers, 37·70; printers, 36·66; clerks, 34·99, and the average population, 39·88.

The accompanying table shows the average yearly decrease of human life out of a given number born, and the "expectation of life," or average number of years persons may expect to live at any period of life. The table was compiled by Dr. Wiggleworth, after many years of intelligent research, and has justly been regarded as authority by the courts in estimating the value of life estates:

Age.	Persons Living.	Decrement of Life.	Expectation of Life in Years and Decimals.	Age.	Persons Living.	Decrement of Life.	Expectation of Life in Years and Decimals.	Age.	Persons Living.	Decrement of Life.	Expectation of Life in Years and Decimals.
At birth.	4893	1264	28.15	34	1772	38	30.24	68	772	87	12.43
1	3629	274	"	35	1737	35	28.22	69	735	37	"
2	3355	188	"	36	1702	35	"	70	693	87	10.06
3	3167	132	"	37	1667	35	"	71	601	37	"
4	3035	84	"	38	1632	35	"	72	624	37	"
5	2951	58	40.87	39	1597	35	"	73	587	37	"
6	2893	55	"	40	1562	35	26.04	74	549	37	"
7	2838	47	"	41	1527	35	"	75	511	37	7.83
8	2791	40	"	42	1492	35	"	76	474	37	"
9	2751	36	"	43	1457	35	"	77	437	37	"
10	2715	28	39.23	44	1423	34	"	78	400	37	"
11	2687	27	"	45	1396	27	23.92	79	363	37	"
12	2660	27	"	46	1369	27	"	80	326	35	5.85
13	2633	27	"	47	1342	27	"	81	291	34	"
14	2606	27	"	48	1315	27	"	82	257	34	"
15	2579	42	36.16	49	1310	27	"	83	223	34	"
16	2537	43	"	50	1288	27	21.16	84	189	34	"
17	2494	43	"	51	1261	27	"	85	155	21	4.57
18	2451	43	"	52	1234	27	"	86	134	21	"
19	2408	43	"	53	1207	27	"	87	113	21	"
20	2365	43	34.21	54	1180	27	"	88	92	20	"
21	2322	42	"	55	1153	27	18.25	89	72	20	"
22	2280	42	"	56	1126	27	"	90	52	8	3.78
23	2238	42	"	57	1099	27	"	91	44	7	"
24	2196	42	"	58	1072	27	"	92	37	7	"
25	2154	40	32.32	59	1045	27	"	93	30	7	"
26	2114	38	"	60	1018	27	15.43	94	23	7	"
27	2076	38	"	61	991	27	"	95	16	6	1.62
28	2038	38	"	62	964	27	"	96	10	5	"
29	2000	38	"	63	937	27	"	97	5	3	"
30	1962	38	30.24	64	910	27	"	98	2	1	"
31	1924	38	"	65	883	37	12.48	99	1	1	"
32	1886	38	"	66	846	37	"				
33	1848	38	"	67	809	37	"				

DWELLINGS AND HEALTH.

Importance of a Healthful Location.—The healthiness of dwellings depends upon their faultless situation, construction, and management. It is, therefore, of primary importance that the foundation of houses be on dry ground free from decaying matters. Houses built upon a soil saturated with putrid moisture, or upon ...d swamps or cess-pools or similar filthy ground, are notoriously unhealthy, because such a soil, especially in the warm season, evolves deleterious exhalations, and vitiates the water of the ground and the air. In the construction of buildings it is also necessary to protect their foundations against dampness from underground, by means either of drainage or of a damp-proof ground floor. A construction conducive to a free and ample supply of light and air is, then, the main condition for a healthy habitation; however large or small, elegant or plain, the house may be, its salubrious condition may be maintained and regulated by these two simple and cheap correctors, Light and Air.

Remove from a Foul District.—If you live in a district soddened with foulness, change. Shoe leather is cheaper than medicine. It will be better to get up at five "to go to work," than to get up at two "to lay somebody out;" besides, you will have better heart for every thing. Read Ruskin's "Athena," if you can; and bear in mind that when you bar out the goddess Athena, Queen of the Air, you bar in a serpent whose subtle poison will shorten the number of your days, lessen your strength, and undermine all the glory which should bless them. Have water that looks clean, tastes clean, and whenever you lift the lid from a kettle or saucepan, smells clean. If in doubt, catch some rain water and filter it. Then remove to another locality.

Location of Dwellings in Cities.—Dwellings which face on free and open streets, are to be preferred to those which open into courts, because the motion of the air is freer in the former. In a closely-built city the corner house, having the sweep of two streets is, in this respect, better located than others in the block. It is not well that high blocks of dwellings should so surround the rear court as to shut out the wind, nor that streets should terminate against the middle of a block at right angles to it.

In the country any open, dry portion of land will make a good building spot. A slight eminence is preferable.

Shade Trees Around Our Dwellings.—Farm-houses or other dwellings, whether for man or beast, should not be closely shaded, as such shade obstructs both sunlight and air currents. The aim should be to so arrange the trees in the lawn as to permit the ingress of the sun's rays, and of the free and healthful air.

High Ceilings and Health.—Lofty ceilings are regarded by some as a principal means of insuring a sufficient measure in cubic feet for each person. Unless ventilation is secured for the upper portion of a room, a lofty ceiling only makes that portion of space above the tops of the windows a receptacle for foul air which accumulates and remains to vitiate the stratum below.

Capacity of Bricks for "Dampness."—As to the capacity for absorption, three bricks from a building in process of erection, took up in twenty-four hours from eight to fifteen ounces. From a certain brick-yard, samples of face-brick and pressed brick absorbed ten and a half and eleven ounces;

and from another, pressed brick drank up twenty and a half and eighteen and a half ounces all in the same time. These results are startling. We cannot suppose that lateral or horizontal absorption, as, from driving rain, could be much different from that which proceeds upward from wet foundations. Cannot some process of brick making be found that will prevent this action?

Damp Walls and Their Relation to Health.—Porous walls in damp locations, absorbing moisture and water, give rise to various evils. Dr. Dean has made some tests as to the absorbent capacity of bricks.* He first examined in dry weather brick from an old one-story building upon high ground, dry, well-sewered, and well exposed to sunshine. A face-brick next above the foundation, contained one ounce of water; four feet higher, one half; and just under the roof, one twelfth. In a building differently circumstanced, notoriously damp and unwholsome, on high but "made" ground, a face-brick in the fourth row from the foundation was found to contain eighteen ounces of water!

Dampness of Other Walls.—Most kinds of sandstone are so porous that water and air easily pass through them. Solid or quarried limestones are scarcely permeable by air, but as they are of irregular shapes, and require much mortar, they are not much more air-tight than walls made of regular bricks and thin layers of mortar. Observations have been taken of the average quantity of mortar used with different building stones. We may suppose that taking the wall as a whole, it is equal to one third with quarried lime stone, one fourth with tufaceous limestone, one fifth to one sixth with bricks and one sixth to one eighth with cubes of sandstone. Thus, the quantity of the mortar used assists in keeping the walls pervious to air to a certain degree.

Why Damp Walls are Injurious.—Wet walls are air-tight, and consequently injurious:—

1. By impeding ventilation and diffusion of gases through their pores being closed up or narrowed by water.

2. By disturbing the heat-economy of our bodies. Damp walls act as absorbents of heat by their evaporation and increase heat-loss by one-sided radiation. Diseases known to be often caused by cold are particularly frequent in damp dwellings: rheumatism, catarrh, and chronic lung disease, Bright's disease of the kidneys, etc.

In a house using one hundred thousand bricks of ten pounds weight each which have absorbed the average quantity of water, one hundred thousand

---

* Damp brick walls are common, especially in houses in the country where they are exposed upon the north and east sides. So common is this that, in many places in the country a strong prejudice exists against brick houses on account of their constant dampness

pounds, or ten thousand gallons, or fifty tons of water, must leave the walls before they become habitable. How is this to got rid of? By full and perfect ventilation.

How to Dry Damp Walls.—The most effective method is by letting them evaporate the water into the air. This is best accomplished by heating all the chimneys and stoves, and the constant ventilation of all the rooms until the necessary degree of dryness is obtained.

Ventilation is also constantly necessary to maintain the proper degree of dryness to counteract their tendency to re-absorb the various gases, and the emanations resulting from inhabitation, and the vapors arising from the culinary department.

How to Prevent Walls from Becoming Damp—A Successful Experiment.—A gentleman having a brick house exposed on all sides, and suffering from dampness in the kitchen, which was in a wing upon the most exposed side, tried an experiment which has proved very satisfactory. A barrel of the best cement * was purchased, and a common tin wash-basin used for mixing it. The cement was mixed with water till about the consistency of cream, and then applied thickly with a large paint-brush. Of course the mixture had to be constantly stirred to prevent the cement from settling t the bottom. And on account of its very rapid settling it could only be mixed in very small quantities; half a gallon is about as large a quantity as can be readily handled at a time. When first dried it seemed somewhat of a failure, because it could be so easily brushed off, but after it had had twenty-four hours to harden it formed a strong, durable coating. The color is a neutral tint, somewhat like Ohio stone. The coating kept the wall perfectly dry, and as it is not expensive and does not need skilled labor in its application, ought to be extensively used. The coating should be brushed into all the crevices and openings of the work, and it may be found desirable to apply two coats in order that all the openings, etc., may be completely closed.

The covering of brick walls with several coats of good oil paint, also prevents them from imbibing moisture. The walls should be first covered with a thorough coat of sizing.

---

* Cement is much stronger than mortar, and can be used to great advantage in many places instead of lime, even in the face of the fact that it is much more costly than lime, except in a few favored localities where it is made. The usual proportions are one part of the cement to five of sand. In pointing, the proportion is sometimes as low as three parts sand to one of the cement. Coarse, clean sand—almost pebbles—can be used to the extent of three parts to one of the cement. Some advise mortar to be allowed to set, and then wet and worked again. This course will not answer with cement, which is greatly injured by such a method of working. The greatest enemy of both mortar and cement is the frost. The power with which water expands at the freezing point is practically unlimited, and where it penetrates into the crevices and pores of mortar and freezes, or when wet mortar is allowed to freeze, its strength is destroyed.

Damp Closets and Health.—All closets should be so constructed that they may be often thoroughly aired. Closets that are damp are dangerous enemies to health. If your closets are damp and engender a mold which encases not only boots and shoes, but also other articles of wearing apparel, obtain a half peck of unslacked lime and put in a shallow dish in the closet, and it will absorb the dampness. When it becomes quite damp it should be renewed.

Caution Against Damp Floors.—Floors of cellars and basements should not be made of brick or similar soft and porous material; apparently these can be easily kept clean, but they absorb and retain moisture, and not only remain cold and damp, but by their porosity expose the impurities of the absorbed moisture to evaporation, and thus pollute the air and render otherwise healthy cellars and basements damp and unwholesome. Floors of water-tight cement or of wood, well ventilated underneath, are therefore preferable.

How to Make Dry Cellar Floors.—For making floors, the following method is said to produce very desirable results: Four parts coarse gravel, or broken stone and sand, and one part each of lime and cement, are mixed in a shallow box, and well shovelled over from end to end. The sand, gravel, and cement are mixed together dry. The lime is slacked separately and mixed with just water enough to cement it well together. Six or eight inches of the mixture is then put on the bottom, and when well set, another coating is put on, consisting of one part cement and two of sand. This will also answer for making the bottom of a cistern that is to be cemented up directly upon the ground without a lining of bricks.

Danger from Vegetables in Cellars.—Most cellars contain a large amount of decomposing vegetable matter in the form of decaying fruits and vegetables, which give off their foul and poisonous gases during the process of decay. These gases give origin to diphtheria, typhoid and scarlet fever, and many other serious illnesses. Then, again, cellars are usually close, unventilated, and unsunned Air which is kept confined and without the purifying influence of sunlight, soon becomes impure and unfit to breathe, and if to this we add the dampness and constantly-escaping gases of decomposing vegetation, we have the condition of the atmosphere of cellars. The cellar should be thoroughly cleansed, aired, and sunned as often as foul air becomes noticeable, and all accumulations of rubbish or vegetable matter should be removed as soon as they begin to decay.

Danger from Wetting Coal in Cellars.—The habit of wetting coal in bulk in the cellar, which is sometimes practiced, causes it to emit poisonous gases deleterious to health, and it should be carefully avoided.

Sitting-Rooms and Bed-Rooms and Health.—Dwellings, and particularly sitting-rooms and bed-rooms, should be so constructed as to allow, at all seasons, regular ventilation, as moisture and the exhalations of their occupants accumulate and are absorbed by the porous walls, by carpets, beds, and furniture. The importance of ventilating bed-rooms is a fact in which every body is vitally interested, and which few properly appreciate. If two men are to occupy a bedroom during a night, let them step upon weighing-scales as they retire, and then again in the morning, and they will find that their actual weight is at least a pound less in the morning. Frequently there will be a loss of two or more pounds, and the average loss throughout the year will be more than one pound; that is, during the night there is a loss of a pound of matter, which has gone off from their bodies, partly from the lungs, and partly through the pores of the skin. The escaped material is carbonic acid and decayed animal matter, or poisonous exhalations.

The Kitchen Sink and Health.—A little sink near a kitchen door step, inadvertently formed, has been known, although not exceeding in its dimensions a single square foot, to spread sickness through a whole household. Hence, every thing of the kind should be studiously obviated, so that there should be no spot about a farm-house which can receive and hold standing water, whether it be the pure rain from the sky, the contents of a wash-basin, the slop-bowl, or the water-pail.

Ripe Fruit in Sitting or Sleeping-Rooms.—Care should be taken not to permit large quantities of ripe fruit in our sitting-rooms. Especially beware of laying it about a sick-chamber for any length of time. That complaint which some people make, of a faint sensation in the presence of fruit, is not fanciful; they may be really affected by it, for two Continental chemists have shown that from the moment of plucking, apples, cherries, currants, and other fruits are subject to incessant transformation. At first they absorb oxygen, thus robbing the surrounding air of its vital element; then they evolve carbonic acid, and this in far greater volume than the purer gas is absorbed, so that we have poison given us in the place of pure air, with compound interest, warmth accelerating it.

The Out-door Parts of the House.—These should be looked after with unremitting and ever-persistent care. If there is a cesspool it must be prevented from emitting any foul odors. Disinfectants must be used promptly until a complete change is effected. The out-door privy, if there is one, should have free access to the air. Exclude all slops or rain-water from it. If there is odor from it, use odorless disinfectants until it is corrected. If too foul for use, cover it over with "calx powder," and have under the seats some receptacle—such as the patent pail, or a half barrel or tub—which can be frequently removed, and alternately replaced by another. A privy built above ground, with water-tight receptacle, by the use of dry earth, powdered wood-charcoal, dry sifted ashes, and occasional copperas-water, is easily kept neat and clean, if cleansed each spring and fall. Heaps of rubbish and decayed wood, fruit or vegetables, should be removed. An offensive pig-sty, "hen-roost," stable, or other inclosure, should be cleansed at once and kept so. To do this will require only a little care.

House Cisterns and Health.—Dr. Stevenson Macadam, F.R.S.E., Lecturer on Chemistry in Edinburgh, has been making a series of researches which throw an interesting light on what is one of the most fertile and frequent, but one of the most easily controlled, sources of the contamination of our house drinking-water. He has made a series of analyses of water drawn from mains and from ordinary house-cisterns in Edinburgh, and by experiment has shown the effect upon the water from the mains of being retained in vessels containing a number of samples of cistern deposits. The results, Dr. Macadam says, demonstrate that the water-supply of a town or populous place, which may be every thing that is desired at the fountain-head, and even at the supply pipe as delivered to the house-holders, is liable to very serious contamination when retained in house-cisterns containing deposits or sediments which are composed in part of finely-divided-lead compound and decaying or putrescent organic matter; and he is confident that in many cases the water-supply of both towns and mansion-houses is rendered unwholesome from being retained in dirty cisterns.

How to Remedy the Evil of Bad Cisterns.—The remedy for the evil lies in the periodic cleansing of the house-cistern, which should be regularly done every month or two, according to its position and its liability to become impregnated with dust and sediment. The cleansing should be carried out with a very soft brush, and every care must be taken that the natural skin of the lead be not disturbed. A cover of wire or perforated zinc might be placed over the cistern to keep out mice, pieces of plaster, etc.; but a tight cover, which hinders the aëration of the water, should not be used. In ordinary cases, it is seldom or never that cisterns are purposely cleaned out, unless there be occasion to run off the water in order to execute repairs, and probably not even then, unless special instructions be given to clean out the cistern. Many towns and populous places are specially favored with water of excellent quality, as delivered into the towns and into the cisterns, and indeed each house is placed on the same footing for water-supply as if the foundations rested on the hills or other country district from which the water is drawn; and it is a matter of regret that gross inattention to the condition of house-cisterns should lead to these receptacles being sources of contamination of the water, which otherwise is of the most wholesome and suitable quality for all domestic purposes.

"Death in the Kitchen Dishcloth."—A lady correspondent of the *Rural World*, having been startled by *typhoid fever* in her neighborhood some time ago, gives the following good advice about dishcloths:—

If they are black and stiff, and smell like a barnyard, it is enough; throw them in the fire, and henceforth and forever wash your dishes with cloths that are white, cloths that you can see through, and see if you ever have that disease again. There are sometimes other causes, but I have smelled a whole house full of typhoid fever in one "dishrag." I had some neighbors once—clever, good sort of folks; one full four of them were sick at one time with typhoid fever. The doctor ordered the vinegar barrels whitewashed, and threw about forty cents' worth of carbolic acid in the swill-pail and departed. I went into the kitchen and made gruel; I needed a dishcloth, and looked around and found several, and such "rags!" I burned them all, and called the daughter of the house to get me a dishcloth. She looked around on the table. "Why," said she, "there was about a dozen here this morning," and she looked in the wood-box and on the mantelpiece, and felt in the cupboard. "Well," I said, "I saw some old black rotten rags lying around and I burned them, for there is death in such dishcloths as those, and you must never use such again." I took turns at nursing that family for weeks, and I believe those dirty dishcloths were the cause of all that hard work.

Therefore, I say to every housekeeper, keep your dishcloths clean. You may only brush and comb your head on Sundays, you need not wear a collar unless you go from home—but you must wash your dishcloths. You may only sweep the floor when the sun gets right; the windows don't need washing, you can look out of the door; that spider's web on the front porch don't hurt any thing—but as you love your lives, wash out your dishcloths. Let the foxtail grass grow in the garden, (the seed is a foot deep anyway;) let the holes in the heels of your husband's foot-rags go undarned; let the sage go ungathered; let the children's shoes go two Sundays without blacking; let the hens set four weeks on one wooden egg—but do wash out your dishcloths. Eat without a tablecloth, wash your faces and let them dry, do without a curtain for your windows and cake for your tea—but, for heaven's sake, keep your dishcloths clean.

Secure General Home Sanitary Inspection.—When families are housed near each other, every family has a right to expect and to demand protection from the civil authorities with regard to the presence of any foul odors arising from the lack of proper care on the part of others. A writer in one of our metropolitan journals has well said that "there will be householders who, from thoughtlessness, ignorance, or poverty, do not secure for themselves or for others the needed sanitary conditions. Charity, the public welfare, and the necessary incidents of city life, require regulated and definite provision against all those nuisances which imperil the life and health of the populace." The same writer very properly insists "upon systematic prevention, instead of waiting for that loss which disease always involves when it is artificial, or when we are compelled to meet an epidemic hurriedly If your authorities do not act, move by voluntary associations, which shall exhibit the facts and so compel action. There is no waste so great as that of preventible disease, which disables not only the sufferers, but puts a tax on labor, capital, and life, much more direful than a well-directed expenditure to prevent it. Epidemics are to be dreaded; but our greatest losses are from a chronic death and sickness rate, which has a permanent base of supply in prevalent unsanitary conditions, not remedied, as they should be and can be. Public health is common wealth. Can you not do something to reduce the tax levy which forced diseases impose upon the citizens of your city, township, and State? To the degree that sickness and invalidism is unnecessary, it means hard times and ill-content. Every motive of comfort and interest require that we plan to prevent all those ailments which are within the range and duty of our control."

SCHOOL-ROOMS AND HEALTH.

Near-Sightedness in Schools.—Prof. Cohn, Dr. of Medicine and Philosophy in the University of Breslau,[*] on examining 10,000 pupils, found 1,004 affected by myopia, or "near-sightedness." All the schools in which he made his investigations included some near-sighted individuals, but in the village schools these unfortunates were found in the proportion of only 1·4 per cent., whilst in city schools 11·4 in every hundred were affected with myopia. Furthermore, in the primary city schools the proportion was 6·7 per cent. In schools of the second grade, myopes were met with in the proportion of 10·5 per cent. In normal schools the percentage rose to 19·7; and in the Gymnasia, or highest schools, to 26·2. In the first class of the Gymnasia *more than half* the pupils were near-sighted.

An Alarming Fact.—From the researches of Prof. Cohn, with those of others, it seems indubitable that the work of reading and writing in imperfectly-arranged school-houses, brings about a lamentable development of myopia. Now it is certain that myopia is hereditary, and that, according to the great law of the extinction of the unfit, the children of myopic parents are predisposed to the development of this disease, so that they will certainly suffer from it, if exposed to conditions which would be apt to engender near-sightedness in normal eyes quite free from any taint of hereditary tendency. We are, therefore, as a people, threatened with an infinite increase of myopia, unless we can devise some efficient sanitary precautions for counteracting the injurious effects of prolonged application in the school-room upon our visual organs.

---

[*] *American Journal of Medical Science*, 1879.

School-rooms and Health.

How to Remedy the Evil.—Among the general deductions reached by Cohn and others, the following are the most important:—

1. In the first place, study-rooms should be well-lighted during the day, and especially toward evening, because a feeble or badly-arranged light compels us to diminish the distance between the eye and the book whilst reading or writing.

2. Light should be allowed to enter from the left side. Illumination from the front is more or less dazzling, and obliges the pupils to bend forward too much, or to sit side-wise in constrained and fatiguing positions. Again, light coming from behind is entirely insufficient, because in great measure cut off by the head or upper part of the body of each scholar.

3. The windows of a school-room should be large and high, be arranged along the left side of the apartment so as to shed the light upon desks placed in rows at right angles to the wall in which they are cut.

4. The light from above furnished by a sky-light is not so good as that derived from lateral illumination. The light of lamps is recommended as being preferable to gas, and the gas-light shining through ground-glass globes is condemned as particularly objectionable.

5. The inclination of the desk at which the pupil sits to read or write is a matter of no small importance. Desks which are horizontal, or only slightly inclined, favor the development of myopia by compelling the scholar to bend the head over a good deal whilst reading or writing. Such a position brings on, as a mere result of weight of the blood, passive congestion of the head and eyes, and this results in an intra-ocular tension, insensible, perhaps, when it first appears, but very marked in its effects when long and constantly continued. Besides, a child who acquires the habit of leaning forward in this manner, is very apt to bend nearer and nearer his book as the muscles of the back become fatigued, and thus, by straining his power of accommodation at short focus, promote the rapid development of myopia. The desks of school children should, therefore, be sharply inclined at an angle of 40° or 45° when used for reading, and their seats should not be too high, and should be furnished with comfortable backs.

How the Evils are Caused.—The faults of school-furniture, which give rise to injurious postures, are so conducive to myopia and asthenopia, as well as to scoliosis or lateral curvature of the spine, are:—

1 Want of, or unsuitable backs.
2 Too great a distance between the seat and the desk.
3. Disproportion; generally too great a difference between the height of the seat and that of the desk.
4. Wrong form and slope of the desk.

Liebreich, * in his lectures in 1878, gives a very clear exposition of the way

---

* Consulting Surgeon in St. Thomas' Hospital, London.

in which these defects cause the diseases already mentioned, and concludes with the subjoined recommendations, which he considers, however, less advantageous than what he calls the American plan of having the seat and desk made to every child's measure; or the Swiss system, when seven or more different sizes of seats and desks are manufactured to suit the different classes: —

"1. One and the same size and model of desk should be used for children and grown-up persons of both sexes.

"2. The adaptation to the height of each child should be effected by varying the height of the seat and the foot-board.

"3. The edge of the table is always to be in a perpendicular line above that of the seat.

"4. No seat is to be without a back, and the top of this is always to be 1 inch lower than the edge of the table for boys, and 1 inch higher than the edge of the table for girls.

"5. In all the classes where the boys change places, the height of the seat is to be regulated in proportion to the average height of the pupils.

"6. In all girls' schools, in all those boys' schools where the children do not change places, in boarding-schools, and in private school-rooms, the seat of each child should be accurately regulated in proportion to its height."

The support for the back should incline only a few degrees from the perpendicular, and be so shaped as to press upon the spinal column just above the hips of the pupil. The breadth of the seat ought to be considerable, in order to support most of the thighs, and its height just such as to allow the feet to rest easily upon the foot-board. The desk should be so arranged, by means of a hinged flap or otherwise, so as to hold the book at an angle of 40° or 45° whilst reading, and the paper at an angle of 20° whilst writing is being performed by the scholars.

CARE OF CHILDREN.

Early Food of Children.—The nursing child finds its earliest and best food in the mother's milk.* In most cases nothing more is needed until the first teeth appear. If the mother's milk is not sufficient, diluted milk from the cow may be used to supply the lack. If the mother does not nurse the child, cow's milk may be substituted. In such case, the milk should consist, for the first month, of milk one part and water two parts, with about a half teaspoonful of pure sugar to a half tumbler of the diluted milk. Condensed milk may be used instead, in which case the proportion should be one part

---

* The exceptions to this rule are when the mother is suffering from disease, or is of a consumptive family or habit.

condensed milk and ten parts water. Experience shows this mixture to be the best first food next to the mother's milk. Unless advised by an experienced physician, no "wet nurse" should be employed. As far as possible the infant should be trained to nursing at regular, though frequent, intervals

Changes of Early Diet—Weaning.—As a rule the child should be weaned when from ten to twelve months old. Except in case of teething the time should not extend beyond that period, and may terminate at the age of eight months. The nursing should not cease at once, as the abruptness of such change might prove unhealthful. It is well to wean the child first from day nursing, later from night nursing. Food may now be given consisting of milk and sweetened water with a little bread or cracker soaked therein. If convenient, arrowroot or rice flour, sago, or weak gruel of oatmeal may be added. It is best that the early food be neither cold nor hot—"milk warm" is better. No tea or coffee or highly-seasoned food should be given. A little tender meat finely divided, or a little beef-tea may be given once a day, *after the teeth for masticating food appear.*

Best Rule as to the Exact Time for Weaning.—Between the dentition of the four anterior *molar* teeth and the *canines* there is an interval of several months. This interval is recommended by that distinguished French medical professor and author, Foussagrives, as the most favorable time for weaning. All mothers should know this fact, and, when possible, weaning should be deferred until the child has twelve teeth. This rule is infinitely better than any one founded on age. Forced weaning at the time of dentition leads to disorders of the digestive passages. Hence it is dangerous to begin weaning during a teething crisis.

Arrangement of Regular Meals for Children.—Later, as well as earlier, these meals should be as regular as possible, and the children should not be allowed to eat "between meals." The younger the child the more frequently should the meals be given. The habit of regularity cannot too strongly be insisted upon. And yet not one mother in ten observes this rule. The exercise of a little care with a little common sense will early enable the mother to arrange the plan of regular meals and keep it.

Is the Mother's Health Injured by Nursing?—The rule is *never*. Dr Beard very properly says: "It is an error to suppose that the constitution suffers from suckling. Very many women have improved health from performing this most feminine of all offices. Many very delicate females have experienced the best effects from nursing their children; and many of the complaints incident to woman are removed or alleviated by it. *Fewer women die when nursing than at any other period.* The spirits during this period are generally more lively and uniform, the temper milder and more even, and the general feeling more healthy and pleasant than before."

The Mother's Food while Nursing.—The mother's food should be simple and easy of digestion. It is an oft-repeated truth that the food which agrees best with the mother's health while nursing also agrees best with the child's health during the same period. The mother's food should be ample, though in respect of quantity as well as quality that which is best for the mother is best for the child. Our Creator has wisely arranged these matters so that there is perfect harmony.

A Common Artificial Food Condemned.—Concerning a very popular favorite article, Dr. Zimmerman, as quoted by Liebig says: "Pap is a poison, the use of which senseless custom has consecrated. Many millions are nourished with pap, but it has also cost the lives of hundreds of thousands. The well-known Parisian physician, Dr. Vandermonde, shares my opinion, that pap is the worst food for children, the source of most of their maladies, their deformities, and death." And adds Liebig, "The evil effect of the much-used 'pap' given to children, both in the country and in towns, is well known to physicians; for it is quite intelligible that good cows' milk is not improved but depreciated, because wheaten flour, on account of its deficiency of the nutritive salts, is a very incomplete sort of food."

Objections of the same serious character apply to nearly to all the kinds of artificial food which are found in common use. They either do not comprise the elements of food in proper or sufficient quantity, or the elements themselves are rendered almost nugatory by dilution or adulteration.

Early Baths for Children.—For convenience, and to prevent chilliness, the child from the first should be washed in a small tub, with the body except the head immersed in milk-warm water. For thorough cleansing this should be done every morning and every evening. Not only is such a bath healthful in itself, but it also accustoms the child to the water. The warm bath should be used until one and a half or two years old, when a cool bath should be substituted. The bath should be very brief—at first not more than "two minutes." The child's body should be quickly wiped dry and quickly clothed. No wet or soiled napkins should be allowed to remain on the child.

Early Clothing for Children.—The clothing should be warm and light. As a rule, let long clothes be worn for about six months; then change, not to short clothes, but to those half-way between short and long; later, (when the child should learn to walk,) to short clothes. Great care should be taken to keep the feet warm and dry. It is well to have fine soft flannel worn next to the skin. This should always be loose.

Early Sleep of Children.—The best-informed medical advisers tell us that, when in health, children for the first month should sleep two-thirds of the time, and then a little less, and so on, until about fifteen months old, when their sleep should be about twelve hours in twenty-four. A child

Care of Children.

should be encouraged as long as possible to take a nap in the middle of the day, though after the age of two years it will be found difficult in many cases to induce a continuance of the habit. Parents should insist that their children go to bed at regular hours. The earlier the hour the better, and nothing, neither callers at home nor company away from home, should allow interruption to the rule.

Shall Children be Rocked to Sleep?—If the child be accustomed to sleep in the crib from the first, it will demand nothing else, and good habits of sleep with less exposure will be likely to continue. The best advisers now urge that the habit of rocking children to sleep, of carrying them about the room in order to entice them to sleep, is a great evil. A child with well regulated habits will sleep much more successfully and pleasantly than in the old and common way of rocking, or carrying, or jolting in the lap or arms. Kindly and tenderly, but certainly, put the child in bed, and leave it there unless seriously ill. Resist its cries which may demand the arms at first. Accustom the child to sleep after nursing, not while nursing.

Shall Feather Pillows be Used for Babies' Heads?—Important testimony in response to this question is given by Dr. Dio Lewis. He says: "The proximate, if not the original, cause of a large proportion of deaths among American babies is some malady of the brain. When we suppose the death to result from dysentery or cholera infantum, the immediate cause of the death is an affection of the brain supervening upon the bowel disease. The heads of American babies are, for the most part, little furnaces. What mischief must come from keeping them buried twenty-four hours out of every twenty-four in feather pillows. It makes me shiver to think of the number of deaths among these precious little ones, which I have myself seen, where I had no doubt that cool straw pillows would have saved them. The hair pillow is inferior to straw, because it cannot, like straw, be made perfectly clean and fresh by frequent change. Do not fail to keep their little heads cool."

Babies' Bow-legs, and How to Prevent Them.—It is well known that "bow-legs" are among the common deformities of humanity, and wise mothers assert that the crookedness in either case arises from the afflicted one having been put upon his or her feet too early in babyhood. But a Manchester physician, Dr. Crompton, who has watched for the true cause, thinks differently. He attributes the first-mentioned distortion to a habit some youngsters get in of rubbing the sole of one foot against that of the other; some will go to sleep with the soles pressed together; they appear to enjoy the contact only when the feet are naked; they never attempt to make it when they are socked or slippered. So the remedy is obvious: keep the baby's soles covered.

Babies' "Knock-knees," and How to Prevent Them.—"Knock-knees," another common deformity, the physician ascribes to a different childish habit: that of sleeping on the side, with one knee tucked into the hollow behind the other. He has found that where one leg has been bowed inwardly more than the other, the patient has always slept on one side, and the uppermost member has been that most deformed. Here the preventive is to pad the inside of the knees, so as to keep them apart, and let the limbs grow freely their own way.

How to Care for Children's Feet.—It has been well said that life-long discomfort, disease, and sudden death often come to children through the inattention or carelessness of the parents. A child should *never be allowed to go to sleep with cold feet*. The thing to be last attended to is, to see that the feet are dry and warm. Neglect of this has often resulted in a dangerous attack of croup, diphtheria, or a fatal sore-throat.

Always, on coming from school, on entering the house from a visit or errand in rainy, muddy, or thawing weather, the child's shoes should be removed, and the mother should herself ascertain if the stockings are the least damp; and if so they should be taken off, the feet held before the fire and rubbed with the hand till perfectly dry, and another pair of shoes be put on, and the other shoes and stockings should be placed where they can be dried, so as to be ready for future use at a moment's notice.

Early Exercise for Children.—They should be much in the open air, and for this purpose the "baby carriages," now largely introduced into all large towns, are a great boon to society. All violent exercise should be avoided. Tossing up and down, or jolting in a chair, is not well, especially during the first months. In carrying the child around in the arms or carriage, it should be kept in a horizontal position.

Giving Spirits or Cordials to Babies.—One of the best known and most successful physicians in America writes: "Spirits given to a baby, or, what is much the same, drank by the mother, is poison for the body, and may be the starting of a habit which leads to ruin. Most of the cordials for children are evil, and only evil, and that continually."

Are Candies Healthful for Children?—Sugar is not injurious, but should not be given to children often, or it will lessen or disturb the appetite. Most candies which are found in the small shops, or which are hawked about the streets, have been adulterated, and are positively injurious. See chapter on "Adulteration of Food." Candies should either be made "at home" or purchased of an honest dealer. The simpler and milder candies are best.

Children in the Care of Servants.—Remarkable testimony upon this question has recently been given. Here is the record: A number of physicians, practicing in New York and Brooklyn, having "compared notes," have concluded that one leading cause of the mortality among children arises from their being left too much to the care of servants. It has been observed that children who are taken care of by their parents, undressed and put to bed by them, and by them dressed in the morning, and kept under a loving mother's eye during the day, are, as a general thing, far more healthy, good-tempered, and intelligent than such as are left almost exclusively to the care of servants. In addition to this, it must be remembered that most of the accidents which happen to children, whereby they are seriously injured, and sometimes crippled, maimed, and rendered idiotic, occur through the negligence of those in whose care they are left by unthinking or unloving parents.

Lack of Appetite in Children.—The Boston *Journal of Chemistry* says that children must have an abundance of out-door exercise, fun and frolic. Make them regular in their habits, and feed them only on plain, nourishing food, and they will seldom, if ever, complain of a lack of appetite. But keep them overtasked at school, confined close to the house the rest of the time, frowning down every attempt at play, feed them upon rich or high-seasoned food, candies, nuts, etc., allow them to eat between meals and late in the evening, and you cannot expect them to have good appetites. On the contrary, you may expect they will be pale, weak, and sickly. Don't cram them with food when they don't want it, or have no appetite for it; such a course is slow murder. If they have no appetite, encourage, and if need be, command them to take exercise in the open air.

Age, Studies, and Habits of Children at School.—The faculty of a Massachusetts medical college, after carefully considering the influence of public schools upon the health of children, authorized the publication of the following opinions:—

1. No child should be allowed to attend school before the beginning of his sixth year.

2. The duration of daily attendance, including the time given to recess and physical exercises, should not exceed four and a half hours for primary schools; five and a half for other schools.

3. There should be no study required out of school—unless at high school; and this should not exceed one hour.

4. Recess-time should be devoted to play outside the school-room—unless during stormy weather—and, as this time rightfully belongs to the pupils, they should not be deprived of it except for serious offenses; and those who are not deprived of it, should not be allowed to spend it in study; no child should ever be confined to the school-room during an entire session. The minimum of recess-time should be fifteen minutes each session, and in primary schools there should be more than one recess in each session.

5. Physical exercise should be used in school to prevent nervous and mus-

cular fatigue, and to relieve monotony, but not as muscular training It should be practiced by both teacher and children in every hour not broken by recess, and should be timed by music. In primary schools every half hour should be broken by exercise, recess, or singing.

6. Ventilation should be amply provided for, by other means than by open windows, though these should be used in addition to special means during recess and exercise time.

7. Lessons should be scrupulously apportioned to the average capacity of the pupils; and in primary schools the slate should be used more and the book less; and the instructions should be given as much as possible on the principl- of "object teaching."

THE SICK-ROOM AND HEALTH.

Light in the Sick-Chamber.—Except in extraordinary cases, light is indispensable to the best relief of the sick. It should be softened and subdued, and not glaring. The light should be admitted in large quantities. It is an element of cheerfulness, and on that account should be admitted to as large an extent as the patient can bear without inconvenience. As shown in a previous chapter, the sun-light has a direct and powerful influence for good upon the physical system, and on this account, also, its presence should be regarded as a prime necessity. Blinds or curtains may be provided to screen the eyes, if the latter are too weak or sensitive to bear the direct rays; but no substitute can perform its powerful service as a sanitary agent in the sick chamber.

Cheerful Walls and Cheerful Prospects.—The walls should be of a cheerful tint; if possible, some sort of out-door glimpse should be visible from the bed or chair where the invalid lies, if it is but the top of a tree and a bit of sky. Eyes which have been traveling for long, dull days over the pattern of the paper-hangings, till each bud and leaf and quirl is familiar —and hateful—brighten with pleasure as the blind is raised. The mind, wearied of the grinding battle with pain and self, finds unconscious refreshment in the new interest.

The Inspiration of Pleasant Contrasts.—Ah, there is a bird's shadow flitting across the pane! The tree-top sways and trembles with soft rustlings —a white cloud floats dreamily over the blue—and now, O delight and wonder! the bird himself comes in sight and perches visibly on the bough, dressing his feathers, and quivering forth a few notes of song. All the world, then, is not lying in bed because we are, is not tired of its surroundings—has not the back-ache! What a refreshing thought! And though this glimpse of another life, the fresh natural life from which we are shut out—that life which has nothing to do with pills and potions, tip-toe movements, whispers, and doctors' boots creaking in the entry—may cause the hot tears to rush suddenly into our eyes, it does us good, and we begin to say, with a certain tremulous thrill of hope, "When I go out again I shall do"—so and so.*

The Healthful Influence of Pleasant Variety.—If friends knew how irksome, how positively harmful, is the *sameness* of a sick-room, surely love and skill would devise remedies. If it were only bringing in a blue flower to-day, and a pink one to-morrow; hanging a fresh picture to vary the monotony of the wall, or even an old one in a new place—something, anything—it is such infinite relief. Small things and single things suffice. To see many of his surroundings changed at once, confuses an invalid; to have one litt e novelty at a time to vary the point of observation, stimulates and cheers. Give him that, and you do more and better than if you filled the apartment with fresh objects.

The Inspiration of Beautiful Flowers.—Many argue that flowers should be carefully kept away from sick people, lest they exhaust the air, or communicate to it some harmful quality. This may, in a degree, be true of such strong, fragrant blossoms as lilacs or garden lilies, but of the more delicately-scented ones no such effect need be apprehended. A well-aired room will never be made close or unwholesome by a nosegay of roses, mignonette, or violets, and the subtle cheer which they bring with them is infinitely reviving to weary eyes and depressed spirits.

Caution as to Reading Aloud in the Sick-Room.—"With regard to reading aloud in the sick-room," says Florence Nightingale, "my experience is, that when the sick are too ill to read to themselves, they can seldom bear to be read to. Children, eye-patients, and uneducated persons are exceptions, or where there is any mechanical difficulty in reading. People who like to be read to have generally not much the matter with them; while in fevers, or where there is much irritability of brain, the effort of listening to reading aloud has often brought on delirium. I speak with great diffidence, because there is an almost universal impression that it is sparing the sick to read aloud to them."

Read Slowly to the Sick.—If the patient desires reading, or if reading aloud is not trying to the nerves, it should be done slowly. "People often think that the way to get it over with least fatigue to him is to get it over in least time. They gabble, they plunge and gallop through the reading. There never was a greater mistake. Houdin, the conjurer, says that the way to make a story seem short is to tell it slowly. So it is with reading to the sick.

---

* *Scribner's Monthly.*

I have often heard a patient say to such a mistaken reader, 'Don't read it to me; tell it me.' Unconsciously he is aware that this will regulate the plunging, the reading with unequal paces, slurring over one part, instead of leaving it out altogether if it is unimportant, and mumbling another."

Read in a Natural, Pleasant, Colloquial Voice.—If the reader lets his own attention wander, and then stops to read up to himself, or finds he has read the wrong bit, then it is all over with the poor patient's chance of not suffering. Very few people know how to read to the sick; very few read aloud as pleasantly even as they speak. In reading they sing, they hesitate, they stammer, they hurry, they mumble; when in speaking they do none of these things. Reading aloud to the sick ought always to be rather slow, and exceedingly distinct, but not mouthing; rather monotonous, but not sing-song; rather loud, but not noisy.

Evil of Reading Aloud Only Fragmentary Paragraphs.—The extraordinary habit of reading to one's self in a sick-room, and reading aloud to the patient any sentences which will amuse him, is exceedingly thoughtless. What does such a reader think the patient is thinking of during his gaps of non-reading? Do you think that the patient amuses himself upon what you have read for precisely the time it pleases you to go on reading to yourself, and that his attention is ready for something else at precisely the time it pleases you to begin reading again? Whether the person thus read to be sick or well; whether he be doing nothing, or doing something else while being thus read to, the self-absorption and want of observation of the person who does it, is equally difficult to understand—although very often the patient is too amiable to say how much it disturbs him.

Evil of a Rough Voice in the Sick-Room.—Many attendants or visitors have little intelligent care as to their voice in the sick-room. A person sometimes has a rough, stentorian voice, and forgets to control it, or mellow it when using it in the presence of the sick. The sick cannot endure, either, the rough or ever "thundering" voice, and will be likely to say, at least in a whisper, when the visitor has gone away: "Never let that man come to me again; never let him enter the door again; his voice was enough to distract my poor head; *I cannot endure it.*

Evil of an Indistinct Voice in the Sick-Room.—The other extreme is also a real evil. The attendants speak gently enough, it may be, yet so *indistinctly* that the poor patient cannot understand what is said. The latter is worn out and distracted with the nervous effort to lay hold of some precious instruction and spiritual comfort, perhaps from the minister, which he strives in vain to understand. A little care upon the part of the speaker will enable him to adjust his voice so as not to tax the nerves of the sick man. Distinctness is very great value under such circumstances.

The Sick-Room and Health. 243

Great Tenderness of Manner Required.—A man lying on a bed of sickness must be treated with a great deal of tenderness and consideration in regard to voice and manner, as well as in regard to the matter and measure of the instruction which you give him. And if a truly consistent Christian comes in to visit him, and his voice is so gentle that it does not disturb him by a loudness which he cannot bear, and, at the same time, is so distinct that, without difficulty, he can catch every word that is spoken, the impression will be quite different. He says, when his instructor is gone, "O, what a nice gentleman that was! How soft and gentle his voice was! and yet so clear and distinct that without the least difficulty I could understand every word that he said. Whenever he comes let me see him."

How to Move a Patient.—Sometimes, when patients are greatly exhausted, or after severe surgical operations, it may be dangerous to bring them into a sitting position, but they may be safely and easily moved if the body is kept horizontal in the following manner: Place the head of one bedstead against the foot of the other. Having procured two hard-wood poles six feet long and one and a half inches in diameter, place one on each side of the patient near the edge of the sheet on which he rests, and roll them firmly into the sheet to within six inches of the patient's body. Two persons should stand on each side of the bed, facing the two on the other side, and grasping the poles firmly with both hands, separated about eighteen inches apart, they should first pull firmly against each other until the sheet on which the patient lies is converted into a stretcher. Then continue to pull, and lifting the body horizontally and moving downward together, they easily deposit the patient in the fresh bed, without danger or suffering. The sheet on which he has been moved can then be readily slipped out from beneath the body. It is astonishing with what ease a thing can be done when done in the right way.

Heat and Ventilation in the Sick-Room.—Where the entire dwelling is heated by a furnace, or by steam, it will probably be unnecessary to have other means of warming the sick-room; but the fire-place should be *always* open, and kept ready for a wood or a coal fire whenever the patient shall express a desire for one. The fire-places are excellent ventilating flues even without a fire, but are nearly perfect when supplied with a wood fire, the brisk blaze of which creates a strong ascending current, and continually carries off the ever-accumulating exhalations of the sick-room. If there is no fire-place, a window opened a short distance from the bottom, in the room in which the patient is lying, and one let down from the top in the other large room, with the doors opened between the two, will form an effectual draught during any but the warm days of summer, and will not be too strong for the most delicate patient who is protected from the direct draught by the high head-board of the bed. In cold weather the window opened from the bottom will often be found sufficient. On very cold days we may trust to an entire change of air several times each day, effected by raising all the windows for a few moments at a time, during which the patient must be thoroughly protected by extra blankets and a shawl about the head.

Cleanliness and Neatness in the Sick-room.—The aphorism that Cleanliness is next to godliness," is nowhere more imperative than in the sick-room. Cleanliness absolutely enforced will stamp out any infectious disease, and mitigate all diseases to a marked degree. In enforcing cleanliness in the sick-room we must look to the patient's bed, the patient's body, the nurse, and all utensils, vessels, etc. In the model sick-room there should be two narrow beds of equal height on easy-rolling castors, having hair mattresses, low headboards, and absolutely free from all abominations in the way of canopies. The patient may thus have a fresh bed for the night and another for the morning. In the morning the freshly-made bed, covered with one sheet, can be trundled up to the bed which has been occupied during the night, and the patient can easily be slid on the same level on to a deliciously fresh bed. The mattress and bedding of the bed vacated can be rolled up, quietly taken into an adjoining room, where, with open windows, they can be shaken, thoroughly ventilated during the day, and made ready for the night.

Directions in Contagious Sickness.—The following general directions are useful for nurses and others in contagious or infectious sickness:—

1. The sick person should be restricted to one room, or a part of the house separated from the other inmates.

2. Secure proper ventilation of the sick-room, without producing draughts. *Smell* is an excellent guide as to the state of air; if the air is *sweet* there is but little dread to be felt.

3. The virulence of any poison which causes the spread of disease is greatly increased by concentration in *close rooms*, and decreased by dilution and free circulation of air.

4. The linen, clothing, bedding, utensils, and every object touched by or in contact with the sick, should be isolated, and, such as will permit, should be thrown into boiling water, there to remain at least for half an hour.

5. The nurse should be restricted to the sick-room or otherwise isolated.

6. Remember that disease is communicated by both the poisoned air about the sick, and by the clothes and other articles used or touched by them.

7. After the patient leaves the sick-room, it should be purified and disinfected. *Boil* every thing that will admit of it; scald all utensils; scrub the floors; whitewash ceiling and walls. Empty the room entirely, and leave doors and windows open for at least a day or two.

Important Qualities of a Good Nurse.—A good nurse will be full of kindness. She will control by gentleness combined with decision. She will be most decisive if no one suspects that she is so at all. It is the triumph of supremacy to become unconsciously supreme. Nowhere is this decision more blessed than in a sick-room.* Where it exists in its genuineness the sufferer is never contradicted, never coerced; all the little victories are assumed. The decisive nurse is never peremptory, never loud. She is distinct, it is true--there is nothing more aggravating to a sick person than a whisper --but she is not loud. Though quiet, she never walks on tip-toe; she never makes gestures; all is open and above-board. She knows no diplomacy of *finesse*, and of course her shoes never creak. Her touch is steady and encouraging. She does not potter. She never looks at you sideways. You never catch her watching. She never slams the door, of course, but she never shuts it slowly, as if she were cracking a nut in the hinge. She never talks behind it. She never peeps. She pokes the fire skillfully, with firm, judicious penetration. She caresses one kind of patient with genuine sympathy; she talks to another as if she were well. She is never in a hurry. She is worth her weight in gold.

Twenty-one Brief Suggestions to Nurses.—Be scrupulously neat in person and dress.

Be cheerful and buoyant to the last degree possible.

A few drops of hartshorn in the water used for *daily* bathing will remove the disagreeable odors of warmth and perspiration.

Never speak of the symptoms of your patient in his presence, unless questioned by the doctor, whose orders you are always to obey *implicitly*.

Remember never to be a gossip or tattler, and "always to hold sacred the knowledge which, to a certain extent, you must obtain of the private affairs of your patient, and the household in which you nurse."

Try to give as little trouble to the servants as possible, and make them feel that you have come to help them in the extra work that sickness always brings.

Never contradict your patient, nor argue with him.

Never let your patient see that you are annoyed about any thing.

Never *whisper* in the sick-room. If your patient be well enough, and wishes you to talk to him, speak in a low, distinct voice, on cheerful subjects.

Don't relate painful hospital experiences, nor give details of the maladies of former patients.

Never startle the patient with accounts of dreadful crimes or accidents that you have read in the newspapers.

Write down the orders that the physician gives you as to time for giving the medicines, food, etc.

Give an account of your patient to the physician in as few words as possible.

---

* *Good Health.*

Keep the room bright (unless the doctor *orders* it darkened).
Let the air be as pure as possible, giving it fresh supplies from outside.
Keep every thing in order, but without being fussy and bustling.
To remove dust, wipe every thing with a damp cloth.
Remember to carry out all vessels covered. Empty and wash them immediately, and keep some disinfectant in them.

Remember, that to leave the patient's untasted food by his side from meal to meal, in hopes that he will eat it in the interval, is simply to prevent him from taking any food at all.

Medicines, beef-tea, or stimulants, should never be kept where the patient can see them, or smell them.

Remember "that we have no power of ourselves to help ourselves," but that God is ever willing to grant us strength to perform our duties, if we pray to him in the name of our Blessed Saviour.

ALCOHOL AND HEALTH.

Alcohol Cannot be Classed as Food.—Omitting in this connection all reference to the social and moral relations of this question, we invite attention to its hygienic aspects. The highest medical and chemical authorities now indorse the conclusion that alcohol is not a food, but a poison, like opium, and a substance abhorrent to the human economy; that it does not in the slightest degree nourish the body, or even prevent the waste of tissue, but that it arrests digestion, destroys the appetite, lessens muscular force and vital heat, excites the lower passions, predisposes the drinker to disease, and retards his recovery.

Liebig's Testimony.—Professor Liebig has shown that alcohol contains no element which can be converted into nutriment; and the experiments of MM. Lallemand, Perrin, Duroy, Dr. Edward Smith, and other physiologists, demonstrate that alcohol is ejected from the system in the state in which it is introduced, no trace of any derivative of alcohol being found in the blood; therefore, no quantity of alcohol can be of benefit to healthy persons; on the contrary, it must, in every case, exercise a poisonous influence.

Dr. Richardson's and Prof. Silliman's Testimony.—Prof. Silliman, M.D., of Yale Medical Institute, quotes Dr. Richardson's conclusion on this question, after thorough investigation, as follows: "Speaking honestly, I cannot, by any argument yet presented to me, admit the alcohols through any gate that might distinguish them as separate from other chemical bodies. I can no more accept them as foods than I can chloroform, or ether, or methylal. That they produce temporary excitement is true, but as their gen eral action is quickly to reduce animal heat, I cannot see how they can supply animal force. I see clearly how they reduce animal power, and can show a reason for using them in order to stop physical or to stupefy mental pain; but that they give strength, that is, that they supply material for the construction of fine tissue, or throw force into tissue supplied by other material, must be an error as solemn as it is wide-spread."

Alcohol not the Source of Physical Force.—The authority quoted above, adds: "The true place of the alcohols is clear; they are agreeable temporary shrouds. The savage, with the mansions of his soul unfurnished, buries his restless energy under their shadow. The civilized man, overburdened with mental labor, or with engrossing care, seeks the same shade, but it is shade after all, in which, in exact proportion as he seeks it, the seeker retires from perfect natural life. To search for force in alcohol is to my mind equivalent to the act of searching for the sun in subterranean gloom until all is night."

Similar Testimony from Others.—Hundreds of testimonies similar in their teachings have been given. "It seems doubtful," says Dr. T. K. Chambers, "if on the healthy nervous system alcohol is ever a stimulant, even in the most moderate dose, and for the shortest periods of time." In another part of his work, on "Renewal of Life," Dr. Chambers says, "It is clear that we must cease to regard alcohol as in any sense an aliment, inasmuch as it goes out as it went in, and does not, as far as we know, leave any of its substance behind." Dr. Edward Smith, F.R.S., asserts that "alcohol is not true food; and it neither warms nor sustains the body." *

Does Alcohol Help Digestion?—Alcohol is said to increase the flow of the gastric secretions when used in moderate quantities, and so to promote the digestion of food. The limit, however, to its acting thus is a very restricted one. If used in any quantity it never fails to irritate the lining membrane of the stomach, and so produce the very opposite effect to that stated; a small quantity, however, soon loses the effect sought; as the amount is increased the deterioration which over-stimulation is certain to induce is brought on, and the terrible indigestion of the tippler is established.

Alcohol Useless in Nearly All Cases.—Put against the above the results of accredited and intelligent experience and observation, that in the long run of surgical ailments no aid is required from stimulants, but, on the contrary, these complaints "*are much better managed without alcohol.*"

A Distinguished Surgeon Uses Alcohol in Only One Case out of Fifty!—"At this moment," says Dr. Macleod, "at the moment I address

---

* ALCOHOL AN ANÆSTHETIC.—In a paper upon "The Use and Abuse of Alcoholic Liquors," Dr. W. L. Schenck supports with considerable ability the idea that alcohol is neither a food nor a stimulant, but a true anæsthetic.

you I have under my care more than fifty surgical cases, and only one—and she is a very weakly woman, with blood poisoning—is taking alcohol. Among the cases I allude to are many who have undergone serious operations, and many old and feeble people. I mention this to show that, while I resolutely defend the use of alcohol in certain cases, I am but little given to its administration in the usual practice of my profession.

Patients Require Food Rather than Stimulants.—If food of a nourishing and concentrated kind can be taken and assimilated, that is what will recuperate our patients and prolong their lives. Alas, it is the want of this power of assimilation which baffles us so frequently in dealing with disease, and *that* is not unfrequently the offspring of previous intemperance.

Careless Use of Alcohol Dangerous.—We cannot be too strenuous in warning persons against the careless way in which too much stimulant is prescribed in the sick-room. Occasionally one hears friends told to "be good to the patient," or to take care and "keep up his system," or to "stimulate him freely." No such lax and injudicious instructions should ever be given, but the exact quantity scrupulously laid down, and care taken that it is adhered to. Weak, nervous, worn-out persons will put a very liberal interpretation on any mere general instruction, and thus you come to discover that food is neglected for alcohol—truly, "One halfpennyworth of bread to this intolerable deal of sack." Never allow the bottle containing the stimulant to be kept in the sick room, but let the precise amount to be consumed in the twenty-four hours be put into a separate phial, so that its progressive use may be judged of accurately.

Alcohol a Brain Poison.—Science has shown that alcohol has a special affinity for the brain. On its introduction into the system it rushes to that vital organ, and makes there its first and most powerful assault upon life. If the quantity is sufficient it causes *instant* death.

In common doses it produces disturbances ranging from trifling congestion to *delirium tremens*. It literally hardens the brain. A professor of surgery assured his class that he could tell the brain of a drunkard in the dark by passing the dissecting knife through it.

An agent classed by all toxicologists with deadly poison, that has an affinity for the brain so strong that it crowds not only the channels of the circulation, but the substance of the brain itself, cannot fail to produce serious disturbances in the delicate organ of thought. And facts agree. Brain diseases, such as congestion, paralysis, apoplexy, epilepsy, and insanity, are caused or aggravated by intoxicating drinks to a fearful extent.

Alcoholic Rheumatism.—A writer in the *British Medical Journal* thus alludes to a disease, new in name if not new in experience, in this country.

1. Alcoholic rheumatism is the result of a distinct cause.

2. It is produced by drinking alcoholic beverages.
3. It is slow in effecting a marked change in the system.
4. It does not usually appear before middle life.
5. Its effects are produced by the accumulation of the alcoholic fluids taken into the system.
6. It causes stupidity, stiffness in the body, hobbling gait, and ultimate lameness.
7. It causes changes of structure and produces chronic alcoholism.
8. The remedy is abstinence from the use of all fermented alcoholic drinks and taking vigorous exercise in the open air.

How Alcoholic Drinks Cause Apoplexy.—It is the essential nature of all wines and spirits to send an increased amount of blood to the brain. The first effect of taking a glass of wine or stronger form of alcohol is to send the blood there faster than common, hence the circulation that gives the red face. It increases the activity of the brain, and it works faster, and so does the tongue. But suppose a man keeps on drinking, the blood is sent to the brain so fast, in such large quantities, that in order to make room for it the arteries have to enlarge themselves; they increase in size, and in doing so they press against the more yielding and flaccid veins which carry the blood out of the brain, and thus diminish their size, their pores, the result being that the blood is not only carried to the arteries of the brain faster than is natural or healthful, but it is prevented from leaving it as fast as usual; hence a double set of causes of death are in operation. A man may drink enough brandy or other spirits in a few hours, or in a few minutes, to bring on a fatal attack of apoplexy.

No Risk in Disusing Alcohol Suddenly and Fully.—It is a very gratifying fact that there is no risk in withdrawing alcohol *at once* and *fully* from inebriates. Indeed, this is generally the only method very hopeful in the direction of recovery. "Half-measures always fail. Let it be absolutely forbidden in any form and quantity, and though I am not very sanguine as to success in the case of confirmed drunkards, yet for those less hopelessly abandoned there is, by following rigid abstinence, a chance of reform. Nourishing, fatty food, sugar, plenty of fresh air, and mental enjoyment, will help to wean the victim from his poison."

Physicians Should Especially Promote Abstinence from Alcohol.—"The medical profession may do much to promote temperance, and it is its bounden duty to exercise its wide-spread influence to such a good end. One of the most painful sights ever seen, was the graves of three young medical practitioners, all victims to intemperance, which lay side by side, on the sunny slope of a Highland hill, beneath the shadow of an ancient cross, which had been erected by the self-denying Anchorites of the early faith.

One after another, they had gone to practice their divine art, and, in succession, fell victims to their self-indulgence, a melancholy picture of neglected talents and wasted lives."

Testimony of a Great Surgeon.—"Gentlemen," said the same lecturer, "let us determine that we will avoid all such vices, and fulfill the old promise which Hippocrates, the father of surgical science, imposed on his disciples, (and which is almost exactly reproduced in the declaration you will all sign on graduation here.) 'I will follow that system of regimen which, according to my ability and judgment, I consider for the benefit of my patients, and *abstain from whatever is deleterious or mischievous*. I will give no deadly medicine to any one, if asked, or suggest any such counsel, and, *with purity and holiness*, I will pass my life and practice my art.' These are, indeed, noble words—which were the sentiments of a Pagan, but they would do honor to the most exalted Christian."

Inconsiderate Prescription of Alcoholic Liquors by Physicians —Testimony of 300 Leading Physicians.—The following opportune document, signed by three hundred of the leading physicians of London, appeared in the papers of that city just before Christmas :—

As it is believed that the inconsiderate prescription of large quantities of alcoholic liquid by medical men for their patients has given rise, in many instances, to the formation of intemperate habits, the undersigned, while unable to abandon the use of alcohol in the treatment of certain cases of disease, are yet of opinion that no medical practitioner should prescribe it without a sense of grave responsibility.

They believe that alcohol, in whatever form, should be prescribed with as much care as any powerful drug, and that the directions for its use should be so framed as not to be interpreted as a sanction for excess, or necessarily for the continuance of its use when the occasion is past. They are also of opinion that many people immensely exaggerate the value of alcohol as an article of diet, and since no class of men see so much of its ill effects, and possess such power to restrain its abuse, as members of their own profession, they hold that every medical practitioner is bound to exert his utmost influence to inculcate habits of great moderation in the use of alcoholic liquids.

Being also firmly convinced that the great amount of drinking of alcoholic liquors among the working classes of this country is one of the greatest evils of the day, destroying—more than anything else—the health, happiness, and welfare of those classes, and neutralizing, to a large extent, the great industrial prosperity which Providence has placed within the reach of this nation, the undersigned would gladly support any wise legislation which would tend to restrict, within proper limits, the use of alcoholic beverages, and gradually introduce habits of temperance. George Burrows, M.D., F.R.S., President of the Royal College of Physicians, Physician Extraordinary to the Queen ; George Busk, F.R.S., President of the Royal College of Surgeons, and others.

General Physiological Effects of Alcohol.—A valuable paper was furnished recently at a meeting of one of our State Medical Associations, in which, after discussing thoroughly the whole question of the physiological effects of alcoholic beverages, the author gave the following, among other conclusions, which he had reached in his researches :—

Alcohol and Health.

1. Alcohol, when present in the blood, causes fatty degeneration of the organs.

2. It dilates the blood vessels, and increases the force and frequency of the heart, by its action on the nervous centers. It does not give additional strength, but merely enables a man to draw on his reserve energy. It may thus give assistance in a single effort, but not in prolonged exertion

3. It has the same effect upon the action of the heart.

4. By dilating the vessels of the skin, alcohol warms the surface at the expense of the internal organs.

5. The symptoms of intoxication are due to paralysis of the nervous system. It is through paralysis of the medulla that alcohol usually causes death.

6. The apparent immunity possessed by drunken men from the usual effects of serious accident, is due to paralysis of the nervous mechanism through which shock could be produced in a sober condition.

Alcoholic Drinks Greatly Shorten Life.—A celebrated French physician, Dr. Everat, has furnished statistics showing that the mortality from this cause is annually 50,000 in England, 40,000 in Germany, 15,000 in Russia, 4,000 in Belgium, 3,000 in Spain, and 15,000 in France. Notwithstanding the universality of this vice among nearly all classes of society, few persons are aware of how materially human life is abbreviated by the use of alcohol.

Interesting Illustrative Statistics.—Mr. F. G. P. Nelson, an actuary, of London, from a series of careful observations, has deduced some valuable statistics regarding this subject, which prove that the average duration of life, after beginning the use of liquor as a beverage, is as follows: Among beer-drinkers, 21·7 years; among spirit-drinkers, 16·7 years; among those who drink spirits indiscriminately, 16·1 years. The death-rate among different drinkers Mr. Nelson found to be: Among beer-drinkers, 4·597 per cent. yearly; among spirit-drinkers, 5·996 per cent. yearly; among mixed-drinkers, 6·194 per cent. yearly.

Table Showing the Comparative Expectation of Life for Drinkers.—The subjoined table, prepared by Nelson, contrasts the "Expectation of Life" for temperate and intemperate persons:—

Ages.	Temperate.	Intemperate.	Loss of Life.
20	44·2 years.	15·5 years	28·7 years.
30	36·5 "	13·8 "	22·7 "
40	28·8 "	11·6 "	17·2 "
50	21·2 "	10·9 "	10·3 "
60	14·3 "	8·9 "	5·4 "

The expectation of liquor-drinkers, from the time of becoming such, varies with the vocation:

Among mechanics, working and laboring men..................18 years.
Among traders, dealers, and merchants....................17 "
Among professional men and gentlemen....................15 "
Among females...14 "

It will be noticed that professional men addicted to strong drink, are shorter lived than drinkers of other pursuits.

Why Some Liquor-Drinkers Have Long Lives.—While the above tables, carefully compiled, show the average of the lives of liquor-drinkers to be much less than that of the abstemious, there are occasional instances in which even the intemperate live to old age. Certain physical constitutions become transformed in the functional condition of the system, so that they live on in an abnormal way, enduring, and even enjoying, a poisonous physical condition. Some persons seem to enjoy better health in a malarious atmosphere than out of it. Their bodies have undergone the transformation of "acclimation." In exceptional cases, such persons may survive, even to old age. The average, however, is in the other direction. No man has a right to place himself in the small prospective list of exceptions.

Alcoholic Intemperance Hereditary.—It is now well-known that intemperance becomes hereditary, and begets various forms of insanity. Dr. George H. B. Macleod, F.R.S.E., Regius Professor of Surgery in the University of Glasgow, and Surgeon in Ordinary to the Queen, in an address on the subject of alcohol in the treatment of the sick, says, concerning the question of inheriting a taste for alcohol: "We perceive, in dealing with the children of intemperate persons, their ailments, mental and corporeal, not unfrequently take a complexion of their own from the habits of the parents. The low vitality, the stunted growth, the late maturity, the epileptic seizures, the hydrocephalus, and numerous other morbid conditions met with, occasionally own the intemperance of the progenitor as their cause."

Darwin Confirms this View.—Darwin writes more strongly on this point. He says: "It is remarkable, that all the diseases that spring from drinking spirituous and fermented liquors are liable to become *hereditary* even to the third generation, gradually increasing, if the cause be continued, till the cause becomes extinct."

Hereditary Drunkenness Illustrated.—Not more pitiful are the approaches of madness than are the well-understood symptoms which signify to the hereditary drunkard the hour of his inherited passion. "I knew in Texas," says a correspondent, "a young man who was heir to such a woeful heritage. He was physically one of the handsomest of men, and possessed of great and varied talents, which he had carefully cultivated. Moreover, he had served his country with distinguished bravery, and was then holding a high position of trust and honor.

"But, with a regularity that was terrible, there came to him—no matter where he was, over his ledger, in the church, by the side of the woman he loved -a craving for brandy that possessed him like a demon, and drove him forth from among his fellows.

"With set lips and despairing face he would deliver to a friend the keys of his office, and betake himself to his room—not as men go to a carousal, but as they go to meet a fearful reckoning—and for two or three days drink in sullen silence, till the craving was appeased. Some one was one day praising, in his presence, his vast stores of acquired information, and his delicate fancy as an artist.

"'Yet I shall die like a brute,' he said, sadly; and the despairing look of a hunted animal came into his eye, as he added: 'My father died drunk; my mother, too, (God forgive her!); my grandfather shot himself in delirium tremens. You know, boys, how poor Patrick died; it will be the same with me.' His prophecy was too soon fulfilled."

Great Peril in Using Alcohol as Medicine.—There is always a very great risk in prescribing spirituous liquors as a medicine, to be used even in small quantities. The history of many a young man shows that, insidiously, the habit grows and the appetite becomes intensified. Multitudes die annually because of the tyrannical power of habits formed while using alcoholic stimulants as a medicine. Physicians, surgeons, and nurses cannot be too cautious in prescribing alcohol.

Sad Results of Prescribing Alcohol.—A pastor furnishes the following narrative: "Some time since, a person who had been for a long period in feeble health, but was of excellent moral character and amiable disposition, recovered from his enfeebled state, and was able to resume his calling in life. It was found, however, to the dismay of his young and lovely wife, and to the bitter grief of his friends, that he was rapidly falling into habits of intemperance, and at length of open and shameless drunkenness. No entreaties of those nearest and dearest to him seemed to be of any avail to stop his dreadful course.

"As the pastor and friend of his family, we were apprised of the melancholy state of things, and besought to use all the influence possible to reclaim and save the sadly-erring and falling man. His business was soon neglected, and at length given up; self-respect was lost; want, that had never been known in his home, began to be felt. For a long time now, never had he read the chapter, or bowed the knee in prayer at the family altar, as had been his custom in the early days of his happy married life; and never now did he come to the house of God. There was an entire change in the circumstances and habits, disposition and character, of the man."

Fruitless Efforts for Recovery.—"As requested, and drawn by a fond desire to do him good, and bring gladness and hope again to that now sad family, we repeatedly saw and conversed and prayed with the changed and unhappy man. When free from the influence of strong drink, he would freely talk with us, at times confess his folly and sin, weep most bitter tears, and make promises almost with the intense earnestness of a desperate man, that he would never touch the accursed drink again. And as we would bow together in prayer for the grace that alone could sustain in keeping from the terrible evil and in doing the right, he would add his most emphatic Amen to the petition. Yet, ere long, he would fall again as low or lower than before, and thus continued reforming and refalling, and becoming more and more the utter wreck and ruin of himself, until at length he died a terrible death."

The Victim's Sorrowful Experience.—"Now, what was the history of this terrible change in that man? This was a question that we often pondered, and after vainly seeking for some time an account of it from himself, he one day spoke in substance as follows: 'Up to the time of my long declining health no man ever had a greater abhorrence of the drunkard's cup and the drunkard's curse than I; never was ardent spirits in any form put into my mouth, and in no sense had I the slightest desire for it. But,' said he, 'after I had been ailing some time, my physician directed me to procure a particular kind of ardent spirits, and take a portion of it every day. I hesitated, however, about it, not from any particular fear, but because I could not bear the taste of it. But he insisted it would do my system good; so we obtained it, and I began to drink it. The effect seemed beneficial, and my physician told me to continue to take it. The repugnance I had to it gradually wore off, and finding it exhilarated me and made me feel better, I more and more willingly took it, and after a time would look forward with pleasure, and even longing, for the appointed season or hour for taking it, and thus it went on; but,' said he, with an awful pause, and a look of indescribable agony and despair, 'why shall I tell you any more? You see the beginning, and here I am a slave to a habit, and a doomed man. I have tried to stop— O, God only knows how hard I have tried!—but I cannot. The desire for it comes upon me at times with an óverpowering force, and I *must* have it— I *must*, I MUST!' and he rushed from the room.

"It was not long after this he died, and sad were the thoughts and feelings of the funeral day."

Dr. Rush's Noble Testimony.—Strong and noble, and even stately, was the course of the excellent Dr. Benjamin Rush in this matter. Long before the temperance reform, a missionary from the West Indies sought medical advice of Dr. Rush, and when an unpalatable medicine was presented, the patient asked if he could not take a little "good old Jamaica" with it.

"No, sir," the doctor decidedly replied.

"Why, sir, what harm will it do?" demanded the West Indian.

"What harm will it do?" continued Dr. Rush. "I am determined that no man shall rise on the day of judgment and say, 'Dr. Rush made me a drunkard.'"

Drinking Paroxysms: Periodic Attacks.—In some cases the drinking paroxysms come on suddenly and after considerable periods of abstinence. Sometimes there is no premonition, but more frequently there is an alteration in appearance and temper that forewarns those who have any thing to do with the patient. In the case of a married man, the wife can almost always tell when an attack is coming on. The length of these attacks varies very much, more especially according to the duration of the disease in the patient. In the early history of the disease, the drinking bouts often last from one to three weeks, and during that time the patient is constantly drinking. As he cannot get the quantities of liquor that he requires outside anywhere, he takes to drinking in his own rooms or house. Nothing will stop him. If his friends or servants try to get him to leave off, he storms and rages and terrifies them into submission to his ways and wants.

The Excuse for these Periodic Paroxysms.—His excuse for drinking is always that he is excessively weak and nervous and requires support, and that it is absolutely necessary for his life that he should have stimulants. His appetite soon disappears, and he only makes vain efforts to partake of any food that is brought to him. Great sleeplessness and restlessness comes on, and, in fact, the patient is often on the verge of delirium tremens when the disease abates, either gradually or suddenly, and he gets fairly well.

Sudden End of the Drinking Paroxysms.—When it ends suddenly, it is generally from an attack of acute or subacute gastritis, for which he requires and seeks medical aid. The craving for drink having also disappeared, he willingly submits to medical direction, and under judicious treatment recovers. When the attacks go off gradually, there are less severe gastric symptoms, and the craving having become less, there is a diminution in the gastric and nervous troubles.

Increase of the Paroxysms.—After patients have lived for several years with these periodical attacks, the duration of attack diminishes in length, and they increase in frequency; the cause of this being chiefly due to the effects on the gastric system. The stomach much sooner resents the large quantities of alcohol put into it, and consequently the drinking fits are cut short by attacks of gastritis, and often also enteritis. But from the attack being shorter, the interval of diminution in drinking also becomes shorter, so that the patient gradually goes from bad to worse.

How Alcohol Injures the Physical System.—Dr. N. S. Davis having instituted a series of sphygmographic observations of the effects of alcohol on the circulation, thus sums up the results in the *Chicago Medical Examiner* —

1. Its presence in the blood directly interferes with the normal play of vital affinities and cell action in such a manner as to diminish the rapidity of nutrition and disintegration, and consequently to diminish the dependent functions of elimination, calorification, and innervation; thereby making a positive organic sedative, instead of a diffusable stimulant, as is popularly supposed, both in and out of the profession.

2. That the alcohol itself acts in the system exclusively as a foreign substance incapable of assimilation or decomposition by the vital functions, and is ultimately excreted or eliminated without chemical change.

The important bearing of these conclusions on the therapeutic and hygienic uses of alcoholic drinks must be obvious to all, and especially demands the careful attention of every member of the medical profession.

Patent "Bitters" are Strong Liquors Drugged.—Nearly all the patent "bitters" are strong liquors drugged and doctored, and labeled medicine, for the sake of those whose appetites are stronger than their temperance principles, and who want their daily dram without being known as even "moderate drinkers." The wine-bottle of the side-board is better than the bitter-bottle in the closet; or, in other words, it is better to drink openly at meals than to drink irregularly and in secret between meals. It is better to drink honest wine than hypocritical bitters.*

Patent "Bitters" the Worst Form of Alcohol.—"If one must drink alcoholic liquors," said a distinguished physician to us lately, "let him drink them pure, not drugged with nameless poisons, and passed off on the community on false pretenses." Of all temperate drinking the drinking of bitters is the most dangerous. And he who gets his prescription for indigestion from the advertising columns of the newspapers, no matter how conclusive the indorsements, nor how respectable the journal, may be morally sure that he is getting gin, whiskey, or rum, under pretense of medicine.

"Cure of Drunkenness."—The first business of the intelligent attendant should be to shut off the supply of liquor, and the second to get the terrible poison out of the patient's system. The former work may be done at once; the latter will require considerable time, the length being proportioned to the extent of the inroads made upon the physical system, and to the thoroughness of the remedial treatment.

---

* *Christian Weekly.*

The "Tapering-off System" Exploded.—The most rigid experiments show that it is better to stop the liquor supply *at once*, instead of gradually diminishing the amount used until all is banished. An eminent physician, after carefully testing both the "gradual stoppage" and the "sudden stoppage" systems, gives the following opinion: "I am firmly convinced that the latter has every advantage over the former, and especially in those cases in which, at first appearance, it seemed that in cutting off at once the entire supply there would be the greatest peril."

Treatment of Inebriates in Delirium Tremens.—In the "Archives Générales de Médicines," November, 1871, Dr. Decaisne wrote: "The use of opium in the treatment of delirium tremens is not unattended with danger on account of the large doses which it becomes necessary to arrive at progressively in the majority of cases. I resolved to submit a certain number of patients to an entirely expectant plan of treatment, to determine whether simple regime and a withholding of the cause of the disease would give a result similar to those caused by the principal medicinal agents recommended for this disease. Eight patients were submitted to the following regime: entire abstinence from wine and spirits: Some beer and an infusion of orange leaves were given as drinks. The diet was low; a warm bath was given every day, and every morning each patient took a purgative draught containing sulphate of magnesia. This mode of treatment is capable of being often used with advantage.

Delirium tremens must be carefully treated, in a way to restore physical strength speedily. If there is vomiting, give lime-water and milk, one teaspoonful of the former to two or three of the latter, with a small piece of ice given every fifteen minutes for two hours. If this fails, then a large mustard plaster, should be given, applied over the abdomen, and the remedy first named repeated. As soon as the stomach will bear it, beef-tea should be given at short intervals, beginning with a tablespoonful and increasing gradually to a teacupful as needed; it can be seasoned with black pepper, salt, and a small pinch of ground cloves. Chicken-tea will sometimes be borne more readily than beef-tea. From fluids we can soon pass on to something more solid, such as eggs, toast, mutton-chops, etc.

What to Avoid.—Two things are to be especially avoided in treatment. 1. The use of tobacco * in any form; and 2. Water, except in *limited quantities;* although the thirst for it may be very great, there is danger in gratifying it. Medical tinctures should not be used; hop-tea, wormwood-tea, capsicum, and highly-seasoned soups can be dispensed with as tending to keep up a desire for drink. Tobacco must be entirely avoided.

---

* Statistics show that *ninety-four per cent. of inebriates use tobacco.*

Sleep and food are the main restoratives in the treatment, and the remedies should be directed to produce sleep, and enable the victim to take proper nourishment and food. A convalescent inebriate possesses usually a great appetite and rapidly gains flesh, and is hungry for his meals for weeks, after having starved his system on alcohol.

TOBACCO AND HEALTH.

Effects of Tobacco on the System.—Some years ago, the French Government directed the Academy of Medicine to inquire into the influence of tobacco on the human system. The report of the commission appointed by the Academy states that a large number of the diseases of the nervous system and of the heart, noticed in the cases of those affected with paralysis or insanity, were to be regarded as the sequence of excessive indulgence in the use of this article. The report also stated that tobacco seems primarily to act upon the organic nervous system, depressing the faculties, and influencing the nutrition of the body, the circulation of the blood, and the number of red corpuscles in the blood. Attention was also called to the bad digestion, benumbed intelligence, and clouded memory of those who use tobacco to excess.

Another Testimony.—A late article in the *Journal of Science Review* gives us the mischievous results of the use of tobacco, as shown by many experiments, and sums up as follows:—

"Tobacco adds no potential strength to the human frame. Its work is destruction, and not construction. It cannot add one molecule to the plasm out of which our bodies are built up. On the contrary, it exerts upon it a most deleterious influence. It does not supply, but it diminishes, vital force. Tobacco belongs to the class of narcotic and exciting substances. It has no food value. Stimulation means abstracted, not added, force. It evolves the narcotic paralysis of a portion of the functions, the activity of which is essential to healthy life.

"It will be said that tobacco soothes and cheers the weary toiler and solaces the overworked brain. All such expedients are fallacious. When a certain amount of brain-work or hand-work has been performed, nature wants time to rest and recuperate, and all such devices for escaping from this necessity will fail. It is a bad policy to set the house on fire to warm our hands by the blaze. Let it then be clearly understood that the temporary excitement produced by tobacco is gained by the destruction of vital force, and that it contains absolutely nothing that can be of use to the tissues of the body."

Other Testimonies.—Dr. Gibbons says: "Tobacco impairs digestion, poisons the blood, depresses the vital powers, causes the limbs to tremble, and weakens and otherwise disorders the heart."

Dr. Willard Parker says that the manufacturers and users of tobacco "cannot recover soon, and in a healthy manner, from cases of injury or fever. They are more apt to die in epidemics, and more prone to apoplexy and paralysis."

Dr. Hassock makes the use of tobacco one cause of "the alarming frequency of apoplexy, palsy, epilepsy, and other diseases of the nervous system."

Another result of the habit is the creation of a thirst, of which Dr. Rush says: "It cannot be allayed by water, for no sedative, or even insipid liquor, will be relished after the mouth and throat have been exposed to the stimulants of the smoke or the use of tobacco."

Dr. Stephenson says that the salivary glands are so exhausted that "brandy, whisky, or some other spirit is called for."

We have before us excerpts, similar to the above, taken from the professional opinions of hundreds of able medical authorities.

Tobacco Specially Harmful to the Young.—A writer in the *Buffalo Medical Journal* puts on record the following warning: "The use of tobacco is bad enough when begun in mature life, but it is infinitely worse when the foundations of the habit are laid in early years, as it seems to be the case here."

A distinguished French physician, (M. Decaisne,) has investigated the effect of smoking on thirty-eight boys, between the ages of nine and fifteen, who were addicted to the habit. Twenty-seven presented distinct symptoms of nicotine poison. In twenty-two there were serious disorders of the circulation, indigestion, dullness of intellect, and a marked appetite for strong drinks. In three there was heart affection; in eight decided deterioration of blood; in twelve there was frequent epistaxis; ten had disturbed sleep, and four had ulceration of the mucous membrane of the mouth.

All assert that its use is most injurious to young persons. Even the "Organ of the Tobacco Trade" admits that "Few things could be more pernicious for boys, growing youths, and persons of unformed constitutions, than the use of tobacco in any of its forms."

Tobacco and Paralysis.—A Buffalo correspondent of one of our dailies reports the following: "A case in my own intimate acquaintance has this very week appalled a large circle of friends in this city. The victim was exactly my own years, and a companion from early childhood. For thirty years, at least, he has been a daily smoker of the choicest cigars, but in all his other habits temperate and regular, and of excellent constitution—one, who, of all men, would have laughed at the suggestion that tobacco was killing him. A week ago last Saturday night he was stricken with a progressive paralysis, characteristic of nicotine, and on Sunday night he died.

Tobacco and Early Physical Weakness.—Says the *Scalpel:* "So far are we from doubting its power over the moral and physical welfare of the race, that we have not a doubt that it has infinitely more to do with the physical imperfection and early death of the children of its votaries, than its great associate, drunkenness itself. The deficiency of virile power in many instances of long-continued smokers is very marked. Every surgeon of experience must have observed it. The local surgical and medical treatment most effective in these cases proves conclusively that it is to the debilitating and exhausting influence of tobacco that these sad consequences are due."

Tobacco Pollutes the Atmosphere.—A person who is saturated with tobacco, or tobacco-poisoned, acquires a sodden or dirty yellow hue; two whiffs of his breath will scent a large room; you may nose him before he takes his seat. Of this he is entirely unconscious; he will give you the full force of his lungs, and for the most part such people have a great desire to approach and annoy you. "We have been followed," writes a physician, "round a large office-table by them, backing continually to escape the nuisance, till we had made a revolution or two before our motive was perceived."

The Tobacco Appetite often Hereditary.—One of the most alarming facts brought out is the hereditary influence of this indulgence. The evil effects of the habit are sometimes scarcely seen in the parent, but are manifest in the children. Not only the appetite, but disease and physical weakness are transmitted to the children. This fact, well authenticated, should awaken thoughtful consideration on the part of parents who are addicted to this useless habit.

The Excuses of Tobacco Users Trivial.—The pleas set forth for the use of tobacco are generally trivial and easily answered. The evil effects are so many and so evident that, as with intoxicating drinks, the only safe plan is total abstinence. The habit is disagreeable to friends, is injurious to the user, and has very little in its favor. Even its victims admit that it is useless, if not positively injurious, and there are thousands who regret that they ever acquired the appetite. The only relief is a prompt and determined abandonment of tobacco, in every form and for all time.

Smoking Worse than Chewing.—Smoking is less filthy than chewing, but is more injurious to health. Dr. Dixon, of the *Scalpel*, in an article strongly condemning the use of tobacco in every form, says:—

"Our remarks apply in a much more forcible manner to smoking than to chewing. Some people are so silly as to suppose, because they do not spit while smoking, that no harm can ensue; but they should remember that the oil of tobacco, which contains the deadly nicotine, is volatilized, and circulates with the smoke through the delicate lining membrane of the mouth at each whiff of the cigar, and is absorbed by the extensive continuation of this membrane that lines the nostrils, and acts upon the whole body. The smoke of tobacco is indeed much more rapid in its stupefying effect, as every professed smoker knows. It is usually called 'soothing' by its votaries; but this is, of course, only the first stage of stupefaction; it acts precisely as opium or other narcotics do "

Tobacco in the Form of Snuff.—" Tobacco in the form of snuff," says Dr. Rush, "seldom fails of impairing the voice by obstructing the air." At a council of physicians held in London, the question of "snuff-using" came up for discussion, but it engaged the attention of the council for only a few minutes, the discussion being broken off by the *unanimous* adoption of a resolution declaring the use of snuff to be "a useless and pernicious habit."

"But I Can't Quit It!"—Let the testimonies of the many thousands who have discontinued the use of tobacco—some of them in advanced age—answer. Said James Parton, who was a slave to the practice for thirty years, and who heroically broke from his chains on the instant of his resolution to do so: " I have less headache, I enjoy exercise more, and step out much more vigorously. My room is cleaner, I think I am better tempered, as well as more cheerful and satisfied. I endure the inevitable ills of life with more fortitude, and look forward more hopefully to the coming years. It did not pay to smoke, but it decidedly pays to stop smoking."

Testimony of John Q. Adams.—" In my early youth I was addicted to the use of tobacco in two of its mysteries—smoking and chewing. I was warned by a medical friend of the pernicious operation of this habit upon the stomach and the nerves; and the advice of the physician was fortified by the results of my own experience. More than thirty years have passed away since I deliberately renounced the use of tobacco in all its forms; and although the resolution was not carried into execution without a struggle of vitiated nature, I never yielded to its impulses; and in the space of three or four months of self-denial, they lost their stimulating power, and I have never since felt it as a privation. I have often wished that every individual of the human race afflicted with this artificial passion could prevail upon himself to try but for three months the experiment which I have made, feeling sure that it would turn every acre of tobacco-land into a wheat-field, and add five years of longevity to the average of human life."

Great Extent of the Tobacco Habit.—A writer in *Blackwood's Magazine* estimates the whole amount of tobacco grown on the face of the globe at *four thousand* millions of pounds; and a close estimate shows that the world's tobacco costs, directly, at least *one thousand* millions of dollars annually. To this has to be added the loss of the land on which it is grown, and of the thousands of persons engaged in its cultivation and manufacture. The wealth-producing power of both land and men is lost, because the product of their toil does not add wealth to the country, or increase the nation's power of producing wealth. Besides, the effect of tobacco growing is to impoverish the soil. Gen. John H. Cooke, of Virginia, says: "Tobacco exhausts the land beyond all other crops. As a proof of this, every homestead from the Atlantic border to the head of tide-water is a mournful monument. It has been the besom of destruction, which has swept over this once fertile region." The use of tobacco is a tax on the health and wealth of the user, and money thus spent is worse than wasted.

OPIUM-EATING AND HEALTH.

Powerful Effects of Opium.—The quantity of opium necessary to cause death varies according to the circumstances and age of the person. Infants can bear a very small quantity—one drop of laudanum has been known to kill a child. Children are extremely susceptible to its influence. Two drams have been known to kill an adult. Opium kills in from four to twelve hours. Liquid preparations of opium and the salts of morphia act very rapidly.

Symptoms of Opium Poison.—The patient trembles, becomes giddy, drowsy, and unable to resist the tendency to sleep, the stupor deepens until insensibility ensues. The pupils become contracted, the eyes and face congested, the pulse becomes slow and feeble. The respiration becomes slow—the breathing stertorous, profuse perspiration occurs, the coma becomes deeper, and death ensues.

Treatment of Poison by Opium.—The stomach should be emptied by the stomach-pump, or by emetics. Twenty grains of zinc, or ipecac, or a tablespoonful of mustard or common salt will suffice to eject the poison. Copious draughts of warm-water should be given to keep up the vomiting. Strong coffee is an antidote, and brandy and ammonia should be frequently given by the mouth, or by injection.

Opium-Chewing.—This terrible habit prevails much more widely than many suspect. The appetite for it is generally caused by the use of the drug in prescriptions during sickness. Physicians and patients should carefully and intelligently guard against such evil effects, and in order to do this the drug should be used sparingly, and only when imperatively needed.

Symptoms of Opium-Chewing.—Persons addicted to the use of opium are recognizable by the face, which is sallow, pinched, and has a parchment-like appearance. The eyes become glassy and receding when deprived of the drug, there is an unsteady, trembling gait, depression of spirits, and great mental and even physical suffering.

Treatment for Cure.—Opium consumers must cut the habit off short; no matter how terrible may be the craving, it is rarely expedient to gratify it. Total abstinence is the sure cure, as the appetite will remain if indulged in ever so little. Large doses of bromide of potassium are recommended as serviceable in counteracting the cravings experienced by the victims of this horrible vice.

CLIMATE AND HEALTH.

Time Required for Complete Change of Body.—We have noted in a previous chapter the fact that our bodies are continually wasting away, and that by food and drink they are as constantly repaired. We lose the fleshy particles of our bodies once a year, and the bones in seven years. Hence, in seven years we have possessed seven bodies of flesh and blood, and one frame of bones. We have not now a particle of flesh and bones we had seven years ago. The water we have drank, the flesh and vegetables we have eaten, being made of the component parts of our bodies, cause us to hanker and long for the same substances of which our bodies are composed. Like substances in us call for like substances without to supply the waste of the system.

The Philosophy of Acclimation Explained.—Now, suppose we suddenly change our climate from forty to thirty degrees north latitude. The air, water, fruits, vegetables, and flesh all differ. The old particles composing our bodies, and brought from forty degrees north latitude, fly off as usual. This produces hunger and thirst, and we supply our wants by the water and food of thirty degrees north latitude, and continue for weeks to do so. This creates a conflict between the old substances of our bodies and the new flesh and blood continually forming, throws the electro-nervous force out of balance, and engenders disease. If we live and struggle on for seven years we become *acclimated*, because our old flesh and bones, formed by the substances of one latitude, have disappeared, and our entire systems are made of the substances of another latitude.

Effects of Dry and Moist Climates.—It is not generally known, but it is nevertheless true, that a pure, moderately-dry air generally produces great mental sprightliness, especially with full-blooded persons. A cloudy and moist atmosphere, on the other hand, produces mental relaxation, and, with many, melancholy. This explains why suicides so often happen when the sky is overcast. The depressed mental state is thus further enhanced. Villeneuve reports that of every ten suicides which were committed in Paris during two years, nine took place in the rainy season. The influence of the climate is also well exemplified in the case of mountaineers. They are quicker, more active, and excitable.

Remarkable Facts Incident to a Moist Climate.—A speaker, in a recent address in one of our chief cities, alluded particularly and approvingly to the fact that the influence of a moist atmosphere is strikingly illustrated in the case of individuals who have been weakened by previous illness, from the great number of suicides committed at the close of the year 1828, in the Dutch places Groningen and Sneek. Most of the unfortunates had suffered from the epidemics of 1826 and 1827. In the city of Sneek, with 6,000 inhabitants, not less than four suicides took place in one week, and among those was a boy eight years old. *

Influence of Climate upon National Characteristics.—The Swiss naturalist, Desor, in a recent essay, describes the climate of North America as very changeable and dry. After having explained a number of phenomena produced by the climate in general, he depicts its influence upon the inhabitant of this country. He derives from the climate his activity, acuteness, his tall stature, his eagerness for gain, his practical talent, and his love of adventure. It is also well known that the inhabitants under a preponderating clear sky possess more talent for art, while those under a gloomy sky have more propensity for speculation and thought.

Influence of Trees upon Climate.—The subject of "foresting," or the planting of trees, upon the climate of a country, and of "deforesting," or destroying the forest growth, continues to excite much interest throughout the world, as it is now well established that the climate of many localities has been materially altered by the one or the other of these processes. Systematic efforts have been made, in different parts of the world, for introducing a growth of trees where these had either disappeared or had never been known, from which important results have followed in many instances. In consequence of which, Egypt, which formerly had only about six rainy days every year, since being replanted on a large scale, has already attained to twenty-four.

Effect of Water upon Climate.—If we are to believe M. Rayet, the climate of the Isthmus of Suez will undergo a transformation in consequence of the arrival of the sea in Lake Timsah and in the basin of the Bitter Lakes, and the creation of two immense sheets of water in a region where there existed nothing but marsh land occasionally inundated by the Nile. This modification of climate has already become observable.† According to the evidence of persons who have resided on the spot as old *employés* of the

---

* Condensed from a report of one of the New York Club meetings.
† *Medical Reporter.*

Suez Company, the rains are much more frequent than they were five or six years since. *Apropos* of this report, M. Buys-Ballot has addressed to the Academy of Sciences of Paris the conclusions of a work published some time since, in which he has shown that the draining of Harlem Lake has modified the climatic condition of the country. The result of numerous investigations is, that since the drying of these 19,000 hectares the temperature has risen half a degree in summer, and has fallen half a degree in winter.

How to Relieve Certain Malarious Districts.—Sixteen square miles of the swampy, unhealthy country along the coast of the Bay of Biscay, in the Department of the Landes, were planted with millions of trees—especially the cork oak and swamp pine—with surprisingly beneficial results. The trees drained the land so as to destroy the swamp fevers, and to change it into a healthy country with pine forests. Biscay law requires that for every tree cut down two shall be planted, and it is said to be executed with rigorous severity.

Evil Effect of Sudden Transitions in Climate.—The diseases especially affected in this way are phthisis, pulmonalis, pneumonia, bronchitis, Bright's disease, diseases of the brain and nervous system, and diseases in general of persons who have reached the age of seventy years and upward. Scarlatina and diphtheria are also subject to the same influences. Persons affected by these diseases, who might live much longer under favorable circumstances, often die suddenly through quickly-succeeding alternations of heat and cold, dryness and dampness. Invalids weakened by old age are naturally more susceptible of these ill effects than others; but children are not particularly affected by them except in cases of pulmonary disease.

Are Frequent Rains Beneficial?—The relative humidity or degree of saturation of the air is of greater sanitary significance than the rainfall, but both are important. In a city the rain washes the air, as well as the streets and sewers, of many impurities, the presence of which would be prejudicial to health. It should be remembered that the relative humidity is not always, or even generally, high when rain falls, which is easily understood when it is borne in mind that the state of the higher atmosphere may be and is very different, generally, from that of the lower. In most of the Middle States, especially those near the sea coast, December is the month in which the relative humidity is highest, but it is the one in which the rainfall is least. The following is the order of the months, according to their mean relative humidity beginning with the one in which it is the highest: December, January, August, November, September, March, October, February, July, (same as last,) June, April, May. The following is the order for 1877: January, October, December, November, September, August, March, June, February, April, May.

The following is the order of the months according to the rainfall, beginning with the one in which it is greatest: July, September, March, November, June, February, October, August, April, January, May, December. The following is the order for 1877: October, July, June, November, March, September, April, January, May, February, December, August.

TEMPERAMENT AND HEALTH.

Varieties of Physical Temperament.—Temperament is the peculiar physical and mental character of an individual arising from the relations and proportion between the constituent parts of the body. The temperament is the visible measure of a man's life-force. Mere vegetative life is the sum total of the powers that resist decay. We call its degree the constitution, and each man has his own in common with other animals. A man has a strong or weak vital force, he breathes powerfully or feebly, he feels to advantage or disadvantage. If he has strong vital force he is usually fond of animal food, and is very active and energetic in his movements. If he is weak in his vital force, or lymphatic in temperament, he is more sluggish in his movements, and is satisfied with food which yields less fibrine and red globules to his blood. Vegetarians are generally "cold-blooded" and phlegmatic. Temperaments are classified as *sanguine, bilious, lymphatic, encephalic,* and *nervous.*

Sanguine Temperament.—A man of fine physical conformation and with plenty of red blood flowing through his face, with clear, bright, blue or gray eyes, capacious lungs, broad shoulders, and wavy brown hair and beard, is of the highest sanguine temperament. He has high vital force, and if he has a well-organized brain and a good early education, he is susceptible to the best influences.

Bilious Temperament.—A lean man with well-defined and hard muscles, and little or no fat, tall and slender-limbed, with brown hair and beard and gray eyes, very active and energetic in his movements, has the highest degree of executive and vital force combined; he is sanguine-bilious, the bile hiding the red blood in his face makes him darker.

Lymphatic Temperament.—A man with full and well-rounded person, and a much paler face, and whiter, straight hair and beard, with short limbs and fingers, and built like a fat person, is slower in his movements and passions, and colder in temperature. He is lymphatic in temperament.

Encephalic Temperament.—This temperament is characterized by an unusual development of the anterior brain. Vital vigor is indicated by a broad base to the head, a broad and full development of the lower brain, a healthy and lively color to the skin. Those possessing the sanguine temperament, with its accompanying mental vigor, have great capacity in executing all the functions of their organs, but they attain a far less degree of longevity than those of the mixed temperaments, encephalic and bilious sanguine.

Nervous Temperament.—The *nervous* temperament is characterized by greater excitability and sensibility than the bilious, by mental activity, by greater delicacy of person, and less muscular development, is produced by a head of less occipital strength than the bilious, and less basilar development than the sanguine. As the basilar organs are not very deep, the person is not very fleshy, nor the muscular system stout. This temperament does not produce the greatest extremes of virtue or vice. It is adapted to pursuits which require intelligence and readiness, with respectable or moderate force of character. It is much more easily affected by medicine than the bilious temperament, and much more liable to diseases from slight causes, but less iable proportionably, to obstinate chronic attacks.

PRECAUTIONS AND HEALTH.

Eating, Sleeping, and Speaking—Simple Precautions.—Never eat hurriedly, because it causes indigestion.

Never dine in excitement, because the blood is called to the brain which ought to aid digestion.

Never swallow food without thorough chewing, because it brings on dyspepsia.

Never eat when you do not want it, because when you shall want you cannot eat.

Never sleep with your mouth open, because the air breathed with carbonic acid disturbs the mucous membranes.

Never go to rest without washing the hands and face, because more dirt accumulates on the skin in the day than in the night, and is re-absorbed during the night.

Never begin a journey until breakfast is eaten.

After speaking, singing, or preaching in a warm room in winter, do not leave it immediately. In leaving, close the mouth, put on the gloves, wrap up the neck, and put on a cloak or overcoat before passing out of the door. The neglect of these simple precautions has laid many a good and useful man into a premature grave.

Never speak under a hoarseness, especially if it requires an effort, or painful feeling.

Danger from Wet Clothes.—Few persons understand fully the reason why wet clothes exert such a chilling influence. It is simply this: Water, when it evaporates, carries off an immense amount of heat, in what is called the latent f rm. One pound of water in vapor contains as much heat as nine or ten pounds of liquid water, and all this heat must, of course, be taken from the body. If our clothes are moistened with three pounds of water— that is, if by wetting they are three pounds heavier—these three pounds will, in drying, carry off as much heat as would raise three gallons of ice-cold water to the boiling point. No wonder that damp clothes chill us.

Danger from Cosmetics.—Ladies who use cosmetics to give an artificial whiteness and softness to their complexions, will do well to read a little pamphlet published by Dr. Lewis A. Sayre, of New York, describing three cases of lead palsy which have come under his notice. In these three cases the disease was clearly attributable to the lead, which is an essential ingredient in nearly all the nostrums sold under the names of "Bloom of Youth," "Beautifying Lotion," and the like. By the use of proper remedies the patients recovered, but for a long time they were as completely palsied as painters are who work much with white lead paint. The poison is absorbed by the skin and penetrates to the nerves.

Danger from Lamp Explosions.—Scarcely a week passes but we read accounts of frightful accidents from kerosene lamps exploding, and killing or scarring for life men, women, and children. A simple knowledge of the inflammable nature of the liquid may put a stop to nearly all the accidents. As the oil burns down in the lamp, inflammable gas gathers over the surface. When the oil is nearly consumed, a slight jar will inflame the gas, and an explosion follows. If the lamp is not allowed to burn over half way down, accidents are almost impossible. "What, then, shall we do?" *Fill your lamps in the morning.*

How to Test Dangerous "Kerosene."—There is one simple, and, for practical purposes, satisfactory method of determining the character of all such mixtures, and which applies equally as well to the common oils. Let a few drops be poured into a saucer, and apply a match; if the material burns, reject it as unsafe. The fact that the material can be set on fire at the ordinary temperature of our dwellings, should be sufficient evidence to a person of ordinary intelligence that, when employed in the household, it may at the first thoughtless or careless act become the cause of a frightful accident.

Caution in Cleansing Wells.—As a rule, never descend into a well without first lowering down a candle or lamp, to be sure that it does not contain foul air. Wells in barn-yards that are used in winter for stock, and seldom used in summer, are very liable to be foul at this season. While the spring-are low, in August or September, is a good time to clean them out, but let no one go down without using the above precaution.* The "foul air" is carbonic acid, and no one can live in it an instant. If a candle or lamp will burn freely, there is no danger. The carbonic acid is heavier than common air, and accumulates at the bottom of wells. The candle will go out as soon as it strikes the carbonic acid, and thus show how much there is in the well. To get it out is not difficult, provided there is water in the well. All that is needed is to pump out the water and dash it in again. The water will absorb an equal volume of carbonic acid, and the agitation will mix sufficient air with it to allow combustion to proceed, and if a bundle of straw is ignited and lowered into the well, the heat will cause the foul air to ascend. We have succeeded in getting out the carbonic acid from a well simply by dropping bunches of burning straw into it. The blaze would at first be extinguished when it struck the carbonic acid, but the heat is more or less retained, and sets the air in motion.

Caution Concerning the "Tea-pot."—When any tin-lined vessel, especially the tea-pot, becomes rusted or blackened inside, there is danger in its use. The acid contained in the tea combines with the iron of the exposed portions of the vessel, and forms a chemical compound, not unlike ink. It corrodes and darkens the teeth, and cannot be inoffensive to the stomach. I have seen the discoloration both of natural and artificial teeth prove so obstinate from this cause as to require several scourings with soap and ashes, with a stiff brush, to remove it. When housekeepers hear any of the family remarking, "This tea tastes like ink," it is time to examine, possibly to throw away, the tea-pot. The most palatable and wholesome tea is made by steeping in a bright tin or porcelain cup, then pouring into a freshly-scalded *earthen* tea-pot. Thus treated it will never acquire the astringent quality so deleterious to the teeth and to health.

Caution About Laughing Gas.—The use of nitrous oxide gas should be avoided in all cases of diseases of the lungs in which the breathing is much embarrassed, and when there is evidence of either serious brain or heart disease.

Caution Concerning Ice-Cream.—An eminent physician in France has investigated the article known in cities as street-corner ice-cream, and finds it to contain poisonous coloring matter, which produces serious symptoms when taken in a continued course, and is a prolific cause of scrofulous eruptions and dropping out of the hair among the lower classes.

Caution in Carrying Lead Pencils.—There is often danger in carrying lead pencils in the pocket. Several cases of deaths are recorded of persons

---

* *American Agriculturist.*

who were pierced by pencils carried in the pocket. We should be careful to place the pencil, or other sharp instrument, in such a way in the pocket as to provide against such danger.

Visiting Infected Rooms.—Avoid entering a sick-room while in the state of perspiration, because in cooling off the pores absorb freely; nor should a person sit between the sick and the fire. Do not approach contagious diseases with an empty stomach.

Dangerous Medicines.—Thousands of deaths take place every year from the unauthorized use of dangerous medicines. They often occur on this wise: A person is suffering; the family physician is called; he writes a prescription; it is taken; grateful relief is experienced; patient desires to know the name of the marvelous remedy, bears it in mind, and if there is something similar he ventures to send for it (the remedy) direct to the druggist. On being relieved again he becomes enthusiastic, and volunteers advice to his friends. They are relieved—sometimes—and forthwith he begins to think he knows "about as much as any of the doctors." A little later, it is not unusual to see a record in the newspapers that Mr. —— was "found dead in his bed this morning." Remember, that a prescription providing a remedy for one disease, may prove perilous in another.

Dangerous Medicines—Two Good Rules.—1. Never to keep dangerous medicines in the house.

2. Never to use a dangerous drug, except by the immediate advice of your family physician.

Mistakes in Prescriptions.—The number of perilous mistakes in putting up prescriptions by druggists has become alarmingly frequent. A physician assures us, that eleven times during the last year his prescriptions were answered by the return of substances not requested. Sometimes mistakes are alleged to be owing to the careless handwriting of the physicians. Not a few of them are said to be made by assistants who were too young to be employed in such business. In some countries the number of apothecary shops is limited by law, and no one can be principal or assistant who has not studied a certain time, and passed certain examinations. The requirements in England and France are very rigid in this respect, as they ought to be in our own country in so serious and responsible a business.

Using Medicines as Stimulants—Danger.—When in the use of any remedy you find yourself inclined to employ it oftener, or in larger quantities, to produce the same effects, whether it be spirits, tobacco, snuff, tea, coffee, chloroform, ether, or any other stimulant or poison, be assured that you are on the very verge of destruction, and that you are liable, any day, to instant death. When you find yourself inclined to "take" anything, even a cup of tea or coffee, to enable you to perform any work in hand, mental or bodily, avoid it as you would a deadly poison. The three greatest men of this century, in our country, in pulpit, bar, and forum, died drunkards; and long before their deaths it was known to their friends that they were "incapable of an effort" without being first "fortified by a glass of brandy."

How to Escape Fever Infections.*—In a properly-chosen, well-lighted, well-aired, well-scrubbed dwelling, with thoroughly-washed inmates, there is comparatively little fear of infectious poisons. But it is well for every one to be acquainted with some of the easiest means of resistance and of escape, when that gigantic evil approaches, or when duty compels us to go within its range. Knowledge of the reality will prevent foolish exaggerations and diminish useless fear.

Fever Infections—Avoid the Poison.—All infectious fevers (typhus, scarlatina, small-pox, etc.) arise from the reception of a subtle poison into the blood, which, spreading through the system, is exhaled from it principally by the skin and lungs. This poison has been actually condensed out of impure air poisoned by filth and decay, and appears in the form of a dirty-looking, half-solid, half-fluid, half-gelatinous stuff, a few drops of which inserted into the veins of a dog will inoculate that dog with typhus fever.

Fever Infections—Ventilation.—The poisonous infection is lighter than air, and ascends. If we allow it to escape at the top of the room the air below is safe. This is the reason why in fever wards few cases of infection occur; without the ventilators in the ceiling they would be dens of death. The circulation of fresh air in a fever-chamber by open doors and windows must be produced several times a day, (care being taken that the patient be not directly exposed to the draught,) or, still better, let the upper part of a window be kept permanently open, and if the patient be in a box-bed let there be several holes bored through the roof of the bed, to allow the exit of infectious vapor in the direction of the open window.

Fever Infection—Avoid Absorbing It.—A person may breathe infection a thousand times over without any bad results; the poison is innocent unless it enters the blood. The thin delicate skin of the lungs, composed of minute cells, is an active absorbent, and whatever is inhaled comes in contact with the absorbing surface, and is liable to pass into the blood. A medical man may be exposed to infection ninety-nine times with impunity, but on the hundredth occasion the absorbent vessels may be peculiarly active, they suck in the poison, and he falls a victim. When the pulse is weak absorption is strong and active; when the pulse is strong absorption is weak; regular and nourishing food and fresh air will, therefore, diminish the risk

---

* Robert Fairman, M.D.

of the poison entering the blood, while want of sleep, and fasting, and impure air, will of course greatly increase it.

When infection is not destroyed or dispersed by proper ventilation, it adheres to articles of furniture and clothing, but especially to cotton and woolen material, and everything must be done to secure its dispersion by *ventilating* these also. They should be exposed to a free current of air, or steeped for twelve hours in cold water before washing, and not folded up for some time. Black or dark substances absorb infection more easily than white; light dresses are therefore safest for nurses, and hence, too, one of the advantages of white-washing in the dwellings of the poor.

Fever Infection and Flannel—Wear Flannel.—Cold, damp, and shivering chilliness also produce debility, which will render the absorbing vessels active; the use of flannel next the skin is therefore of the greatest importance. It is stated that the ancient Italians who lived near the poisonous Pontine marshes of Italy, suffered less from fever than the moderns, as they wore warm and fleecy clothing, and that now the evil has been greatly arrested by flannel again coming into use. Laborers in such places fall victims in great numbers unless this precaution be adopted.

Fever Infection and Fear.—As far as possible avoid fear. Fear is also a fruitful source of infection, for it weakens the pulse and the whole frame. Travelers in the East have told that when a dog is suddenly bitten by a rattlesnake, the wound is not considered half so deadly as when the dog has seen the reptile, and stood trembling before it; fear in this case aids and quickens the poison. Charms and amulets, met with occasionally among the poor of our country, and frequently in foreign ones, may thus actually be useful by inspiring confidence, although it is the confidence of superstition.

Poisonous Soap.—A common and annoying form of skin-disease, "ekzema," is sometimes produced by bad soap. The soap that seems to suffer most in analytical experiments is the cheaper kind of "Old Brown Windsor," which is made from putrid animal matter extracted from heaps of decaying bones, which are described as emitting a stench that is intolerable. The brown color which is given to the higher-priced Brown Windsor by artificial means this cheaper soap gets quite sufficiently from the filthy fat from which it is made; and the stench, which even the saponifying process does not quite remove, is disguised by the perfume which is afterward added.

Death from Nicotine.—A case of death from nicotine recently occurred under the following circumstances: The father of a little girl, in an endeavor to "heal a sore on her lip," applied to it the contents of a "rank" pipe-stem. The victim was almost immediately seized with the peculiar symptoms of tobacco-poisoning, and died a few hours afterward.

Poison of Quinces.—In France, recently, a lady was poisoned to death by the exhalations of quinces. She slept in a room in which they were kept, with doors and windows closed, and died in a short time. The odor of quince blossoms is also highly injurious.

Orange Peel Poisonous.—Fatal consequences may follow the swallowing of the rind of oranges The oil of the rind is highly acrid, and adds greatly to the noxious quality of the indigestible mass.

Quite recently a child something over a year old was attacked with violent dysenteric symptoms, for which no cause could be assigned. The attack came on during the passage of a steamer from San Diego. The symptoms were so identical with those which arise from poisoning by orange peel, that the physician inquired particularly if the child had had an opportunity of getting this substance in its mouth. He was informed that it had been playing with an orange, and nibbling at it, just before the attack of the disease. The discharges from the bowels were frequent, and consisted of blood and mucus. After a week of severe enteric inflammation the child died. Though but a small quantity must have been swallowed, yet a very small quantity of such an indigestible and irritating substance will often produce most serious consequences.

Danger in Carrying Friction Matches.—Many persons have the habit of carrying friction matches loosely in their pockets, and using these at the same time quite indiscriminately for carrying tobacco, candies, cakes, and other eatables. Aside from the danger of ignition of the matches, which might cause serious burns, a greater danger arises from the fact that the tips of the matches, highly charged with phosphorus, are liable to break off and mix with those eatables in the pocket, and in that way find their way into the stomach, and occasion fatal accidents of poisoning. Several such cases have occurred, and point to the necessity of greater care in carrying and using matches.

Care Concerning Poisonous Candies.—In no class of articles intended for consumption is the use of poisons so free as in candies and confections. Arseniate of copper, copperas, white lead and litharge, (or red lead,) and the aniline colors, red, green, or blue, and other poisons, mineral and vegetable, are frequently employed in the manufacture of candies. There are confectioners who do not use such dangerous drugs, or who use them so sparingly that they work no immediate appreciable harm to the consumer; but others are neither so scrupulous nor so well informed about the real nature of the poisons which impart the desired vividness of color or fineness of flavor to their products. Bright, highly-colored, handsome candies always sell better than dull, plain varieties. The beautiful tints can be had most cheaply and satisfactorily by the use of the virulent mineral poisons—chiefly arseniates and preparations of copper and lead. Be cautious, therefore, in purchasing candies to buy only of manufacturers or dealers who are scrupulously careful in their preparation.

Death from Chloroform.—Dr. Charles Anderson, of Cincinnati, calls attention, in the *American Journal of Medical Science*, to a very singular circumstance attending the inhalation and use of chloroform. Many of those who have died from its use have taken it repeatedly, and often for a considerable time, without any unpleasant symptoms, whereas, an attempt to give it a short time afterward has proved fatal. Thus, one patient who had taken it frequently during ten years, died from forty drops. Another had taken it one hundred times, and had once been under its influence five hours; the last dose, which was fatal, consisted of an inhalation or two from a chloroformed handkerchief. Dr. Anderson expresses the opinion that in these cases there exists a sort of floating idiosyncrasy—"one that may be in him to-day, and off to-morrow; but if, while under its influence, he inhales the vapor of chloroform, he is almost sure to die. I was on the point of saying, that if he inhales the slightest quantity of the vapor of chloroform it will prove fatal."

Care Concerning Ice-Cream.—Ice-creams may be colored as freely as any other confections. The brilliant red tint of strawberry cream may be attained by litharge or rosaline; the splendid green tint of pistachio cream (so-called) may be derived from arseniate of copper more economically than from the pistachio nut. It does not follow that the confectioners who make these colored creams know that they are using poisonous ingredients for producing tints or flavors. They may obtain the articles from other persons who manufacture and sell them.

Danger of Green-Colored Materials.—In the use of green papers, tarlatans, artificial flowers, and other green-colored materials, great care and discrimination should be exercised, as the color frequently contains arsenic in the form of the brilliant, but very poisonous, arseniate of copper, known as Schiele's Schweinfurt, and Paris Green. Such paper is sold in many stores for ornamental purposes, and even used in wrapping candies, and for Kindergarten material and toys. These colors and materials containing them, among which are green wall-paper and window-shades, and the bright green tarlatans and crapes used for evening dresses, etc., are not only dangerous in the hands of children, lest they may get particles of the poisonous color into their mouth or inhale its dust, but also from the comparatively large amount of arsenic they contain, and by the fact that the color is slowly decomposed by moisture and heat, and passes poisonous arsenious gases into the air. The use of bright green wall-papers and window-shades in sitting and sleeping-rooms should never be permitted, unless the color be tested and found free

Precautions and Health.

of arsenic. Wall-paper in particular has caused many deaths and cases of severe illness.

How to Detect Arsenic in Colors.—The green arsenious colors are soluble in ammonia water, (hartshorn;) if, therefore, a little ammonia water is poured on strips of the paper or crape in a plate, a disappearance of the color or such a change in it as indicates the removal of green, makes the presence of arsenic probable. To identify its presence, strips of the paper or fabric should be immersed in a little ammonia water for a few minutes, about ten drops of the water are then poured upon a glass pan or plate, and a small crystal or piece of a crystal of nitrate of silver is placed in the center of the liquid. If a yellow turbidity forms around the crystal, it indicates the presence of arsenic.

Be Cautious of Poisonous Vegetables.—There are many beautiful and innocent-looking forms of vegetable life to be met with in our gardens and hedges, which are yet full of deadly poison, while others, from their close resemblance to nutritious articles of food, are often partaken of by mistake, and fatal accidents are consequently of too frequent occurrence. Here is a partial list of them: "Monkshood," or aconite; "fool's-parsley," a species of hemlock; buttercups (often poisonous to children's hands;) laburnam seeds; deadly-nightshade (half a berry of the dark purple has caused death;) belladonna (poison lies in the fruit answering to the potato apple;) leaves of the common laurel; the wild arum; and one kind of mushrooms. The mushrooms proper to be used in cookery grow in the open pasture land, for those that grow near or under trees are poisonous. The eatable mushrooms first appear very small, and of a round form on a little stalk. They grow very rapidly, and the upper part and stalk are white. As they increase in size, the upper part gradually opens, and shows a fringed fur of a very fine salmon color, which continues more or less till the mushroom has gained some size, and then turns to a dark brown. These marks should be attended to, and likewise whether the skin can be easily parted from the edge and middle, and whether they have a pleasant smell. Those which are poisonous have a yellow skin, and the under part has not the clear flesh-color of the real mushroom; besides which they smell rank and disagreeable, and the fur is white or yellow.

ANTIDOTES FOR POISONS—HYDROPHOBIA.

Animals Affected by Hydrophobia.—Man, and many of the lower animals, are subject to madness, or hydrophobia. In animals the disease is called rabies, or canine madness. Dogs, cats, and wolves are mostly its subjects, but sometimes goats, pigs, horses, and cows are the victims. The poison is communicated by means of the saliva through wounds made by the teeth, and may occur at any season of the year.

Period of Development.—The period of its development, after the subject has been bitten, and the virus communicated, varies considerably Usually it appears within two months. Cases have been mentioned, where the disease did not develop for ten, or twelve, or fifteen months.

Symptoms of Hydrophobia.—In hydrophobia, the victim becomes melancholy, and his fear keeps him on the watch for some development of the disease. If the part bitten becomes painful, and begins to inflame, his anguish becomes intensified. The skin becomes hot and dry, the pulse rapid and weak, and there is much thirst. In two or three days the muscles of the throat, especially those of deglutition, become sore and stiff. Attempts to swallow are attended with spasmodic contraction of these muscles, and of the respiratory muscles. Convulsive movements become more frequent, and easily excited by pouring out water, cold currents of air, changing of bed-clothes, or shutting doors hastily. Sometimes general convulsions occur. The thirst becomes intense, but the patient fears to relieve it, for fear of bringing on the spasms, or of choking. The eyes are blood-shot and staring, saliva flows from the mouth, the voice is husky, and the countenance manifests extreme terror. As death approaches, the skin becomes clammy and cold, the pulse almost gone, and respiration irregular. Convulsions, or exhaustion, soon terminate the sufferings of the unfortunate victim.

Treatment of Hydrophobia.—1. The wound inflicted by the bite of an animal suspected of rabies should be washed and sucked as in cases of wounds incurred in dissections, and afterwards cauterized thoroughly. Cutting out the wounded part is better, in most cases, than cauterizing. Some recommend a tight ligature placed around the limb above the wound, before washing, and excision, to prevent absorption of the poison. This is more useful when the bite is on the finger or toes. The excision should extend some distance into the healthy tissue, and the wound be afterward thoroughly cauterized. Resort should be had to a physician the first moment possible—washing and sucking the wound is of the first importance.

2. Spirits of hartshorn is said to be an excellent remedy. The wound should be bathed constantly with it, and three or four doses taken inwardly during the day. The hartshorn decomposes chemically the virus insinuated into the wound, and immediately alters and destroys its deleteriousness.

3. The following is *reported* as a "sure cure" for hydrophobia: "The bite must be bathed, as soon as possible, with warm vinegar and water, and when this has dried, a few drops of muriatic acid poured upon the wound will destroy the poison of the saliva, and relieve the patient from all present and future danger."

Antidotes for Poisons—Hydrophobia.

4. The following remedy was habitually used by the late Mr. Youatt, a well-known veterinary surgeon, who was bitten by mad dogs eight times. The remedy was to allow the common nitrate of silver, easily procured, to filter into the wound. It decomposes the saliva, and in doing this destroys the virus. Sir Benjamin Brodie acted upon this, with complete success, in a case where a mad dog had licked the inside of a child's mouth. The best mode of application of the nitrate of silver is by introducing it solidly into the wound.

5. A new cure for rabies was recently discovered by chance in France. A farmer, whose horse was affected, had him taken to a steep bank of a lake and thrown off into the water, supposing that the sudden plunge, and the fall together would kill the animal speedily. A few moments after, the horse rose to the surface, and the farmer was surprised to find that all symptoms of madness had vanished, and the horse soon made for the shore. On being taken out, he was found perfectly docile, and continued so, to the farmer's great delight, no traces of the disease ever reappearing. The theory resulting from this incident is this: Hydrophobia, or rabies, is a disease of the brain, in which fear is predominant. In the case of the horse, the terror produced by the sudden plunge into the cold water was so far superior to that of the disease, as to act homeopathically upon the animal, and when the overpowering effect had passed, and the animal was fairly in the water, the cooling plunge had a beneficial effect.

It is a mistake to suppose that mad dogs will always shun the water. On the contrary, they will often rush eagerly to it, and try to drink, although they are generally unable to do so, because of paralysis of the jaw.

ANTIDOTES FOR POISONS—SNAKE AND INSECT BITES.

What Snakes are Poisonous.—Among the principal venomous reptiles may be enumerated the whip-cord snake, cobra di capello, rattlesnake, viper, and adder. According to Dr. J. W. Howe, the bites of the first two produce a fatal result more quickly than the others. Rattlesnake bites stand next in order of virulence. Viper and adder bites are fatal only to very young animals, or to children of tender years. In the more deadly classes the symtoms following a bite, and the action of a poison, are the same. Rattlesnake bites are not uncommon in the Southern and Western States, and the mortality attending them is very great. The venom of this reptile is contained in a small sac situated at the base of the sharp tooth or fang. The tooth is channeled throughout the center to make a place of exit for the poison. When the tooth is inserted into the tissues, the poison-sac is compressed, and the venom ejected into the wound.

Symptoms of Snake-Poison.—Persons bitten by one of these reptiles experience after a few minutes a feeling of great depression and faintness. The wound begins to swell rapidly, very soon, sometimes becoming of dark red color, and sometimes a bluish black. A sharp and intense pain is felt in the wound extending along the course of the principal nerves. Sometimes there is congestion of the brain and there may also be congestion of the lungs and mucous membrane of the stomach and intestines. The pulse is feeble, intermittent, and rapid. The pupils of the eyes become dilated, pain is felt over the abdomen, and vomiting and sometimes purging takes place. Delirium generally appears. The surface and extremities of the body grow cold and clammy, and breathing becomes difficult, stupor sets in, growing worse rapidly, and death terminates the sufferings soon.

Antidotes for Snake-Bites.—1. The general treatment should be the same as that pursued in cases of hydrophobia. Various internal remedies may be recommended, of which the best is carbonate of ammonia in doses of ten or twenty grains every half hour. Friction to the surface of the body, with pieces of flannel dipped in hot alcohol, is also beneficial.

2. Sweet oil is a very good remedy. A plain farmer says: "It is now over twenty years since I learned that sweet oil would cure the bite of a rattlesnake, not knowing it would cure other kinds of poison. Practice, observation, and experience have taught me that it will cure poison of any kind, both on man and beast. The patient must take a spoonful of it internally and bathe the wound for a cure. To cure a horse it requires eight times as much as for a man. One of the most extreme cases of snake-bites occurred eleven years ago. It had been thirty days standing, and the patient had been given up by his physician. I gave him a spoonful of the oil, which effected a cure."

3. Dr. Wier, of Philadelphia, states that the application of carbolic acid, immediately on the receipt of the injury, prevents both local and general poisoning. The pure acid, however, if applied in too great quantity, is liable to produce sloughing and even dangerous symptoms; hence it is best used in the proportion of two parts of acid and one of alcohol. Given internally, or applied to the wound at a late period, it produces no effect. It is believed to act, not by neutralizing the poison, but by causing contraction of the small vessels, and thus preventing its absorption.

4. Prof. Halford, of the University of Melbourne, Australia, has found an antidote for snake-poison which has proved successful in the most critical cases. It is simply liquid ammonia ejected into the veins. A small syringe, with a sharp point for the purpose of making the injection, is manufactured and sold in Melbourne, and now few travel in that country without one.

Bites of Venomous Insects.—Among the symptoms following the bites of scorpions, tarantulas, centipedes, spiders, bees, hornets, etc., are head ache, vertigo, dimness of sight, and feverishness. Sometimes the wound is not much inflamed, while in other cases it becomes red, painful, and swollen, ending in suppuration.

Treatment of Insect-Bites.—1. Cleanse the wound and sponge it thoroughly with a strong solution of ammonia, and afterward cover it with linen or other suitable cloth, wet with solution of ammonia.

2. Poison from bees, hornets, spider-bites, etc., is instantly arrested by the application of equal parts of common salt and bicarbonate of soda, well rubbed in on the place bitten or stung.

ANTIDOTES FOR POISONS—MISCELLANEOUS.

Poison Ivy and Oak: Remedies.—1. The common wild turnip, or "Jack-in-the-Pulpit," as it is called, is an excellent remedy when scraped and applied to the poisoned part. When the blisters have flattened, apply cold cream to heal them sooner.

2. A good remedy for poison by ivy is to dissolve a tablespoonful of copperas in two thirds of a teacup of boiling water, and when cold apply with a cloth to the poisoned places.

3. Rubbing frequently with sweet oil is one of the best remedies. Some use salt and water, and find relief from that.

4. A standing antidote for poison by dew, poison oak, ivy, etc., is to take a handful of quick lime, dissolve in water, let it stand half an hour, then paint the poisoned parts with it. Three or four applications will never fail to cure the most aggravated case.

5. Olive oil is said to be a certain cure. In severe cases it is to be taken inwardly as well as applied externally. Dose: two tablespoonfuls three times a day, keeping the affected parts well oiled all the time. Anointing exposed parts with the oil will prevent poisoning.

6. A few drops of kerosene oil, rubbed in with the point of the finger or a piece of sponge, is a certain and speedy cure for the effects of the poison oak. Repeat for three or four days.

Lead Poisoning.—In cases where people frequenting freshly-painted rooms are affected in a disagreeable manner, the poisoning is due to the presence of lead in the paint. Painters are often poisoned by washing paint from their hands by means of turpentine. The turpentine brings the particles of lead into such a condition that they are easily absorbed by the skin. Lead is also found in hair dyes in large quantities, and the glazed visiting cards, so much in vogue a few years ago, owe their resemblance to "mother of pearl" to salt of lead.

Antidotes for Lead Poisoning.—The topical application of cold in lead poisoning has been tried in Clichy, by Professor Monneret, in over forty cases with complete success. Iced drinks and injections, the cold shower-bath two or three times a day, and ice-bags or ice-poultices (of fragments of ice laid in dry linseed meal) are used. The pain and other symptoms disappear, "as if by enchantment," and in two or three days the bowels are natural. A red-lead manufacturer of France has discovered that the use of milk at their meals, which he has made obligatory on his workmen, to the extent of one liter daily, preserves those employed in lead works free from any symptoms of lead-disease.

Poisoning by the Filling of Teeth.—A young lady of St. Louis has been suffering for several years past from symptoms of mercurial poisoning. For a long time no cause could be ascertained, but a dentist finding that she had her teeth filled with mercurial amalgam, came to the conclusion that the chlorine contained in her saliva might have generated corrosive sublimate. He therefore removed the amalgam and put in gold. She has since recovered her health.

Poisoning by Wall-Paper.—The habit of putting on the wall layer after layer of wall-paper is very pernicious. Several cases have been discovered lately where there was a mass of decayed paste and paper two inches thick, with a large growth of fungi. The sickness of several members of the families was attributed to the paper.

Phosphorus Poisoning.—Commercial oil of turpentine is a good antidote for poisoning by phosphorus. There is no fatty degeneration of the tissues, nor is there any free phosphorus found in the system of the animals experimented on. Phosphorus and turpentine oil form in the stomach a compound resembling spermaceti, which is readily excreted.

Poisoning by Opium.—1. Bisulphide of carbon will cure serious cases of poisoning by opium. Cloths should be saturated with it, and laid along each side of the spinal column its entire length, and covered to prevent evaporation.

2. Fluid extract of belladonna, administered in doses of twenty drops every ten minutes, will arrest the progress of the opiate.

3. Electricity will cure where everything else fails.

How to Act when Poison has been Swallowed: General Directions.
—1. Whatever is done must be done quickly. The instant a person is known to have swallowed poison, by design or accident, give water to drink, cold or warm, as fast as possible, a gallon or more at a time, and as fast as vomited drink more; tepid water is best, as it opens the pores of the skin and promotes vomiting, and thus gives the speediest cure to the poisonous article. If pains begin to be felt in the bowels, it shows that part, at least, has passed downward; then large and repeated injections should be given, the object in

both cases being to dilute the poison as quickly and as largely as possible. Do not wait for warm water; take that which is nearest at hand, cold or warm, for every second of time saved is of immense importance; at the same time send instantly for a physician, and as soon as he comes turn the case into his hands, telling him what you have done. Drinking a gallon or two of simple water will not cure every case of poisoning, but it will cure many.

2. If a poison swallowed is known to be an acid by the name on the bottle, or by the discolored spots on the dress, or having a sour taste when the tongue is applied, alkalies will be the proper antidote—such as chalk, magnesia, soda, whiting mixed with milk, or plaster torn from the wall, if nothing better is at hand. If, on the other hand, poisoning has occurred by an alkaline substance, such as pearl-ash, vinegar would arrest its progress. The antidote for corrosive sublimate, is eggs; and for sugar-of-lead, epsom salts.

3. A poison of any conceivable degree of potency which has been swallowed intentionally or by accident, may be rendered instantly harmless by swallowing two gills of sweet oil. An individual with a very strong constitution should take twice the quantity. This oil will neutralize every form of vegetable or mineral poison with which physicians or chemists are acquainted.

4. Arsenic may be rendered inactive in the stomach by a dose of hydrated peroxide of iron, which is prepared by pouring a solution of green vitriol boiled with nitric acid, or of chloride of iron, into ammonia or soda, and washing the precipitate. Both arsenic and peroxide of iron can then be removed by the stomach pump or an emetic.

EMERGENCIES—HOW TO MEET THEM.

Loss of Blood a Real Loss.—Many deaths from wounds might be prevented if the means were immediately at hand for stopping the flow of blood. In any case the loss of blood is a disaster from which it takes a long time to recover. The means to be taken to save life must be adopted instantly, before a surgeon can be called, and therefore ought to be very commonly understood.

Bleeding from Veins.—1. Ordinary bleeding from small cuts or injuries may be stopped by cold water, or ice, or pressure, until a clot has had time to form. The wisdom of our Maker has made this wonderful provision, that as soon as blood ceases to circulate in its proper channels, or comes in contact with the air, it will coagulate. By this means a plug is formed at the mouth of an open vessel to stop the flow of blood. Cold water and various styptics, like sulphate of iron, tannin, alum, and matico, hasten this result.

2. It is said that bleeding from a wound, on man or beast, may be stopped

by a mixture of wheat flour and common salt, in equal parts, bound on with a cloth If the bleeding be profuse, use a large quantity, say from one to three pints. It may be left on for hours, or even days, if necessary.

Bleeding from Arteries.—Blood may often be seen to flow from one small point of the wound. This indicates the opening of a small artery. Slight pressure with one finger, or the ball of the thumb over the spot, will stop it as long as the pressure is kept up, and often altogether, even after the pressure is removed.

2. Bleeding from a larger artery is indicated at once, by coming in jets at each beat of the heart, and being of a bright scarlet color instead of purple. If the wound be of such a character that the end of the artery can be seen, it can be readily taken up with a hook, or sharp-pointed fork, by any one *who keeps his wits about him in spite of the sudden alarm*, and tied with a strong thread. Otherwise, tie the limb between the wound and the heart, the simplest device being to bind the handkerchief around, and running a stick beneath the knot, twisting it up until the requisite pressure be attained to stop the bleeding.

Bleeding from the Teeth.—The following is an excellent remedy for hemorrhage arising from the extraction of teeth: Cut a piece of clean *dry* sponge into cone shape. This should be compressed tightly and introduced into the cavity left by the tooth. As soon as the sponge is dampened it begins to swell, and thus will, in most cases, effectually close the cavity, and prevent bleeding.

N. B.—For remedy for bleeding from the nose, see page 146.

Rupture of a Large Blood-vessel.—In case a large artery or vein is cut, especially in a limb, make a knot in a handkerchief, and tie it loosely about the limb, placing the knot on the wound. Then with a stick twist the handkerchief until the flow of blood ceases. A pad can be used instead of a knot. If the artery is ruptured, apply the pressure between the wound and the heart. If a vein, beyond the wound.

Fracture of the Skull.—Send for the physician. If there be a collapse, hot bottles and blankets should be applied to the extremities, and the circulation stimulated by friction with the hands. Diluted injections may be given. These efforts must cease when reaction is secured.

Partial Fainting, and its Relief.—In mild cases of fainting, where partial consciousness remains, stimulating substances, as vapor of ammonia or cologne-water, may be inhaled, and cold water sprinkled in the face, and fresh air introduced into the apartment.

Apparent Insensibility.—No violent measures should be used to arouse a patient who may, or may not, be insensible. Lay him in bed, loosen his clothes, and let him have a free access of air, notice whether the breathing is quiet or noisy, regular or irregular, whether there are any convulsive movements of the limbs, whether the urine or feces are passed involuntarily, whether the pupils of both eyes are alike, or larger or smaller than usual, or whether the patient will bear to have his eyes touched, and whether he can be aroused at all. In all cases of apparent insensibility, the attendant should be careful to say nothing to the patient within his hearing, for while he can neither speak nor move, he may yet be perfectly conscious of all that is passing around him, and the effort to speak may do him great injury.

Complete Unconsciousness and its Remedy.—Place the patient immediately in a recumbent position, with the head lower than the shoulders. Remove all superfluous clothing from the chest and throat. Neck-ties, collars, etc., hinder recovery. Moisten the nostrils with ammonia. Throw cold water into the face, and strike the palms of the hands, and rub them rapidly. Dip a plate in hot water and place it over the stomach and breast-bone. Should all these means fail, try galvanism, placing one pole of the battery at the upper part of the spinal column, and move the other up and down, over the back-bone and the breast-bone.

Dislocation, and its Treatment.—This is the displacement of two or more bones where articular surfaces have lost wholly, or in part, their natural connection, either owing to external violence, or to disease of some of the parts about the joint. Dislocation is complete when the bones have entirely lost their connection; incomplete, when they partly preserve it; and compound, when a wound communicates with the dislocated joint. The first thing to be done is to reduce the protruded bone to its original place, then to retain it in that position by means of splints, ligatured as tightly as the circulation will allow. The circulation must, by no means, be impeded, otherwise mortification will ensue.

Sprains, and How to Cure Them.—A sprain is often more painful and dangerous than a dislocation. It requires immediate attention. The injured part should be wrapped in flannels wrung out of hot water, and covered with a dry bandage, or, what is better, oiled silk. The limb should not be allowed to hang down, but kept in a quiet, easy position, until after all pain has ceased.

Fracture of the Collar-Bone.—If the *collar-bone* is fractured, the attendants must keep the patient in bed without a pillow, with the arm on the injured side folded across the chest. Keep the part moist with water "until the doctor comes."

Fracture of the Ribs.—If the *ribs* are fractured, the patient should remain in bed, have a spittoon within reach, so that the expectorations may be duly noted by the physician when he arrives.

Dislocations.—The limbs must be extended by force, until the contraction of the muscles is overcome, when the bone may be readily pushed into its proper place. In case of dislocation of the jaw, the operator must thrust both thumbs (covered by linen cloths) as far as possible into the mouth, while the fingers press externally the jaw; then press downward and backward until the back end of the jawbone is restored to its place.

Clothing on Fire—Presence of Mind Needed.—Many persons lose their lives by want of presence of mind when a small portion of their clothes catches fire; and many lives are lost by others in the room also losing their presence of mind. The first impulse of fear is to ring the bell, rush madly about the room, or into passages full of draughts, so that the fire is fanned, and in a few minutes the unfortunate sufferer is hopelessly burned.

Clothing on Fire—What to Do.—The first thing to do is to snatch up a hearth-rug or table-cloth, or any woolen thing that may be nearest, and roll it tightly round the person. This will exclude the air, and extinguish the flame. If water is within reach, it should be sluiced over the burning parts. Do not go in search of it—a moment's delay is fatal. If a person is alone in a room, and there is nothing better to be had, the best plan is to roll over and over on the carpet till the fire is extinguished.

To Prevent Clothing from Taking Fire.—There is a very simple process by which muslins, used for ladies' and children's dresses, can be prevented from getting on fire. Dissolve a small piece of alum in the water in which muslins are rinsed. When dry, if a light be put to them, they will smoulder slowly away, but not break out into a blaze. And this, so far from being injurious to muslin, improves its appearance greatly.

Cures for Lock-jaw.—Take a small quantity of turpentine, warm it, and pour it on the wound, no matter where it is, or of what nature it is, and relief will follow in less than one minute. Lobelia has been successfully used in several cases of lock-jaw.

Relief from Choking.—1. To relieve choking, break an egg into a cup and give it to the patient to swallow. The white of the egg seems to catch around the obstacle and remove it. If one egg does not answer the purpose try another. The white is all that is necessary.*

2. Often a smart blow between the shoulders, causing a compression of the chest and a sudden expulsion of air from the lungs will throw out the substance.

---

* EGGS IN CASE OF TROUBLE.—The white of an egg is said to be a specific for fishbones sticking in the throat. It is to be swallowed raw, and will carry down a bone easily and certainly. There is another fact touching eggs which it will be well to remember. When, as sometimes by accident, corrosive sublimate is swallowed, the white of one or two eggs taken will neutralize the poison, and change the effect to that of a dose of calomel.

3. If the person can swallow, give plenty of bread and potatoes, and water to wash it down.

4. Press upon the tongue with a spoon when perhaps the substance may be seen and drawn out with a pair of dull scissors.

5. If these fail, give an emetic of ipecac, or mustard and water.

Frost-Bites—Instant Remedy.—Frost-bites are frequently so sudden that one is not aware when they occur. In Canada, it is not uncommon for persons meeting in the street to say, "Mind, sir, your nose looks whitish." The blood cools and runs slowly, and the blood-vessels become choked and swollen. *Keep from the heat.* Rub the part quickly with snow, if necessary for hours, till the natural color is restored. If one is benumbed with cold, take him into a cold room, remove the wet clothes, rub the body, dry, cover with blankets, and give a little warm drink. On recovering, let him be brought to a fire gradually.*

General Treatment for Burns and Scalds.—In both large and small burns, protect carefully from the air. Cover the wound immediately with cotton-batting, or dredge it with flour. A piece of oil silk will do good service. Wrap a dry bandage upon the outside. Remove the patient to a bed warmly-covered. Do not remove the bandage until it becomes stiff and irritating; then remove gradually, and redress and cover quickly. Do not expose any wound to the dust and infinitesimal living germs of the air. *Put no salve on a burn.*

1. A solution of bi-carbonate of sodium applied to burns promptly and permanently relieves pain.

2. Cotton-batting saturated with a solution of carbolic acid is very good in cases of severe burning. It is also good in cases of gunpowder burns, as it prevents discoloration of the skin.

3. It is said of oakum as a dressing for burns, that it induces the healing of extensive sores with remarkable rapidity; it induces healing action in those indolent ulcers that are the result of defective hygienic conditions; it prevents all smell; it is cheap, saves time and trouble; and most important of all, the resulting scars do not contract.

4. In cases of scalding or burning the body, immersing the part in cold water gives entire relief, as instantaneously as the lightning. Meanwhile, get some common dry flour, and apply it an inch or two thick on the injured part the moment it emerges from the water, and keep sprinkling on the flour

---

* STEELE.—If you are caught in a snow-storm, look for a snow-bank in the lee of a hill, or a wood out of the wind, or a hollow in the plain filled with snow. Scrape out a hole big enough to creep into, and the drifting snow will keep you warm. Men and animals have been preserved after days of such imprisonment. Remember that if you give way to sleep in the open field, you will never awake.

through any thing like a pepper-box cover, so as to put it on evenly. Do nothing else, drink nothing but water, eat nothing, until improvement commences, except some dry bread softened in very weak tea of some kind. Cures of frightful burnings have been performed in this way, as wonderful as they are painless.

5. A varnisher of metals, in Paris, one day got his hand badly burned, and in his agony thrust it into a pot of varnish at his side. To his astonishment the pain at once ceased, and the wound rapidly healed. This cure being reported around, persons in the neighborhood who had got burned, came to the varnisher and were cured in like manner. The news circulated far and wide, and finally reached the medical faculty, and the varnisher was sent for to try his skill in the hospital. He responded to the call and succeeded in curing all on whom he operated. The philosophy of the cure is, the varnish keeps the burn from the air, and gives nature a chance to supply a new skin under its protection.

6. The white of an egg has proved of late the most efficacious remedy for burns. Seven or eight successive applications of this substance soothe the pain and effectually exclude the burn from the air. This simple remedy seems preferable to collodion or even cotton. Extraordinary stories are told of the healing properties of a new oil which is easily made from the yelks of hens' eggs. The eggs are first boiled hard, the yelks are then removed, crushed, and placed over a fire, where they are carefully stirred until the whole substance is just on the point of catching fire, when the oil separates and may be poured off. It is in general use among the colonists of Southern Russia as a means of curing cuts, bruises, and scratches.

7. A bath in oil is one of the best remedies for serious burns. A German ballet-girl, whose dress had caught fire, and who had been horribly burned in consequence, was put into a bath full of oil by the chief physician of the Leipsic Hospital. She was suffering excruciating agonies, but the oil caused her pains to cease almost immediately. She remained in the bath nine days and nights, the oil being renewed five times during that period, and her burns were then so far healed that she could be taken out without pain or danger. Three weeks after she had completely recovered. This is an admirable form of cure, because it suppresses the intolerable tortures which do more to kill the victims by fire than the actual gravity of the wounds. Unfortunately, like most good things in life, it is a remedy beyond the reach of small purses.

Cut-Wounds—How to Heal Quickly.—Protect the wounded parts from the air and dust instantly if possible. Press the parts together and keep them so by adhesive plaster or bandage, and give them instant and permanent rest till healed, which in most cases will be rapidly accomplished. It is the inherent property of all wounds (on surface or deep) to heal by "first intention."

How to Relieve Pain from Wounds.—A correspondent of the *Country Gentleman* gives the following remedy for painful wounds: "Take a pan or shovel with burning coals, and sprinkle upon them common brown sugar and hold the wounded part in the smoke. In a few minutes the pain will be allayed, and recovery proceed rapidly.

Pain from Nail in the Foot—Instant Remedy.*—The same writer says: "In my own case a rusty nail had made a bad wound in the bottom of my foot. The pain and nervous irritation was severe. This was all removed by holding it in the sugar-smoke for fifteen minutes, and I was able to resume my reading in comfort. We have often recommended it to others with like results. Last week one of my men had a finger-nail torn out by a pair of ice-tongs. It became very painful, as was to be expected. Held in sugar-smoke for twenty minutes, the pain ceased, and it promises speedy recovery."

Sunstroke—Its History.—The earliest case on record is the one mentioned in the Bible.

"Manassas was her husband, who died in the early harvest: for as he stood among them and bound sheaves in the field, the heat came upon his head, and he fell on his bed, and died in the city of Bethulia." The second instance relates to the son of the Shunamite woman, who was restored to life by the prophet Elisha: "And when the child was grown, it fell on a day that he went out with his father to the reapers. And he said unto his father, '*My head, my head.*' And when he had taken him and brought him to his mother, he sat on her knees till noon, and then died."

Sunstroke Does not Follow Short Exposure.—It does not depend upon a short exposure to the direct rays of the sun; the exposure must have been continued for a day or two. Nor does sunstroke necessarily arise from solar heat. Prolonged confinement in the heated atmosphere of a building may likewise produce it.

Most Dangerous Time for Sunstroke.—About the third or fourth day from the commencement of a heated term, sunstrokes usually appear. The sufferers in most cases are exposed to the heat for some days preceding the attack. In the summer of 1866, the majority of sunstroke cases—generally laboring-men—were brought to Bellevue Hospital in the morning or *early in the day*.

Premonitory Symptoms of Sunstroke.—The *symptoms of sunstroke*

---

* Here is another, which comes strongly endorsed: "To relieve from the terrible effects of running a nail in the foot of man or horse take peach-leaves, bruise them, apply to the wound, and confine with a bandage. They cure as if by magic in most cases. Renew the application twice a day, if necessary, but one application usually does the work. It has cured both man and horse in a few hours, when they were apparently on the point of having the lock-jaw. This recipe, remembered and practiced, will save many valuable lives."

are usually headache, vertigo, dimness of vision, nausea, often developing into coma, or even delirium or convulsions, ending in many cases in insanity, softening of the brain, or death.

Hints for the Prevention of Sunstroke.—For the *prevention of sunstroke*, the following are hints, especially when there is tendency to a hot brain :

Wear a light-colored, well-ventilated hat.

Avoid meats and other heating foods. Eat plenty of fruit.

Wet the hair on the temples and top of the head often, but not behind.

If the hot brain pressure is felt coming on, dash cold water on the face and temples, or in the absence of that, clasp and squeeze both temples with the fingers to crowd the blood back, and rub the back of the neck powerfully to draw the blood from the brain.

Where special danger is apprehended, wear a cool, wet bandage around the forehead and head.

Treatment of Sunstroke.—The patient should be removed at once to a cool room, and placed in a recumbent position near an open window. The clothes are then stripped off, and a stream of water poured over the body. The vessel containing the liquid is to be held four or five feet above the patient, in order that he may receive the benefit of the shock. The stream of water should at first be directed on the head, then on the chest and abdomen, and finally on the extremities, and thus alternating from one part to another, until consciousness returns. Ice rubbed over the body is liked by some; the cold douche is, however, preferable.

Internal medication is useful in all cases. Among the numerous drugs employed, bromide of potassium has been found most efficient. The best results were obtained from its use in Bellevue Hospital, in the years 1866 and 1868. This drug may be administered in all stages of the affection. When the patient is unable to swallow, it can be given by injection, always remembering to increase the dose one quarter more than when given by mouth. In mild cases, from five to ten grains may be given, at intervals of from half an hour to one hour, until the grave symptoms disappear. In several forms from ten to thirty grains may be administered every half hour; when the pulse becomes weak or intermittent, stimulants are needed. Stimulation should be resorted to in all cases where exhaustion is the prominent feature. Brandy and milk, or brandy with ammonia, must be introduced into the stomach or rectum. The cold douche must be sparingly employed in this latter class of cases. If the skin is cold, it will do no good whatever.

Treatment of Sunstroke after Recovery.—After consciousness has returned, mustard plasters or blisters are to be applied to the back of the neck. The bromide need not be discontinued for one or two weeks. As soon as convenient, the patient should be sent to a cool district in the country, and kept free from excitement. The brain must rest from all work. Exercise in the open air and nourishing diet are essential; regular habits must be rigilly enforced. A continuance of this treatment for several months prevents, or at least lessens, the danger from nervous affections which follow sunstroke.

Lightning Stroke: Preliminary Dangers: Important Hints.—After a thorough examination, an able medical professor states that "when persons happen to be overtaken by a thunder-storm, although they may not be terrified by lightning, yet they naturally wish for shelter from the rain which usually attends it; and, therefore, if no house be at hand, generally take refuge under the nearest tree they can find. But in doing this they unknowingly expose themselves to a double danger; first, because their clothes being thus kept dry, their bodies are rendered more liable to injury, the lightning often passing harmlessly over a body whose surface is wet; and, secondly, because a tree or any elevated object, instead of warding off, serves to attract and conduct the lightning, which in its passage frequently rends its trunks or branches, and kills any person or animal who happens to be close to it at the time. Instead of hay-rick, pillar, wall, or hedge, the person should either pursue his way to the nearest house, or get to a part of the road or field which has no object that can draw lightning toward it, and remain there until the storm has subsided.

"It is particularly dangerous to stand near leaden spouts or iron gates at such times; metals of all kinds have so strong a conducting power for lightning as frequently to lead it out of the course it would otherwise have taken.

"When in the house avoid standing near a window, door, or walls during a thunder-gust. The nearer you are placed to the middle of a room the better.

"When a person is struck by lightning, strip the body and throw buckets full of cold water over it for ten or fifteen minutes; let continued frictions and inflations of the lungs be also practiced; let gentle shocks of electricity be made to pass through the chest, when a skillful person can be procured to administer them; and apply blisters to the chest."

Apoplexy: Nature and Cause. *—Apoplexy is caused by an unnatural amount of blood in the brain. Whatever sends too much to the brain may cause apoplexy. Whatever keeps the blood from coming from the brain dams it up, and may cause apoplexy. This is the kind of apoplexy which seems

---

* From the suddenness of the attack and the apparent causelessness of it, the Greeks connected it in their minds with the idea of a stroke of lightning as coming from the Almighty hand; it literally means "a stroke from above." As instantaneous as the hurling of a thunderbolt in a clear sky, there comes a loss of sense, and feeling, and thought, and motion; the heart beats, the lungs play, but that is all—they soon cease forever. The Romans considered the person to be "thunderstruck" or planet-struck, as if it were of unearthly origin.—J. W. HOWE.

to come without any apparent adequate cause. Tying a cord around the neck, or holding the head downward too long, can bring on an attack of apoplexy, by damming up the blood in the brain, and keeping it from returning to the body. A sudden mental emotion can send too much blood to the brain, or too great mental excitement does the same thing.

Immediate Treatment of Apoplexy.—When a man is asleep his pulse beats and his lungs play; he is without sense, and can be easily awakened.

If a person faints, he too is without sense, but he has no pulse, and does not breathe. Apoplexy is between the two; the heart beats, the lungs play as in sleep, and there is no sense as in fainting, but you can't shake the man back to life.

In sleep the face is natural.

In a fainting fit it has the pallor of death.

In apoplexy it is swollen, turbid, and fairly livid.

If a man is asleep, let him alone; nature will wake him up as soon as he has got sleep enough.

When a person faints, all that is necessary is to lay him down on the floor, and he will "come to."

In apoplexy *set a man up.** Then give him rest. Keep the head raised, and put cool cloths upon it. Put mustard plasters on the calves of the legs. These may draw the blood from the head. In difficult cases, strong purgatives should be given, and sometimes these should be accompanied by electric or galvanic action. After recovery the extent of the liability of another attack cannot be estimated. In a majority of cases, among persons of prudent, careful life, there is no relapse.

How to Treat Delirious Patients.—Avoid any roughness in dealing with such cases, but be firm, and do not permit them to know you are afraid of them or inclined to let them have their own way. Do not attempt to argue with them or contradict any of their assertions, but at the same time it is well to appear interested in their conversation. See that all escape is prevented See that there are no knives or dangerous weapons within reach. Immediate aid should be within call.

Convulsions, and How to Stop Them.—Some children are liable to convulsions from derangement of the digestive organs. They sometimes occur when a child is teething. The attack is often preceded by involuntary

---

* In apoplexy, as there is too much blood in the head, every one can see that the position is to set a man up, and the blood naturally tends downward—as much so as water will come out of a bottle when it is turned upside down, if the cork is out.

If, then, a man is merely asleep, let him alone, for the face is natural.

If a man has fainted, lay him flat on his back, for his face is deadly pale.

If a man is apoplectic, set him in a chair, because the face is swollen and livid with its excess of blood.

movements of the mouth or eyelids; then the eyes become fixed and the body rigid, the breathing is irregular, often suspended for a few moments, and the face and surface of the body becomes dark red or livid. This is followed by twitching or jerking of the limbs, and often the arms and the legs, and the muscles of the face. The attendant should at once prepare a warm bath, and the child be immersed in the water up to the head, which should have cold water applied to it. It should be kept in the bath until the convulsions cease, keeping up the temperature to about 98°. After the bath, wrap the child in a warm blanket.

EMERGENCIES—DROWNING.

What to Do in Case of Drowning.*—When a drowned person is taken from the water he must be treated on the spot, in the open air. On no account waste precious time by removing him to a house, unless the weather is intensely cold. Secure a return of breathing first—protecting him from the severe cold by coats, blankets, etc., if necessary—and then take him into a house Keep bystanders off twelve or fifteen feet, while three (or, at most, four) stout persons manage the patient. Loosen all tight clothing.

To Restore Breathing.—Place the patient *upon his face*, with his chest

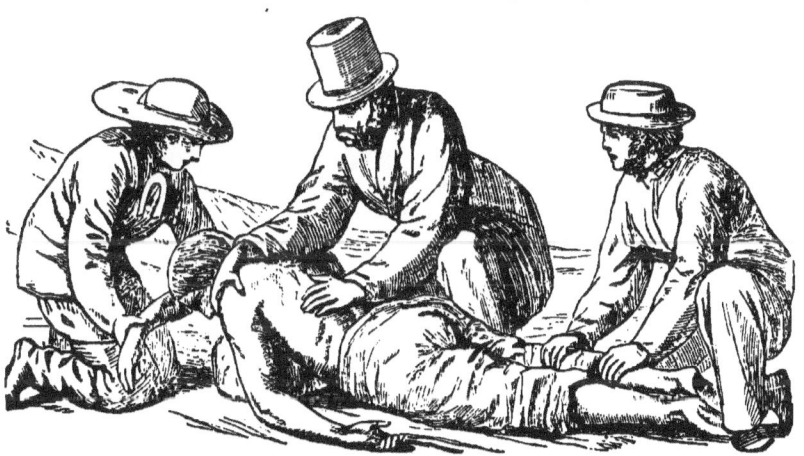

Fig. 1.

resting on a good cushion, (as a coat folded,) and one arm brought under his forehead, (see Fig. 1.) In this position the fluid will escape from the mouth,

---

* Reprinted from *The Physio-Medical Recorder*, Cincinnati, by the courtesy of whose editor and publisher, Wm. H. Cook, M.D., the article, with its illustrations, is here inserted.

throat, and mostly from the lungs. The tongue itself will also fall forward, and thus leave the entrance to the windpipe free. The mouth may be wiped out quickly with a fold of the handkerchief over one's forefinger. Press gently between the shoulder-blades and on the sides. On no account lift the patient to his feet, or even to a sitting posture, even for a moment, as such a position causes the water to sink to the bottom of the lungs, and might utterly strangle a patient who was gasping for breath.

Possibly the patient may struggle into breathing so soon as the water escapes from his mouth. If so, manage him as hereafter described for this stage of recovery. If he should not now recover, do not keep him on his face more than *one-fourth of a minute* at the furthest; but remove the hands from making pressure on the sides and back, and turn him fully upon one side, no matter whether right or left, as in Fig. 2. Support the head

Fig. 2.

while doing this, and also hold up the arm that was previously under the forehead. Some smelling-salts or snuff may be placed to the nose in the hope of exciting a breathing effort, but not too abundantly; or a feather may be used to tickle the throat. Be careful not to roll the patient so far upon his back as to have the tongue fall back upon the windpipe; and if it is observed thus to fall, pull it forward quickly.

The position upon the side must not be maintained longer than a few seconds. If the patient then show no signs of returning life, he must be rolled upon the face, precisely as in the position first named—making pressure between the shoulder-blades and upon the sides of the chest, as before. This position upon the face causes (or imitates) the natural action of lungs and chest in the *expiration* of breath; while the position upon the side imitates

Emergencies—Drowning.

the *inspiration* of breath. These two movements may now be repeated regularly, as a close resemblance to the natural act of breathing. They should be made at the rate of not more than fifteen times in a minute, or once in four seconds. There is much liability that they will be made oftener; but this must be carefully guarded against. The turning upon the side had better be alternated from right to left. At the moment of turning from the face to the side, all pressure must be removed from the trunk; and it will be well also to lift upward the free arm, so that its weight shall not drag across the chest and compress the lungs. If the tongue should be disposed to fall backward, it had better be drawn pretty well forward by passing a cord behind its thick part and out of the corners of the mouth—then tying the cord under the chin. Smelling salts may be applied occasionally, but not too often nor too freely.

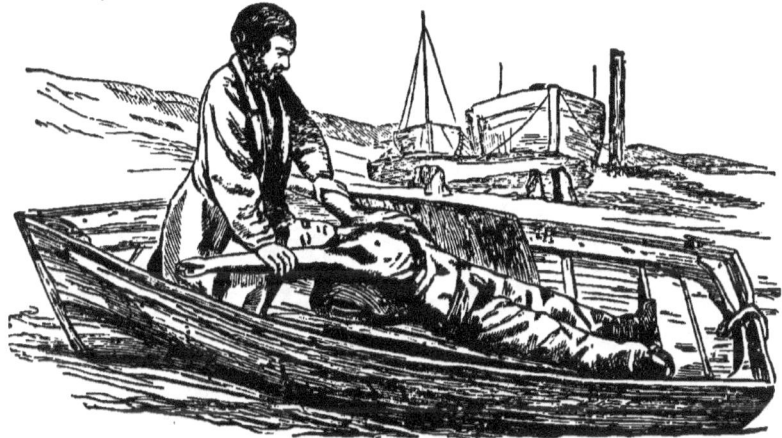

FIG. 8.

While carrying on the above operations, dry the hands and feet gently without much rubbing, and gently put on dry clothing; and be sure not to let the act of changing the clothes interfere in the least with either the regularity or the completeness of the above movements. These movements often suffice to restore signs of life in a few minutes. If no such signs are apparent after eight or ten minutes of such efforts, the position may be changed, and different movements made as follows:—

The water being thoroughly worked out of the lungs by the above movements, place the patient upon his back upon a board or other flat surface. Let this incline upward a little from the feet to the head. Support the head and shoulders on a small but firm cushion, extending down to the lower edge of the shoulder-blades, such as a folded coat. Draw the patient's tongue strongly forward, even beyond the lips, and keep it thus by a tape or string, as before named. Now take a position at the patient's head, grasp his arms just above the elbows, and draw them gently (but steadily and firmly) upward, as in Fig. 3. Keep them well stretched in this position for two seconds. This movement elevates the whole ribs, enlarges the capacity of the chest, and puts the parts in a position favorable for the *ingress* of air. Next bend the patient's elbows, turn the arms downward, and press them gently but firmly against the sides of the chest, as in Fig. 4. Keep them in this position for two seconds, during which time the air will be *pressed out* of the lungs. The first or upward position of the arms is now to be resumed; and these movements are thus to be continued perseveringly at the rate of not more than *fifteen times to the minute.* This latter plan is called the Sylvester plan.

These movements must be continued without any remission whatever; nor should such efforts cease because signs of life do not return soon. It is not

FIG. 4

uncommon for such efforts to prove successful at the end of two hours; and several cases are on record in which no symptoms of returning life were seen until the fourth, and even the fifth, hour of unremitting labor, and then the attendants were rewarded by the recovery of the patient.

To Restore Circulation.—The above measures are directed wholly to restoring the breath. This is the first necessity. There should be no rubbing of the surface, except gently, to dry it, while this is going on. Should the inclemency of the weather demand the removal of the patient in-doors, the above movements must be kept up, even while he is being removed; and on no account should he be taken into a warm or crowded room.

When the patient begins to breathe, commence rubbing the limbs. Rub them *upward* with considerable briskness and pressure. Use flannels some what warmed; throw a quilt or blanket over the patient, and continue friction under this. Put two or three layers of warm flannel on the stomach; and warm bricks, or bottles of warm water, may be put at the feet, between the thighs, and under the arm-pits; but be very careful not to have these things too warm, or much above the temperature of the healthy body. As they get cool, replace them with others of the right warmth. As consciousness returns, give him a spoonful of weak ginger-tea every five minutes, and, as he gets stronger, use the tea stronger and in larger quantities, or give a tea of composition instead of ginger. Brandy, and other alcoholic drinks are the worst stimulants that could be given. Black pepper, red pepper, or allspice, are far better. When the pulse has been restored, encourage a disposition to sleep.

Recovery Twelve Hours after Drowning.—A correspondent of the *Christian Advocate* sends us an account of the drowning at Osceola Mills, some five years ago, of two little boys, Willie and Charlie, aged four and six years. They were on the bank of the Big Moshanon Creek, fishing, and both fell in. They were seen by the father, near by, who hastened to their relief, but were not recovered until life was apparently extinct. Charlie was under water eight or ten minutes. The correspondent adds:—

The children were carried home by the parents, a physician sent for to Philipsburgh, a distance of five miles. In the meantime a fire was made in the cook-stove, a lounge placed behind it, and Charlie placed thereon, rolled up in warm blankets, and thoroughly rubbed with brandy; brandy was also forced down his throat. The physician came, but could do nothing more than had been done. The neighbors came and went until midnight, leaving Charlie for dead. Though all others gave up the hope of restoring Charlie, the mother continued to rub him, and keep him warm until three o'clock the next morning, when he opened his eyes, and, looking his mother in the face, exclaimed, "Mamma, what am I doing here?" The accident happened about three o'clock the previous afternoon, making twelve hours from the time he was drowned until he showed life, or spoke.

How to Bring a Drowning Person to Shore.—The proper method of bringing a drowning man to shore, is to approach him from behind. Seize him with your left hand by the hair, coat-collar, or shoulder. Turn him upon his back, and then place his head upon your chest, and, with your right arm free, swim upon your back to the land. (If by the left hand alone it be too difficult to turn him upon his back, apply, in addition, the right hand to his right shoulder, and the turning will be easily accomplished.) If he be conscious, encourage him, and direct him to straighten out his legs. *

---

* If the drowning man be out of sight under the water, watch carefully for the rising of a bubble upon the surface; he will usually be found directly below it.

296 HOME AND HEALTH.

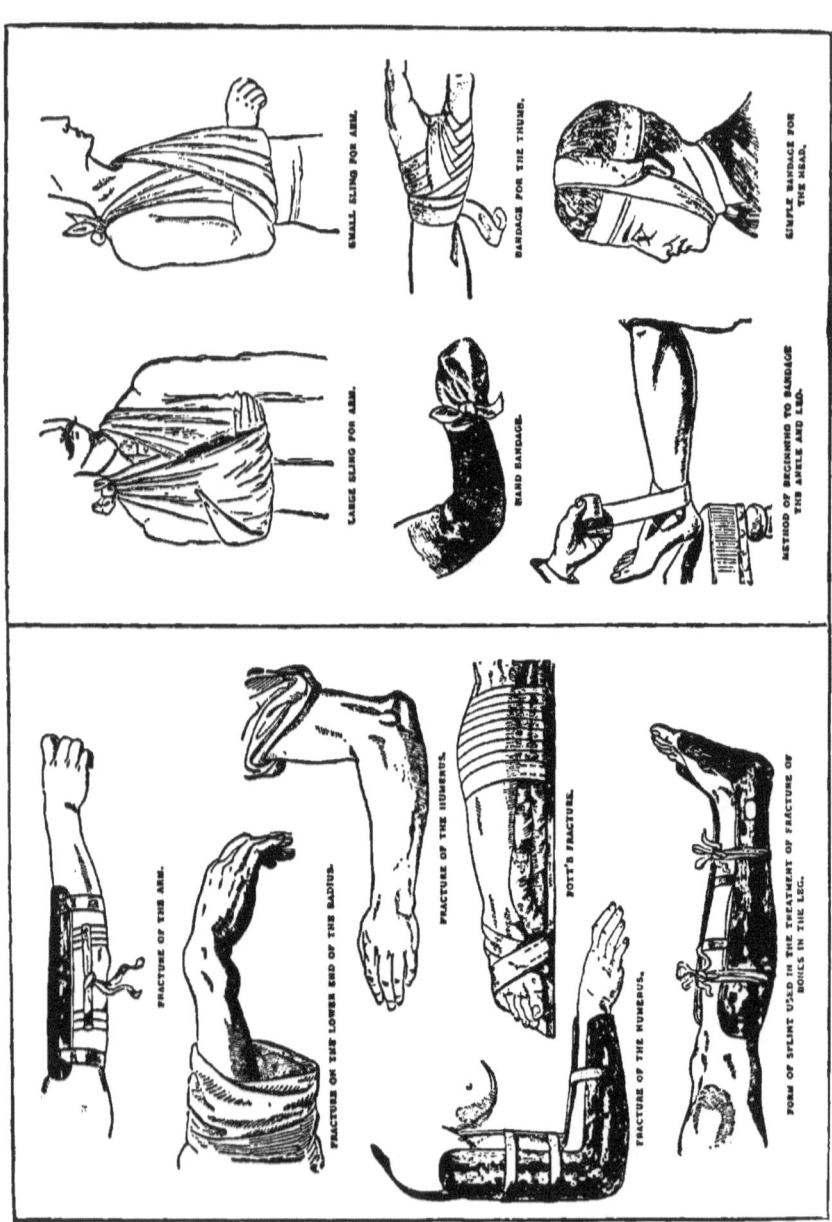

BANDAGES. (See also page 354.)

POULTICES AND THEIR APPLICATION.

General Purpose of a Poultice.—The use of poultices is to promote warmth and moisture; hence those which keep warm and moist the longer are the best. They are employed in the treatment of abscesses, suppurating wounds, inflammation, and pain. In making them the attendant should have them smooth, light, and as hot as they can be made without burning in their application.

1. *Bread Poultice.* Cold, light wheat bread, soaked in sweet milk, makes good ones.

2. *Beet Poultice.* A beet fresh from the garden, and pounded fine, makes an excellent poultice.

3. *Linseed-meal Poultice.* In preparing this, the basin should be scalded in which it is made. Pour in boiling water, according to the size of the poultice required. Add gradually sufficient linseed-meal to form a thick paste, stirring it one way until it is of the proper consistency and smoothness; then spread it on linen or muslin, and apply it.

4. *Charcoal Poultice.* Take two ounces of bread in crumbs, soak for ten minutes in boiling water—say ten ounces; then mix and add gradually a half an ounce of pulverized charcoal and a half an ounce of linseed-meal, well stirred together; spread as above, and apply.

5. *Chlorinated Soda Poultice* is made like linseed-meal poultice; consisting of two parts of linseed-meal poultice, to one of chlorinated soda, mixed with boiling water.

6. *Yeast Poultice* is made by mixing a pound of flour or linseed-meal with half a pint of yeast; heat it, and stir it carefully. All poultices are made with boiling water, except yeast, and with this the temperature should not be over 100°.

7. *Mustard Poultice.* Take a sufficient quantity of powdered mustard to make a thin paste of the required size. It should be mixed with boiling water, with a small quantity of vinegar added, if a very strong poultice is required. Spread it on brown paper or linen, with a piece of thin muslin over it. It should be kept on from ten to twenty minutes. If the skin is very irritable afterward, a little flour should be sprinkled over it. By mixing the mustard with the white of an egg, the poultice will not cause a blister.

8. *Mustard and Linseed Poultice.* These poultices are often mixed with linseed-meal when a milder form is required than of mustard alone. After the use of any kind of mustard poultice, the skin should be carefully wiped with something very soft, so that no mustard be left behind. One of the best mustard poultices is the paper plaster now sold by every druggist. It is always ready, and can be carried by a traveler. It has only to be dipped in water, and applied at once.

BRIEF CURES FOR VARIOUS DISEASES.

Colds—Seven Important Remedies.—A cold, like measles or mumps, or other similar ailments, will run its course of about ten days in spite of what may be done for it, unless remedial means are employed within forty-eight hours after its inception. Many a useful life will be spared to be increasingly useful by cutting a cold "short off" before it has taken firm hold on the system. The following are safe, simple, and authenticated remedies:—

1. On the first day of taking a cold there is a very unpleasant sensation of chilliness. The moment you observe this, go to your room and stay there; keep it at such a temperature as will entirely prevent this chilly feeling, even if it requires a hundred degrees of Fahrenheit. In addition, put your feet in hot water, half a leg deep, as hot as you can bear it, adding hot water from time to time for a quarter of an hour, so that the water shall be hotter when you take your feet out than when you put them in it: then dry them thoroughly, and then put on warm, thick woolen stockings, even if it be summer, for summer colds are the most dangerous; and for twenty-four hours eat not an atom of food, but drink as largely as you desire of any kinds of warm teas, and at the end of that time, if not sooner, the cold will be effectually broken without any medicine whatever.

2. Dio Lewis's remedy is the use of *cold* water as follows: "Eat no supper. On going to bed drink two tumblers of cold water. On rising in the morning drink freely of cold water. For breakfast eat a piece of dry bread as large as your hand. Go out freely during the morning. For dinner eat about the same as you ate at breakfast. During the afternoon take a sharp walk, or engage in some active exercise which shall produce a little perspiration. Go without your supper and retire early, drinking, before you jump into bed, as much cold water as you can swallow."

3. Many colds are from over-eating or eating gross food. Strong persons with large lungs who exercise a great deal and breathe much, can dispose of a large quantity of food, but the feeble and sedentary must eat moderately, or break down early; for this kind of a cold one preventive is worth a dozen cures, namely, *cut off the supplies.*

4. Dr. Paillon, of France, announces what he considers to be a new method of curing a cold in the head. It consists in inhaling through the nose the emanations of ammonia contained in a smelling-bottle. If the sense of smell is completely obliterated, the bottle should be kept under the nose until the pungency of the volatile alkali is felt. The bottle is then removed, but only to be reapplied after a minute; the second application, however, should not be long, that the patient may bear it. This easy operation being repeated seven or eight times in the course of five minutes, but always very rapidly, except the first time, the nostrils become free, the sense of smell is restored,

Brief Cures for Various Diseases.

and the secretion of the irritating mucus is stopped. This remedy is said to be peculiarly advantageous to singers.

5. Borax has proved a most effective remedy in certain forms of colds. In sudden hoarseness or loss of voice in public speakers or singers, from colds, relief for an hour or so, as by magic, may be often obtained by slowly dissolving and partially swallowing a lump of borax the size of a garden pea, or about three or four grains, held in the mouth for ten minutes before speaking or singing. This produces a profuse secretion of saliva, or "watering" of the mouth and throat, probably restoring the voice or tone to the dried vocal cords, just as "wetting" brings back the missing notes to a flute when it is too dry.

6. The following is an excellent and safe remedy for children: Take onions, slice thin, and sprinkle loaf-sugar over them; put in the oven, and simmer until the juice is thoroughly mixed with the sugar. It makes a thick syrup, very nice. Give a teaspoonful as seems to be needed, four or five times a day.

7. Dr. George M. Beard, (Allopathist,) a well-known medical lecturer and writer, strongly recommends the following formula or prescription, suggested originally by one of his patients, and since often given by Dr. B. Take of camphor, two parts; powdered opium, one part; carbonate of ammonia, two parts. Dissolve the camphor to the thickness of cream, and then add the opium and ammonia. Let it be prepared by the druggist. Keep the bottle tightly corked, and take a dose just before retiring at night. Dose, from three to six grains in a little water. The druggist who puts up the powder will show the buyer the quantity to be taken. It should be kept on hand at all times, and should be first taken immediately after being chilled through, and should be repeated the following night.

How to Relieve Severe Coughs—Seven Good Recipes.—1. The paroxysm of coughing may often be prevented or cured by using a little dry salt as a gargle. Let those who doubt try it. It will relieve the *tickling* in the throat.

2. Equal parts of hoarhound, elecampane root, comfrey root, spikenard, and wild-cherry bark. Boil in one gallon soft water down to one quart; strain, and add one pound of honey. Take a tablespoonful three times a day, or when the cough is troublesome.

3. Roast a lemon very carefully without burning it; when it is thoroughly hot, cut and squeeze it into a cup upon three ounces of sugar, finely powdered. Take a spoonful whenever your cough troubles you. It is good and agreeable to the taste. Rarely has it been known to fail of giving relief.

4. Take one quart thick flaxseed tea, one pint of honey, half pint of vinegar, two spoonfuls saltpeter. Boil all together in a new earthen pot that is well glazed, until it becomes a pretty thick syrup; keep stirring while boiling with

a pine stick; if fresh from a green tree the better. Dose, one tablespoonful three or four times a day.

5. A medical writer says: "We are often troubled with severe coughs, the result of colds of long standing, which may turn to consumption or premature death. The remedy I propose has been often tried by me, with good results, which is simply to take into the stomach before retiring for the night a piece of raw onion, after chewing. This esculent in an uncooked state is very heating, and tends to collect the waters from the lungs and throat, causing immediate relief to the patient."

6. Common sweet cider, boiled down to one half, makes a most excellent syrup for coughs and colds for children—is pleasant to the taste, and will keep for a year in a cool cellar. In recovering from an illness, the system has a craving for some pleasant acid drink. This is found in cider which is placed on the fire as soon as made, and allowed to come to a boil, then cooled, put in casks, and kept in a cool cellar.

7. Take a handful of hops, put it into three pints of hot water; let it boil one half hour, or until the strength is out. Strain and add one and one half cups of best kind of molasses, and one cup of white sugar. Boil down slowly in a bright dish or enameled kettle to about one quart. Then bottle up, and it is ready for use. Drink a little when you cough.

Cures for Sore Throat.—1. Powdered potash held on the tongue and allowed to dissolve is very good for sore throat when there are "white spots."

2. For clergymen's sore throat, use fluid extract Callinsonia and simple syrup, equal parts. Take a teaspoonful three or four times a day.

3. Take the whites of two eggs and beat them in with two spoonfuls of white sugar; grate in a little nutmeg, and then add a pint of luke-warm water. Stir well and drink often. Repeat the prescription, if necessary. A practical physician thinks it will cure the most obstinate case of hoarseness in a short time.

4. One of the best of cures is a cold-water compress. Before going to bed, wet a cotton-rag in cold water and wring it partially dry. Put it closely around the throat, and wrap around it a large piece of flannel to keep the moisture in. In the morning, bathe the throat in cold water and rub briskly with a coarse towel to prevent catching cold.

5. Every body has a cure for this trouble, but simple remedies appear to be most effectual. Salt and water is used by many as a gargle, but a little alum and honey dissolved in sage-tea is better. Others use a few drops of camphor on loaf sugar, which very often affords immediate relief. An application of cloths wrung out of hot water and applied to the neck, changed as often as it begins to cool, has the most potency in removing inflammation.

Headache—Five Different Remedies Suggested.—1. Much sick-headache is caused by overloading the stomach—by indigestion. It may be relieved by drinking very freely of warm water, whether it produces vomiting or not. If the feet are cold, warm them or bathe them in water as hot as you can bear it. Soda or ashes in the water will do good. If the pain is very severe, apply a cloth wrung out of hot water to the head—pack the head as it were. To prevent it, let plainness, simplicity, and temperance preside at your table. In some cases medicine is necessary; but if the above is properly carried out, almost immediate relief is experienced.

2. One-fourth of a grain of ipecac, repeated every half hour or hour, has relieved many cases of nervous sick-headache, and if the ipecac is continued in one to three-grain doses three or four times daily, a cure will frequently result—at least the intervals will be prolonged.

3. "The people about the Jumna and Tonsee rivers, India," says Mr. Wilson, "have this way of treating a common headache: They lie down by the fire, and with the forehead as near to it as bearable. It is a very good one, I believe. I have tried it myself with success when my own remedy failed.*

4. Dr. Warburton Begbie, of Edinburgh, advocates the use of turpentine in the severe headache to which nervous and hysterical women are subject. "There is, moreover," he says, "another class of sufferers from headache, and this is composed of both sexes, who may be relieved by turpentine. I refer to the frontal headache, which is most apt to occur after prolonged mental effort, but may likewise be induced by unduly sustained physical exertion—what may be styled the headache of a fatigued brain. A cup of very strong tea often relieves this form of headache, but this remedy with not a few is perilous, for, bringing relief from pain, it may produce general restlessness, and, worst of all, banish sleep. Turpentine in doses of 20 to 30 minims, given at intervals of an hour or two, will entirely remove the headache.

5. A much simpler cure than any of the above, and one more likely to be permanently effective, is *to stop drinking tea. Try it.* See our chapter on "Tea and Coffee and Health," p. 103.

Indigestion and Dyspepsia—Four Remedies.—1. Many of the Welsh peasants live almost wholly upon oatmeal-cakes and buttermilk, and seldom suffer from indigestion. The acid (*lactic acid*) in the buttermilk is regarded as a promoter of digestion.

2. Dyspepsia is cured by muscular exercise, voluntary or involuntary, and in no other way can it be cured, because nothing can create or collect the gastric juice except exercise; it is a product of the human machine. Nature only can make it.

---

* *Medical and Surgical Reporter.*

3. A dyspeptic once read that by sending a dollar to a person in New York he would receive a cure for dyspepsia. On sending the money he was sent a printed slip with these words: "Stop drinking and hoe in the garden." The man was angry at first, then laughed, and finally stopped drinking and "hoed in the garden." The result was in a short time he was as well as ever. There is more in this cure than would appear at first sight.*

4. A Southern gentleman says: "For something near two years I had suffered with dyspepsia and soreness of the gastric organs. During that time I used several different preparations, and advised with every physician I met, but still could get no permanent relief. Four or five months ago I commenced the use of a remedy that has proved very beneficial to me. Here it is: Every night before I retire, and every morning just as soon as I rise, I give myself a good pounding all over the breast and stomach, breathing long, full breaths frequently during the operation, and throwing my arms in every direction. I followed this course energetically for some time. Now I have no symptoms of dyspepsia, and the soreness in my stomach, which gave me an untold amount of annoyance, has almost entirely disappeared. Of course the pounding must be light and moderate at first. This remedy is simple, and can be used by all."

Biliousness—Its Symptoms and Cure.—Bad blood, too much blood, giving headache, bad taste in the mouth mornings, variable appetite, sickness at stomach, chilliness, cold feet, and great susceptibility to taking cold; no one person may have all these symptoms when bilious, but one or more is always present.

Sometimes a bilious person has a yellow tinge in the face and eyes called "bilious," because the bile, which is yellow, is not withdrawn from the blood; it is the business of the liver to do that, but when it does not do it it is said to be lazy, does not work, and the physician begins at once to use remedies which are said to "promote the action of the liver."

It has been discovered within a few years that acids "act on the liver," such as nitric acid, elixir vitriol, vinegar; but these are artificial acids, and do not have the uniform good effect of natural acids—those which are found in fruit and berries.

Almost all persons become bilious as the warm weather comes on; nine

---

* A VERY SUGGESTIVE CURE.—If any dyspeptic young lady will take five pounds of loose-waistedness, four of short skirtedness, three of bodily cleanliness and warmly-clothedness, and with these take a stomach moderately full of unseasoned fruits and vegetables, and unbolted, unfermented bread, two or three times a day, with nothing between excepting occasionally a gill, or half a gill, of pure soft water, mixed well with out-of-door exercise, pure fresh air, and plenty of sunshine for both soul and body, she will be cured of the dyspepsia, or almost any other ill that flesh is heir to, without "aloes," "alcohol," or any other poisonous abominations.

times out of ten nature calls for her own cure, as witness the almost universal avidity for "greens," for "spinach," in the early spring, these being eaten with vinegar; and soon after, by the benign arrangement of Providence, the delicious strawberry comes, the raspberry, the blackberry, the whortleberry; then the cherries and peaches and apples, carrying us clear into the fall of the year, when the atmosphere is so pure and bracing that there is general good health every-where.

The most beneficial anti-bilious method of using fruits and berries as health promoters is to take them at dessert, after breakfast and dinner; to take them in their natural, raw, ripe, fresh state, without cream or sugar, or any thing else beside the fruit themselves.

Half a lemon eaten every morning on rising, and on retiring, is often efficacious in removing a bilious condition of the system, giving a good appetite and greater general health.

First, on getting up and going to bed, drink plenty of cold water. Eat for breakfast, until the bilious attack passes, a little stale bread, say one slice, and a piece as large as your hand of boiled lean beef or mutton. If the weather is warm, take instead a little cracked wheat, or oatmeal porridge. For dinner take about the same thing. Go without your supper. Exercise freely in the open air, producing perspiration, once or twice a day. In a few days your biliousness is all gone. This result will come, even though the biliousness is one of the spring sort, and one with which you have, from year to year, been much afflicted. Herb drinks, bitter drinks, lager-beer, ale, whisky, and a dozen other spring medicines, are simply barbarous.*

Diarrhœa and Dysentery—Nine Remedies.—1. In all cases of diarrhœa, dysentery, etc., perfect rest should be enjoined, which adds more to the removal of the difficulty than the too-frequent use of medicine. A recumbent position is best.

2. Parched corn and meal, boiled in skimmed milk, and fed frequently to children suffering from summer diarrhœa, will almost always cure, as it will dysentery in adults, and often the cholera in its earliest stages.

3. Common rice, parched brown like coffee, and then boiled and eaten in the ordinary way, without any other food, is, with perfect quietude of the body, one of the most effective remedies for troublesome looseness of the bowels.

4. Put a quarter pound of oat-meal, an ounce and a half of sugar, half a teaspoonful of salt, and three pints of water, into a stew-pan, boil slowly twenty minutes, stir continually. Before serving, add one pint boiled milk, one ounce butter, and a little pounded spice.

---

* Dio Lewis.

5. A spoonful or two of pure, raw wheat-flour, thinned with water so it can be easily drunk. Three or four doses, taken at intervals of ten or twelve hours, will generally cure any case not absolutely chronic. To make the dose palatable for children, it can be sweetened, and flavored with some drops not acid.

6. A physician says: "My attention was called, a short time since, to a novel, but nevertheless successful, remedy. While rendering medical assistance to an extremely sick patient with an obstinate attack of cholera morbus, all my remedies were of no effect until, by request, a large onion was peeled and cut in half, and one half placed in each arm-pit. In several attacks since that time have I seen this remedy promptly control the incessant vomiting, and relieve the distressing nausea."

7. Take one gill of rice, and place in a spider over the fire, stirring it constantly until thoroughly brown. Do not *burn* it. As soon as it is thoroughly brown, fill the spider with boiling water, and let it boil till the mass is of the consistency of *thin* paste. If the rice is not cooked perfectly soft, add a little more water and let it boil away again. Be careful at the last moment that it does not burn on the bottom. When cooked soft, turn into a bowl, sweeten with loaf or crushed sugar, and salt to suit the taste. Eat in milk.

8. For diarrhœa in children, take one cup wheat flour, and tie in a stout cloth, and drop in cold water; then set over the fire and boil three hours steadily. After it is cold, remove the cloth and crust formed by boiling. The ball thus prepared can be kept ready for use for any length of time. To use, grate a tablespoonful for a cupful of boiling water and milk—each one-half. Wet up the flour with a very little cold water; stir in, and boil five minutes. Sweeten to taste. Use a little salt, if desired.

9. Nothing is easier to check than chronic diarrhœa, if it is of the genuine kind, which you may know by the symptom of a clean, very smooth tongue. If the tongue is not clean and smooth, the diarrhœa may be an effort of nature to clean you out, and you had best let it alone. If it is really chronic diarrhœa, take pills of opium and tannin, (provided they are prescribed by your physician,) one grain of each, at intervals during a few days, and it will stop the trouble. But stop using the pills as soon as possible, or you may have trouble of an opposite kind.

Constipation—Cause and Cure.—Over-indulgence in *animal* food is a frequent cause of constipation. No nation consumes such quantities of flesh meats, and so many times a day, as the American. Dyspepsia and constipation result. The rapidity with which we eat, and which causes dyspepsia, is equaled by the carelessness, the hurry, and the neglect which we inflict upon the colon and rectum. A neglect of a regular and proper hour to evacuate the bowels often induces constipation.

Abstain from tea and coffee, eat plenty of fresh vegetables, drink a glass of water immediately after rising in the morning, eat slowly, and masticate the food well, avoid salt meats and salt fish, and take one tablespoonful of sulphur every other night upon retiring.

Cures for Boils.—1. An experienced and well-known New York physician * prescribes the following cure for boils: Procure one ounce horse-radish root, one ounce yellow-dock root, and one quart of cider. Boil ten minutes. Drink a wine-glassful three times a day. The physician referred to hinted, *sub rosa*, that the cider need not be continued after the boils are cured.

2. As soon as the characteristic culminating point of a boil makes its appearance, put in a saucer a thimbleful of camphorated alcohol, and, dipping the ends of the middle fingers into the liquid, rub the inflamed surface, especially the middle portion, repeating the operation eight or ten times, continuing the rubbing at each time for about half a minute. Then allow the surface to dry, placing a slight coating of camphorated olive-oil over the affected surface. One such application, in almost all such cases, causes boils to dry up and disappear. The application should be made at morning, noon, and in the evening. The same treatment will cure whitlows, and all injuries of tips of fingers. As soon as pain and redness appear, the fingers should be soaked for ten minutes in camphorated sweet-oil. The relief is said to be immediate, and three applications are generally enough to afford a cure.

To Prevent and Cure Ulcers.—1. Dried and pulverized clay applied to an ulcer will cure it in a short time, and leave no scar.

2. Petroleum has been used, with good results, as an external application to ulcers and wounds. It may be used undiluted or diluted with equal parts of oil or glycerine.

3. Ulcers caused by cyanide of potassium, so much used by photographers, may be guarded against by rubbing the hands, when soiled with it, with a mixture of photo-sulphate of iron reduced to a very fine powder, and linseed oil.

Felons—Eight Thoroughly-Tested Cures.—1. Take a pint of common soft soap, and stir in air-slaked lime till it is of the consistency of glazier's putty. Make a leather thimble, fill it with this composition, and insert the fingers therein, and a cure is certain.

2. As soon as the parts begin to swell, get the tincture of lobelia, and wrap the part affected with a cloth saturated thoroughly with the tincture, and the felon is dead. An old physician says he has known it to cure in scores of cases, and it never fails if applied in season.

---

* Dr. Walter Palmer.

3. As soon as the disease is felt, put directly over the spot a fly blister, about the size of your thumb-nail, and let it remain for six hours, at the expiration of which time, directly under the surface of the blister, may be seen the felon, which can be instantly taken out with the point of a needle or a lancet.

4. When the felon first appears, procure some poke root, and roast a piece sufficient to cover your finger. When it is roasted tender, cut it open and bind it on the felon as hot as can be borne; repeat this when the root becomes dry, until the pain subsides. If the felon is too far advanced to "put back," this same remedy will hasten it on and cure it in a few days, as it softens the skin.

5. Probe the swelling of the finger, making a small incision where the pain appears greatest. The pain of the operation may be lessened by the local application of ether or inhalation of chloroform. The after-treatment is equally simple. The small wound is to be covered with lint and carbolic acid, and bathed morning and evening in tepid water. In a few days it is perfectly healed.

6. Take an earthen crock, put in a quantity of live coals, throw on a handful each of hops, rye flour, and brown sugar; then steam the affected part for about fifteen minutes, repeating two or three times, by holding it over the vessel. The better way is to bore a hole through a board, thus having the affected part only coming in contact with the steam. This is guaranteed as a certain cure.

7. Elder Evans, the Shaker, says: "For the past ten years we have treated felons with hot water, and with unerring success. No cutting, no blistering, no any thing, but immersing the finger, hand, or even the whole arm if necessary, in water as hot as can be borne, until the pain is gone, and the core is loosened and drawn from the bone. When rusty nails have produced wounds, the same course has been pursued. If on the hand or foot, keep it in hot water."

8. Take the root of the plant known as dragon root, Jack-in-the-pulpit, or Indian turnip, either green or dry; grate about one half a teaspoonful into four tablespoonfuls of sweet milk; simmer gently a few minutes, then thicken with bread crumbs, and apply as hot as possible. This can be heated again two or three times, adding a little milk each time. If the felon is just starting, this will drive it back; if somewhat advanced, it will draw it out quickly and gently. It is well to put a little tallow on the poultice, especially after opening, to prevent sticking. This same poultice is good for a carbuncle or any other rising.

Cancers—Important Methods of Prevention and Relief.—1. Gastric juice has effected remarkable cures. External applications must be made three times a day for about twenty days. The first application causes much pain, but this may be lessened by the use of almond oil.

2. Several cases of cancer, and other malignant tumors, have been speedily cured by the application of acetic acid. In some instances of cure by this prescription, the cancers and tumors had been of long standing.

3. Take an egg and break it; pour out the white, retaining the yoke in the shell; put in salt, and mix with the yoke as long as it will receive it; stir them together until the salve is formed; put a portion of this on a piece of sticking-plaster, and apply to the cancer about twice a day.

4. The exquisite pain which belongs to open cancer is found to be best relieved by the stramonium ointment which is employed in London. The following is the formula: Half a pound of fresh stramonium leaves, and two pounds of lard; mix the bruised leaves with the lard, and expose to a mild heat until the leaves become friable, and strain through lint. The ointment thus prepared is spread upon lint, and the dressing changed three times a day.*

5. A large majority of the cases of cancerous tumors may be cured, or entirely arrested and brought within safe limits, by the following management:

(1.) Wear a wet compress, covered with half a dozen thicknesses of dry flannel, every night over the tumor.

(2.) Go out much in the sun.

(3.) Breathe *full* of the purest air day and night.

(4.) Eat the best beef and bread, and no trash.

(5.) Go to bed at eight o'clock, and sleep as long as possible. Lie down an hour in the middle of every day, and try to sleep.

(6.) Cultivate a cheerful, jolly temper.

(7.) Exercise freely every day in the open air.

(8.) Keep your skin open by a regular morning bath in soap and water.

Treatment of Scabies.—With regard to the efficacy of sulphur in the treatment of this disease, Dr. Carl H. Smith, of Kenton, Ohio, writes the Boston *Medical and Surgical Journal* that he has employed it, mixed with glycerine, to the consistence of an ointment, in upwards of five hundred cases, in civil and army practice, with unfailing success. In three or four days the disease disappeared, in every instance, one or two applications having been made daily.

Whooping-Cough—Two Views of Giving Medicine.—1. Dr. Arnold, of Maryland, discussed recently, at a meeting of the Medical Association, the question of whooping-cough, in the following strain: "I am more and more impressed with the little reliability of therapeutic remedies in this disease. We have so many medicines presented for our acceptance; some based upon

---

* *Medical and Surgical Reporter.*

certain pathological theories; some upon no theory at all, and others upon a delusion. In my own family this disease prevailed; I did nothing for it, and it got well in six weeks. If I had used medicines I would have thought that I had cured it. We know nothing of its cause; there is great diversity in regard to its pathology, and no unanimity of treatment. Many popular remedies are in use, but in bad cases no remedy seems to be of any great benefit."

2 T. Prestwick, in the *Lancet*, (December 9, 1871,) reports over thirty cases showing the value of cod-liver oil in whooping-cough. The improvement following the use of the oil in his practice has been such that he considers it as a specific for whooping-cough. As the spasmodic attacks of this complaint are almost always preceded by inflammatory or catarrhal symptoms, these he treats in the usual manner, and afterward administers the oil. It is a remarkable circumstance that not one death has occurred when the oil has been administered and has been retained on the stomach.

Croup—Six Methods of Instant Relief.—One teaspoonful of molasses and a teaspoonful of goose-oil, given to a child inclined to the croup, will generally relieve it at once.

For speedy relief, take a knife or grater, and shave or grate off in small particles about a teaspoonful of alum; mix it with about twice the quantity of sugar or honey, to make it palatable, and administer as quickly as possible. This will give almost instant relief.

A lady correspondent of the *Maine Farmer* says the following is an effective remedy for croup: "Half a teaspoonful of pulverized alum in a little molasses. It is a simple remedy, one almost always at hand, and one dose seldom fails to give relief. If it should, repeat it after one hour."

French physicians claim the discovery of a perfect cure for croup in flour of sulphur exhibited in water. M. Lagauterie gives in croup teaspoonful doses of a mixture of sulphur and water (a teaspoonful to a glass of water) every hour with wonderful effects. Seven severe cases were cured in two days.

J. K. Holloway, M.D., in a letter to the *Medical and Surgical Journal*, describes the successful cure of a very extreme case of croup by causing the patient to inhale the evaporations of lime-water. The patient had been suffering for thirty-six hours with membraneous croup, and without relief from other medicines. No time was to be lost. Lime unslaked was put into a pitcher. A blanket was then so thrown over the patient and the pitcher as to cause the inhalation of the free lime vapor. In twenty minutes the patient was fully relieved.

Dr. D. W. Williams, of Liverpool, communicates the following to the *British Medical Journal* on the use of quinine in croup:—

"In 1862 I examined the trachea of three children who died of croup, and found the mucous membrane covered with a yellowish-white substance like gruel, (muco-putriform matter,) the membrane itself being reddened. A crowquill could have been passed down the tube without touching the substance which lined its walls. There was nothing like blocking, nothing like tubes of false membranes, (lymph,) yet my little patient died of slow suffocation.

"While thinking of these cases, one of my own children took the croup. The usual remedies were adopted; but in a few hours the result could be but too easily foretold; she was slowly choking. The restlessness and anxiety so well known was great, and I asked myself these questions : 'Is this child dying from inflammation and blocking of the trachea, or from a blood-poison, which manifests itself in local inflammation and spasms?' Inclining to the latter opinion, I gave her a grain of quinine, a large dose for a child twelve months old. In twenty minutes the relief was surprising; the restlessness, etc., abated. In an hour a second grain was given, and the child fell asleep, and made an excellent recovery, the quinine being continued in smaller doses. Since this I have treated several cases in the same way, with similar result. In bronchitis and pneumonia also, I find quinine of great value when the distress is out of proportion to the amount of disease."

Hay-fever—Class of Persons Affected.—In a book entitled "Experimental Researches on the Causes and Nature of Catarrhus Æstivus," (Hay-fever or Hay-asthma,) Mr. Blackley published some very interesting conclusions respecting this singular disease. He finds that it is peculiar to the educated classes, but is not aristocratic, like the gout, being more common in proportion to the spread of mental culture and the intensity of intellectual occupation. And yet a highly-organized state of the mind is not the only element in its propagation, for race-qualities seem to have a marked effect upon it. Thus in Europe, it is most common in England, after which follow Germany, France, Belgium, Switzerland, Scotland, Italy, Russia, and Ireland. Climate, therefore, has no influence upon its propagation, for England and Ireland, which are geographically contiguous, form the extremes of the above list. Out of 152 patients, 81 were English, 36 Germans, and only 1 Irish.

Hay-fever—Causes.—As to the actual inciting cause of the disease, it has been referred to summer heat, dust, ozone, the odors of flowers, the pollen of blossoms, and especially of grasses. The author's experiments led him to the conclusion that it is to the pollen of flowering plants (including grasses) that the disease is due. He collected pollen-grains from the atmosphere, and gives curves showing the number of grains which gathered on a square centimeter of surface, from May 28 to August 1, 1866—the highest number, 880, falling on June 28.

Hay-fever—Localities Most Affected.—By using kites he ascertained the proportionate amount of pollen at high levels in the atmosphere, with the somewhat remarkable result, that at 1,500 feet above the earth the pollen was found to be more abundant than on the surface. The author found that germs and spores of other plants generally outnumbered the pollen, and he thinks that "if these should resemble pollen in its capacity for absorbing water and discharging granular matter under the influence of moisture, we may have a form of finely-divided vegetable and animal matter thrown into the air which the best modern instruments might fail to discover the nature and origin of, but which might, nevertheless, be a powerful cause of disease." As to the places least likely to be affected by the disease, the author found hay-fever least common in those localities where pollen is least likely to be plentiful, such as the centers of large cities, the sea-shore, and high-lying districts given up to pasturage.

Remedies for Hay-fever.—Dr. George M. Beard, in a new treatise on the subject of hay-fever, expresses the opinion (formed after extensive observation and investigation concerning over two hundred cases) that the disease is not amenable to any specific remedy; that the leading indications are prevention—avoidance of heat, light, worry, dust, vegetable and animal irritants, and other exciting causes, fortifying the system by tonics, before and during the attack, and relieving the symptoms by sedatives and anodynes; indications which are best met by resort to the sea-shore or to a sea-voyage, high latitudes, and—for those who cannot avail themselves of such changes —cool, closed, dark rooms.

Eruptive Fevers.—For the early stages, when the skin is hot, a warm bath, or tepid sponging will be useful. Cleanse the eyes and nostrils with water and a piece of lint as often as necessary. If small-pox, and the pustules have burst, this is all that is practicable. Light poultices to the face will prevent pitting. To allay itching, oil the pustules on the face and neck with olive-oil and cold cream. The same will apply in scarlet-fever. In small-pox, the nurse must examine the body; and if she finds any signs of abscesses forming, should report to the physician; she should, also, use every precaution against bed-sores.

Symptoms and Preventives of Fever.—Fevers, and many acute diseases, are often preceded by a loss of appetite, headache, shivering, "pains in the bones," indisposition to work, etc. In such cases, sponge with tepid water, and rub the body till all aglow. Go to bed, place hot bricks to the feet, take nothing but a little gruel, or beef-tea, and drink moderately of warm, cream-of-tartar water. If you do not feel better the next morning, call a physician. If that be impossible, take a dose of castor-oil, or Epsom-salts.

Relief of Sea-sickness.—A distinguished physician writes: "In the greater number of instances I allow the stomach to discharge its contents once or twice, and then, if there is no organic disease, I give five drops of chloroform in a little water, and, if necessary, repeat the dose in four or six hours. The almost instant effect of this treatment, if conjoined with a few simple precautions, is to cause an immediate sensation, as it were, of warmth in the stomach, accompanied by almost total relief of the nausea and sickness, likewise curing the distressing headache, and usually causing a quiet sleep, from which the passenger awakes quite well."

To Avoid Sea-sickness.—While sitting, avoid resting the feet on the floor. Be seated so that the roll of the ship shall not pitch you forward or backward, but from side to side. Whenevever the premonitory symptoms of sea-sickness occur, do not fix attention on any near object; omit reading or writing; go to meals regularly; eat sparingly, of plain food.

Temporary Relief for Neuralgia.— 1. A New Hampshire gentleman says: "Take two large table-spoonfuls of cologne, and two tea-spoonfuls of fine salt; mix them together in a small bottle; every time you have any acute affection of the facial nerves, or neuralgia, simply breathe the fumes into your nose from the bottle, and you will be immediately relieved."

2. Prepare horse-radish by grating and mixing in vinegar, the same as for the table, and apply to the temple, when the face or head is affected; or to the wrist, when the pain is in the arm or shoulder.

Cure of Stammering.—The effectual cure mainly depends upon the determination of the sufferer to carry out the following rule: Keep the teeth close together, and before attempting to speak, inspire deeply; then give time for quiet utterance, and, after very slight practice, the hesitation will be relieved. No spasmodic action of the lower jaw must be permitted to separate the teeth when speaking.

MISCELLANEOUS HEALTH NOTES.

Pine Woods and Health.—The pleasant odor emitted by fir-trees in a sunny atmosphere has long been thought serviceable to invalids, and the vicinity of pine woods has been declared salubrious.

Danger of Cold Water in the Face.—It is dangerous to wash the face in cold water when much heated. It is not dangerous, but pleasantly efficacious, if warm water is used.

A Most Refreshing Bath.—Sun baths cost nothing, and are the most refreshing, life-giving baths that one can take, whether sick or well. Read carefully our chapter on "Sunlight and Health."

To Prevent Harm from Drinking Cold Water.—It is a very safe rule to wet your wrists before drinking cold water if at all heated. The effect is immediate and grateful, and the danger of fatal results may be warded off by this simple precaution.

How to Avoid Pneumonia.—Never allow yourself to be chilled "through and through;" it is this which destroys so many every year, in a few days' sickness, from pneumonia, called by some lung-fever, or inflammation of the lungs.

Position After Being Tired.—If very tired physically, lie on the back knees drawn up, the hands clasped above the head, or resting on the elbows, the fore-arm at right angles, and the hands hanging over by the bend of the wrists.

Opening Abscesses Under Water.—According to the Vienna correspondent of the *Chicago Medical Examiner*, opening abscesses and buboes under water, and applying plaster of Paris, is being tried there with satisfactory results.

Pie-crust and Dyspepsia.—Whoever eats heavy pie-crust commits a crime against his physical well-being, and must pay the penalty. The good house-wife should see to it that all pastry and cakes are light; no others should be eaten.

Little Things and Health.—The little causes must be looked for. There are the little errors in diet, the little violations in our habits of exercise, study, sleep, dress, etc., etc. The wise and prudent will carefully attend to the *little* things.

Guarding against Diphtheria.—People cannot be too careful in regard to diphtheria. No disease is so difficult to guard against after it has once entered a household. But where people live comfortably and cleanly, slight precautions are sufficient to keep it away entirely.

Eating at Certain Intervals.—After fifty years of age, if not a day-laborer, and sedentary persons after forty, should eat but twice a day—in the morning and about four in the afternoon; persons can soon accustom themselves to a seven hours' interval between eating, thus giving the stomach rest, for every organ without adequate rest will "give out" prematurely.

Time Required for Digesting Food.—The following is the time required to digest certain articles of food: 1 pound of meat, 3 hours; cheese, $3\frac{1}{2}$ hours; milk, 2 hours; eggs, 3 hours; veal, 4 hours; fowls, 4 hours; pork, 4 hours; tripe, 1 hour; bread, $3\frac{1}{2}$ hours; boiled potatoes, $3\frac{1}{2}$ hours, roasted, 2 hours; cabbage, $4\frac{1}{2}$ hours; beans, $2\frac{1}{2}$ hours.

Cold or Warm Drinks.—Whoever drinks no liquors at all, will add years of pleasurable existence to his life. Of cold or warm drinks, the former are the most pernicious. Drinking at meals induces people to eat more than they otherwise would, as any one can verify by experiment, and it is excess in eating that devastates the land with sickness, suffering, and death.

Miscellaneous Health Notes.

How to Remove Bitter Taste.—To swallow a pill, place it under the tip of the tongue and take a drink of water. The largest will go down almost without knowing it. The taste left in the mouth after taking such bitter medicines as quinine, aloes, etc., is instantly neutralized by chewing a piece of liquorice root.

Most Healthful Seat in a Car.—Other things being equal, the forward seats in a street or railway car are the most healthful. The forward motion of the car causes a current of air backward, carrying with it the exhalations from the lungs of the forward passengers. In all cases avoid as much as possible inhaling another's "breath."

Causes of Lung Congestion.—The causes that produce congestion of the lungs are—cold feet, tight clothing, costive bowels, sitting still until chilled after being warmed with labor or a rapid walk, going too suddenly from a close room into the air, especially after speaking, too hasty walking, or running to catch a train, etc.

Spread of Pestilence is possible through the rag-picker, who takes contagion to the very door of the rich man. The breath of the wretched beggar, craving arms of the lady at her carriage-step, may waft to her the seeds of death. The little street-wanderer, in brushing past your child, may render vain the anxious care of years. The highly-recommended nurse-maid may carry the infant into scenes and atmospheres the most dangerous.

Sewing-Machines and Health.—Dr. Decaisne (*L' Union Medicale*) states, after a careful investigation of the cases of six hundred and sixty-one female operatives upon the sewing-machine, that they were not more subject than other working-women to disease, and that certain other cases which had been reported were evidently simple coincidences, and the results of labor too severe for the women's strength.

A Specific for Scrofula.—Cranberry wine, taken internally and applied externally, is announced as a cure for scrofula. To make the wine, take the ripe berries, mash them in a mortar to a fine pulp, put into a stone jar, add one quart of water to two quarts of berries, stir it well, set away and let it stand a week; then strain it through cotton, and you have a beautiful wine, which, with a little sugar, makes at once a cooling and palatable drink. It does not ferment.

Important Suggestion to Parents about Sitting.—A very common position in sitting, especially among men, is with the shoulders against the chair-back, with a space of several inches between the chair-back and the lower portion of the spine, giving the body the shape of a half hoop; it is the instantaneous, instinctive, and almost universal position assumed by any consumptive on sitting down, unless counteracted by an effort of the will·

hence parents should regard such a position in their children with apprehension, and should rectify it at once.

Improper Sitting and its Evils.—Consumptive people, and all afflicted with spinal deformities, sit habitually crooked, in one or more curves of the body. There was a time in all these when the body had its natural erectness, when there was not the first departure on the road to death. The make of our chairs, especially that great barbarism the unwieldy and disease-engendering rocking-chair, favors these diseases, and undoubtedly, in some instances, leads to bodily habits from which originate the ailments just named, to say nothing of piles, fistula, and the like. The painful or sore feeling which many are troubled with incessantly for years at the extremity of the backbone, is the result of sitting in such a position that it rests upon the seat of the chair at a point several inches forward of the chair-back.

Chewing Between Meals.—The habit of chewing substances of any kind between meals is always harmful to health. The chewing over-taxes the organs which secrete the saliva, and exhaust them so that the chief agent in promoting the digestion of food is diminished in quantity and efficiency. The act of chewing always excites the flow of saliva. Persons who chew gum soon become sensible of the exhaustion and fatigue of the salivary glands. The same is true of those who chew tobacco. In order to the best condition of these glands they should rest " between meals."

Remedy for Feverishness.—When persons are feverish and thirsty beyond what is natural, indicated in some cases by a metallic taste in the mouth, one of the best "coolers" is to take a lemon, cut off the top, sprinkle over it some loaf-sugar, working it down into the lemon with a spoon, and then suck it slowly. Invalids with feverishness may take two or three lemons a day in this manner with most marked benefit, manifested by a sense of coolness, comfort, and invigoration. A lemon or two thus taken at "tea-time" is for some an excellent substitute for the ordinary supper in summer.

Cause and Cure of Leanness.—Leanness may be caused by insufficient food, or over-exertion, or both. But the usual cause is disease; the vital powers being more occupied in removing impurities and poisons, and overcoming abnormal conditions, than in digesting and assimilating nutrient material. The patient should eat all the plain nutritious food that he can assimilate. Those lean persons who are not accustomed to fruit will find baked sweet apples a good addition to each meal to begin with. Oat-meal mush, with a slice of wheat-meal bread, and two or three baked apples, make a breakfast with which any lean individual may be justly content.

Cure of Obesity.—The diet advised for fat persons, by the best authorities, consists of food containing a large percentage of nitrogen, to which some vegetables without starch, and cooked fruit are to be added, for the purpose of moderating the excitation due to animal nourishment. Beer is forbidden. Use very little sugar. Cheese, potatoes, rice, beans, peas, maize, macaroni, tapioca, arrowroot, and soups are not allowed. The use of sulphate of soda is recommended, as moderating the transformation of nitrogenous materials and stimulating the oxidation of fat; and the use of mineral waters containing the sulphate of soda in solution is considered of the greatest importance in this respect. The waters of Marienbad,* which are especially rich in this salt, are stated to have, usually, the most happy effect. Their use, together with that of some alkaline pills, and a strict adherence to the conditions above mentioned, caused a decrease in weight of from twenty-five to sixty pounds in different individuals in the course of a few weeks.

Chief Causes of Sudden Death.—Very few of the sudden deaths which are said to arise from diseases of the heart do really arise from that cause. To ascertain the real origin of sudden deaths, an experiment was tried and reported to a Scientific Congress at Strasburg. Sixty-six cases of sudden death were made the subject of a thorough post-mortem examination; in these cases only two were found who died from disease of the heart. Nine out of sixty-six had died from apoplexy, while there were forty-six cases of congestion of the lungs—that is, the lungs were so full of blood they could not work, there not being room enough for a sufficient quantity of air to enter to support life.

Medical Qualities of Pumpkins.—A prominent physician of New York city, speaking of the properties of pumpkins, says that in his travels in Syria he found pumpkin-seeds almost universally eaten by the people on account of their supposed medical qualities. Not because they are diuretic, but as an antidote against animalculæ which infest the bowels. They are sold in the streets as apples and nuts are here.

It is a medical fact that persons can be cured of tape-worm by the use of pumpkin-seeds. The outer skin being removed, the seeds are bruised in a mortar into an oily, pasty mass. It is swallowed by the patient after fasting some hours, and it takes the place of chyle in the stomach, and the tapeworm lets go its hold on the membrane and becomes gorged with this substance, and in some measure, probably, torpid. Then a large dose of castor-oil is administered, and the worms are ejected before they are enabled to renew their hold.

To Keep White Hands.—Our readers need not suffer from having their hands affected by water or soapsuds if the hands are dipped in vinegar-water or lemon-juice immediately after. The acid destroys the corrosive effect of the alkali, and makes the hands soft and white.

A Good Tooth-wash.—Dissolve two ounces of borax in three pints of

---

* Mr. Schind, in *Harpers' Weekly.*

boiling water, and before it is cold add one or two teaspoonfuls of spirits of camphor, and bottle for use. A tablespoonful mixed with an equal quantity of tepid water, and applied daily with a soft brush, purifies and beautifies the teeth, tends to prevent the formation of tartar, and induces a healthy action of the gums.

To Remove Moth from the Face.—The principal causes of moth spots are biliousness, and a torpid liver. A distinguished and successful physician prescribes this remedy: "Put ten drops of elixir of vitriol into half a tumbler of water, and drink the whole dilution twice daily."

Pimples on the Face.—Pimples about the face are extremely common and very annoying. Dr. Dio Lewis writes: "The number of persons who have written me about this difficulty must be thousands. In the absence of any definite information about the particular condition of the general health, I have always to say that the only remedy is to be sought in the improvement in the systematic tone. Eating in moderate quantities nourishing and simple food, keeping the bowels regular, exercising and sleeping wisely; in brief, observing the laws of health, elevating and purifying the system, is the only cure. The skin must be thoroughly bathed with soap and water every night on going to bed, or every morning, as may be more convenient."

To Strengthen the Hair.—Dilute an ounce of borax and an ounce of camphor in two quarts of water, and wash the hair thoroughly twice a week, clipping the ends off occasionally. It will quickly grow long, thick, and even.

To Cool a Room.—Wet a cloth of any size, the larger the better, and suspend it in the room. Let the ventilation be good, and the temperature will sink from ten to twenty degrees in less than an hour.

Protection from Damp Walls.—Boil one pound of powdered sulphur in two quarts of water for half an hour. Apply with a brush while still warm, and you will prevent the damp and unwholesome oozings from the brick walls of your workshops.

To Make a Good Court-Plaster.—Balsam of benzoin one part, alcohol twelve parts, mix—then isinglass two parts, and water barely sufficient to dissolve. Strain the two solutions separately, then mix them. For use, place the bottle in warm water, and give the silk, previously strained on rollers, ten or twelve coats with a brush; when dry, give it a coat of the following: Ohio turpentine one part, tincture of benzoin two parts.

To Relieve Whooping-Cough.—Dr. Snow has suggested the use of *carbolate of lime*. It has apparently produced a marked effect in diminishing the frequency and severity of the paroxysms of coughing. Small quantities of the carbolate of lime are placed in saucers in the room where the child sleeps; merely sufficient to make the odor perceptible. The odor is like coal tar, and if not too strong is not unpleasant. The carbolate of lime is about the same price as chloride of lime, and for all disinfecting purposes is far more valuable than the chloride of lime.

Diphtheria—Its Symptoms.—Diphtheria is a kind of sore throat in which matter exudes from the mucous membrane. This stiffens into a peculiar white substance, patches of which may be seen in the back part of the mouth. Fever and debility accompany the disease, which is so sudden and insidious in its advances as to be exceedingly dreaded.

Cause of Diphtheria.—Recents reports go to show that the principal causes of this ailment are polluted wells, foul and wet cellars, or no cellar at all; and bad sewage, and cold, wet lands seem to afford the most favorable conditions for its existence. A preceding summer's drought, with ensuing low water in the wells and springs, have been noticed in connection with epidemic prevalence. In one family, two fatal cases originated during extreme lowness of the water in the well, and while the water looked milky, and was refused by the cow, that would suffer thirst for days before she would drink it.

Treatments of Diphtheria.—1. The neck should be wrapped in a wet bandage and covered with red flannel or a woolen stocking. Gargle the throat with a solution of a teaspoonful of salt in a pint of water, or thirty grains of chlorate of potash in a wine-glass of water.

2. Treatment consists in thoroughly swabbing the back of the throat with a wash made thus: "Table salt, two drachms; black pepper, golden seal, nitrate of potash, alum, one dram each. Mix and pulverize, put into a tea-cup, which half fill with boiling water, stir well, and then fill up with good vinegar. Use every half hour, one, two, and four hours, as recovery progresses. The patient may swallow a little each time. Apply an ounce each of spirits turpentine, sweet oil, and aqua ammonia, mixed, to the whole of the throat and to the breast bone every four hours, keeping flannel to the parts.

3. A simple and successful treatment of diphtheria may be found in the use of lemon juice. Gargle the throat freely with it, at the same time swallowing a portion, so as to reach all the affected parts. A French physician claims that he saved his own life with this pleasant remedy.

4. It is said that diphtheria may be speedily arrested, and sometimes cured, by swallowing lumps of ice, *continuously*, until relief is afforded; let them, as much as possible, melt in the throat. Common sore throat is cured in the same way sometimes.

5. A treatment which has the advantage of being short, if nothing else, consists in simply using a gargle of phenic acid and distilled water, with external applications of new flannel; the food and drink to be taken cold.

Infection Carried by Pet Animals.—Hair and fur absorb and retain in a remarkable degree odors, gases, and minute substances discharged into, and transmitted by, the air. Attention has recently been called to a number of cases where scarlet fever has been proved to be conveyed, even after quite a time, from one person to another by pet dogs and cats.

Flies as Poison Carriers.—Similar carriers of contagious material are flies, which with great indifference for the most odious substances, pass quickly from one surface to another, and from any diseased or foul matter to material used for food or drink. They may thus convey, by means of their feet and probosces, one substance to another, and it is, therefore, considered highly probable that the communication of contagious or septic poisons by their agency, is not by any means rare.

To Prevent After-taste of Quinine.—The mastication of some acid fruit, as an apple or a pear, will permanently remove the disagreeable aftertaste of quinine. The first mouthful of food should be well masticated and rolled through the mouth, so as to cleanse the teeth, etc., and then ejected. The second morsel may be swallowed, when it will be discovered that all taste of the quinine will be removed.

Inflation of the Lungs.—Five minutes spent in the open air, after dressing, inflating the lungs by inhaling as full a breath as possible, and gently pounding the breast during the inflation, will greatly enlarge the chest, strengthen the lung power, and very effectually ward off consumption.*

Diet for Dyspeptics.—If inclined to be dyspeptic, avoid mince pie, sausage, and other highly-seasoned food. Beware of eating too freely of soup; better to eat food dry enough to employ the natural saliva of the mouth in moistening it. If inclined to over-eat, partake freely of rice, cracked wheat, and other articles that are easily digested. Eat freely of ripe fruit, and avoid excessive use of meats. Eat at regular hours, and lightly near the hour of going to bed. Eat slowly. Thoroughly masticate the food. Do not wash it down with continual drink while eating.

Personal Health Tests.—New methods are receiving attention in these later years, given to health foods and health methods. Many intelligent writers are furnishing the publishing public with the result of careful and thorough experiments along the line of "practical hygiene." "How many meals shall we eat daily?" Test this for yourself, and do it thoroughly. Remember that as a rule the stomach is overtaxed both in times and quantity. If the new teacher advises the omission of the "breakfast" as a habit, try it and see. If some ministerial friend whose opinion you value tells you that since he adopted the plan of omitting his morning meal until after the morning sermon he preaches with greater vigor of thought to himself and to his congregation than hitherto, and with less tax upon his physical strength, why may you not test the value of the suggestive hint thus received by this statement?

HOME ECONOMICS.

WASTE IN THE KITCHEN.

WASTE in the kitchen is often very great from apparently trivial sources. Housekeepers should read and ponder :—

In cooking meats, the water is thrown out without removing the grease, or the grease from the dripping-pan is thrown away.

Pieces of bread in the bread-box, and cake in the cake-box, are left to dry and mold.

Scraps of meat are thrown away.

Cold potatoes are left to sour and spoil.

Preserves are opened, forgotten, and left to mold and ferment.

Dried fruits are not looked after, and become wormy.

Vinegar and sauce are left standing in tin.

Apples are left to decay for want of "sorting over."

Corks are left out of the molasses and vinegar jugs.

The tea-canister is left open.

Victuals are left exposed to be eaten by mice.

Bones of meat and the carcass of turkey are thrown away, when they could be used in making good soups.

Vegetables and puddings left from the dinner are thrown away.

Sugar, tea, coffee, and rice are carelessly spilled in the handling.

Soap is left to dissolve and waste in the water.

Dish-towels are used for dish-cloths.

Napkins are used for dish-towels.

Towels are used for holders.

Brooms and mops are not hung up.

Coal is wasted by not sifting the ashes.

More coal is burned than necessary, by not arranging dampers when not using the fire.

Lights are left burning when not used.

Tin dishes are not properly cleansed and dried.

Knives and forks get rusty, for want of care.

Nice ones are spoiled by use in the kitchen.

Pails and wash-tubs fall to pieces, because left dry.

Potatoes in the cellar grow, and thus become unfit for eating.

Ashes are thrown out and wasted, when they could be utilized in different ways.

Carpets are swept with stub brooms which wear out the carpet texture.
Good new brooms are used in scrubbing the kitchen-floors.
Sheets are scorched and injured by being used in ironing.
Silver spoons are used in scraping kettles.
Good forks are used and ruined in toasting bread.
The flour is sifted in a wasteful manner, or the bread-pan left with dough sticking to it.
Pie-crust is left and laid by to sour, instead of making a few tarts for tea, etc.
Cold puddings are considered good for nothing, when often they can be steamed for the next day, or, in case of rice, made over in other forms.
Vegetables are thrown away that would warm for breakfast nicely.
Cream is left to mould and spoil.
Mustard is left to spoil in the cruse, or rust, etc.
Vinegar is allowed to stand until the tin vessel becomes corroded and spoiled.
Pickles become spoiled by the leaking out or evaporation of the vinegar.
Pork spoils for want of salt, and beef because the brine wants scalding.
Hams become tainted, or filled with vermin, for the want of care.
Cheese molds, and is eaten by mice or vermin.
Lard is not well tried in the fall, and becomes tainted.
Tea and coffee-pots are injured on the stove.
Soap-suds are thrown away instead of being used as a valuable addition to the soil in the garden.
Potatoes are "peeled" before boiling, thus losing a large fraction of the substance. It is much more economical to boil before the rind is removed; then only the *thin* rind is lost.
Wooden-ware is unscalded, and left to warp and crack.
N. B.—The above list is partial. It could easily be extended.

KITCHEN FURNITURE.—CLEANING.

Heating New Iron.—*New iron* should be very gradually heated at first. After it has become inured to the heat, it is not so likely to crack.

To Prevent Crust in Tea-kettles.—Keep an oyster-shell in your tea-kettle. By attracting the stony particles to itself, it will prevent the formation of a crust.

To Clean Tea-kettles.—Kerosene will make your tea-kettle as bright as new. Saturate a woolen rag and rub with it. It will also remove stains from clean varnished furniture.

Glass should be washed in cold water, which gives it a brighter and clearer look than when cleansed with warm water.

Glass Vessels, and other utensils, may be purified and cleaned by rinsing them out with powdered charcoal.

To Clean Coal-oil Cans.—After cleansing them as much as possible with wood ashes and hot water, use nitric-acid in moderate quantities, which will soon remove the difficulty.

Washing Knives and Forks.—Do not let knives be dropped into hot dish-water. It is a good plan to have a large tin pot to wash them in, just high enough to wash the blades *without wetting* the handles.

To Clean Knives.—Cut a small potato in two; dip one half in the brick-dust, and rub the knives, and rust and stain will disappear like magic from their surfaces.

Scouring Knives.—Place a quantity of brick-dust on a board, and having the knife perfectly dry, press it down hard and rub it back and forth *cross-wise of the blade.* When bright, turn and scour the other side. Then wipe off with chamois leather. Knives thus treated will retain their brightness much longer, and have a *new* look after years of usage.

To Extract Stains from Silver.—Sal ammoniac, one part; vinegar, sixteen parts. Mix and use this liquid with a piece of flannel, then wash the plate in clean water.

Silver Soap.—For cleaning silver and Britannia: One half pound of soap; three tablespoonfuls of spirits of turpentine, and half a tumbler of water. Let it boil ten minutes; add six tablespoonfuls of spirits of hartshorn. Make a suds of this, and wash silver with it.

To Clean Silver.—Cleansing silver is not an easy task; the use of kerosene will greatly facilitate the operation. Wet a flannel cloth in the oil, dip in dry whiting, and thoroughly rub the plated or silverware; throw it into a dish of scalding soapsuds, wipe with a soft flannel, and polish with a chamois skin.

Another Method of Cleaning Silver.—Silver door-plates are most expeditiously cleaned with a weak solution of ammonia and water; say one teaspoonful of ammonia to a tea-cup of water, applied with a wet rag. It is equally useful in cleaning other silver-plate and gold jewelry.

Cleaning Tinware.—An experienced housekeeper says the best thing for cleaning tinware is common soda. She gives the following directions: Dampen a cloth, and dip in soda, and rub the ware briskly, after which wipe dry. Any blackened ware can be made to look as well as new.

To Clean Tin Covers.—Get the finest whiting; mix a little of it powdered with the least drop of sweet oil, rub the covers well with it, and wipe them clean; then dust over them some dry whiting in a muslin bag, and rub bright with dry leather. This last is to prevent rust, which the cook must guard against by wiping them dry, and putting them by the fire when they come from the dining-room, for if but once hung up damp the inside will rust.

To Polish Tins.—First rub them with a damp cloth; then take dry flour and rub it on with the hands; afterward take an old newspaper and rub the flour off, and the tins will shine as well as if half an hour had been spent rubbing them with brick-dust or powder, which spoils the hands.

Papier-Mache Articles should be washed with a sponge and cold water, without soap, dredged with flour while damp, and polished with a flannel.

Japanned Ware.—Wet a sponge in warm water, and dampen it over; then wipe off with a soft cloth. If a tray becomes spotted, take a bit of woolen cloth and dip into a little sweet oil, and rub it as hard as possible, and the marks, if effaceable, will disappear.

Cleaning Floor-boards.—Scrubbing them with a mixture made by dissolving unslaked lime in boiling water, will have the desired effect. The proportions are, two tablespoonfuls to a quart of water. No soap need be used.

Another Method.—Lime, one part; sand, three parts; soft soap, two parts. Lay a little on the boards with a scrubbing-brush, and rub thoroughly. Rinse with clean water, and rub dry. This will keep the boards of a good color, and will also keep away vermin.

To Clean Painted Wainscot, or Other Wood-work.—Fuller's earth will be found cheap and useful; and on wood not painted, it forms an excellent substitute for soap.

Cleaning Old Brass.—The best liquid for cleaning old brass is a solution of oxalic acid.

To Clean a Brass Kettle.—Do this before using it for cooking; use salt and vinegar.

To Clean Brasses, Britannia Metals, Tins, Coppers, Etc.—These are cleaned with a mixture of rotten-stone, soft-soap, and oil of turpentine, mixed to the consistency of stiff putty. The stone should be powdered very fine and sifted; and a quantity of the mixture may be made sufficient to last for a long while. The articles should first be washed with hot water, to remove grease. Then a little of the above mixture, mixed with water, should be rubbed over the metal; then rub off briskly, with dry, clean rag, or leather, and a beautiful polish will be obtained.

To Keep Iron from Rusting.—Kerosene applied by means of a moistened cloth to stoves, will effectually keep them from rusting during the summer. It is also an excellent material to apply to all iron utensils used about the farm. Give plows, cultivators, and the like, a coating before they are put away in the fall.

Paper for Cleaning Stoves, Tinware, Furniture, Etc.—After a stove has been blackened, it can be kept looking very well for a long time by rubbing it with paper every morning. Rubbing with paper is a much nicer way of keeping the outside of a tea-kettle, coffee-pot, and tea-pot, bright and clean, than the old way of washing them with suds. Rubbing with paper is also the best way of polishing knives, tinware, and spoons; they shine like new silver. For polishing mirrors, windows, lamp-chimneys, etc., paper is better than a dry cloth.

Cleansing Bottles.—Many persons clean bottles by putting in some small shot, and shaking them around. Water dissolves lead to a certain extent, and a film of this lead attaches itself to the sides of the bottle so closely that the shaking or rinsing with water does not detach it, and it remains to be dissolved by any liquid which has the least sourness in it, and if drank, lead poison may be the result. Sometimes a shot becomes wedged in at the bottom of a bottle, to be dissolved by wine or cider. Therefore, it is better to wash every bottle as soon as emptied with warm water and wood ashes, or saleratus, and put the bottle away, mouth open and downward; but be careful to wash again when used, as flies and other insects frequently get into open bottles. Or, chop up a large potato very fine, and put it into the bottle with some warm water, and shake it rapidly until it is clean.

SOAPS AND WASHING FLUIDS.

Hard Soap.—Five pails soft soap, two pounds salt, and one pound resin. Simmer together, and when thoroughly fused, turn out in shallow pans so as to be easily cut.

Soft Soap.—Boil twenty-five pounds of fried grease in two pails of strong lye. Next day add another pailful of hot lye; also on the following day, if there is grease on the top of the soap. Afterward add a pailful of hot water each day until the barrel is filled.

Excellent Soft Soap.—Take 16 quarts of lye of sufficient strength to float an egg; 8 pounds of clean grease; 1½ pounds resin; put the whole into a five-pail kettle and boil it. At first it is apt to rise, in which case add a little strong lye, and so continue to do until the materials are incorporated. Then remove it from the fire, and add, by degrees, weak lye, stirring it at every addition, till the kettle is full.

Common Hard Soap.—Put in an iron kettle five pounds unslaked lime, five pounds soda, and three gallons soft water; let it soak over night; in the morning pour off the water, then add three and a half pounds of grease, boil till thick, turn into a pan until cool, and then cut in bars.

Labor-Saving Soap.—Take two pounds sal-soda, two pounds yellow bar-soap, and ten quarts of water; cut the soap into thin slices, and boil together two hours; strain, and it will be fit for use. Put the clothes to soak the night before you wash, and to every pail of water in which you boil them add a pound of soap. They will need no rubbing; merely rinse them out, and they will be perfectly white and clean.

Honey Soap.—Cut thin two pounds of yellow soap into a double sauce-pan, occasionally stirring it till it is melted, which will be in a few minutes, if the water is kept boiling around it; then add a quarter of a pound of palm-oil, quarter of a pound of honey, ten cents' worth of true oil of cinnamon; let all boil together another six or eight minutes; pour out and stand it by till next day, it is then fit for immediate use.

Using Soap.—Hard soap is fittest for washing clothes, and soft soap for floors. It is a good plan to soap your dirtiest clothes, and soak them over night in soft water. If you are at a loss to procure soft water for washing, fill a barrel half full of wood ashes, and fill it up with water, and you will have a lye whenever you want it. A gallon of strong lye put into a great boiler of hard water, will make it quite soft. Some use pearl-ash, or pot-ash; but either injures the texture of the cloth.

Suggestions.—A tablespoonful of turpentine boiled with white clothes, will greatly aid the whitening process.

Boiling starch is much improved by the addition of sperm, or salt, or both, or a little gum-arabic, dissolved.

Washing Fluid.—Five pounds of sal-soda, one pound of borax, one-half pound of fresh unslaked lime, four ounces of liquid ammonia. Pour one gallon of boiling water upon the soda and borax; when it has dissolved and has cooled, add the ammonia. Slake the lime in one gallon of hot water, and let it stand until entirely settled, when the clear fluid must be carefully poured off. Turn it upon the solution of soda and borax, and add to the mixture eight gallons of cold water. Put the clothes to soak the night before washing-day, with six tablespoonfuls of this fluid to a tub full of clothes.

To Make Hard Water Soft.—Dissolve one pound of white rock pot-ash in one gallon of water, and then use half a gill of the preparation to a tub of water.

To Clear Muddy Water.—A little dissolved alum is very effective in clearing muddy water. If thrown into a tub of soap-suds, the soap, curdled and accompanied by the muddy particles, sinks to the bottom, leaving the water above clear and pure. In times of scarcity of water this may be used again for washing clothes.

WASHING CLOTHES.

To Clean a White Lace Veil.—Put the veil into a strong lather of white soap and very clear water, and let it simmer slowly for a quarter of an hour. Take it out and squeeze it well, but be sure not to rub it. Rinse it in two cold waters, with a drop or two of liquid blue in the last. Have ready some very clear gum-arabic water, or some thin starch, or rice water. Pass the veil through it, and clear it by clapping. Then stretch it out even, and pin it to dry on a linen cloth, making the edge as straight as possible, opening out all the scallops, and fastening each with pins. When dry, lay a piece of thin muslin smoothly over it, and iron it on the wrong side.

To Wash Fine, Colored Fabrics.—To wash colored stockings, or any delicate colored fabrics, table-linen, lawns, or cambrics, etc., dissolve one tablespoonful of sugar of lead in one gallon water. Soak the articles thoroughly in the solution; then dry.

To Wash Merino Stockings.—Boil the soap to make a lather, wash them in this warm, and rinse in a second lather. If white, mix a little blue. Never rinse in plain water, or use cold water.

To Make the Colors stand in Delicate Hose.—Turn the stockings right side out, and wash in a lather of lukewarm water and white castile soap; then wash the wrong side. If very much soiled, two waters will be required. Rinse in lukewarm water and then in cold water; dry as soon as possible by heat, not by sun. It is better not to iron them, but when nearly dry, smooth and pull them into shape by hand.

To Wash Chintz.—Boil two pounds of rice in two gallons of water till soft, and pour it into a tub; let it stand until it subsides into a moderate warmth; put the chintz in and wash it (without using soap) until the dirt disappears; then boil the same quantity of water and rice as before, but strain off the rice and mix it in warm water. Wash the chintz in this till quite clean; afterward rinse it in the water the rice was boiled in; this will answer for starch, and dew will not affect it.

Washing Prints.—To a sufficient quantity of hot water for washing a dress add a tablespoonful of ox gall. Let the dress remain in this a few minutes, then cool enough to wash out like other prints. Rinse immediately in cold water and dry as quickly as possible in the open air. If there are spots to be removed, apply soap when dry.

Another.—Dissolve half an ounce of alum in sufficient water to rinse two print dresses. Dip your prints in, and when sure that every part is wet, wring them out; then have a warm soapsuds, in which wash quickly and rinse in cold water. Then in second rinsing-water mix your starch, rinse, wring quickly, and hang to dry, not in the sun, but on a line where the wind will dry them quickly. Immediately they are dry enough, iron them; or if this is not convenient, let them get quite dry and iron them through a damp cloth. Prints should never be sprinkled.

To Make Use of Faded Prints.—Dingy print dresses can be bleached and made into something serviceable and pretty. When the season of soap-making approaches, have faded dresses ready to scald in lye. Let them be washed and boiled in hot suds until all the color possible is extracted, then finish the work by scalding with lye, washing with suds, and laying them on the first young grass.

Cleansing Blankets.—Put two large tablespoonfuls of borax and a pint of soft soap into a tub of cold water. When dissolved, put in a pair of blankets, and let them remain over night. Next day, rub and drain them out, and rinse thoroughly in two waters, and hang to dry. Do not wring them.

To Wash Flannel.—Never rub soap upon it. Make a suds by dissolving the soap in warm water. Rinse in warm water; very cold or hot water will shrink flannel. Shake them out several minutes before hanging to dry. Blankets are washed in the same way.

Restoring White Flannel.—To restore the appearance of white flannel which has turned yellowish by lying for a long time or by wear, soak for one hour in a weak solution of bisulphate of soda, then add a little diluted muriatic acid, stir well, and cover the vessel for twenty minutes. After this take the flannel out, rinse in plenty of soft water, and dry in the sun.

Washing Woolen Clothing.—Articles of woolen washed in ordinary soap and water not only shrink, but acquire a peculiar fatty odor, due to the decomposition of the soap by the lactic and acetic acids present in the perspiration, and consequently precipitation of the greater part of the fat of the soap in the fiber of the wool. To prevent these effects steep the articles for several hours in a warm, moderately-concentrated solution of washing soda, then after the addition of warm water and a few drops of ammonia, wash and rinse them in lukewarm water.

How to Wash Table-Linen.—Put a teaspoonful of sugar of lead into two-thirds of a pail of water, and when dissolved, soak the table-linen in it fifteen or twenty minutes. Be careful in wringing the article from this water that there is no cut or sore on the hands, as the sugar of lead is poisonous. Every thing that is liable to fade must be washed quickly, and not allowed to soak in suds or rinsing-water, and hung in a shady place to dry. Never wash flannel, silk, or colored things on a wet or cloudy day, but lay them aside for a fair day; and when washing such articles do not let them stand and soak, but wash, rinse, starch (if needed) and hang out each thing as fast as possible, and then take the next.

To Preserve Clothes-Pins.—Clothes-pins, boiled a few moments, and quickly dried, once or twice a month, become more flexible and durable. Clothes-lines will last longer and keep in better order if occasionally treated in the same way.

STARCHING, FOLDING, AND IRONING.

To Prepare Starch.—Take two tablespoonfuls of starch dissolved in as much water; add a gill of cold water; then add one pint of boiling water, and boil it half an hour, adding a small piece of spermaceti, sugar, or salt; strain, etc. Thin it with water.

Flour Starch.—Mix flour gradually with cold water, so that it may be free from lumps. Stir in cold water till it will pour easily; then stir it into a pot of boiling water, and let it boil five or six minutes, stirring it frequently. A little spermaceti will make it smoother. This starch will answer very well for cotton and linen. *Poland starch* is made in the same manner.

Glue Starch.—Boil a piece of glue, four inches square, in three quarts of water. Keep it in a bottle well corked. Use for calicoes.

Gum-arabic Starch.—Get two ounces of fine, white gum-arabic; pound it to powder; put it into a pitcher, and pour a pint or more of boiling water upon it; cover it well. Let it stand all night, and the next morning pour it carefully from the dregs into a clean bottle; cork it, and keep for use. A tablespoonful stirred into a pint of starch made in the ordinary manner will restore lawns to almost their original freshness; and it is also good for thin white muslin and bobbinet.

Starching Clothes.—Muslins look well when starched, and clapped dry, while the starch is hot, then folded in a damp cloth, till they become quite damp, before ironing them. If muslins are sprinkled, they are apt to be spotted. Some clap muslins, then dry them, and afterward sprinkle them.

Sprinkling Clothes.—They should be sprinkled with clear water and laid in separate piles; one of flannels, one of colored, one of common, and one of fine articles.

Folding Clothes.—Fold the fine articles, and roll them in a towel; then fold the rest, turning them all right side outward. Lay the colored articles separate from the rest. They should not remain damp long, as the colors might be injured. Sheets and table linen should be shaken and folded.

Gloss for Linen.—"Starch Luster" is a substance used for washing purposes, which, when added to starch, causes the linen to which it is applied to assume not only a high polish, but a dazzling whiteness. A portion, of the size of a copper cent, added to half a pound of starch, and boiled with it for two or three minutes, will produce the best results. This substance is nothing more than stearine, paraffine, or wax, colored by a slight admixture of ultramarine blue. The latter may be added at will.

To Make Flat-irons Smooth.—Rub them with clean lard, and wipe dry; or rubbing them with a little beeswax while hot will have the desired effect.

Another.—Rub them with fine salt, and it will make them perfectly smooth.

To Preserve Irons from Rust.—Melt fresh mutton suet, smear over the irons with it while hot, then dust it well with unslaked lime, powdered and tied up in muslin. When not used, wrap the irons in baize, and keep them in a dry place. Use no oil on them at any time except salad oil.

To Remove Starch or Rust from Flat-irons.—Have a piece of yellow beeswax tied in a coarse cloth. When the iron is almost hot enough to use, but not quite, rub it quickly with the beeswax, and then with a clean, coarse cloth. This will remove it entirely.

Ironing.—In ironing a shirt, first do the back, then the sleeves, then the collar and bosom, and then the front. Calicoes should be ironed on the right side, as they thus keep clean for a longer time. In ironing a frock, first do the waist, then the sleeves, then the skirt. Keep the skirt rolled while ironing the other parts, and set a chair to hold the sleeves while ironing the skirt, unless a skirt-board be used. Silk should be ironed on the wrong side, when quite damp, with an iron which is not very hot, as light colors are apt to change and fade. In ironing velvet, turn up the face of the iron, and after dampening the wrong side of the velvet, draw it over the face of the iron, holding it straight. Always iron lace and needlework on the wrong side.

Starching — Clear-starching, Etc.— To Make Starch for Linen, Cotton, Etc.—To one ounce of the best starch add just enough soft cold water to make it, by rubbing and stirring, into a thick paste, carefully breaking all the lumps and particles. When rubbed perfectly smooth, add a pint of boiling water, with blueing to suit, and boil for at *least half an hour*, taking care to have it well stirred all the time, to prevent its burning. When not stirring, keep it covered, to prevent the accumulation of dust, etc. Also keep it covered when removed from the fire, to prevent a scum from rising upon it. To give the linen a fine, smooth, glossy appearance, and prevent the iron from sticking, add a little spermaceti—a piece as large as a nutmeg—to the starch when boiling, and half a teaspoonful of the finest table-salt. In ironing linen collars, shirt bosoms, etc., their appearance will be much improved by rubbing them, before ironing, with a clean white towel, dampened in soft water. All starch should be strained before using.

To Clear-starch Lace, Etc.—Starch for laces should be thicker and used hotter than for linens. After your laces have been well washed and dried, dip them into the thick, hot starch in such a way as to have every part properly starched. Then wring all the starch out, and spread them out smooth on a piece of linen; roll them up together, and let them remain for about half an hour, when they will be dry enough to iron. Some think that laces should never be clapped between the hand, as it injures them. Cambrics do not require so thick starch as net or lace. Some people prefer cold or raw starch for book-muslin, as some of this kind of muslin has a thick clammy appearance, if starched in boiled starch. Fine laces are sometimes wound round a glass bottle to dry, which prevents them from shrinking.

Ironing Laces.—Ordinary laces and worked muslin can be ironed by the usual process with a smoothing or sad-iron; finer laces cannot be. When the lace has been starched and dried, ready for ironing, spread it *out as smooth as possible* on an ironing-cloth, and pass over it, back and forth, as quickly as you can, a smooth, round glass bottle containing hot water, giving the bottle such pressure as may be required to smooth the lace. Sometimes you may pass the laces over the bottle, taking care to keep them smooth. Either way is much better than to iron.

REMOVING STAINS.

Grease-spots.—Cold rain-water and soap will remove machine-grease from washable fabrics.

Stains from Acids can be removed by spirits of hartshorn, diluted. Repeat, if necessary.

Wine Stains may be taken out of articles by holding the spots in milk while it is boiling.

Sal-volatile, or hartshorn, will restore colors taken out by acid. It may be dropped upon any garment without doing harm.

Iron Rust.—Dip the rusty spots in a solution of tartaric or citric acid; or wet the spots with lemon-juice, and rub on hard, white soap, expose it to the heat; or apply lemon-juice and salt, and expose it to the sun.

To Take Out Scorch.—Lay the article scorched where the bright sunshine will fall upon it. It is said it will remove the spot, and leave it white as snow.

Mildewed Linen.—This may be restored by soaping the spots; while wet, covering them with fine chalk scraped to powder, and well rubbed in.

To Remove Mildew.—Remove mildew by dipping in sour butter-milk and laying in the sun.

Another Method of Removing Mildew.—Pour one quart of boiling water on two ounces of chloride of lime, and strain through a cloth; then add three quarts of cold water. Let the articles stand in this twelve hours, then rinse thoroughly. It will not injure the cloth.

Coffee Stains.—Pour on them a small stream of boiling water before putting the article in the wash.

Grass Stains.—Wash the stained places in clean, cold, soft water, without soap, before the garment is otherwise wet.

Tea Stains.—Clear, boiling water will remove tea stains, and many fruit stains. Pour the water through the stain, and thus prevent its spreading over the fabric.

Medicine Stains.—These may be removed from silver spoons by rubbing them with a rag dipped in sulphuric acid, and washing it off with soap-suds.

Fruit Stains.—Freezing will take out all old fruit stains, and scalding with boiling water will remove those that have never been through the wash.

Fruit Stains on Napkins, Table-cloths, etc.—Pour hot water on the spots; wet with hartshorn or oxalic acid—a teaspoonful to a teacup of water.

For Fruit and Wine Stains, mix two teaspoonfuls of water and one of spirit of salt, and let the stained part lie in this for two minutes; then rinse in cold water; or wet the stain with hartshorn.

Ink Stains.—Ink stains may sometimes be taken out by smearing with hot tallow, left on when the stained articles go to the wash.

How to take Marking-Ink out of Linen.—A saturated solution of cyanuret of potassium, applied with a camel's-hair brush. After the marking-ink disappears, the linen should be well-washed in cold water.

Ink in Cotton, Silk, and Woolen Goods.—Saturate the spots with spirits of turpentine, and let it remain several hours; then rub it between the hands. I. will crumple away, without injuring either the color or the texture of the article.

Ink Stains on Mahogany.—Put a few drops of spirits of niter in a teaspoonful of water, touch the spot with a feather dipped in the mixture, and when the ink disappears, rub it over at once with a rag dipped in cold water, or there will be a white mark not easily effaced.

Ink Stains on Silver—The tops and other portions of silver ink-stands frequently become deeply discolored with ink, which is difficult to remove by ordinary means. It may, however, be completely eradicated by making a little chloride of lime into a paste with water, and rubbing it upon the stains. Chloride of lime has been misnamed "the general bleacher," but it is a foul enemy to all metallic surfaces.

Ink and Iron Mould.—This may be taken out by wetting the spots in milk, then covering them with common salt. It should be done before the garment has been washed. Another way to take out ink, is to dip it in melted tallow. For fine, delicate articles, this is the best way.

How to Remove Stains from Floors.—For removing spots of grease from boards, take equal parts of fuller's-earth and pearl-ash, a quarter of a pound of each, and boil in a quart of soft water, and, while hot, lay it on the greased parts, allowing it to remain on them for ten or twelve hours; after which it may be scoured off with sand and water. A floor much spotted with grease should be completely washed over with this mixture the day before it is scoured. Fuller's-earth or ox-gall boiled together, form a very powerful cleansing mixture for floors or carpets. Stains of ink are removed by strong vinegar, or salts of lemon will remove them.

To Preserve Steel Goods from Rust.—After bright grates have been thoroughly cleaned, they should be dusted over with unslaked lime, and thus left until wanted. All the coils of piano-wires are thus sprinkled, and will keep from rust for many years. Table-knives, which are not in constant use, ought to be put in a case in which sifted quick-lime is placed, about eight inches deep. They should be plunged to the top of the blades, but the lime should not touch the handles.

To Remove Paint Stains on Windows.—It frequently happens that painters splash the plate or other glass windows when they are painting the sills. When this is the case, melt some soda in very hot water and wash them with it, using a soft flannel. It will entirely remove the paint.

Stains on the Hands.—A few drops of oil vitriol (sulphuric acid) in water, will take the stains of fruit, dark dyes, stove blacking, etc., from the hands without injuring them. Care must, however, be taken not to drop it upon the clothes. It will remove the color from woolen, and eat holes in cotton fabrics.

To remove ink or fruit stains from the fingers, take cream of tartar, half an ounce; powdered salt of sorrel, half an ounce; mix. This is what is sold for salts of lemon.

To Preserve Polished Iron Work.—Such work may be preserved from rust by a mixture, not very expensive, consisting of copal varnish mixed with as much olive oil as will give it a degree of greasiness, adding nearly as much spirits of turpentine as of varnish.

If **Rust** has made its appearance upon grates or fire-irons, apply a mixture of tripoli, with half its quantity of sulphur, mixed on a marble slab, and laid on with a piece of soft leather. Emory and oil may be applied with an excellent effect. This will not only clean but polish.

To Extract Grease Spots from Books.—Gently warm the greased or spotted part of the book or paper, and then press upon it pieces of blotting-paper, one after another, so as to absorb as much of the grease as possible. Have ready some fine, clear, essential oil of turpentine heated almost to a boiling state, warm the greased leaf a little, and then with a soft, clean brush, apply the heated turpentine both sides of the spotted part. By repeating this application, the grease will be extracted. Lastly, with another brush, dipped in rectified spirits of wine, go over the place carefully, until the paper becomes smooth and clean.

Removing Tar Spots.—The old remedy for removing tar is butter; tar is soluble in fat, and especially in butter; when this is left on the tar-spot for some time, both butter and tar are easily washed out by a sponge, with soap and water. It is the same with resinous wagon-grease. A creamy mixture of powdered extract of liquorice, with oil of anise-seed, will easily dissolve tar, resin, pitch, Venice turpentine, etc. It is afterward washed out with soap and warm water.

Ammonia for Renovation.—Keep constantly in the house some strong spirits of hartshorn in a ground-glass stoppered bottle. A teaspoonful in a tablespoonful of water will clean combs and brushes.

In any case where an acid has taken the color from a fabric, ammonia will restore it. Washing a carpet in ammonia-water—say a tablespoonful of concentrated ammonia to a quart of warm suds—will take almost any stain out of it.

In cleaning paint, glass, silver, or gold, it is invaluable, as well as for keeping the hands soft and white after cleaning all these other things.

For cleaning windows, put a teaspoonful of strong ammonia in a half pint of clear warm water, wring a cloth out, and rub sashes and glass, then rub with a dry cloth.

Stains, pencil-marks, fly-specks, and all manner of dirt, disappear under the ammonia treatment, with no injury to paint or varnish if not used too strong.

Removing Grease from Silk.—Apply a little magnesia to the wrong side, and the spots will disappear.

To Remove Grease from Coat Collars.—Wash with a sponge moistened with hartshorn and water.

To Restore Crape.—A bit of glue dissolved in skim-milk will restore crape. Ribbons of every kind should be washed in cold suds, and not rinsed.

To Clean Furs.—Shake and whip them well; then brush; boil some flax-seed; dip a rag in the water and wipe them slightly. This makes them look nearly as good as new.

To Preserve Furs.—First, hang them out in the sun for a day or two; then give them a good beating and shaking-up, to be sure no moth is in them already. Then wrap up a lump of camphor in a rag, and place in each; then wrap up each in a sound newspaper and paste together, so that there is no hole or crevice through which a moth can gain entrance.

To Clean Velvet.—Wet a cloth and put it over a hot flat-iron, and a dry one over that, then draw the velvet across it, brushing it at the same time with a soft brush, and it will look as nice as new.

To Restore Silk.—The best method to make old silk look like new, and one that is employed by millions, is to sponge over the outside with strong, cold black tea. The silk should afterward be ironed outside.

Wrinkled Silk may be rendered nearly as beautiful as when new, by sponging the surface with a weak solution of gum-arabic or white glue; then iron on the wrong side.

To Bleach White Silks or Flannels.—Wash the articles clean, rinse in suds, and smoke with brimstone while wet; the silk must be brushed or washed with a sponge; if rubbed it will never press smoothly; expose the goods to the air, and the odor will soon pass off.

To Clean White Ostrich Feathers.—Wash them well in soft water with white soap and blue, if you can get the blue; if not, use the white soap alone; rub them through white, clean paper, beat them on the paper, shake them before the fire, dry them in the air by waving them with the hand to and fro. Afterward curl them.

To Clean Feathers.—Dissolve four ounces of white soap, cut small, in four pounds of water, moderately hot, in a basin, and make the solution into a lather by beating with a small rod. Then introduce the feathers, and rub them well with the hands for five minutes. They are next to be washed in clean water as hot as the hand can bear it.

To Make Cloth Water-proof.—In a pail of soft water put half a pound of sugar of lead, half a pound of alum; stir this at intervals until it becomes cool; then pour it into another pail and put the garment therein, and let it be in for twenty-four hours, and then hang it up to dry without wringing it.

To Clean Black Cloth.—Dissolve one ounce of bicarbonate of ammonia in one quart of warm water. With this liquid rub the cloth, using a piece of flannel or black cloth for the purpose. After the application of this solution, clean the cloth well with clear water, dry and iron it, brushing the cloth from time to time in the direction of the fiber.

Cleaning Silk and Merinos.—Grate two or three large potatoes, add to them a pint of cold water, let them stand a short time, pour off the liquid, clear, or strain it through a sieve, when it will be ready for use. Lay the silk on a flat surface, and apply the liquid with a clean sponge till the dirt is well separated; dip each piece in a pail of clear water, and hang up to dry without wringing. Iron, while damp, on the wrong side.

To Color Kid Gloves.—Put a handful of logwood into a bowl, cover with alcohol, and let it soak until it looks strong—one day, perhaps. Put one glove on the hand, dip a small woolen cloth or sponge into the liquid, wet the glove all over, rub it dry and hard until it shines, and it will be a nice purple. Repeat the process, and it will be black.

To Clean Kid Gloves.—Have ready a little new milk in one saucer, a piece of white soap in another, a clean cloth folded two or three times. On the cloth lay out the glove smooth and neat. Take a piece of flannel, dip it in the milk, then rub off a good quantity of soap on the wetted flannel, and commence to rub the glove toward the fingers, holding it firmly with the left hand. Continue this process until the glove, if white, looks of a dingy yellow, though clean; if colored, till it looks dry and spoiled. Lay it to dry, and the operator will soon be gratified to see that the old glove looks nearly new. It will be soft, glossy, smooth, and elastic.

Washing Kid Gloves.—First, see that your hands are clean, then put on your gloves, and wash them as though you were washing your hands, in a basin of spirits of turpentine. This method is used in Paris. The gloves should be hung in the air, or some dry place, to carry away the smell of turpentine.

To Extract Grease from Papered Walls.—Dip a piece of flannel in spirits of wine and rub the greasy spots gently once or twice.

To Clean Wall-Paper.—Tie a soft cloth over a broom, and sweep down the walls carefully.

WHITEWASHING AND PAINTING.

Cracks in Plastering.—In some cases the plasterer has used too little real plaster and too much lime. Pure plaster of Paris will never crack; but as it sets too quickly for the convenience of the operator, a little lime is mixed with it. If you try to plaster with lime alone, it will crack all over in drying, and come off in patches. This indicates the necessity of always using as little lime as possible, either in the sand used for brick-laying or in the plaster used for coating the walls.

To Fill Holes in Walls.—Small holes in white walls can easily be repaired without sending for a mason. Equal parts of plaster of Paris and white sand, such as is used in most families for scouring purposes, mixed with water to a paste, applied immediately after removing the loose particles of the walls, and smoothed with a knife or flat piece of wood, will make the broken place as good as new. As the mixture hardens very quickly, it is best to prepare but a small quantity at a time.

Brilliant Zinc Whitewash.—The *Manufacturer and Builder* says: "Mix oxide of zinc with common sizing, and apply it with a whitewash brush to the ceiling. After this apply in the same manner a wash of the chloride of zinc, which will combine with the oxide to form a smooth cement with a shining face."

Cheap Whitewash.—Slake the lime as usual, except that the water used should be hot, and nearly saturated with salt; then stir in four handfuls of fine sand, to make it thick like cream. Coloring matter can be added to both, making a light stone-color, a cream-color, or a light buff.

Making Paper Stick to Whitewashed Walls.—Make a sizing of common glue and water, of the consistency of linseed oil, and apply with whitewash or other brush to the wall, taking care to go over every part, and especially top and bottom. Apply the paper in the ordinary way.

New Recipe for Whitewash.—The following recipe for whitewashing has been found by experience to answer on wood, brick, and stone, nearly as well as oil-paint, and is much cheaper: Slake half a bushel of unslaked lime with boiling water, keeping it covered during the process. Strain it and add a peck of salt, dissolved in warm water; three pounds of ground rice put in boiling water, and boiled to a thin paste; half a pound of powdered Spanish whiting, and a pound of clear glue, dissolved in warm water; mix these well together, and let the mixture stand for several days. Keep the wash thus prepared in a kettle or portable furnace, and when used put it on as hot as possible, with a painters' or whitewash brush.

A Brilliant Stucco Whitewash.—Take clean lumps of well-burnt lime, slake in hot water in a small tub, and cover it to keep in the steam. It should then be passed through a fine sieve in a fluid form to obtain the flour of lime. Add a quarter of a pound of whiting or burnt alum, two pounds of sugar, three pints of rice-flour made into a thin and well-boiled paste, and one pound of glue dissolved over a slow fire. It is said to be more brilliant than plaster of Paris, and will last fifty years. It should be put on warm with a paint brush.

To Color and Prevent Whitewash from Rubbing Off.—Alum is one of the best additions to make whitewash of lime which will not rub off. When powdered chalk is used, glue-water is also good, but would not do for outside work exposed to much rain. Give it the desired color by small quantities of lamp-black, brown sienna, ocher, or other coloring material.

Paint for Kitchen Walls.—Paint on the walls of a kitchen is much better than kalsomine, whitewash, or paper, since it does not absorb odors or peel off, and can be quickly and perfectly cleaned. Any woman who can whitewash can paint her own kitchen. The wall needs first to be washed with soapsuds, then covered with a coat of dissolved glue, and then with paint. A broad, flat brush does the work quickly.

Fire and Water-Proof Paint.—Slake stone lime by putting into a tub, covered to keep in the steam; when slaked pass the powder through a fine sieve, and to every six quarts add a quart of rock salt and a gallon of water; then boil and skim clear; to every five gallons of liquid add pulverized alum, one pound; pulverized copperas, one half pound, and stir slowly; add powdered potash, three fourths pound; very fine sand, or hickory ashes, four pounds; then use any coloring matter desired, and apply with a brush. It looks better than any ordinary paint, and is as durable as slate; will stop small leaks in roofs, prevent moss from growing thereon, make it incombustible, and render brick impervious to water.

POLISHING FURNITURE.

Best French Naphtha Polish.—Solution of shellac three pounds, and of wood naphtha three quarts.

Best French Spirit Polish.—Shellac, two pounds; powdered mastic and sandarac, of each one ounce; copal varnish, half a pint; spirits of wine, one gallon. Mix in the cold till dissolved.

Polish or Mahogany Color.—Two ounces of beeswax, cut fine; spirits of turpentine, one ounce; one dram of powdered resin; melt at a gentle heat, and add two drams of Indian red to give it a mahogany color.

Simplest Polish for Oiled Furniture.—Rub oiled furniture with a woolen cloth saturated slightly with oil.

Oil for Red Furniture.—Take linseed oil, put it into a glazed pipkin with as much alkanet root as it will cover. Let it boil gently, and it will become of a strong red color; when cool it will be fit for use.

Polish of Oil and Alcohol.—One pint of linseed oil, one wine-glass of alcohol; mix well together; apply to the cloth with a linen rag; rub dry with a soft cotton cloth, and polish with a silk cloth. Furniture is improved by washing it occasionally with soap-suds. Wipe dry and rub over with a very little linseed oil upon a clean sponge or flannel. Wipe polished furniture with silk.

Polish for Leather Cushions, etc.—Beat well the yelks of two eggs and the white of one; mix a tablespoonful of gin and a teaspoonful of sugar thicken it with ivory black, add it to the eggs, and use as common blacking; the seats or cushions being left a day or two to harden. This is good for dressing boots and shoes.

To Give a Fine Color to Cherry-Tree Wood.—Take one ounce of orchanetta; cut it in two or three bits, and put it to soak for forty-eight hours in three ounces of good olive oil. With this oil anoint your cherry-tree wood after it is worked and shaped as you intend it, and it will give it a fine luster.

To Stain Black Walnut.—To impart to common pine the color and appearance of black walnut the following composition may be used: One quarter of a pound of asphaltum, one half a pound of beeswax, to one gallon of turpentine. If found too thin, add beeswax; if too light in color, add asphaltum, though that must be done with caution, as a very little will make a great difference in the shade, and black walnut is not what its name implies, but rather a rich dark brown. Varnishing is not essential, as the wax gives it a good gloss.

Imitation Ebony Stain.—Mix up a strong stain of copperas and extract of logwood, about equal parts; add powdered nutgalls, one-fourth part; stain wood with solution, dry, rub down well, oil; then use French polish made tolerably dark with indigo or finely-powdered stone blue.

To Ebonize Various Woods.—Apple, pear, and walnut wood, especially if fine-grained, may be "ebonized" by the following process: Boil in a glazed vessel, with water, four ounces of gall-nuts, one ounce of logwood chips, half an ounce of vitriol, and a half an ounce of crystallized verdigris; filter while warm, and brush the wood with the hot solution a number of times. The wood, thus stained black, is then to be coated two or three times (being allowed to dry completely after each coating) with a solution of one ounce of iron filings in a quart of good wine vinegar. This is to be prepared hot and allowed to cool before use.

Water and Varnished Furniture.—Water should never be applied to varnished furniture, but the slats of bedsteads can be washed and dried, and kerosene applied to the ends or joints of the bedsteads. Varnished furniture should be cleaned with a woolen cloth dipped in linseed oil.

Cleansing Polish for Furniture.—Cold drawn linseed oil, one quart; gin or spirits of wine, half a pint; vinegar, half a pint; butter of antimony, two ounces; spirits of turpentine, half a pint; this mixture requires to be well shaken before it is used. A little of it is then to be poured upon a rubber, which must be well applied to the surface of the furniture. Several applications will be necessary for new furniture, or for such as has previously been French polished or rubbed with beeswax.

Where and How to Varnish.—Varnish should always be applied in a warm room, as warm as a person can work in comfortably. At a lower temperature there is always moisture in the air, and an invisible dew, which gives the varnish a milky and cloudy appearance. This will happen even on a fine summer day, and the only preventive is to employ artificial heat to produce a temperature of at least seventy-five degrees Fahrenheit. At this temperature the moisture is not precipitated until the alcohol of the varnish has sufficiently evaporated to leave a thin and smooth film of shellac. The gloss and durability are entirely dependent upon this.

Varnish for Unpainted Wood.—A good surface may be produced on unpainted wood by the following treatment: Sand-paper the wood thoroughly as for French polishing, size it, and lay on a coat of varnish, very thin, with a piece of sponge or wadding covered with a piece of linen rag. When dry, rub down with pumice dust, and apply a second coat of varnish. Three or four coats should produce a surface almost equal to French polish, if the varnish is good and the pumice be well applied between each coat. The use of a sponge or wadding instead of a brush, aids in preventing the streaky appearance usually caused by a brush in the hands of an unskilled person.

Blacking for Stoves.—May be made with half a pound of black lead finely powdered, mixed with the whites of three eggs well beaten; then dilute it with sour beer or porter till it becomes as thin as shoe-blacking; after stirring it, set it over hot coals to simmer for twenty minutes; when cold it may be kept for use.

Brunswick Black for Varnishing Grates.—Melt four pounds of common asphaltum, and add two pints of linseed oil and one gallon of oil of turpentine. This preparation is usually put up in stone-ware bottles for sale, and is used with a paint brush. If too thick, more turpentine may be added.

To Clean Bronzed Chandeliers, Lamps, etc.—These articles should only be dusted with a feather brush, or soft cloth, as washing will take off the bronzing.

For Cleaning Brasses Belonging to Mahogany Furniture.—Use for this purpose, either powdered whiting or scraped rotten-stone, mixed with sweet-oil, and rubbed on with a chamois-skin.

To Clean Sinks.—Copperas, dissolved in boiling-water and applied with a whisk-broom, is good for cleaning iron sinks and drains. For zinc, take one fourth muriatic acid and three fourths water, thickened with whiting and applied with a cloth. Scour well with this mixture and then wash with warm water.

ARTICLES FOR THE TOILET.

Rose Oil.—Put any quantity of dried rose-leaves into an earthenware pipkin, cover them with olive-oil, and keep hot for some hours. The oil will extract both odor and color.

Cologne Water.—A very fair article, that will improve with age, may be made as follows: One pint of alcohol, add twelve drops each of oils of bergamot, lemon, neroli, orange-peel, rosemary, and one dram of cardamom seed.

Another recipe: One pint of alcohol, sixty drops of lavender, sixty drops of bergamot, sixty drops of essence of lemon, sixty drops of orange-water. To be corked up and well shaken. This also is better for considerable age.

To Wash Hair Brushes.—Hair brushes, however dirty, may be washed and kept good for years, without loss of stiffness, by putting a small handful of soda into a pint jug of boiling water. When the soda is melted, put in the brush and stir it about till clean. Rinse it in cold water, and dry in the sun or by the fire. The quicker it dries, the harder the bristles will be.

A Paste for Sharpening Razors.—Take prepared putty one ounce, saturated solution of oxalic acid enough to make a paste; this composition is to be rubbed over the strop, and when dry, a little water may be added. The acid having a great attachment for iron, a little friction with this powder gives a fine edge to the razor.

Shaving Cream.—Take one pound of soft-soap in a jar; add to it one quart best alcohol; set the jar in a vessel of boiling water until the soap is dissolved. Perfume with essential oil to suit. This is a good article for shaving, especially for those troubled with pimples on the face. Two or three drops rubbed on the face with the end of the finger is enough for shaving. Dip the end of the brush in a little hot water, brush the face briskly, and it will raise a rich lather.

To Curl Hair.—Take two ounces of borax, one dram of powdered gum senegal, one quart of hot water, (not boiling;) mix, and as soon as the ingredients are dissolved, add two ounces of spirits of wine strongly impregnated with camphor; on retiring to rest, wet the hair with the above mixture and roll it in papers as usual; leave them till morning, when untwist and form into ringlets.

To Remove Tight Rings.—To remove tightly-fitting rings from a finger without pain, (says the London *Lancet*,) pass the end of a portion of rather fine twine underneath the ring, and evenly encircle the finger from below upward (as whip-makers bind lashes on) with the remainder, as far as the center of the finger, then unwind the string from above downward by taking hold of the end passed under the ring, and it will be found that the ring will gradually pass along the twine toward the tip of the finger.

Rose Lip-Salve.—No. 1. Oil of almonds, three ounces; alkanet, half an ounce. Let them stand together in a warm place until the oil is colored, then strain. Melt one ounce and a half of white wax, and half an ounce of spermaceti with the oil, stir till it begins to thicken, and add twelve drops of attar of roses. No. 2. White wax, one ounce; almond oil, two ounces; alkanet, one dram. Digest in a warm place till sufficiently colored. Strain, and stir in six drops of attar of roses.*

BIRDS AND BIRD-FOOD.

To Distinguish Canaries.—To distinguish the male bird from the hen, observe the bird when it is singing, and if it be a cock you will perceive the throat heaving with a pulse-like motion, a peculiarity which is scarcely perceptible in the hen.

Place for Cages.—Place the cages so that no draught of air will strike them. Avoid placing them near the stove, fire-place, or register. About half way between the floor and the ceiling is best, as the temperature there is preferable. The room should never be heated above seventy degrees.

Size of Cage Perches.—Very many mean to give their birds all things needed to make them bright and happy, and at the same time are guilty of great cruelty in regard to perches. The perches in a cage should be each one of different size, and the smallest as large as a pipe-stem. If perches are of the right sort, no trouble is ever had about the bird's claws growing too long; and of all things keep the perches clean.

Food for Canary Birds.—Give nothing to healthy birds but rape and canary seed, water, cuttle-fish bone, and gravel-paper or sand on the floor of the cage, no hemp-seed, and a bath three times a week. When moulting (shedding feathers) keep warm; avoid all draughts of air. Give plenty of German rape-seed; a little hard-boiled egg, mixed with crackers grated fine, is excellent. Feed at a certain hour in the morning. By observing these simple rules, birds may be kept in fine condition for years. For birds that are sick or have lost their song, procure bird-tonic at a bird-store.

Care of Young Canaries.—Feed young canaries with white and yelk of hard eggs, mixed together with a little bread steeped in water. This should be pressed and placed in one vessel, while in another should be put some boiled rape-seed, washed in fresh water. Change the food every day. When they are a month old, put them in separate cages.

---

* For other articles for the toilet consult previous chapters on health.

Parasites upon Canaries.—The red mite, a minute insect, almost invisible to the naked eye, but easily seen through the microscope, is found in large numbers in nearly all the cages containing canaries, particularly those which are kept in dark rooms away from the light. These tiny creatures shun the light, and generally leave the birds during the day, concealing themselves in the cracks and crevices of the cage until darkness arrives, when they sally forth to attack the canaries. By continually irritating them, they cause a loss of sleep which occasions many diseases and very often is the source of their death.

How to Destroy these Parasites.—The presence of these insects is indicated by the uneasy manner the birds exhibit, becoming dispirited, and sitting in a drooping position on the perches or on the ground. It is difficult to get rid of them. A plan simple and effectual is to place in the cage a hollow reed with three or four gimlet holes along it, as a substitute for the ordinary perch. The mites hide in the reed with the return of light, and can be readily shaken from it. In a short time the insects can all be destroyed by this easy process.

Food for Mocking-Birds.—1. One medium-sized boiled potato (without salt) and the yolk of one hard-boiled egg, chopped together very fine when warm. In cold weather this may last two days, but in summer should be made fresh daily.

2. Ground or bruised hemp-seed, sixteen ounces; ground or bruised rice, four ounces; dust of butter crackers, eight ounces; flax-seed meal, two ounces; mix and put in a pan with two ounces of lard, and cook until it has a brown color, stirring with a spoon to keep it from sticking or getting into lumps. One or two tablespoonfuls a day, with grated carrot, is sufficient.*

To Distinguish Thrushes—Food.—The male bird may be distinguished from a hen by a darker back and the more glossy appearance of the feathers. The breast also is white. Their natural food is insects, worms, and snails. In a domesticated state they will eat raw meat, but snails and worms should be procured for them.

Care of Young Thrushes.—Young birds are hatched about the middle of April, and should be kept very warm. They should be fed with raw meat, cut small, or bread mixed in milk with hemp-seed well bruised; when they can feed themselves give them lean meat cut small, and mixed with bread or German paste, plenty of clean water, and keep them in a warm, dry, and sunny situation.

Food of Bullfinches.—Old birds should be fed with German paste, and

---

* *Forest and Stream.*

occasionally rape-seed. The Germans occasionally give them a little poppy-seed, and a grain or two of rice, steeped in Canary wine, when teaching them to pipe, as a reward for the progress they make. Bird-organs, or flageolets, are used to teach them to sing.

Care of Young Bullfinches.—Bullfinches breed three or four times a year. The young require to be kept very warm, and to be fed every two hours, with rape-seed, soaked for several hours in cold water, afterward scalded and strained, bruised, mixed with bread, and moistened with milk. One, two, or three mouthfuls at a time.

Linnets and their Food.—Male birds are browner on the back than the hens, and have some of the large feathers of the wings white up to the quills. Canary and hemp-seed, with occasionally a little groundsel, water-cress, chickweed, etc., constitute their food.

Blackbirds and their Food.—The cock-bird is of a deep black, with a yellow bill. The female is dark brown. It is difficult to distinguish male from female birds when young; but the darkest generally are males. Their food consists of German paste, bread, meat, and bits of apple. The same treatment as given for the thrush applies to the blackbird. .

To Distinguish Skylarks.—The male bird is recognized by the largeness of his eye, the length of his claws, the mode of erecting his crest, and by marks of white in the tail. It is also a larger bird than the hen.

The Cages of Skylarks.—The cage should be of the following proportions: Length, one foot five inches; width, nine inches; height, one foot three inches. There should be a circular projection in front, to admit of a fresh turf being placed every two or three days, and the bottom of the cage should be plentifully and constantly sprinkled with river sand. All vessels containing food should be placed outside, and the top of the cage should be arched and padded, so that the bird may not injure itself by jumping about.

Food of Skylarks.—Their food, in a natural state, consists of seeds, insects, and also buds, green herbage, as clover, endive, lettuce, etc., and occasionally berries. When confined, they are usually fed with a paste made in the following manner: Take a portion of bread, well-baked and stale, put it into fresh water, and leave it until quite soaked through, then squeeze out the water and pour boiled milk over it, adding two-thirds of the same quantity of barley-meal well sifted, or, what is better, wheat-meal. This should be made fresh every two days. Occasionally the yelk of a hard-boiled egg should be crumbled small and given to the birds, as well as a little hemp-seed, meal-worms, and elderberries. Great cleanliness should be observed in the cages of these birds.

RULES FOR CARVING.

Carving Knives.—These should always "be put in edge" before the guests are called to the table. Let them be light as well as sharp. Dispense if possible with the "steel" after the guests are seated. However closely the guests are compelled to sit, give the carver plenty of room.

Carving Dishes.—Joints which require carving should be placed on plates of ample size, and the dish should be so placed as to give the operator complete command over the joint.

To Carve a Fowl.—To carve a fowl (which should always be laid with the breast uppermost) place the fork in the breast, and take off the wings and legs without turning the fowl; then cut out the "merry-thought," cut slices from the breast, take out the collar bone, cut off the side pieces, and then cut the carcass in two. Divide the joints in the legs of a turkey.

To Carve a Fillet.—To carve a fillet of veal, begin at the top, and help to the stuffing with each slice. In a breast of veal separate the breast and brisket, and then cut them up, asking which part is preferred.

To Carve a Round of Beef.—First cut away the irregular outside pieces, to obtain a good surface, and then serve thin and broad slices. Serve bits of the udder fat with the lean.

To Carve a Sirloin.—In carving a sirloin, cut thin slices from the side next to you, (it must be put on the dish with the tenderloin underneath,) then turn it, and cut from the tenderloin. Help the guests to both kinds.

To Carve a Leg.—In carving a leg of mutton or a ham, begin by cutting across the middle to the bone. Cut a tongue across, not lengthwise, and help from the middle part.

To Carve a Pig.—In carving a pig it is customary to divide it and take off the head before it comes to the table, as to many persons the head is revolting. Cut off the limbs and divide the ribs. The ribs are considered very choice.

To Carve a Calve's Head.—Carve across the cheek, and take pieces from any part that is easily reached. The tongue and brain-sauce are served separate.

To Carve a Saddle of Mutton.—Cut thin slices parallel with the backbone; or slice it obliquely from the bone to the edge. Saddles of pork or lamb are carved in the same manner.

To Carve a Spare-Rib.—A spare-rib of pork is carved by separating the chops, which should previously have been jointed. Cut as far as the joint, then return the knife to the point of the bones, and press over to disclose the joint, which may then be relieved with the point of the knife. Hams are cut in very thin slices from the knuckle to the blade.

To Carve Fish.—Fish are served with a fish-slice, or the new fish-knife and fork, and requires very little carving, care being required, however, not to break the flakes, which from their size add much to the beauty of cod and salmon. Serve part of the roe, milk, or liver to each person. The heads of cod and salmon, sounds of cod, are likewise considered delicacies.

ILLUSTRATIONS ON CARVING—ADDITIONAL NOTES.

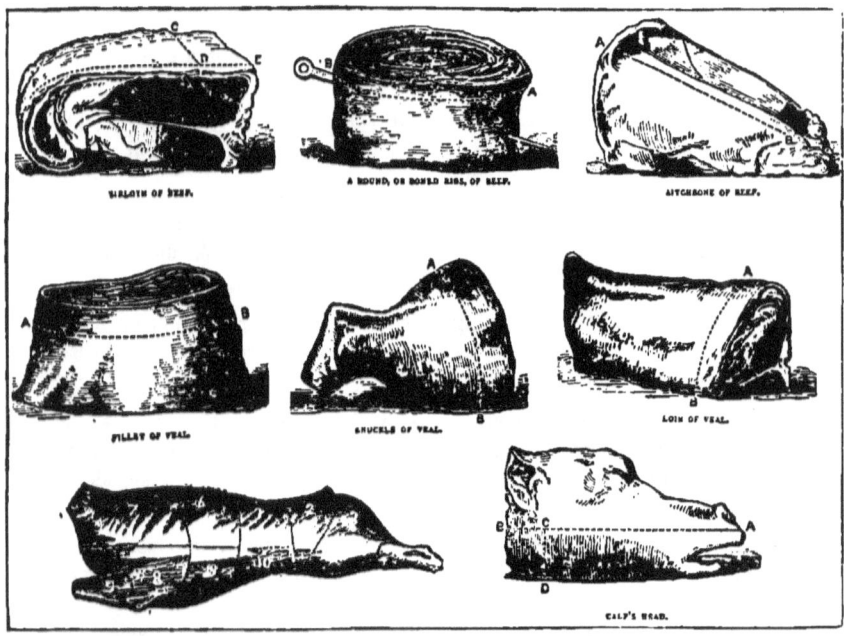

NOTES.—The dotted lines above, in connection with the previous directions, explain themselves. Some carvers cut the top of the sirloin of beef from C to D; but this is a wasteful method; the one from E to F is to be preferred; in case of the under piece (the tenderloin) the cross line only should be observed. Cut the aitchbone of beef from A to B, slicing "thin" from top to bottom. In carving the fillets, slice round from the top. The numerals in the seventh illustration show the method of cutting up and designating the carcass of veal, thus: *Hind-quarter:* 1. Loin, prime joint; 2. Chump end of loin, roasts or cutlets; 3. Fillet, best cutlets; 4. Hind knuckle, for boiling or stewing; 10. Flank, for stews. *Fore-quarter:* 5. Fore knuckle; 6. Neck, best end of neck; 7. Shoulder, roasting; 8. Bladebone, roasting; 9. Breast, braized or stew; 11. Head, eaten in various ways.

ROASTING AND CARVING POULTRY AND GAME BIRDS.

Ducks are carved very much as turkeys, geese, and other fowls. If the bird be a young duckling it may be carved like a fowl, namely, by first taking off the leg and wing on either side; but in cases where the duckling is very small it will be as well not to separate the leg from the wing, as they will not then form too large a portion for a single serving. After the legs and wings are disposed of the remainder of the duck will be also

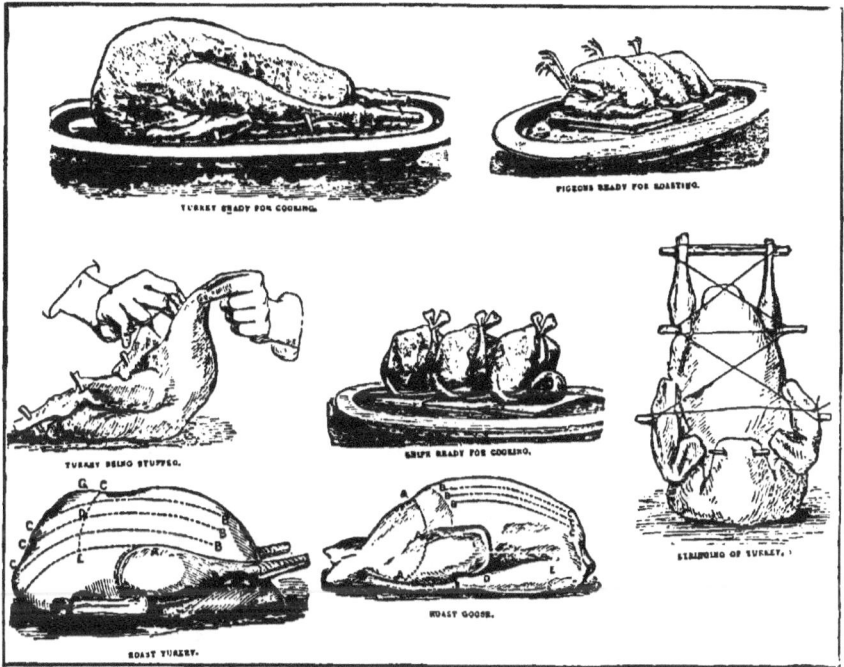

NOTE.—In the roast turkey, G, C, D, show place of the "Merrythought," which can be easily removed; in the goose, A, A, A, the line for the knife in severing the apron covering the stuffing. By a little care all the other parts may also be readily disjointed and removed.

carved in the same manner as a fowl, and not much difficulty will be experienced, as ducklings are tender, and the joints are easily broken by a little forcing, or penetrating by the knife. In cases where the duck is a large bird the better plan to pursue is then to carve it like a goose. As to the prime parts of a duck, it has been said that the "wings of a flyer and the legs of a swimmer" are severally the best portions.

CARVING FISH—ILLUSTRATIONS.

Salmon.—Run the knife along the side of the fish from A to B and C to D. Then help the thick part lengthwise from A to B and the thin part breadthwise from E to F, supplying each person with a piece of each. The thin part is from the belly, where lies the fat and rich piece of the fish.

Mackerel.—Run the knife sidewise from C to B down the backbone so as as to divide the fish into halves; remove the backbone neatly without

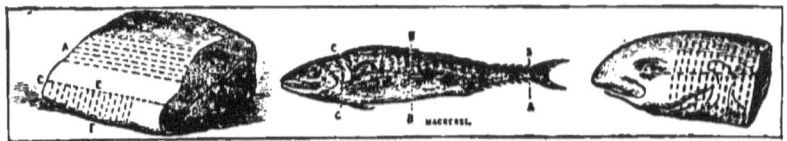

SALMON. MACKEREL. COD'S HEAD AND SHOULDER.

breaking the flakes, then crosscut at A, A, and C, C, and as needed at intermediate places. Be careful not to leave any of the choice and delicate bits on the backbone, as that would be regarded as a real loss.

Cod's Head and Shoulder.—Run the knife as indicated, and bear in mind the fact that lovers of the cod regard the parts around the head as the greatest delicacies of that fish.

THE DINNER TABLE.

Cutting Up Beef.

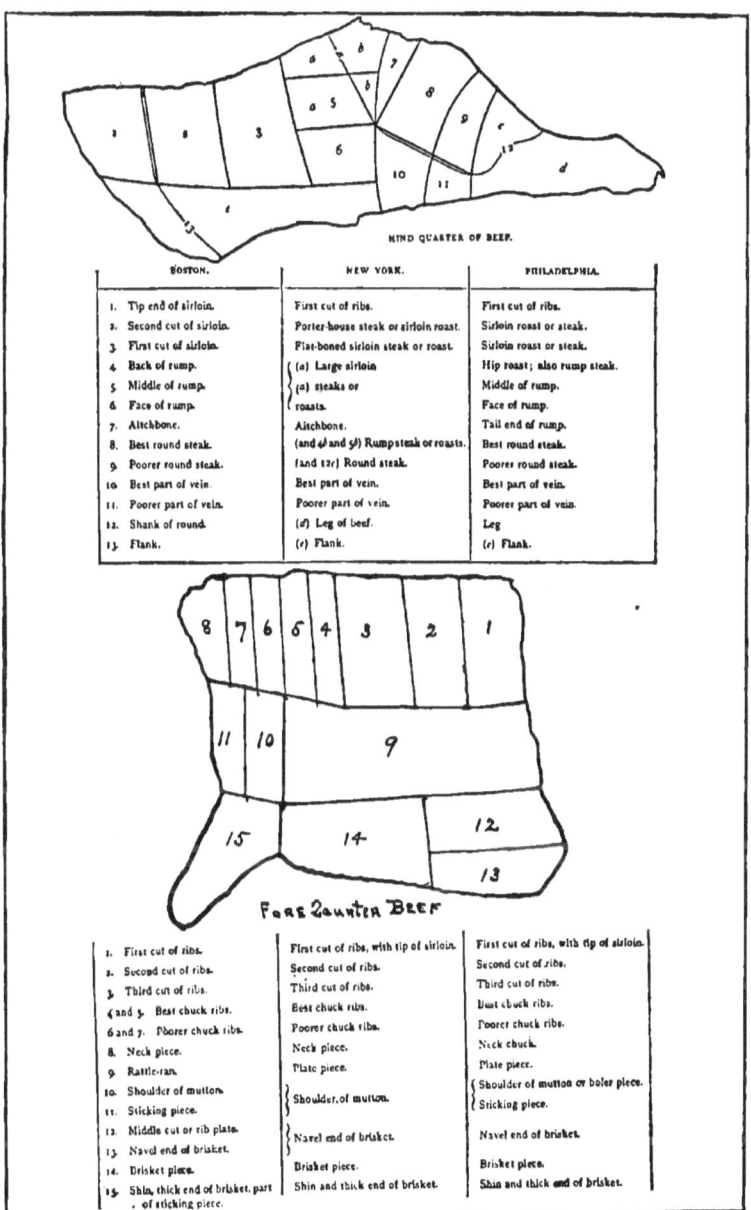

HIND QUARTER OF BEEF.

BOSTON.	NEW YORK.	PHILADELPHIA.
1. Tip end of sirloin.	First cut of ribs.	First cut of ribs.
2. Second cut of sirloin.	Porter-house steak or sirloin roast.	Sirloin roast or steak.
3. First cut of sirloin.	Flat-boned sirloin steak or roast.	Sirloin roast or steak.
4. Back of rump.	(a) Large sirloin	Hip roast; also rump steak.
5. Middle of rump.	(a) steaks or roasts.	Middle of rump.
6. Face of rump.		Face of rump.
7. Aitchbone.	Aitchbone.	Tail end of rump.
8. Best round steak.	(and 4 and 5b) Rump steak or roasts.	Best round steak.
9. Poorer round steak.	(and 12c) Round steak.	Poorer round steak.
10. Best part of vein.	Best part of vein.	Best part of vein.
11. Poorer part of vein.	Poorer part of vein.	Poorer part of vein.
12. Shank of round.	(d) Leg of beef.	Leg
13. Flank.	(e) Flank.	(e) Flank.

FORE QUARTER BEEF

1. First cut of ribs.	First cut of ribs, with tip of sirloin.	First cut of ribs, with tip of sirloin.
2. Second cut of ribs.	Second cut of ribs.	Second cut of ribs.
3. Third cut of ribs.	Third cut of ribs.	Third cut of ribs.
4 and 5. Best chuck ribs.	Best chuck ribs.	Best chuck ribs.
6 and 7. Poorer chuck ribs.	Poorer chuck ribs.	Poorer chuck ribs.
8. Neck piece.	Neck piece.	Neck chuck.
9. Rattle-ran.	Plate piece.	Plate piece.
10. Shoulder of mutton.	Shoulder of mutton.	Shoulder of mutton or boler piece.
11. Sticking piece.		Sticking piece.
12. Middle cut or rib plate.	Navel end of brisket.	Navel end of brisket.
13. Navel end of brisket.		
14. Brisket piece.	Brisket piece.	Brisket piece.
15. Shin, thick end of brisket, part of sticking piece.	Shin and thick end of brisket.	Shin and thick end of brisket.

PASTE AND CEMENTS.

Rice Flour Cement.—This cement, much used in China and Japan, is made by mixing fine rice-flour with cold water, and simmering over a slow fire until a thick paste is formed. This is superior to any other paste either for parlor or workshop purposes. When made of the consistence of plaster, clay models, busts, bass-reliefs, etc., may be formed of it, and the articles when dry, are susceptible of high polish, and very durable.

Paste that will Keep a Year.—Dissolve a teaspoonful of alum in a quart of warm water. When cold, stir in flour to give it the consistency of thick cream, being particular to beat up all the lumps. Stir in as much powdered resin as will lay on a silver dime, and throw in a half a dozen cloves. Have on the fire a tea-cup of boiling water; pour the flour mixture into it, stirring well all the time. In a few minutes it will be the consistency of mush. Pour it into an earthen or china vessel; let it cool; lay a cover on, and put it in a cool place. When needed for use take out a portion and soften it with warm water.*

Liquid Glue.—Dissolve one ounce of borax in a pint of boiling water, add two ounces of shellac, and boil in a covered vessel until the lac is dissolved. This forms a very useful and cheap cement; it answers well for pasting labels on tin, and withstands damp much better than the common glue. The liquid glue made by dissolving shellac in naphtha is dearer, soon dries up, and has an unpleasant smell.

A Lasting Paste.—Buy at a druggist's an ounce of the best gum tragacanth—the whitest is best. Pick it clean, and put it into a wide-mouth glass or white-ware vessel which will hold a quart. Pour on a pint and a half of clear, cold soft water. Cover the vessel, and let it stand till next day. The gum tragacanth will then be much swollen, and nearly to the top of the vessel. Stir it down to the bottom with a stick, and add two or three drops of oil of wintergreen or sassafras. This will prevent the paste from becoming sour or moldy. Stir it several times during that day, but afterward do not stir it at all, leaving it to form a smooth, white mass, like a very thick jelly. Then cover it closely, and set it away for use.

Paste for Labels.—Take linseed oil, varnish, and turpentine, of each half an ounce, of glue an ounce, and of rye flour one pound. Make a paste of the rye flour in the usual way, dissolve the glue and put it in, add the other ingredients, and mix all thoroughly. This will hold labels fast to bottles in damp cellars. The mucilage used on most of our envelopes is made by taking two ounces of glue, ten of water, four of rock candy, and one and a half of gum arabic. Dissolve all together and mix thoroughly.

Paste and Cements.

To Prevent Glue from Smelling Badly.—A teaspoonful of saltpeter added to a large pot full of glue will effectually prevent it from smelling badly; besides, it causes it to dry faster and harder than it would without it.

Cement for Iron and Stone.—Glycerine and litharge stirred to a paste hardens rapidly, and makes a suitable cement for iron upon iron, for two stone surfaces, and especially for fastening iron to stone. The cement is insoluble, and is not attacked by strong acids.

Diamond Cement.—The diamond cement which is so useful in joining china, wood, leather, etc., is formed as follows: White glue, (or gelatine,) four lbs.; white lead, (dry,) one lb.; soft water, four qts.; alcohol, one qt. Boil the glue and lead in the water by means of a water-bath; when the glue is dissolved, add the alcohol and stir until the whole is well mixed. Pour into vials for use.

Cement for Metal and Glass.—The following cement will firmly attach any metallic substances to glass or porcelain: Mix two ounces of a thick solution of glue with one ounce of linseed-oil varnish, or three fourths of an ounce of Venice turpentine; boil them together, stirring them until they mix as thoroughly as possible. The pieces cemented should be tied together for two or three days.

Glue for Uniting Card-Board, etc.—For uniting card-board, paper, and small articles of fancy work, the best glue, dissolved with about one-third its weight of coarse brown sugar in the smallest quantity of boiling water, is very good. When this is in a liquid state it may be dropped in a thin cake upon a plate, and allowed to dry; when required for use, one end of the cake may be moistened by the mouth and rubbed on the substances to be joined.

A Cement Withstanding Heat and Moisture.—Pure white lead, or zinc white, ground in oil, and used very thick, is an excellent cement for mending broken crockery-ware; but it takes a long time to harden. It is well to put the mended object in some store-room, and not to look at it for several weeks or even months. It will then be found so firmly united that if ever again broken it will not part on the line of the former fracture.

Cement for Crockery.—To make a good cement for crockery, take one pound of white shellac pulverized; two ounces of clean gum mastic; put these into a bottle, and then add one half pound pure sulphuric ether. Let it stand half an hour, and then add half a gallon ninety per cent. alcohol, and shake occasionally until it is dissolved. Heat the edges of the article to be mended, and apply the cement with a pencil-brush; hold the article firmly together till the cement cools.

To Make Compound Glue.—Take very fine flour, mix it with white of eggs, isinglass and a little yeast; mingle the materials; heat them well together; spread them, the batter being made thin with gum-water, on even tin plates, and dry them in a stove, then cut them out for use. To color them, tinge the paste with Brazil or vermillion for red; indigo or verditer etc., for blue; saffron, turmeric, or gamboge for yellow.

HOUSEHOLD ORNAMENTS.

Pretty Hanging Ornaments.—Take a common pine cone, and plant in its crevices a few canary seeds; place this half way in a hyacinth water-glass, and the seeds will sprout, and throw out delicate little green feathery blades shortly, filling the whole upper portion with a little festoon of verdure.

Take a large turnip and scrape out the inside, leaving a thick wall all around. Fill the cavity with earth, and plant in it some clinging vine or morning-glory. Suspend the turnip with cords, and in a little time the vines twine around the strings, and the turnip, sprouting from below, will put forth leaves and stems that will turn upward and gracefully curl around the base.

Take a common tumbler or fruit can and fill it nearly full of soft water. Then tie a bit of coarse lace or cheese-sacking over it, and press down into the water, covered with a layer of peas. In a few days they will sprout, the little thread-like roots going down through the lace into the water, and the vines can be trained up to twine around the window; or, what is prettier, a frame may be made for the purpose.

The sweet-potato vine is also a curiosity; few would believe, until they have tried it, how pretty a sight might be made of it. Put a sweet potato in a tumbler of water, or any similar glass vessel; fill with water; keep the lower end of the tuber about one or two inches from the bottom of the vessel; keep on the mantel shelf; sun it for an hour or two each day, and soon little roots will appear—the eye will throw up a pretty vine, and grow rapidly over any trellis-work above.

The morning-glory is one of the prettiest climbers for parlor windows. Give it plenty of sun.

Pretty Mantel Ornaments.—A very pretty mantel ornament may be obtained by suspending an acorn, by a piece of thread tied around it, within half an inch of the surface of some water contained in a vase, tumbler, or saucer, and allowing it to remain undisturbed for several weeks. It will soon burst open, and small roots will seek the water; a straight and tapering stem, with beautiful, glossy green leaves, will shoot upward, and present a very pleasing appearance.

Chestnut trees may be grown in this manner, but their leaves are not as beautiful as those of the oak. The water should be changed once a month, taking care to supply water of the same warmth; bits of charcoal added to it will prevent the water from souring. If the leaves turn yellow, add one drop of ammonia into the utensil which holds the water, and it will renew their luxuriance.

Take a saucer and fill it with fresh green moss. Place in the center a pine cone, large size, having first wet it thoroughly. Then sprinkle it thoroughly with grass seed. The moisture will close the cone partially, and in a day or two the tiny glass spires will appear in the interstices, and in a week you will have a perfect cone of beautiful verdure. Keep secure from the frost, and give it plenty of water, and you will have a "thing of beauty" all the winter.

Rules for Arranging Cut Flowers.—The first thing to be considered in arranging cut flowers is the vase. If it is scarlet, blue, or many-colored, it must necessarily conflict with some hue in your boquet. Choose rather pure white, green, or transparent glass, which allows the delicate stems to be seen. Brown Swiss-wood, silver, bronze, or yellow straw conflict with nothing. The vase must be subordinate to what it holds. Use a bowl for roses; tall-spreading vases for gladiolus, fern, white lilies, and the like; cups for violets and tiny wood flowers. A flower-lover will in time collect shapes and sizes to suit each group.

Colors should be blended together with neutral tints, of which there are abundance—whites, grays, purples, tender greens—and which harmonize the pink, crimsons, and brilliant reds into soft unison.

Certain flowers assort well only in families, and are spoiled by mixing. Of these are balsams, hollyhocks, and sweet-peas, whose tender liquid hues are as those of drifting sunset clouds. Others may be massed with good effect. In arranging a large basket or vase it is well to mentally divide it into small groups, making each group perfectly harmonious with itself, and blending the whole with green and delicate colors. And above all, avoid stiffness. Let a bright tendril or spray of vine spring forth here and there, and wander over and around the vase at its will.

The water should be warm for a winter vase—cool, but not iced, for a summer one. A little salt or a bit of charcoal should be added in hot weather, to obviate vegetable decay, and the vase filled anew each morning. With these precautions your flowers, if set beside an open window at night, will keep their freshness for many hours even in July, and reward by their beautiful presence the kind hand which arranged and tended them.

To Crystallize Grasses.—The best rule is to put in as much alum as the water will dissolve; when it will take no more, it is called a saturated solution. Then pour it into an earthen jar, and boil it slowly until evaporated nearly one half. Now suspend the grasses in such a manner that their tops will be under the solution. Put the whole in a cool place where not the least draught of air or motion will disturb the formation of crystals. In twenty-four or thirty-six hours take out the grasses, and let them harden in a cool room. Beautiful blue crystals can be made by preparing blue-vitriol or sulphate of copper in the same manner; but don't let it drop on your dress or the carpet. Gold-colored crystals can be produced by adding turmeric to the alum solution, and a few drops of extract of log-wood will make rich, purple crystals.

To Take Leaf Impressions.—Hold oiled paper in the smoke of a lamp, or of pitch, until it becomes coated with the smoke; then take a perfect leaf, having a pretty outline; after warming it between the hands, lay the leaf upon the smoked side of the paper, with the under side down, press it evenly upon the paper, that every part may come in contact; go over it lightly with a rolling-pin, then remove the leaf with care to a plain piece of white note-paper, and use the rolling-pin again; you will then have a beautiful impression of the delicate veins and outline of the leaf. And this process is so simple that any person, with a little practice to enable him to apply the right quantity of smoke to the oil paper and give the leaf proper pressure, can prepare leaf impressions such as a naturalist would be proud to possess. Specimens can be neatly preserved in book form, interleaving the impressions with tissue paper.

Rockeries, Vases, and Hanging-Baskets.—They can, if properly made, and furnished with suitable, healthy plants, be made very ornamental additions to the lawn and piazza. Artificial rockeries should partake of a natural appearance as much as possible. Ferns, alpine plants, cypress-vines, vincas, lobelia, dwarf stocks, etc., are good plants for these. Vases, and hanging-baskets, whatever their design, should be at least ten or twelve inches in diameter, and six inches or more in depth. Be sure the drainage is good. Glazed pots, and those without outlet for water, are not good. The soil should not be over-rich, as it forces the growth too much for beauty and gracefulness. Climbing and drooping vines may, however, be stimulated. A good composition is one-third "scouring-sand," the rest dark loam and leaf-mold. The fallings around pine-trees are excellent. For the center plant, dracena or achyranthus, or coleus, or centaurea is good. Next to center, begonias of all sorts, pilea, verbenas, petunia, vincas, sedunes. For edges, oxalis-lobelia, and various ivies and grasses. Water regularly.

Vases for Cut Flowers.—To the average person a bunch of flowers in a vase must be harmonious and beautiful under all circumstances. The artistic and educated taste knows that it is quite as easy for the combination to be most unpleasing.

In a paper on the relations of vases to the cut flowers which they will hold, a writer in *Garden and Forest* shows quickly that the subject is worthy of consideration. "A flat circular dish," he says, "is needed for waterlilies, and as the flowers are in this case large the containing vessel must be ample in size, not merely to hold the flowers, but to preserve a proper sense of proportion. Tall spikes require tall vases, which should not be cylindrical, but should be sensibly wider at the top than at the bottom. Roses and flowers with comparatively short stems require low, broad vessels, flaring at the top so as to admit of the graceful drooping which is so attractive with both leaves and flowers. Not more than four or five differently shaped flower vases are really necessary, the types of form being either flat or low circular vessels, which may be widely fluted upon the edges to break the too great uniformity of a plain circular rim, or round vessels which spread more or less as the sides rise from the bottom, and which may also be widely fluted at the top. All forms which bulge below, or which are in the smallest degree bizarre in shape, must be rejected."

"If, with the Japanese, we consider a single beautiful flower enough at a time, a narrow containing vessel may be used. The Japanese use a piece of bamboo, which, from its irregular surface, loses the stiffness of the cylindrical form. We have no bamboo to use, and imitations in glass, china, or earthenware are, like all imitations, offensive to good taste. Flower vases should always be of some opaque material, and, all things considered, good unglazed earthenware is to be preferred, only it should be impermeable to water and not coarse in texture. It should also be without ornamentation of any kind, and of a single and uniform tint of color."

"Opaque white" vases usually present too strong a contrast, and all colored glasses are to be rejected, together with white or colorless glasses, which show the "usually unsightly" stem of the flower. To this last rule, however, there is an admitted exception.

Umbrella Covers.—Cut a circle from paper of the desired diameter, and cut this into eight triangular pieces. Take one of these pieces and fold the two sides together ; begin at the bottom of the triangle and cut off an inch, narrowing the strip cut off till it reaches a point midway between the base and the apex of the triangle. This makes the umbrella curve down when it is opened. If not thus trimmed it will be flat on top. When the pattern is cut lay it on the goods so that the selvage will be at the base of each triangular section. Experiment with old muslin first, and then new goods may be used. Sew the sections together with strong thread doubled, and long enough to reach the entire length of the seam. With some ingenuity and patience almost anyone can cover an umbrella and make a very passable job of it.

Fractures. — There are simple, compound, and comminuted fractures. When a bone is broken in one place, without any external wound, it is a simple fracture; when there is an external wound leading down to the broken bone, it is compound; and when a bone is broken in two or more places, as when a splinter of bone is broken off, the fracture is comminuted.

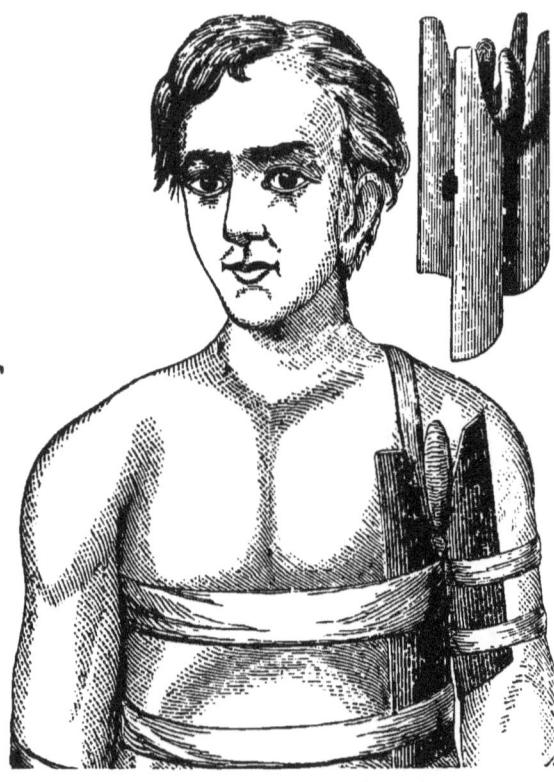

As soon as the fracture is suspected, the surgeon should be summoned. He will be able at once to determine the nature and extent of the injury, and to summon to his aid one of the various appliances which have been invented for relief of patients in such an emergency. The accompanying cuts will illustrate the construction and application of some of the most useful "splints" * for fractures thus far brought to the attention of the public.

The first splint is for the arm, the second for the leg. Both bear the highest commendation, and are in extensive use by the medical profession, and may be purchased at small cost.

---

* Invented by H. L. Richardson, M.D., Physician and Surgeon, West Washington Place, New York.

INDEX.

HOME.
	PAGE
Only Man has a Home	9
Virtues of the Hearth are the Securities of the People	9
Home Builds the House	9
Origin of the Family	10
How the Family Develops Character	10
The Family often Ripens Rapidly those who Carry its Burdens	11
The Family Multiplies Happiness	11
The Family Blesses in Necessitating Housekeeping	12

MARRIAGE.
What God thinks of Marriage	13
Principles Governing Marriage	13

HOW TO PERPETUATE THE HONEY-MOON.
Continue your Courtship	16
Do not Assume a Right to Neglect your Companion More after Marriage than you did Before	16
Have no Secrets that you Keep from your Companion	16
Do not Conceal your Marriage for an Hour	16
Avoid the Appearance of Evil	16
Once Married never open your Mind to any Change	16
Make the best of the Inevitable	16
Keep Step in Mental Development	16
Keep a Lively Interest in the Business of the Firm	16
Gauge your Expenses by your Revenues	17
Start from where your Parents Started Rather than From Where they Now Are	17
Avoid Debt	17
Do not Both get Angry at the Same Time	17
Do not Allow yourself Ever to Come to an Open Rupture	17
Study to Understand your Companion's Disposition, in Order to Please and Avoid Friction	17
Study to Conform your Tastes and Habits to those of your Companion	17
Chang and Eng were the Siamese Twins	17

HOW TO BE A GOOD HUSBAND
	PAGE
Honor your Wife	17
Love your Wife	17
Show your Love	17
Suffer for your Wife if Need be	18
Consult with Her	18
Study to Keep her Young	18
Study with Her	18
Help to Bear Her Burdens	18
Make yourself Helpful by Thoughtfulness	18
Express your Will, not by Commands, but by Suggestions	18
Study your own Character as Husband	18
Seek to Refine your Nature	19
Be a Gentleman, as Well as Husband	19
Remember the Past Experience of your Wife	19
Level Up	19
Stay at Home	19
Take your Wife with You into Society	20

HOW TO BE A GOOD WIFE.
Reverence your Husband	20
Love Him	20
Do not Conceal your Love from Him	20
Forsake All for Him	20
Confide in Him	20
Keep His Love	20
Cultivate the Modesty and Delicacy of Youth	20
Cultivate Personal Attractiveness	21
Cultivate Physical Attractiveness	21
Do not Forget the Power of Incidental Attention	21
Make your Home Attractive	21
Preserve Sunshine	22
Study your Husband's Character	22
Cultivate His Better Nature	22
Study to meet your Duties as a Wife	23
Seek to secure your Husband's Happiness	23
Study his Interest	23
Practice Economy	23

FACTS FOR PARENTS.
Paternity is Earth's Highest Dignity	23
Children are Boons	23
Children Give New Life to a Home	23

	PAGE
Children are Great Teachers of Theology	24
Parents put their Image and Superscription upon their Character	24
Prepare for the Duties of the Parental Relation	24
Conduct your Home for your Children	24
Remember that Children do Grow Old	24
Recall, as distinctly as Possible, your own Youth	24

FAMILY GOVERNMENT.

Forty-two Hints	24

SUGGESTIONS TO CHILDREN.

Reverence your Parents	29
Appreciate your Parents	29
Do not shorten Childhood by Haste	28
Confide in your Parents	29

MEMBERS OF THE FAMILY.

Brothers in the Family	29
Sisters in the Family	29
How to Treat the Aged	20
A Mother-in-law in the Family	30
A Step-mother in the Family	30

SERVANTS IN THE FAMILY.

A good Master makes a good Servant	30
May expect Promotion from showing Capacity	31
Should Identify Himself with the Interests of his Employer	31
Should Preserve the Strictest Fidelity	31
Should Serve them out of Sight as Scrupulously as when under the Employer's Eye	31
May Secure his wishes by Requests, not by Commands	31
Should Seek to meet the Wishes of the Employer in Spirit	31
Should Secure Permanence of Engagement by making himself Necessary	31
Should Carefully study the Duties Assigned	31
Should avoid Habits and Manners distasteful to his Employer	31
Should avoid Talking Much	31
Should seek to Gain and Retain Respect	31

HINTS TO EMPLOYERS.

Employer should remember that all Rights do not center in Himself	31
Identify himself with the Interests of his Employés	81
Pay Honestly what he would Expect in a Reversed Case	81
Pay Promptly	81
Watch over the Morals of his Employés	81
Inspire Respect	81

	PAGE
Encourage the Worker	81
Instruct With Kindliness	81
Correct in Authority and Gentleness	81

MISTRESS IN THE FAMILY.

Should Remember that her Position gives her Certain Dignity	32
She Must Preserve Good Temper	32
Avoid Fault-finding	32
Improve your Servants by showing them how they can do Better	32
Secure their Confidence in Your Kindness	32
Keep them in Self-respect	32
Put your Servants into the Way of Self-care	82
Inspire Them with the Sense of Life's Worth	82

SUPERIORS AND INFERIORS.

Proper Respect for Superiors is a due Part of Liberty	82
Children should be Subordinate to Parents	32
Superiors in Age, Office, and Station, have Precedence	32
A Parent, Teacher, or Employer, may Admonish	32
A Superior may use Language and Manners of Freedom	82
Respect is Due from All to All	33
It is the most Exalted Philosophy to accept Facts	33

TRAINING CHILDREN FOR GIVEN ENDS.

What is your Purpose in Training	83
Training for Usefulness	83
Training for Wealth	33
Training for Greatness	84
Training for Refined Society	34
Training for Heaven	84

CHOOSING A CALLING.

But few are Elected to any one Particular Calling or Trade	84
Study your Natural Proclivities	34
Study Providence	34
Do not Fret over your Natural Qualifications	34
Wishes are often Presentiments of Capabilities	35
Having Settled the Calling, let it Remain Settled	35
Pith	35

HOW TO CONDUCT FAMILY PRAYER.

Conduct it according to your Strength	85
Have Family Prayer	85
Collect your Household	35
Have each Member take Part	85

INDEX.

If the Father is not a Professing Christian, the Duty of Leadership Devolves upon the Mother............ 35
If the Father cannot command Courage to Lead in Prayer.................. 36
It is a valuable Custom on the Sabbath Morning for the Worship to be Varied................................. 36
It is Helpful to have a Room where all Meet for Prayer 36

GRACE AT THE TABLE.

Render unto God Thanks for Daily Bread............................... 36

HOW TO PROFIT BY HABIT.

Habit Becomes Destiny................ 36

HINTS AND HELPS IN CONVERSATION.

Eighty-four Hints and Helps..........37–41

GOOD MANNERS.

Politeness is Loving thy Neighbor as Thyself............................ 41
Affectation is the Foe of Good Breeding 41
The Divine Law of Politeness......... 41
Gentleman and Gentlewoman......... 42
Good Manners are Important Helps.... 42
American Manners.................... 42
Study, Observation, and Experiment... 42
Should be Taught to Children Gradually 42
A Few Brief Rules should be Suspended in Every School-room................ 42

TABLE MANNERS.

Cleanliness is the First Element of Decency............................... 42
Children should be Trained in the Family 43
Table Rules........................... 43
Table Improprieties. (44 described).... 44

CHURCH MANNERS.

Thirteen Rules....................... 46

INTRODUCTIONS—HOW TO GIVE THEM.

Not Necessary to Introduce Every body to Every body....................... 46
Business Men......................... 46
Inferior should be Introduced to the Superior................................. 46
In Presenting Persons, Speak Names Plainly.............................. 47
If you are the Inferior, be not First to Extend the Hand..................... 47
In Introducing Members of your own Family, Always Mention the Name... 47
If you are a Gentleman................ 47

SALUTATIONS, AND HOW TO MAKE THEM.

Salutation the Touchstone of Good Breeding............................. 47
A Great Rudeness not to Return a Salutation................................. 47

RECEPTIONS—BEST METHODS.

The Duty of Receiving Visitors........ 47
When one Enters, Rise Immediately... 47
If the Master Receives................ 47
If Several Come at Once.............. 48
If Visitor is a Stranger............... 48
If Some who are Present Withdraw.... 48

VISITS AND CALLS.

Visits of Ceremony, Congratulation, Condolence, and Friendship............. 48
Visits of Ceremony.................... 47
Visits of Congratulation.............. 48
Visits of Condolence.................. 48
Visits of Friendship.................. 48
Visiting Cards....................... 48
A Gentleman Attending Ladies Making Calls............................... 48
In Terminating a Call................ 48
Morning Call......................... 48
Soiled Over-shoes and Wet Wraps...... 48
Gentlemen Attending should be Prompt 48
Twenty-eight Rules................... 48

HOSTS AND GUESTS.

Hosts should give Guests Home Feeling 50
Guests should Show Hosts the Home Feeling.............................. 50

APPOINTMENTS.

Dinner Parties........................ 51
Evening Parties...................... 51
Christmas............................ 51
The New Year......................... 52

WEDDINGS.

Custom gives Liberty to Follow Taste.. 53
For a Stylish Wedding................ 53
For a Formal Wedding................ 53
In a Well-ordered Wedding........... 53
When Ceremony is performed in Church 53
Following Bridesmaids and Groomsmen 54
Order of Approach.................... 54
If the Ring is used................... 54
Have only Ushers..................... 54
Order Changes with Fancy............ 54
When Ceremony is Ended............. 54
If Ceremony performed in House...... 54
Bridegroom takes early occasion to Thank Clergyman................... 54

FUNERALS.

When Member of Family Dies......... 54
A Funeral Service.................... 54
Minister Not Expected to go to Grave.. 54

INDEX.

IMPORTANT RULES OF CONDUCT.
	Page
Always Respectful to Parents	55
Courteous to Brothers and Sisters	55
Delicate Attentions of Lover	55
Mutual Kindness between Employers and Employed	55

POLITENESS.
Seventy-two Important Rules for	55

AMUSEMENTS—THEIR IMPORTANCE.
To Keep Enemy out of Fort, Occupy It Yourself	58
When Amusements become Sinful	58

HOME ENTERTAINMENT.
Provide in the Home not only Instructive, but also Entertaining, Reading	58
Provide Good Supply of Pictures and Toys for very young Children	59
Enter into the Sports of your Children	59
Lead Children to Cultivate Fruits and Flowers	59
Cultivate Music, Vocal and Instrumental	59
Collect Shells, Plants, and Specimens in Geology and Mineralogy	59
Give the Boys Boxes of Tools	59
Give Little Girls Dolls, and nice Large Dolls to Larger Girls	59
Interest the Children in Decorating the Home	59
Celebrate Birthdays, Holidays, and Anniversaries	59
As far as possible let Each Child have a Companion near its own Age, with Congenial Tastes	59
Use Hospitality	60
Establish a Reading Circle	60
Keep Up Family Relations After Leaving Home	60

HOW AND WHAT TO READ.
The Use of Books	60
A Course of Reading	60
A Few Books may Give Culture	60
Choosing Books is Important Business	60
Some Books should be Read Whether we Like Them or Not	61
Never Read Second-class Stories	61
Never Read what you Do Not Wish to Remember	61

HEALTH AT HOME.
Health is Wealth	62
Special Home Ministry	63
Ministry must Begin Early	63
Ministry Illustrated	63
Another Illustration	63

CHOOSING A PHYSICIAN.
	Page
Select the Physician Early	64
Select a Physician of Integrity	64
Choose a Physician of Clean Lips	64
Having Chosen Him, Give Him Your Confidence	64
He should be Able, Thorough as a Student, of Untiring Industry	64
Which School of Medicine	65
Be Considerate of his Time and Rest	65
Don't Abuse his Confidence by Trivial Calls	65
Physician in the Intervals of Sickness	65
Better to care for a Man's Health than for his Disease	65
Why do Successful Medical Men often Die Prematurely?	66
Physician should be Reverential	66
Qualities of a Good Doctor, by a Doctor	66

PREVENTION OF DISEASE.
Early and Strange Notions of Disease	67
What is Disease?	67
Many Diseases may be Avoided	67
Methods of Prevention	68
Responsibility of Health Commissioners	68
The Divine Plan	68
Why Medicine is Taken	68

THE BLOOD—ITS RELATION TO LIFE AND HEALTH.
Change and Waste	75
Supply from the Blood	75
Quantity of the Blood	75
Effects Produced by Loss of Blood	76
Transfusion of Blood	76
Composition of Blood	76
Water of the Blood	76
Mineral Ingredients	76
Albumen in the Blood	77
Albumen	77
Quantity of Albumen	77
Fibrine	77
Other Substances	77
Described Globules of the Blood	77
Remarkable Characteristics of the Globules	78
Color of Blood Globules	78
Opacity of the Blood	78
White Globules	78
Coagulation of the Blood	79
Time for Coagulation	79
Cause of Coagulation	79
Serum of the Blood	79
A "Clot" of Blood	80
Importance of Coagulation	80
Coagulation Stops Bleeding	80
Coagulation in the Interior of the Body	80
Ligature and Coagulation	81
Coagulation Spontaneous	81
Why Coagulation does not Stop Circulation	81
Two Different Kinds of Blood in the Body	82

INDEX. 359

FOOD AND HEALTH.

	Page
Food Makes Blood for the Body,	82
Amount of Food Daily Needed	82
Kinds of Food Needed	83
Process of Digestion	83
Nutritious and Healthy Articles of Food	83
A Suggestive Conversation	84
Onions	84
Tomatoes	85
Healthful Bread	85
Unground Wheat	85
A Very Nutritious Bread	86
Fresh or Stale Bread. Which?	86
Oat Meal	86
Poisonous Properties of Moldy Bread	87
Healthfulness of Fruit	87
Fruit Saves Doctors' Bills	87
Danger of Eating Fruit to Excess	88
Special Danger in Summer Vacation	88
Are Nuts Healthful?	88
Salt with Nuts	88

HINTS ABOUT HEALTHFUL EATING.

A Good Appetite Healthful	89
Appetite not an Infallible Guide	89
Evil of Rapid Eating	89
How to Regulate the Quantity of Food	89
Eating too Much	90
Food should be Thoroughly Chewed	90
Hint about "Small Mouthfuls"	90
How Much shall we Eat?	90
Loss of Appetite, and How to Recover it	91
Rest Before and After Eating	91
Eating Between Meals	91
Best Times for Meals	91
Comparative Value of Different Modes of Cooking	92
Variety of Vegetables at the Same Meal	92
"How Long to Starve"	93

FOOD FOR THE SICK.

Toast Water	93
Barley Water	93
Barley Gruel	93
Oatmeal Gruel	93
Parched Corn Gruel	94
Ground Rice Milk	94
Bread Jelly	94
Iceland Moss Jelly	94
Apple Tapioca	94
Tapioca Jelly	94
Meat Jelly	94
To make Arrow-root	95
Apple Water	95
Apple Tea	95
Currant Drink	95
Beverage of Figs and Apples	95
Ice Cream and Beef Juice	95
Broth from Fowls	95
Chicken Broth	95
To Cook birds for Convalescents	96
Mutton Broth	96
A Strong Broth	96
Calves' Feet	96
Nourishing Soup	96

	Page
Honey	96
Isinglass	96
Brewis	96
Suet and Milk	97
Mucilage of Gum-arabic	97
Strong Tonic Drink	97
Bran Tea	97
Savory Custard	97
Raw Beef	97
Recipe for Beef Tea	98

WATER—ITS RELATION TO HEALTH.

Its Source	99
Spring and Well Water in the Country	99
How Water Becomes Polluted	99
Caution in Locating Wells	100
Care in Constructing Cisterns	100
How to Examine Suspected Water	100
Purifying Water with Alum	100
Is Soft Water Better than Hard Water for Drinking Purposes?	101
Water Cure or Hydropathy	101
Water a Powerful Absorbent	101
Caution concerning Standing Water	101
Distilled Water	101
Do Lead Pipes Poison the Water	102

ICE-WATER AND HEALTH.

Ice-Water Hinders Digestion	102
Ice Drinks affecting the Head	102
Other evils of Iced Drinks	103
A Suggestive Caution about Ice	103
How to Cool Drinking Water Without Ice	103

SUMMER BEVERAGES.

Avoid All Alcoholic Drinks	104
Good Cool Water	104
To Allay Thirst without Drinking	104
The Best kind of Water	104
Lemonade and Lemons	104
Lemon Sugar for Traveling	105
Lemons for Excessive Thirst	105
Lemons for Invalids	105
Lemons at "Tea-time"	105
Organic Matter in Drinking Water	105
Various Drinks	106
Orangeade Medically Prescribed	106
Ices and Ice-cream	107

TEA, COFFEE, AND HEALTH.

How Tea is Grown	107
Preparation of Tea for Market	107
Tea Plant in Respect of Quality	108
Tea and Digestion	108
Tea-drinking and Sick Headache; an Illustration	108
The Doctrine Stated	109
A Home Case	109
Was the Case Hereditary?	109
Failure of Remedies	109
More Careful Investigation	110
The True Cause Suspected	110

	PAGE
The Usual Answer	110
First Efforts for Relief	110
Relief at Last	110
Relapse and Recovery	111
Was the Case "Peculiar"	111
A Remarkable Test	111
A Second Remarkable Test	112
A Third Remarkable Test	112
Relief for Most Headache Sufferers	112
The Kinds of Tea Used	113
Other Suspected Bad Effects of Tea	113
Tea a Powerful Excitant	113
Tea a Powerful Astringent	113
How to Test Each Case Properly	113
How to Stop Drinking Tea	114
The Old Cry Stated	114
How Tea was Banished from a Minister's Table	114
Is Tea Good for Well People?	115
Coffee as a Beverage	115
Substitute for Coffee	116

THE AIR WE BREATHE.

The Wonder of Breathing	116
Fresh Air Constantly Needed	116
What is Pure Air?	117
How Fresh Air Purifies the Blood	117
Capacity of the Lungs for Air	118
Amount of Air We Breathe	118
Healthful Respiration	118
Relief from Hiccough	119
How to Check Sneezing, Coughing, etc.	119
Evil Effect of Breathing Respired Air	120
Air in Rooms Vitiated by Lighted Fires	120
Impure Air in Small Rooms and Tenement Houses	120
How to Ventilate Houses	121
Air in Sick Rooms	121
Bad Air in School and Lecture Rooms	121
Teachers and Bad Air	122
Foul Air in Churches	122
How to Remove the Foul Air from Churches	122
Bad Air versus Religion	122
Night Air Healthy	124
Water as a Purifier	124
Sea Air	124
Air at the Seaside	124
Are Winds Healthful?	134
Dampness of the Air and Health	125
Sea and Mountain Air Compared	125
Mutual Diffusion of Air	125
Our Great Enemies, the Marshes	126

DISINFECTANTS — HOW TO PREPARE AND USE THEM.

Fresh Air and Sunlight	126
Water	126
Charcoal	127
Charcoal and Lime	127
Clay	127
Quicklime and Gypsum	127
Sifted Ashes	127
Surface Soil	127

	PAGE
Fresh Stone-lime	127
Copperas	127
Chloride of Lime	128
Salt and Lime Paste	128
Carbolic Acid	128
Salt and Nitrate of Lead	128
"Disinfecting Mixture"	128
General Disinfecting Compound	128
Coffee as a Disinfectant	129
Sunflowers as Disinfectants	129
Boiling for Infected Clothing	129
Soaking for Foul Clothing	129
Boiling after Disinfection	129
Carbolic Acid for Clothing	130
How to Fumigate Rooms	130
To Disinfect Water-closets	130
To Disinfect Dead bodies	131
Comparative Permanent Value of Different Disinfectants	131
Caution in Removing Foul Air from Wells	132
Precautions in Ventilating Infected Rooms	132
Heat and Steam	132
A New Disinfectant	132

SUNLIGHT AND HEALTH.

Power of Sunlight	133
Seclusion from Sunlight	133
Philosophy of the Influence of Sunlight	133
Sunlight and Plants	133
Sunlight and Domestic Animals	133
Sunlight and Human Life	134
Another Testimony	134
Sunlight and Miners	135
Paralysis cured by Sunlight	135
Neuralgia, Rheumatism, and Hypochondria, Cured by Sunshine	135
Florence Nightingale on Sunlight	135
Sunlight Shut out by Parasols	136
The Sunlight and the Blinds	136
The Sun brings Flies	137
Sunlight and Sleep	137
Sunlight and Cars	137
Give the Children Sunlight	137
Sunlight in the School-room	137
The "Solaries" of the Ancients	138
Sunlight and Digestion—an Illustration	138

CARE OF THE EYES.

Strange Neglect of the Eyes	142
How the Eye is Kept Clean	143
How the Eye is Protected from Irritation	143
How to Improve the Eyelashes	143
Overstraining the Eyes	143
Eye Strain sometimes the Cause of Headache	144
Danger of Too Continuous Use	144
Proper Distance of the Object	144
Proper Quantity of Light	144
Best Direction of the Light	145
The Use of Colored Glasses	145

INDEX.

	PAGE
Relieving Near and Far-sightedness	145
Changing Light not a Cause for Alarm	146
Use Glasses as Soon as Needed	146
Double Glasses sometimes useful	146
Squinting and its Remedy	146
Near-Sightedness in Children	147
How to Remove Foreign Bodies from the Eye	147
"Eye Stones," or Grain of Flaxseed for the Eye	147
"Wild Hairs"	147
"Cataract" in the Eye	147
Color-Blindness	147
Color-Blindness Explained	147
The Question of Color-Blindness important	148
Cure of Color-Blindness	148
Medical Treatment of Color-Blindness	148
False Sight Explained	148
How to treat a Sty	149
Important hints Concerning Eyesight	149

CARE OF THE EAR.

How Sound is Produced	152
Careful Attention and Treatment	152
Temporary Deafness	152
Insect in the Ear	153
Other Small Bodies in the Ear	153
Fungus in the Ear	153
Remedy for Fungus	153
Singing in the Ear	153
Remedies for Earaches	154
Earache Relieved by Arnica	154
Don't Treat the Ear for Toothache	155
Don't "Box the Ears"	155

CARE OF THE NOSE—SMELLING.

The Sense of Smell	155
The Object may be Distant	156
Foreign Substances in the Nose	156
Bleeding from the Nose	156
Treatment of Excessive Nose-bleed	156
Simple Remedy for Nose-bleed	156
Catarrh of the Nose	156
Treatment of Nasal Catarrh	157

CARE OF THE TEETH.

Number of the Teeth	157
How the Teeth are Classified	157
Order and Period of their Growth	157
The Composition of Teeth	158
Causes of Decay	158
Want of Cleanliness	158
Deposit of Tartar Injurious	158
How to Care for Permanent Teeth	159
How to Care for the Teeth Early	159
How Often should the Teeth be Washed?	159
Use of Aromatic Water	159
A Mixture for the Teeth	159
Tooth-powders Often Injurious	160
Cracking Nuts with the Teeth	160
Importance of Healthful Gums	160
Teething	160

	PAGE
"Toothache Cures"	160
What to do with Decayed Teeth	161
Artificial Teeth	162

CARE OF THE HAIR.

Growth of the Hair	162
How to Preserve the Hair	162
Why Ladies are not Bald	162
Why the Hair Falls Out	162
How to Prevent the Hair from Falling Out	162
"Organic Baldness" Incurable	163
"Functional" Baldness Curable	163
How to Cure Functional Baldness	163
Avoid Hair Dyes	163
Caution in Using "Hair Oils"	163
A Good Hair-dressing	163
Value of Castor Oil for the Hair	163
A Preparation of Glycerine and Rose-water Recommended	164
Relative Value of Other Oil Preparations	164
How to Prevent the Hair from Turning Gray	164
Washing the Hair with Soda-Water Relieves Headache	164
Sudden Changes in the Color of the Hair	164
A Remarkable Case in Berlin	164
A Remarkable Case in Rotterdam	165
Sudden Changes of Color Without Fright	165
Utility of Beards	165
To Remove Dandruff	166

CARE OF THE FEET.

Warm Feet Essential to Health	166
How to Cure the Habit of Cold Feet	166
How to Sleep with Warm Feet	166
Waking Up with Cold Feet	166
To Keep the Feet Dry	167
Short and High-heeled Shoes	167
Cause of Chilblains	167
To Cure Chilblains	167
How to Prevent, and How to Remove, Corns	168
Cause of Ingrowing Toe-Nail	169
Remedies for Ingrowing Nails	169
Remedy for Blistered Feet	170
Bunions	170
To Cure Frosted Feet	170
Treatment of Scalded Feet	170

CARE OF THE SKIN.

Use of the Skin	170
Color of the Skin	171
The Pores of the Skin	171
Keeping the Skin Clean	172
Diseases of the Skin—Warts	172
Grafting the Skin	172
To Remove Warts	173
Chapped Lips and Hands	174
Freckles	174
Tan and Sunburn	174
Cause and Cure of Moles	174
Pimples and Sores	174

INDEX.

BATHING AND HEALTH.
	PAGE
Bathing in Ancient Times	175
The Object of the Ancient Bath	175
The Bath a Public Benefit	175
Fresh and Salt-Water Bathing	176
Bathing at the Sea-side	176
Tonic Value of Sea-side Air	176
A Caution in Sea-side Bathing	176
Peril at Crowded Sea-side Resorts	177
Season for Sea-Bathing	177
Duration of the Sea Bath	177
Proper Limitation of Sea-Bathing	177
Plunge Bathing	178
Surf Bathing	188
Best Hour of the Day for Bathing	178
Condition of the Body Before Bathing	178
Helpful Accessories to Bathing Exercise	178
Avoid Exposure	179
Bathing Indoors	179
Benefit of a "Towel Bath"	179
Temperature of Baths	179
The Best Bath for Children	179
Turkish and Russian Baths	180
Medicated Baths	180
Convenient Vapor Baths	180
Electric Baths	180
Hot Sand Baths	180
Bathing Dresses	181
Twenty-two Brief Hints to Bathers	181

SLEEP AND HEALTH.
Sleep a Necessity	182
What Sleep will Cure	183
How we go to Sleep	183
Position During Sleep	183
Why High Pillows are Injurious	183
Sleeping on the Back or Side. Which?	184
Evil Effects of Sleeping Exclusively on One Side	184
Amount of Sleep Necessary	184
Testimony of an Experienced Farmer	184
Waking Children	185
Best Hours for Sleeping	185
Kiss the Children a "Happy Good Night"	185
The Great Pleasure of Sleep	185
Sleeping Alone	186
Are Feather Beds Unhealthful?	186
In What Direction shall the Bed Stand?	186
Sleep for the Invalid	186
Lack of Sleep Causes Leanness	186
Sleeplessness—How to Prevent it	188
Sleeplessness—How to Cure it	188
An Eminent Clergyman's Advice	189
Slumber at Will	190
Sleep Procured by Medicine	190
"A Pillow for the Sleepless"	190
Sleeping Hints	191
Short Sleepers	191
Living Without Sleep	191
Curious Cases of Long Sleeping	192
Soft or Hard Beds. Which?	192
Warm or Cold Sleeping-rooms. Which?	193
Thorough Ventilation of Sleeping-rooms	193
Time Required for Airing Beds	193
Dreaming and Somnambulism	193

	PAGE
The Cause of Nightmare	193
Snoring, and How to Stop it	194
Are Plants in Sleeping-rooms Injurious?	195
Plants give out Carbonic Acid During the Night	195
Flowering Plants More Injurious than Others	196
Plants Exhale Other Noxious Substances	196
Sleep and Death	196

CLOTHING AND HEALTH.
Most Healthful Clothing	197
Flannel in Summer as well as Winter	197
Best Color for Clothing	197
Texture of Clothing should not be Close	198
Evil of Insufficient Clothing	198
Evil of Low-necked Dress	198
High-heeled Boots and Shoes	198
Newspapers as Protectors from Cold	199
Warm Clothing for the Feet	199
Frequent Change of Clothing for the Feet	199
How to Wear Underclothing	200
Bad Effects from Using "Garters"	200
Muffling the Throat	200
Remove Wet Clothing	200
Poisonous Clothing—Gloves	201
Other Cases of Glove-Poisoning	201
Poisonous Socks	201
Other Poisonous Clothing	201
How to Avoid such Poisoning	201
How to Cure such Clothing	202
How to Protect the Public from such Clothing	202
Injurious Dress of Many School-Girls	202
How Fashionable Dress Interferes with Education	202
Increasing Demand for Healthy Clothing	203
The Tyranny of Fashion	203

TIGHT-LACING AND HEALTH—IMPORTANT TESTIMONY.
Physical Effects of Tight-pressing Garments	204
Effect on Respiration	204
Effect on Size	204
Investigations by Herbst	204
High Medical Testimony	204
Case Reported by the "British Medical Journal"	205
Tight Lacing Pollutes the Blood	205
Weak and Silly Excuses Described	206
Tight Lacing and General Weakness	207
Absurdity of Tight Lacing	207
The General Question Illustrated	208

EXERCISE AND HEALTH.
Toil and Activity Necessary to Health	213
Severe Exercise after Eating Injurious	213
Light Exercise after Eating is Healthful	214
These Rules Apply also to Mental Exercise	214

INDEX.

Early Walking and Its Value.......... 214
How to Make the Walk most Healthful 214
Walking Combined with Useful Investigation 214
In Walking the Dress should be Loose.. 214
Walk Untrammeled................... 215
Effect of Tight Lacing on Walking..... 215
Exercise for Delicate Women.......... 215
Wear the Right Kind of Shoes.......... 215
Exercise a Cure for Many Diseases..... 216
Exercise "About the House" Not Enough............................. 216
Exercise by Rule Firmly Observed..... 216
Exercise as a Cure for Low Spirits...... 216
Abuse of Physical Exercise............ 217
False Criticism concerning Exercise Answered 217
Riding and Rowing, and other kinds of Exercise............................. 218
Swimming as Exercise................ 218

CRYING, LAUGHING, AND SINGING.

Crying and Health.................... 219
Laughing and Health................. 219
The Laughing Cure 219
Physical Influence of Singing.......... 219
Age for Vocal Training................ 220

OCCUPATIONS AND HEALTH—VITAL STATISTICS.

Mental Labor and Health. An Illustration 221
There are Hundreds of Similar Cases... 221
Average Longevity of Diverse Avocations............................... 222
Order of Mortality in Certain Classes of Manual Labor...................... 222
Comparative Ages of Persons Active in Business............................ 222
Vital Statistics—Births 223
Vital Statistics—Marriages............ 223
Vital Statistics—Deaths............... 223
Expectation of Human Life............ 223

DWELLINGS AND HEALTH.

Importance of a Healthful Location ... 224
Remove from a Foul District 225
Location of Dwellings in Cities........ 225
Shade Trees around our Dwellings..... 225
High Ceilings and Health............. 225
Capacity of Bricks for Dampness....... 225
Damp Walls and their Relation to Health 226
Dampness of Other Walls............. 226
Why Damp Walls are Injurious........ 226
How to Dry Damp Walls.............. 227
How to Prevent Walls from Becoming Damp. A Successful Experiment.... 227
Damp Closets and Health............. 228
Caution Against Damp Floors......... 228
How to Make Dry Cellar Floors....... 228
Danger from Vegetables in Cellars..... 228

Danger from Wetting Coal in Cellars... 228
Sitting-rooms and Bedrooms and Health 228
The Kitchen Sink and Health.......... 229
Ripe Fruit in Sitting or Sleeping-rooms 229
The Out-door Parts of the House...... 229
House Cisterns and Health............ 230
How to Remedy the Evil of Bad Cisterns 230
"Death in the Dishcloth "............. 230
Secure General House Sanitary Inspection 231

SCHOOL-ROOMS AND HEALTH.

Near-sightedness in Schools........... 232
An Alarming Fact..................... 232
How to Remedy the Evil 233
How the Evils are Caused............. 233

CARE OF CHILDREN.

Early Food of Children................ 234
Changes of Early Diet—Weaning...... 235
Best Rule as to the Exact Time for Weaning........................... 235
Arrangement of Regular Meals for Children............................. 235
Is the Mother's Health Injured by Nursing?.............................. 235
The Mother's Food while Nursing..... 236
A Common Artificial Food Condemned. 236
Early Baths for Children.............. 236
Early Clothing for Children. 236
Early Sleep of Children............... 236
Shall Children be Rocked to Sleep?.... 237
Shall Feather Pillows be Used for Babies' Heads?....................... 237
Babies' Bow-legs and How to Prevent them............................... 237
Babies' Knock-knees, and How to Prevent them 238
How to Care for Children's Feet....... 238
Early Exercise for Children........... 238
Giving Spirits or Cordials to Babies.... 238
Are Candies Healthful for Children?... 238
Children in the Care of Servants...... 238
Lack of Appetite in Children.......... 239
Age, Studies, and Habits of Children at School............................. 239

THE SICK-ROOM AND HEALTH.

Light in the Sick-Chamber............ 240
Cheerful Walls and Cheerful Prospects. 240
The Inspiration of Pleasant Contrasts... 240
The Healthful Influence of Pleasant Variety................................ 241
The Inspiration of Beautiful Flowers... 241
Caution as to Reading Aloud.......... 241
Read Slowly to the Sick 241
Read in a Natural, Pleasant, Colloquial Voice............................. 242
Evil of Reading Aloud only Fragmentary Paragraphs................... 242
Evil of a Rough Voice in the Sick-Room 242

364   INDEX.

	PAGE
Evil of an Indistinct Voice	242
How to Move a Patient	243
Great Tenderness of Manner Required	243
Heat and Ventilation in the Sick-Room	243
Cleanliness and Neatness	244
Directions in Contagious Sickness	244
Important Qualities of a Good Nurse	244
Twenty-one Brief Suggestions to Nurse	245

ALCOHOL AND HEALTH.

Alcohol cannot be Classed as Food	246
Liebig's Testimony	246
Dr. Richardson's and Prof. Silliman's Testimony	246
Alcohol Not the Source of Physical Force	247
Similar Testimony from Others	247
Does Alcohol Help Digestion?	247
Alcohol Useless in Nearly All Cases	247
A Distinguished Surgeon Uses Alcohol in only One Case out of Fifty	247
Patients Require Food rather than Stimulants	248
Careless Use of Alcohol Dangerous	248
Alcohol a Brain Poison	248
Alcoholic Rheumatism	248
How Alcoholic Drinks Cause Apoplexy	249
No Risk in Disusing Alcohol Suddenly	249
Physicians should Promote Abstinence	249
Testimony of a Great Surgeon	250
Inconsiderate Prescription of Liquors by Physicians—Testimony of 300 Leading Physicians	250
General Physiological Effects of Alcohol	250
Alcoholic Drinks Greatly Shorten Life	251
Interesting Illustrative Statistics	251
Table Showing the Comparative Expectation of Life for Drinkers	251
Why Some Liquor-drinkers have Long Lives	252
Alcoholic Intemperance Hereditary	252
Darwin Confirms this View	252
Hereditary Drunkenness Illustrated	252
Great Peril in Using Alcohol as Medicine	253
Sad Results of Prescribing Alcohol	253
Fruitless Efforts for Recovery	254
The Victim's Sorrowful Experience	254
Dr. Rush's Noble Testimony	254
Drinking Paroxysms: Periodic Attacks	255
The Excuse for these Periodic Paroxysms	255
Sudden End of the Drinking Paroxysms	255
How Alcohol Injures the Physical System	256
Patent "Bitters" are Strong Liquors Drugged	256
Patent "Bitters" the Worst Form of Alcohol	256
"Cure of Drunkenness"	256
The "Tapering-off System" Exploded	257
Treatment of Inebriates in Delirium Tremens	257
What to Avoid	257

TOBACCO AND HEALTH.

	PAGE
Effects of Tobacco on the System	258
Another Testimony	258
Other Testimonials	259
Tobacco Specially Harmful to the Young	259
Tobacco and Paralysis	259
Tobacco and Early Physical Weakness	260
Tobacco Pollutes the Atmosphere	260
The Tobacco Appetite Often Hereditary	260
The Excuses of Tobacco Users Trivial	260
Smoking Worse than Chewing	260
Tobacco in the Form of Snuff	261
"But I Can't Quit It"	261
Testimony of John Q. Adams	261
Great Extent of the Tobacco Habit	261

OPIUM-EATING AND HEALTH.

Powerful Effects of Opium	262
Symptoms of Opium Poisoning	262
Treatment of Poison by Opium	262
Opium Chewing	262
Symptoms of Opium Chewing	262
Treatment for Cure	263

CLIMATE AND HEALTH.

Time Required for Complete Change of Body	263
The Philosophy of Acclimation Explained	263
Effects of Dry and Moist Climates	263
Remarkable Facts Incident to a Moist Climate	264
Influence of Climate upon National Characteristics	264
Influence of Times upon Climate	264
Effects of Water upon Climate	264
How to Relieve Certain Malarious Districts	265
Evil Effect of Sudden Transitions in Climate	265
Are Frequent Rains Beneficial?	265

TEMPERAMENT AND HEALTH.

Varieties of Physical Temperament	266
Sanguine Temperament	266
Bilious Temperament	266
Lymphatic Temperament	266
Encephalic Temperament	266
Nervous Temperament	267

PRECAUTIONS AND HEALTH.

Eating, Sleeping, and Speaking—Simple Precaution	267
Danger from Wet Clothes	268
Danger from Cosmetics	268
Danger from Lamp Explosions	268
How to Test Dangerous Kerosene	268
Caution in Cleansing Wells	268
Caution Concerning the Tea-pot	269
Caution about Laughing Gas	269
Caution Concerning Ice-Cream	269

INDEX. 365

Caution in Carrying Lead Pencils...... 269
Visiting Infected Rooms 270
Dangerous Medicines............. 270
Dangerous Medicines — Two Good
  Rules 270
Mistakes in Prescription................ 270
Using Medicines as Stimulants—Danger.................................. 270
How to Escape Fever Infections........ 271
Fever Infections—Avoid the Poison.... 271
Fever Infection—Ventilation........... 271
Fever Infection—Avoid Absorbing It.. 271
Fever Infection and Flannel 272
Fever Infection and Fear.............. 272
Poisonous Soap....................... 272
Death from Nicotine 272
Poison of Quinces 273
Orange Peel Poisonous 273
Danger in Carrying Friction Matches .. 273
Care Concerning Poisonous Candies.... 273
Death from Chloroform 274
Care Concerning Ice Cream............ 274
Danger of Green-Colored Materials.... 274
How to Detect Arsenic in Colors....... 275
Be Cautious of Poisonous Vegetables .. 275

ANTIDOTES FOR POISONS—HYDROPHOBIA.

Animals Affected by Hydrophobia 275
Period of Development................ 276
Symptoms of Hydrophobia 276
Treatment of Hydrophobia 276

ANTIDOTES FOR POISONS—SNAKE-BITES AND
INSECTS.

What Snakes are Poisonous............ 277
Symptoms of Snake Poison............ 278
Antidotes for Snake-bites.............. 278
Bites of Venomous Insects 278
Treatment of Insect Bites............. 279

ANTIDOTES FOR POISONS—MISCELLANEOUS.

Poison Ivy and Oak: Remedies........ 279
Lead Poisoning 279
Antidotes for Lead Poisoning.......... 280
Poisoning by the Filling of Teeth 280
Poisoning by Wall Paper... 280
Phosphorus Poisoning................. 280
Poisoning by Opium.................. 280
How to Act When Poison has been
  Swallowed......................... 280

EMERGENCIES—HOW TO MEET THEM.

Loss of Blood a Real Loss.... 281
Bleeding from Veins 281
Bleeding from Arteries 282
Bleeding from the Teeth.............. 282
Rupture of a Large Blood-Vessel....... 282
Fracture of the Skull................. 282
Partial Fainting, and its Relief......... 282
Apparent Insensibility 282

Complete Unconsciousness, and its Remedy 283
Dislocation, and its Treatment 283
Sprains and how to Cure Them........ 283
Fracture of the Collar-bone 283
Fracture of the Ribs 283
Dislocations........................ 284
Clothing on Fire—Presence of Mind
  Needed............................ 284
Clothing on Fire—What to do 284
To Prevent Clothing from Taking Fire . 284
Cures for Lock-jaw................... 284
Relief from Choking.................. 284
Frost Bites—Instant Remedy.......... 285
General Treatment for Burns and
  Scalds............................. 285
Cut Wounds—How to Heal quickly.... 286
How to Relieve Pain from Wounds.... 287
Pain from Nail in the Foot 287
Sunstroke—its History................ 287
Sunstroke does not Follow Short Exposure 287
Most Dangerous Time for Sunstroke ... 287
Premonitory Symptoms of Sunstroke .. 287
Hints for the Prevention of Sunstroke.. 288
Treatment of Sunstroke 288
Treatment of Sunstroke after Recovery . 288
Lightning Stroke: Preliminary Dangers 289
Apoplexy: Nature and Cause......... 289
Treatment of Apoplexy............... 290
How to Treat Delirious Patients........ 290
Convulsions, and How to Stop Them... 290

EMERGENCIES—DROWNING.

What to do in Case of Drowning....... 291
To Restore Breathing 291
To Restore Circulation................ 294
Recovery Twelve Hours After Drowning... 295
How to bring a Drowning Person to
  Shore............................. 295

EMERGENCIES—FRACTURES.

Definitions and Illustrations ....

POULTICES AND THEIR APPLICATION.

General Purpose of a Poultice......... 297

BRIEF CURES FOR VARIOUS DISEASES.

Colds—Seven Remedies............... 298
How to Relieve Severe Coughs—Seven
  Good Recipes...................... 299
Cures for Sore Throat................. 300
Headache........................... 301
Indigestion and Dyspepsia 301
Biliousness 302
Diarrhœa and Dysentery.............. 303
Constipation. 304
Cures for Boils........ 305

INDEX.

	PAGE
To Prevent and Cure Ulcers	305
Felons	305
Cancers	306
Treatment of Scabies	307
Whooping-Cough	307
Croup	308
Hay-fever—Class of Persons Affected	309
Hay-fever, Causes	309
Hay-fever—Localities Most Affected	309
Remedies for Hay-fever	310
Eruptive Fevers	310
Symptoms and Preventives of Fever	310
Relief of Sea-sickness	310
To Avoid Sea-sickness	311
Temporary Relief for Neuralgia	311
Cure of Stammering	311

MISCELLANEOUS HEALTH NOTES.

Pine Woods and Health	311
Danger of Cold Water in the Face	311
A Most Refreshing Bath	311
To Prevent Harm from Drinking Cold Water	311
How to Avoid Pneumonia	312
Position After Being Tired	312
Opening Abscesses Under Water	312
Pie-crust and Dyspepsia	312
Little Things and Health	312
Guarding Against Diphtheria	312
Eating at Certain Intervals	312
Time Required for Digesting Food	312
Cold or Warm Drinks	312
To Remove Bitter Taste	313
Most Healthful Seat in a Car	313
Causes of Lung Congestion	313
Spread of Pestilence	313
Sewing Machines and Health	313
A Specific for Scrofula	313
Suggestion to Parents about Sitting	313
Improper Sitting and its Evils	314
Chewing Between Meals	314
Remedy for Feverishness	314
Cause and Cure of Leanness	314
Cure of Obesity	314
Chief Causes of Sudden Death	315
Healthfulness of Pumpkins	315
Medical Qualities of Pumpkins	315
To Keep White Hands	315
A Good Tooth-wash	316
To Remove Moth from the Face	316
Pimples on the Face	316
To Strengthen the Hair	316
To Cool a Room	316
Protection from Damp Walls	316
To Make a Good Court-Plaster	316
To Relieve Whooping-cough	316
Diphtheria—Its Symptoms	317
Cause of Diphtheria	317
Treatments of Diphtheria	317
Infection Carried by Pet Animals	317
Flies as Poison Carriers	318
To Prevent After-taste of Quinine	318
Inflation of the Lungs	318
Diet for Dyspeptics	318

HOME ECONOMICS.

	PAGE
Waste in the Kitchen	319

KITCHEN FURNITURE.—CLEANING.

Heating New Iron	320
To Prevent Crust in Tea-kettles	320
To Clean Tea-kettles	320
Glass	321
Glass Vessels	321
To Clean Coal-oil Cans	321
Washing Knives and Forks	321
To Clean Knives	321
Scouring Knives	321
To Extract Stains from Silver	321
Silver Soap	321
To Clean Silver	321
Another Method of Cleaning Silver	321
Cleaning Tinware	321
To Clean Tin Covers	321
To Polish Tins	322
Papier-mache Articles	322
Japanned Ware	322
Cleaning Flour Boards	322
Another Method	322
To Clean Painted Wainscot	322
Cleaning Old Brass	322
To Clean a Brass Kettle	322
To Clean Brasses, Britannia Metals, Etc.	322
To Keep Iron from Rusting	322
Paper for Cleaning Stoves, Tinware, Etc.	323
Cleansing Bottles	323

SOAPS AND WASHING FLUIDS.

Hard Soap	323
Soft Soap	323
Excellent Soft Soap	323
Common Hard Soap	323
Labor-saving Soap	324
Honey Soap	324
Using Soap	324
Suggestions	324
Washing Fluid	324
To Make Hard Water Soft	324
To Clear Muddy Water	324

WASHING CLOTHES.

To Clean a White Lace Veil	325
To Wash Fine, Colored Fabrics	325
To Make Merino Stockings	325
To Make Colors Stand in Delicate Hose	325
To Wash Chintz	325
Washing Prints	325
Another	325
To Make Use of Faded Prints	326
Cleansing Blankets	326
To Wash Flannel	326
Restoring White Flannel	326
Washing Woolen Clothing	326
To Wash Table-linen	326
To Preserve Clothes-pins	327

INDEX. 367

STARCHING, FOLDING, AND IRONING.

	PAGE
To Prepare Starch	327
Flour Starch	327
Glue Starch	327
Gum-arabic Starch	327
Starching Clothes	327
Sprinkling Clothes	327
Folding Clothes	327
Gloss for Linen	327
To Make Flat-irons Smooth	328
Another	328
To Preserve Irons from Rust	328
To Remove Starch or Rust from Flat-irons	328
Ironing	328
Starching—Clear-starching, Etc.	328
To Clear-starch Lace, Etc.	328
Ironing Laces	329

REMOVING STAINS.

Grease Spots	329
Stains from Acids	329
Wine Stains	329
Iron Rust	329
To Take Out Scorch	329
Mildewed Linen	329
To Remove Mildew	329
Another Method	330
Coffee Stains	330
Grass Stains	330
Tea Stains	330
Medicine Stains	330
Fruit Stains	330
Fruit Stains on Table-linen	330
Fruit and Wine Stains	330
Ink Stains	330
To Take Marking-ink Out of Linen	330
Ink in Cotton, Silk, and Woolen Goods	330
Ink Stains in Mahogany	330
Ink Stains on Silver	330
Ink and Iron-mould	331
To Remove Stains from Floors	331
To Preserve Steel Goods from Rust	331
To Remove Paint Stains on Windows	331
Stains on the Hands	331
To Preserve Polished Iron Work	331
If Rust	331
To Extract Grease Spots from Books	332
Removing Tar Spots	332
Ammonia for Renovation	332
Removing Grease from Silk	332
Removing Grease from Coat Collars	332
To Restore Crape	332
To Clean Furs	332
To Preserve Furs	333
To Clean Velvet	333
To Restore Silk	333
Wrinkled Silk	333
To Bleach White Silks or Flannels	333
To Clean White Ostrich Feathers	333
To Clean Feathers	333
To Make Cloth Waterproof	333
To Clean Black Cloth	333
Cleaning Silk and Merinos	334

	PAGE
To Color Kid Gloves	334
To Clean Kid Gloves	334
Washing Kid Gloves	334
To Extract Grease from Papered Walls	334
To Clean Wall Paper	334

WHITEWASHING AND PAINTING.

Cracks in Plastering	334
To Fill Holes in Walls	334
Brilliant Zinc Whitewash	335
Cheap Whitewash	335
Making Paper Stick to Whitewashed Walls	335
New Recipe for Whitewash	335
A Brilliant Stucco Whitewash	335
To Color and Prevent Whitewash from Rubbing Off	335
Paint for Kitchen Walls	336
Fire and Water-Proof Paint	336

POLISHING FURNITURE.

French Naphtha Polish	336
French Spirit Polish	336
Polish or Mahogany Color	336
Simplest Polish for Oiled Furniture	336
Oil for Red Furniture	336
Polish for Oil and Alcohol	336
Polish for Leather Cushions, etc.	336
To Give a Fine Color to Cherry-Tree Wood	337
To Stain Black Walnut	337
Imitation Ebony Stain	337
To Ebonize Various Woods	337
Water and Varnished Furniture	337
Cleansing Polish for Furniture	337
Where and How to Varnish	338
Varnish for Unpainted Wood	338
Blacking for Stoves	338
Brunswick Black for Varnishing Grates	338
To Clean Bronzed Chandeliers, etc.	338
For Cleaning Brasses Belonging to Furniture	338
To Clean Sinks	338

ARTICLES FOR THE TOILET.

Rose Oil	339
Cologne Water	339
To Wash Hair Brushes	339
A Paste for Sharpening Razors	339
Shaving Cream	339
To Curl Hair	339
To Remove Tight Rings	339
Rose Lip-Salve	340

BIRDS AND BIRD-FOOD.

To Distinguish Canaries	340
Place for Cages	340
Size of Cage Perches	340
Food for Canary Birds	340

	PAGE		PAGE
Care of Young Canaries	340	To Carve a Spare-Rib	343
Parasites upon Canaries	341	To Carve Fish	343
To Destroy Parasites	341	Order of Serving	343
Food for Mocking-Birds	341		
To Distinguish Thrushes—Food	341	**PASTE AND CEMENTS.**	
Care of Young Thrushes	341		
Food of Bullfinches	341	Rice Flour Cement	348
Care of Young Bullfinches	342	Paste that will Keep a Year	348
Linnets and Their Food	342	Liquid Glue	348
Blackbirds and Their Food	342	To Prevent Glue from Smelling Badly	349
To Distinguish Skylarks	342	Cement for Iron and Stone	349
The Cages of Skylarks	342	Diamond Cement	349
Food of Skylarks	342	Cement for Metal and Glass	349
		Glue for Uniting Card-Board, etc	349
		A Cement Withstanding Heat and Moisture	349
RULES FOR CARVING.		Cement for Crockery	349
Carving Knives	343	To Make Compound Glue	350
Carving Dishes	343		
To Carve a Fowl	343	**HOUSEHOLD ORNAMENTS.**	
To Carve a "Fillet"	343		
To Carve a Round of Beef	343	Pretty Hanging Ornaments	350
To Carve a Sirloin	343	Pretty Mantel Ornaments	350
To Carve a Leg	343	Rules for Arranging Cut Flowers	351
To Carve a Pig	343	To Crystallize Grasses	351
To Carve a Calf's Head	343	To Take Leaf Impressions	352
To Carve a Saddle of Mutton	343	Rockeries, Vases, and Hanging-Baskets	352

INDEX TO ILLUSTRATIONS—SUPPLEMENTAL.

PAGE

The Human Skeleton—three cuts, graphically illustrating the location and name of the various bones of the human body.. 69
Muscles of the Human Body—three cuts, showing the names and location of the principal muscles.. 70
The Nervous and Arterial Systems of the Body—two cuts, with ample explanatory notes...71–73
The Brain and Cranial Nerves, with a large number of explanatory notes........73–75
The Human Eye—three illustrations, with explanatory notes...................... 140
The Human Ear—three illustrations showing how we hear.....................149–152
The Human Skin—showing the various departments of it, including the papillæ, sweat ducts, sweat glands, and other parts of the skin, as seen under a powerful microscope.. 175
The Method of Preparing and Applying Various Bandages in Case of Fractures—eleven cuts.. 206
The Method of Carving Meats—eight illustrations................................ 344
The Method of Roasting and Carving Poultry and other Game Birds—seven illustrations.. 345
The Method of Carving Fish—three cuts.. 346
The Method of Cutting and Designing the parts of Beef—two illustrations........ 347
Snoring, and How to Stop It—two cuts.......................................194, 195
Tight Lacing and Health—four cuts.. 200
Emergencies—Drowning—four cuts..201–204

www.ingramcontent.com/pod-product-compliance
Lightning Source LLC
Chambersburg PA
CBHW020318240426
43673CB00039B/843